Dictionary
of Saints

Dictionary
of Saints

Editor: Martin Manser
Associate Editor: David Pickering

Collins

First published in 2004 by
Collins
A division of HarperCollins*Publishers*
77–85 Fulham Palace Road,
Hammersmith, London W6 8JB

www.collins.co.uk

ISBN 0 00 716950 7

Set in Palatino by
Rowland Phototypesetting Ltd,
Bury St Edmunds, Suffolk

Printed in Great Britain by
Clays Ltd, St Ives plc

CONTENTS

Introduction

In its broadest contemporary sense the word *saint* may describe any person whose nature or behaviour suggests exceptional holiness or goodness. More precisely, it may refer to any person deemed to have been granted admittance to heaven after their death on account of their virtuous life while on earth.

In biblical times, the term *saint* was interpreted somewhat differently, being understood to refer exclusively to those individuals within the early Christian community who had rejected sin and led lives in a state of sanctity. (According to the Bible itself, the term *saint* refers to holy people, that is, those who are consecrated to God; in New Testament terms, all followers of the Christian way.) In more general use, the term came to be applied especially to those martyrs who had died for their faith and who, being now in heaven, could represent before God the pleas of the faithful. As the Roman persecutions of early Christians came to an end the word *saint* began to be applied more widely to other notable religious figures who did not necessarily die martyrs' deaths (technically, *confessors*), such as the Desert Fathers and other early monks and nuns. In later centuries the term *saint* gradually evolved until it came to include all manner of individuals deemed to have dedicated their lives to God and to be worthy of special respect, be they martyrs, hermits, theologians, popes, bishops, priests or humble lay people.

Estimates of the total number of saints acknowledged either locally or throughout the church vary but a figure of around 10,000 is often quoted. Of these only some 300 have actually been officially canonized by a pope. The vast majority of saints were originally acknowledged as such by popular acclaim rather than through any formal procedure, their shrines becoming sites of pilgrimage and their bones becoming treasured relics. Some became the focus of universal veneration, while many more were destined to remain the object of local cults. All might be petitioned in prayer for divine aid, protection or guidance.

The lives of some early saints became confused with one another and the details of many were forgotten entirely, or became shrouded in legend. Some lives, it would appear, were wholly fictitious, inspired by the discovery of an old grave, the product of local folklore or the mistranslation of an ancient written text. The need to formalize saint-making resulted in due course in the process of canonization (that is, the listing of saints in an official catalogue, or canon). The first such lists, chiefly martyrologies, were drawn up at an early date and today the identification of saints depends upon consultation of many such catalogues, including martyrologies and church calendars.

The first official canonization by a pope was that of St Ulrich in 993, under the aegis of Pope John XV, and by the 13th century it was accepted that the pope alone could officially confer sainthood (although this only usually happened after a local cult had become well established). In 1588 a special body within the Roman Catholic church was created specifically to investigate candidates for sainthood. From these investigations has evolved the modern (and often very lengthy) process of canonization, which involves detailed investigation into the life of a proposed saint. If initially successful, the individual concerned is granted the title 'Venerable', upon which he or she goes through further investigation before achieving beatification, being declared 'Blessed' and assigned an official feast day (usually, though not always, falling on the day of their entry into heaven). After a final investigation the individual may be formally canonized as a saint (meaning he or she is deemed worthy of universal veneration). In the course of these investigations it must be proved that the individual in question lived a life of heroic service to virtue or piety, though they need not have been completely faultless. Other requirements include the validation of at least two posthumous miracles.

The Roman Catholic church and the Orthodox Eastern churches all have their own canonization procedures, with varying demands being made upon the evidence presented. The process of canonization was discontinued altogether in the Anglican and Protestant churches several centuries ago, but even here established saints are still respected and the term *saint* is used without reservation as, for instance, in the names of parish churches.

From time to time the church has altered the official standing of saints in response to doubts about the authenticity of their lives. A number of saints were removed from the official martyrology of the Roman Catholic Church with the publication of a revised Roman calendar in 1969, replacing that of 1584, and their importance was reduced (as was the case with the popular but largely legendary saints Christopher, Nicholas and Valentine). New saints have, however, been regularly added (especially under Pope John Paul II).

In the modern church the lives of the saints are often used as exemplars for the faithful to model their own lives upon. The saints have also retained their role as patrons, being commonly regarded as sources of divine protection and guidance. To this day thousands of children around the world are given the names of saints in the belief that this will ensure the special favour of the saint in question. The saints also have enormous cultural significance all round the world as a feature of national folklore and legend.

In selecting entries for this book the emphasis has been placed upon the more important and interesting saints in the canon. These include all the most familiar names, although space has also been made for some of the more obscure figures who, for instance, may be known today only through local placenames. Special attention has been given to the saints of Britain and Ireland.

Each entry includes birth and death dates (where known), details of the life, career and death of the saint in question, together with information about their achievements, character and significance. To these are added details of their patronage, emblems and feast day. It should be noted that feast days may vary widely, with different dates being given in different sources or in different churches. The Roman calendar is followed in this book (though even here there is considerable scope for variation). The main text is followed by a number of indexes listing feast days, emblems, patrons and locations in Britain and Ireland associated with saints.

Martin H. Manser
David H. Pickering

A

Achilleus   *See* NEREUS AND ACHILLEUS.

Adalbert of Magdeburg   (d.981) German bishop. In 961 Adalbert, a monk of Trier, was selected to lead a band of Christian missionaries into Russia at the invitation of St Olga, princess of Kiev. The mission ended in disaster, however, when Olga's pagan son Svyatoslav attacked the group, killing several of them. Adalbert survived and returned to Germany, where he was appointed abbot of a monastery at Weissenburg. He promoted learning among the monks and went on to become archbishop of Magdeburg in 968. He remained in the post for 13 years, dedicating himself to the evangelization of the Wends.
Feast Day: 20 June.

Adalbert of Prague   (*c*.956–997) Bohemian bishop and martyr. Born Voytech into a noble family of Libice, Bohemia, he took the name Adalbert in homage to ADALBERT OF MAGDEBURG by whom he was educated. He rose to the rank of bishop of Prague before the age of 30 and devoted his energies towards the dissemination of Christianity through Bohemia and Hungary. Political opponents forced him into exile in 990, however, and he retreated to Rome and became a monk. Pope John XV ordered him back to Prague to renew his work. Supported by Duke Boleslas of Poland, he founded the Benedictine abbey of Dievnov, which he modelled upon the great monastery at Cluny, but once again fell foul of the local nobility and ended up back in Rome (995). Having given up all hope of making progress in Prague he spent his last years engaged in missionary work among the pagan Prussians in Pomerania with the assistance of his friend Emperor Otto III, only to be murdered as a suspected Polish spy in the vicinity of Konigsberg. He is honoured as the patron saint of Prussia and Poland.
Feast Day: 23 April.

Adamnan   (*c*.628–704) Irish abbot. A distant relative of St COLUMBA, Adamnan (or **Adomnan**) was born in Donegal and became abbot of the monastery on Iona in 679. Some years later he fell out with the monks in his charge when he decided to support the Roman dating of Easter and

after 692 spent much of his time elsewhere, chiefly in Ireland, although he
also conducted missions in Northumbria. In Ireland he may have founded
the monastery of Raphoe and also pushed through a law guaranteeing
protection for the clergy, women and children in times of war. He earned
a reputation as a peacemaker and was widely respected for his humility
and wisdom. His writings included the books *On the Holy Places* and *Life of
St Columba*. He died on Iona, allegedly consumed with despair at the
intransigence of the monks there. The Roman dating of Easter was finally
accepted on Iona some 12 years after Adamnan's death.
Feast Day: 23 September.

Adauctus   *See* FELIX AND ADAUCTUS.

Adelaide   (931–999) French empress of Germany. The daughter of
Rudolf II of Burgundy, Adelaide became the wife of Prince Lothair of Italy
and, after his death, married Otto the Great of Germany (951). Otto was
crowned emperor by Pope John XII shortly afterwards, with Adelaide as
his empress. Otto's family, led by his daughter Theophano, resented
Adelaide's influence and, after Otto's death, spent the next 20 years working to alienate Otto's son, the emperor Otto II, from his mother, finding
fault, for instance, with her unstinting generosity to the poor. Adelaide
was obliged to live for a time in retirement from the court but was
reconciled with Otto before his death, after which she had to go into
retreat once more. After Theophano's death in 991 Adelaide finally
returned as regent and used her authority to revitalize the religious
establishment, founding and restoring monasteries and promoting the
evangelization of the Slavs. She died at a convent she had founded at
Seltz in Alsace.
Feast Day: 16 December.

Adomnan   *See* ADAMNAN.

Adrian and Natalia   (d. *c*.304) Martyrs of Nicomedia. According to
legend, Adrian was a Roman officer stationed at Nicomedia who was so
moved by the courage of the Christians he persecuted that he declared
himself to be a Christian also. He was thrown into prison, where he was
visited by his Christian wife Natalia. Further visits were barred after
Adrian was sentenced to death, but Natalia continued to see him by
disguising herself as a boy and bribing the gaoler. She attended her
husband's execution and retrieved his remains, which she buried at
Argyropolis on the Bosporus. She tended his grave for the rest of her life

and at her own death was laid to rest among the martyrs herself. The relics of Adrian were eventually moved to Constantinople and thence to Rome and Flanders.
Feast Day: 8 September.

Adrian of Canterbury   (d.710) African-born English abbot. While serving as abbot of the monastery at Nerida in Italy he was twice offered the post of archbishop of Canterbury by Pope Vitalian, but turned down the offer both times. On the second occasion, however, he agreed to accompany the eventual choice, the Greek monk Theodore, to England and once there accepted the post of abbot of the monastery school of SS. Peter and Paul (later renamed St Augustine's) in Canterbury. Over the following 40 years he went on to consolidate his reputation as a scholar and administrator and to bolster the standing of Canterbury as a centre of religious learning, where students might study subjects ranging from Greek and Latin to theology, law and astronomy. His pupils included many future abbots and bishops. He proved an invaluable adviser and helper to Theodore and the church prospered under their joint leadership.
Feast Day: 9 January.

Aegidius   *See* GILES.

Aelfheah   *See* ALPHEGE.

Aelred   (1109–1167) English abbot. Aelred (otherwise called **Ailred** or **Ethelred**) was born at Hexham the son of a parish priest and spent much of his youth at the court of King David of Scotland. At the age of 24 he decided to become a monk and joined the newly founded Cistercian abbey of Rievaulx in Yorkshire. Despite his frail health, he quickly became known for his piety and sensitivity and 10 years later was appointed abbot of Revesby in Lincolnshire. After four years in the post he returned to Rievaulx as abbot and went on to oversee a massive increase in the abbey's size and reputation. He placed great emphasis upon charity and love of Christ and left behind some of his thoughts in the writings *On Spiritual Friendship* and *Mirror of Charity*. As well as exercising a strong influence upon the English church he also visited religious establishments in Scotland and France, earning the nickname 'St Bernard of the north'.
Feast Day: 3 March.

Aethelburh   *See* ETHELBURGA OF BARKING.

Afra   (d. *c*.304) German martyr. According to legend, Afra was a prostitute

persecuted as a Christian at Augsburg during the reign of Diocletian.
When she refused to make sacrifice to the gods she was burned to death
on an island in the river Lech. She submitted uncomplainingly to her
executioners, admitting that her body had sinned and deserved punishment but maintaining that her soul remained unpolluted. Her remains
were retrieved by her mother Hilaria and three servants and buried, for
which deed they were also arrested and burned to death. She is honoured
as the patron saint of penitent women.
Feast Day: 5 August.

Agape, Chionia and Irene (d.304) Macedonian martyrs. Agape, Chionia
and Irene were three sisters of Salonika in Macedonia who were arrested
as Christians after they refused to eat meat that had been offered in sacrifice to the gods. When brought before the governor of Macedonia, Agape
and Chionia refused once again to eat the food and were accordingly
sentenced to death and burned alive. Because of her youth Irene was
spared and thrown into prison, but subsequently brought before the
governor again on charges of possessing Christian texts. Confessing her
crime, she was stripped and sent to a soldiers' brothel, but no man would
go near her and she was instead dragged out and burned alive, together
with her books.
Feast Day: 3 April.

Agatha (3rd century) Sicilian martyr. The story of Agatha, a maiden of
Catania in Sicily, is largely shrouded in legend. Tradition has it that she
was of noble birth but as a young woman incurred the wrath of a consul
called Quintian after she refused his advances, having dedicated her
virginity to Christ. Charging her with being a Christian, Quintian handed
her over to a brothel-keeper but, when she emerged uncorrupted, he then
had her savagely tortured. When her breasts were cut off, a vision of
St PETER appeared to heal the wound. Her death in prison (she was rolled
over hot coals) was preceded by an earthquake. Today Agatha is honoured
as the patron saint of Catania, of wet-nurses and also of bell-founders (an
association that evolved from the similarity in shape between a breast and
a bell). Her emblem is a dish bearing a pair of breasts.
Feast Day: 5 February.

Agnes (d. *c.*304) Roman martyr. Despite her fame, little is known for
certain about the life of St Agnes beyond the fact that while still a child
she died the death of a virgin martyr in Rome. She was buried in the

cemetery on the Via Nomentana, where a church dedicated to her memory was later erected. She was first venerated as a martyr within a few years of her death. Various reasons for her arrest and execution have been given to embellish the bare facts of her life story. According to one of these she was a beautiful young girl of around 12 years old who offered her life voluntarily in exchange for those of other victims of persecution. Another suggests she was put to death as a Christian after refusing all suitors on the grounds that she had dedicated her virginity to Christ: undaunted by threats of torture and humiliation she was taken to a public stadium and died after having her throat cut with a sword. She never once displayed any sign of fear and became a lasting symbol of chastity and innocence and is honoured today as the patron saint of betrothed couples, virgins and gardeners. Her emblem is a lamb.
Feast Day: 21 January.

Agnes of Assisi   *See* CLARE OF ASSISI.

Agnes of Montepulciano   (*c.*1268–1317) Italian nun. Born into a wealthy family of Gracchiano Vecchio in Tuscany, Agnes was brought up by the nuns of Montepulciano and in due course became bursar and superioress of a new convent at Proceno. Widely known both for her humble life style (she slept on the ground with a rock for a pillow) and for her visions, she was persuaded back to Montepulciano and there established a new convent in a former brothel, which she subsequently attached to the Dominican order and was appointed prioress in 1306. She remained in her post as head of the convent for the rest of her life, overseeing its rapid growth both in size and reputation. She also became well-known for her prophecies and as a worker of miraculous cures. She was canonized in 1726 and is honoured as the patron saint of Montepulciano.
Feast Day: 20 April.

Agostina Pietrantoni   (1864–1894) Italian nun. Born in Pozzaglia Sabina in Rieti, Italy, Agostina Pietrantoni joined the Sisters of Charity and devoted herself to the care of the sick, working in the Hospital of Santo Spirito in Rome, where many of the patients were convicts. From 1866 she concentrated upon treatments of the critically ill, exposing herself to and often contracting the diseases they were suffering from, including tuberculosis. Transferring to the tubercular ward of the hospital, she continued her work until stabbed to death by one of the patients. As she died she prayed for forgiveness of her murderer. She is honoured as the patron saint of martyrs and victims of abuse.

Feast Day: 13 October.

Aidan (d.651) Irish missionary. Aidan (or **Aedan**) served as a monk in the monastery on Iona before being sent to Northumbria as a missionary around the year 635. Raised to the rank of bishop, he chose the island of Lindisfarne as his base and there founded a monastery that became in due course one of the most influential religious centres in Britain. From Lindisfarne he conducted numerous evangelizing journeys through the mainland, establishing many churches and monasteries with the support of St OSWALD, king of Northumbria, and his successor Oswin. A gentle and discreet man, according to the VENERABLE BEDE, Aidan won many converts through his generosity towards the needy and through his opposition to slavery. He died at Bamburgh soon after the death of his close friend Oswin and was buried on Lindisfarne. His emblem is a stag (a reference to his great love of animals).

Feast Day: 31 August.

Aidan of Ferns *See* MAEDOC OF FERNS.

Ailred *See* AELRED.

Alban (3rd century) English martyr. Alban was a prominent citizen of the Roman city of Verulamium (modern St Albans) who was beheaded for his faith around the middle of the 3rd century, during the reign of Diocletian. According to the VENERABLE BEDE, Alban converted to Christianity after offering shelter to a priest hiding from Roman soldiers, impressed by the man's piety and devotion. When the soldiers eventually called at his house to arrest the priest Alban donned the fugitive's gown and was arrested in his stead, allowing the real priest to escape. When the imposture was discovered the authorities insisted that Alban make sacrifice to the gods and, when he refused, sentenced him to be tortured and put to death. Legend has it that on the day of his execution the river at Verulamium dried up at Alban's approach and the executioner threw down his sword and chose to die with the prisoner rather than be responsible for his demise. A second executioner struck off the saint's head, upon which his own eyes are said to have fallen from their sockets. A substantial church (later abbey) was subsequently erected on the site where Alban died, and he became the first martyr of the British Isles. He is honoured as the patron saint of converts and victims of torture.

Feast Day: 22 June.

Albert the Great   (1206–1280) German theologian and bishop. Born into a wealthy family in Swabia, Germany, Albert the Great (or **Albertus Magnus**) began his career in the church at the age of 16, when he became a Dominican friar. He spent the next 20 years teaching in Paris and at various German Dominican universities, earning a wide reputation as a scholar, his pupils including St THOMAS AQUINAS. Today he is recognized as a founder of medieval scholastic philosophy, although he also wrote on a variety of other subjects, including mathematics, physics, astronomy, geography, mineralogy, chemistry, biology, botany, politics, economics and alchemy. His conclusions included the revolutionary notion that the world was spherical rather than flat. He held a number of ecclesiastical posts between 1254 and 1262, among them theologian to the pope and bishop of Regensberg, but felt he was not suited to administrative roles and eventually gave up his see. He passed his final years teaching in Cologne, although he also returned to Paris (1277) in order to conduct a defence of the work of his recently deceased student Thomas Aquinas. He was canonized in 1931. Nicknamed the 'Universal Doctor', he is honoured as the patron of students of natural science.
Feast Day: 15 November.

Aldhelm   (c.640–709) English scholar and bishop. Born into a royal family of Wessex, Aldhelm received his religious education in Malmesbury and was for a time a pupil of St ADRIAN OF CANTERBURY and St THEODORE OF CANTERBURY in Canterbury. He was appointed abbot of Malmesbury around 675 and became bishop of Sherborne in 705. He also visited Pope Sergius I in Rome. During his brief time as bishop he founded several monasteries and earned a reputation as an evangelist, combining serious moral teaching with singing and other forms of entertainment. He is remembered as much as a scholar and lover of language as an administrator, although nothing survives of his many writings in English. Of his writings in Latin various pieces are still in existence, among them a letter concerning the dating of Easter and a number of riddles. He was buried at Malmesbury abbey.
Feast Day: 25 May.

Alexander   (d.326) Bishop of Alexandria. As bishop of Alexandria from 312, Alexander faced opposition from Meletius of Lycopolis, who disagreed with his lenient attitude towards lapsed Catholics. Further problems arose through the activities of a priest named Kolluth who had assumed the power to ordain deacons and priests and, even more

seriously, from another priest called Arius, whose ideas about Christ's divinity and sinless nature diverged from those of the orthodox church and in due course evolved into full heretical form under the title Arianism. Alexander's initial approach to Arius was gentle persuasion, but when this did not work he summoned a synod of Egyptian bishops to condemn and excommunicate him. Arius whipped up support throughout the East and it was not until 325, when Emperor Constantine sided with Alexander at the council of Nicea, that the Arian heresy was officially condemned. Alexander died soon afterwards, naming ATHANASIUS as his successor.
Feast Day: 26 February.

Alexander Nevsky (1219–1263) Russian prince. Born at Pereaslavl, Alexander succeeded his father as Prince of Novgorod in 1236 and spent much of his reign resisting invading armies. He defeated the Swedes at the river Neva (the source of his name Nevksy) in 1240, beat the Teutonic knights at the lake of Peipous in 1242, forced the Lithuanians into retreat and managed to fend off attack by the Tartars. Respected for his strong religious faith, he became a monk shortly before his death and was buried at the monastery of Vladimir-Kljazma. He was canonized in 1381 and Peter the Great placed St Petersburg under the saint's protection in 1710. His memory was also invoked in World War II through the Alexander Nevsky division financed by the Russian Orthodox Church in the struggle to fight off the country's Nazi invaders. He is honoured as the patron saint of St Petersburg.
Feast Day: 23 November.

Alexis (5th century) Beggar of Mesopotamia. The life of Saint Alexis, if he existed at all, is largely a matter of legend. The story (seemingly dating only from the 10th century) goes that he was the son of a wealthy Roman nobleman who abandoned his bride on their wedding day to go on pilgrimage and ultimately opted for a life of poverty in Syria. He willingly shared everything he received with other needy people. A further legend claims that he spent the last years of his life living incognito as a servant in his father's household in Rome. Nicknamed 'the man of God', his cult enjoyed a peak in popularity during the medieval period. The legend of Alexis may have resulted from confusion with a similar story concerning a Roman nobleman, Saint John Calybata, or with another legend about an impoverished monk of aristocratic Roman birth living in Edessa.
Feast Day: 17 July.

Alipius   (*c*.360–*c*.430) African bishop. Born into a pagan family of Tagaste in Numidia, Alipius was a pupil and close friend of St AUGUSTINE OF HIPPO in Carthage. He accompanied Augustine when he went to Rome and there joined his friend in converting to Christianity. On their return to Tagaste, he and Augustine pursued a life of faith both there and in Hippo, where Augustine became bishop. Alipius himself was ordained as a priest and conducted a pilgrimage to the Holy Land, meeting St JEROME, before accepting the post of bishop of Tagaste.
Feast Day: 18 August.   .

Aloysius   (1568–1591) Italian Jesuit student. Born Aloysius Luigi Gonzaga into a noble family of Lombardy, he attended military school before experiencing life at the court of the duke of Mantua. Such was the disgust he felt at the immorality of the court he refused to accept his inheritance and opted instead for a life of prayer and self-denial. He defied the wishes of his family and in 1585 joined the Jesuits, who succeeded in persuading him to give up the more excessive practices of mortification that he favoured. From his mentor St ROBERT BELLARMINE he learned to love his fellow men and renewed his faith in Christ. Though he suffered from a kidney complaint, he dedicated himself to tending victims of the plague in Rome and in due course died of the disease himself, aged just 23. Canonized in 1726, he was named the patron saint of students in 1729 and subsequently was identified as the patron of all Christian youth. He is also honoured as the patron saint of those suffering from or involved in the treatment of AIDS.
Feast Day: 21 June.

Alphege   (*c*.954–1012) English bishop and martyr. Alphege (otherwise called **Aelfheah** or **Elphege**) began his career in the church as a monk at Deerhurst in Gloucestershire and, after a period living as a hermit in Somerset, as abbot of Bath. A kindly, generous man, he rose in due course to the position of bishop of Winchester, some 20 years later, and ultimately to that of archbishop of Canterbury. His term of office witnessed the hardships caused by Danish raiders who even captured Canterbury itself and took Alphege prisoner, carrying him off to Greenwich. When Alphege forbade the paying of a ransom to secure his release the infuriated Danes turned on him, beating him with ox bones and then killing him with a blow from an axe.
Feast Day: 19 April.

Alphonsus de Orozco   (1500–1591) Spanish mystic and spiritual writer. Born in Oropesa, Avila, in Spain, he spent much of his early life in solitude. In a vision the Virgin Mary had ordered him to write extensively upon such matters as prayer and the Christian way of living. His works include his *Confessions*, in which he recounts his own spiritual journey. He became an Augustinian friar at Salamanca in 1522 and dedicated much of his time to prayer. In 1583, however, he accepted the post of prior of four Augustinian houses and in 1554 became head of the Augustinian community in Valladolid. King Philip II recruited him as court chaplain in 1556 and he spent the remaining 35 years of his life preaching to the Spanish nobility in Madrid and hearing their confessions, exercising a strong influence upon many prominent figures in contemporary public life. *Feast Day: 19 September.*

Alphonsus Liguori   (1696–1787) Italian bishop, theologian and mystic. Born in Marianella, near Naples, Alphonsus Marie Liguori pursued a highly successful career as a lawyer in Naples prior to losing a high-profile court case in 1723 and giving up the profession in humiliation. As the result of a vision he defied the wishes of his family and joined the Fathers of the Oratory, being ordained in 1717 and earning a wide reputation as a preacher. In 1732 he went on to found his own order, called the Congregation of the Most Holy Saviour, popularly known as the Redemptorist Congregation. As director and then superior general of the order, he guided the Congregation through years of political turbulence, despite his own poor health. Appointed bishop of Sant' Agata dei Goti (Beneventum) at the age of 66, he was always a controversial figure within the church establishment and some time before his death was even excluded from the Redemptorist community he had founded. He also wrote numerous books and pamphlets, of which the most influential included *Moral Theology* and *Victories of the Martyrs*. He was canonized in 1839 and is revered today as a Doctor of the Church. He is honoured as the patron saint of confessors and moral theologians.
Feast Day: 1 August.

Alphonsus Rodriguez   (1533–1617) Spanish Jesuit laybrother. Born in Segovia in Spain, Alphonsus Rodriguez had a troubled childhood, having to help his mother run the family wool business after the death of his father when he was 14. He married at the age of 23 but his wife died three years later, shortly followed by his mother and his two children. When his business failed he attempted to join the Jesuits at Valencia but was refused because of his lack of education. Despite his relatively advanced age, he took up Latin studies and in 1571 was finally admitted by the Jesuits as a laybrother. He spent the next 45 years serving as doorkeeper at the Montesione College on Majorca, earning a wide reputation as a spiritual adviser. Those who profited from his guidance included St PETER CLAVER, who was inspired by the advice of Alphonsus to take up missionary work. Though Alphonsus Rodriguez himself complained of being constantly tormented by sexual temptations and at the end of his life concluded he had been of no use to anyone, he was canonized in 1888 and is honoured today as the patron saint of Majorca.

Feast Day: 30 October.

Amand   (*c*.584–679) French missionary bishop. Born in Poitou, Amand defied the wishes of his family in order to adopt the life of a monk at the island monastery of Yeu and in due course was ordained at Tours. Subsequently he lived as a hermit at Bourges for some 15 years before conducting a pilgrimage to Rome and being consecrated bishop in 628. He was not granted a specific see but was instead instructed to preach the gospel to the heathen population of Flanders and the surrounding area. He had considerable success in this demanding role but proved relatively ineffectual when appointed bishop of Maastricht (646) and soon returned to the life of a wandering evangelist. With the support of the Frankish kings he doggedly pursued the conversion of the people of Flanders and northern France. Over the years he attracted thousands of converts to the Christian faith and established numerous monasteries and convents to support such work, in one of which (the abbey of Elnone) he eventually died. His *Testament*, written at Elnone in the last years of his life, still survives. Amand is honoured today as the patron saint of brewers and winemakers (a reference to the wine and beer-making industries of the region in which he worked).

Feast Day: 6 February.

Ambrose   (*c*.339–397) German-born bishop. Born in Trier in Germany, Ambrose was the son of the prefect of Gaul and studied law, literature, philosophy and Greek in Rome. He served in a variety of secular posts, including that of Roman governor, in northern Italy before being acclaimed bishop of Milan in 374. His appointment by public acclamation came as a considerable surprise as Ambrose had not even been baptized, having been sent to Milan simply to maintain peace between rival Catholics and supporters of the Arian heresy. As bishop, however, he gave away his possessions and dedicated himself to the study of Christianity. He soon earned a reputation as a powerful preacher and scholar and also emerged as the leading opponent of Arianism in the West, driving its adherents out of Milan. In 383, at the request of the Empress Justina, he acted in a diplomatic role in dissuading the usurper Maximus from attacking Rome. On another occasion he rebuked the emperor Theodosius for the massacre of thousands of men, women and children at Thessalonica and insisted that he perform public penance for the deed (which he did). Ambrose also encouraged kindliness and piety in his congregation. His influential writings, which did much to promote the growth of Christianity in western Europe, included the treatise *To Gratian Concerning the Faith*, sermons, commentaries and hymns. Notable figures who were deeply influenced by his example included St AUGUSTINE, who met him in Milan in 386 and was inspired by him to convert to Christianity. Ambrose came to be revered as one of the four great Latin Doctors of the Church and is honoured today as the patron saint of learning and of beekeepers and candlemakers. *Feast Day: 7 December.*

Ammonas the Hermit   (d. *c*.350) Egyptian hermit. Born in or near Alexandria in Egypt, Ammonas (or **Ammon**) was forced to marry (by a wealthy uncle) at the age of 22 but persuaded his bride to take a vow of chastity. Subsequently the couple worked together as brother and sister to establish religious communities for men and women in the desert of Nitria outside Alexandria. These loosely organized communities flourished and the saintly reputation of Ammonas and his wife attracted thousands of hermits, each of whom lived in his own cell but came together for meals and to observe religious services. The community for men, called Kellia, numbered some 5000 at its peak and was dubbed 'The City of God' by St JEROME.
Feast Day: 4 October.

Anacletus   *See* CLETUS.

Anastasia   (d.304) Martyr of Sirmium. Little is known of the life of Anastasia beyond the tradition that she was tortured and burned alive for her faith in Sirmium (Srem Mitrovica in modern Serbia) in 304. Legend furnishes the additional detail that earlier in her life she was twice rescued from death by the reformed prostitute St Theodota, who on one occasion piloted Anastasia's ship to safety after she was abandoned at sea. Anastasia is sometimes confused with another martyr of the same name who

was tortured and executed in Rome around 249 during the reign of the Emperor Valerian.
Feast Day: 25 December.

Anastasius the Persian   (d.628) Persian martyr. A soldier, he served in the army of King Chosroes II of Persia when it seized Jerusalem in 614 but there converted to Christianity and became a monk. He was subsequently arrested for preaching to other soldiers in Caesarea, and tortured and strangled to death at Bethsaloe on the Euphrates after he refused to recant.
Feast Day: 22 January.

André, Brother   (1845–1937) Canadian healer. Born Alfred Bessette in Montreal, he joined the Congregation of the Holy Cross at the age of 15 and, because he was never in good health himself and had virtually no education, was made doorkeeper at the Notre Dame College, Mount Royal. He remained in this post for some 40 years, becoming widely respected as an adviser and healer. When the numbers of people coming to him threatened to disrupt life at the college, he founded (1910) the Oratory of St Joseph on a hill nearby and there received his many visitors, who numbered some 10,000 people over the next 27 years. By the time of his death at the age of 91, Brother André was an internationally known figure. He was beatified in 1987.
Feast Day: 6 January.

Andrew   (1st century AD) Apostle and martyr. Andrew appears in the Bible as the first of the 12 apostles who attended Christ through the events leading to the Crucifixion. According to St John's Gospel 1:35–42, he heard about Christ from John the Baptist and met him the following day. According to Mark 1:16–20, however, he encountered Christ for the first time while fishing beside the Sea of Galilee, and with his brother Simon (renamed Peter) responded to his summons to become "fishers of people". Andrew became one of the leaders of the disciples and played a role at the miracle of the feeding of the five thousand and later in Jerusalem. Different sources claim that after the Crucifixion Andrew spread the gospel in Greece or founded the see of Constantinople. Other legends have him preaching in Kiev (hence his identification as patron saint of Russia) and after his death being taken to Scotland (another country that claims him as its patron saint). He is supposed to have been crucified himself on an X-shaped cross at Patras in Achaia. As well as being patron saint of Russia and Scotland, which commemorates Andrew's crucifixion in the X-shaped saltire of the national flag, Andrew is also honoured as patron saint of Greece, of fishermen and of old maids. His emblems are a fishing net and a cross saltire.

Feast Day: 30 November.

Andrew of Crete (*c*.660–740) Monk and bishop of Jerusalem. Born in Damascus, he lived as a monk in Jerusalem for 10 years before being sent to Constantinople as head of an orphanage and old men's home there. Widely respected as a preacher and sacred poet, he was appointed archbishop of Gortyna in Crete around 700. His poetic output included numerous hymns, some of which are still in use in the Byzantine church today. Another St Andrew of Crete was murdered in Constantinople in 766 after criticizing the emperor Constantine V.

Feast Day: 4 July.

Andrew Avellino (1521–1608) Italian priest. Born Lancellotto Avellino at Castronuovo near Naples, he decided to enter the church at a young age and became a priest in 1547, working initially in the church courts. In 1556 he encountered difficulty after taking on the reorganization of a notorious convent and instead, changing his name to Andrew, joined the recently-established congregation of Theatine clerks regular in Naples. A friend of St CHARLES BORROMEO, he earned a reputation as a preacher and confessor and went on to found Theatine houses in Milan and Piacenza. He was canonized in 1712. He is honoured as the patron saint of Naples and of stroke victims.

Feast Day: 10 November.

Andrew Bobola (1591–1657) Polish Jesuit martyr. Born into an aristocratic Polish family, he joined the Jesuit order at Vilna in 1609 and in due course became head of the house at Bobruysk. He distinguished himself by his service to plague victims and dedicated himself to missionary work. He met his death after rebellious Cossacks occupied his house at Janov near Pinsk and subjected him to savage interrogation. When he refused to bow to their will he was scorched, flayed, mutilated and beheaded. He was canonized in 1938.

Feast Day: 16 May.

Andrew Corsini (1301–1373) Italian bishop. Born in Florence, he had an unruly youth before reforming and becoming a Carmelite friar in Florence in 1318. He soon earned a reputation as a preacher and healer and in 1360 was chosen as the new bishop of Fiesole. Initially he sought to refuse this

office before capitulating and proving himself highly effective in the role, winning particular respect for his ability to reconcile quarrelling parties (as when he mended relations during civil unrest in Bologna). He was much loved for his humility and his generosity towards the poor and lived in conditions of considerable austerity himself. He was canonized in 1629.
Feast Day: 4 February.

Andrew Dung-Lac   *See* VIETNAM, MARTYRS OF.

Andrew Fournet   (1752–1834) French priest. Born near Poitiers, he showed little interest in religion in his youth before an uncle persuaded him to take up the priesthood. As curé for Maillé, where he was born, he continued to minister in secret after the French Revolution until arrested in 1792. Subsequently he assisted St ELIZABETH BICHIER in founding the Daughters of the Cross, providing a rule for them to live by. He maintained his links with the order until his death and was variously credited with a number of miracles in his service of the sisters and those in their care.
Feast Day: 13 May.

Andrew Kim Tae-Gon   *See* KOREA, MARTYRS OF.

Angela of Foligno   (*c.*1248–1309) Italian visionary. Born at Foligno in Italy, Angela married a wealthy husband and as a young adult indulged in a life of luxury and sensuality. In 1285, however, she suddenly repented her sinful ways and dedicated herself to penance and prayer. After the death of her husband, mother and sons from plague she joined the Franciscan Third Order in 1291. She demonstrated a special sympathy for the poor and the sick and became well-known for her visions, details of which she dictated to her confessor, Brother Arnold. According to him, Angela of Foligno saw her life as a tortured spiritual journey of 30 steps. During her lifetime she attracted a number of disciples, to whom she offered spiritual guidance.
Feast Day: 28 February.

Angela Merici   (*c.*1474–1540) Italian foundress of the Ursuline order. Born at Desenzano in Lombardy and orphaned at an early age, Angela Merici emerged as a leading figure in the Catholic Reformation in northern Italy. Though a laywoman herself, she spent much of her life occupied with the establishment of communities of unmarried women of all classes who desired to live a celibate, Christian life. From these communities evolved the Company of St URSULA (founded in 1535). Members of the Ursulines lived by a rule devised by Angela Merici herself, dedicating their lives to God, while continuing to live at home with their families, and seeking opportunities to do charitable acts on behalf of their neighbours. The order, which had 24 groups by the time of its founder's death in Brescia, was organized on military lines and earned a lasting reputation as the oldest teaching order for women in the church. Angela Merici herself was canonized in 1807.

Feast Day: 27 January.

Ann   *See* JOACHIM AND ANN.

Anselm   (*c.*1033–1109) Italian bishop. Born into a noble family of Piedmont in Italy, he attended monastery school from the age of five. In 1060 he was admitted as a monk to the Benedictine order at Bec Abbey in Normandy, where he established a reputation as a preacher, scholar and teacher. In due course he rose to the rank of prior and abbot (1078). In 1093 he was appointed archbishop of Canterbury, in which role he proved a vigorous defendant of the English church against secular interference, frequently resisting the wishes of William II and Henry I and even having to go into temporary exile on two occasions because of his outspoken criticism. A particular cause of argument was his insistence upon his right to appoint bishops without interference from the king. He was also a dedicated opponent of slavery and in 1102 secured a resolution of the ecclesiastical council at Westminster condemning the practice. His influential theological treatises include *Cur Deus Homo?*, in which he discussed the incarnation of Christ, *Monologium* and *Proslogium*, in which he defended the concept of the existence of God. Among those profoundly influenced by his writings were such notable figures as St THOMAS AQUINAS. Anselm was identified as a Doctor of the Church in 1720. His emblem is a ship (a reference to his independent spirit).

Feast Day: 21 April.

Anskar   (801–865) French missionary. Born into a noble family near Amiens, Anskar (or **Ansgar**) served as a monk at Corbie in Picardy and Corvey in Westphalia before conducting the first of many ambitious missionary journeys, touring Denmark in 826 under the patronage of the Christian King Harold. Forced to flee Denmark, he subsequently had more success spreading the gospel in Sweden. In 831 he accepted the post of bishop of Hamburg, with responsibility for all of Scandinavia. When the

Danes laid Hamburg to waste in 845 he was entrusted with the see of Bremen, with the rank of archbishop. Respected as a preacher and known for his generosity to the poor, he continued to go on evangelical missions to Sweden and Denmark until his death and was credited with many miracles. He is honoured today as the patron saint of Denmark and Iceland.

Feast Day: 3 February.

Anthelm   (1107–1178) French bishop. Born near Chambéry, he served as a priest in Belley in south-east France until the age of 30, when he enrolled as a Carthusian monk. Such was the respect Anthelm attracted as a reformer and organizer that within two years (1139) he was appointed abbot of the mother house, La Grande Chartreuse. Under his guidance the monastery flourished as never before, benefiting from extensive rebuilding and from the construction of an aqueduct supplying running water as well as from a general improvement in relations between the various charter-houses of the order. After 24 highly successful years in this post, during which time he profoundly influenced the future development of the Carthusian order and passed on his ideas through such pupils as St HUGH OF LINCOLN, Anthelm left in order to become bishop of Belley. In this role too he proved a highly capable administrator and reformer, unflinching in the face of opposition. In 1175, for instance, he caused a furore by excommunicating the powerful Count Humbert of Maurienne for various misdeeds and even had to withdraw from his see for a time. Plans for Anthelm to go to England to mediate between Henry II and St THOMAS BECKET were never realized and Anthelm spent his final years caring for lepers and the needy in Belley. Visitors to Anthelm on his deathbed included Count Humbert of Maurienne, who finally came to repent of his earlier crimes.

Feast Day: 26 June.

Anthony   *See* ANTONY.

Antonino   (1389–1459) Italian bishop. Born in Florence, Antonino Pierozzi (otherwise referred to as **Antonius** or **Antoninus**) determined upon a life in the church at an early age and in 1405, defying poor health, became a member of the Order of Friars Preacher. Over the following 40 years he lived at various Dominican houses throughout Italy, sometimes taking charge of the community in which he resided and earning a reputation as a preacher. He served as vicar-general of the Dominicans of the Strict

Observance (1432–35). In 1436, with the assistance of Cosimo dei Medici, he founded the friary of San Marco in Florence. It became an important cultural and religious centre of the Renaissance, complete with frescoes by Fra Angelico. Antonino was appointed archbishop of Florence in 1446 and in this role proved both generous to the needy and incorruptible in dispensing justice. Widely respected for his great wisdom and integrity, he was also consulted for advice regarding public and civil matters. Observing the strictest poverty in his own life, he spent his last years serving as an ambassador for Florence and contributing towards the reform of the Roman court. His influential writings included the treatise entitled *Summa*, in which he discussed issues of moral theology. He was canonized in 1523. His emblem is a pair of scales.
Feast Day: 10 May.

Antony   (251–356) Egyptian hermit. Born at Coma near Memphis in Egypt, Antony (or **Anthony**) underwent an intense religious experience while listening to the proclamation of the gospel at mass at the age of 20. He responded to this by giving away all his considerable possessions and taking up the life of a hermit in a hut just outside Memphis, dedicating himself to prayer and contemplation and resisting the torments and temptations of daily life. After 15 years there he felt the need for greater solitude and withdrew to an isolated mountain in the Libyan desert, thus becoming one of the founders of the monastic tradition. Aged 55 he gathered around him a community of like-minded hermits and founded a loose community of monks who met for worship and teaching. Becoming widely respected for his piety and wisdom, Antony was often consulted for his advice and from time to time he entered Alexandria in order to lend his support against various heresies. He is said to have died at the age of 105. His emblem is a pig.
Feast Day: 17 January.

Antony Daniel   *See* NORTH AMERICA, MARTYRS OF

Antony of Padua   (*c.*1196–1231) Portuguese preacher and theologian. Born in Lisbon, Antony of Padua entered an Augustinian monastery at Coimbra near Lisbon in 1210 and there earned a reputation as a scholar and preacher. At the age of 25 he joined the Franciscans with the ambition of serving as a missionary with them. Illness, however, prevented him from performing such work overseas and he had to content himself with preaching in central Italy. He became one of the most celebrated preachers of his day, attracting huge audiences wherever he went. Impressed by Antony's gifts, St FRANCIS appointed him teacher of theology to the Franciscan order (the first person to be given the post). He spent his final years in Padua before his premature death at the age of 36, preaching and promoting reform there. He was canonized in 1232 and for his scholarly achievements ranks among the Doctors of the Church. He is honoured today as the patron of Portugal and of lost articles (a reference to the legend that when a young friar stole a valuable manuscript from the saint a terrifying demon menaced the youth, obliging him to return the manuscript to its owner). *Feast Day: 13 June.*

Antony Mary Claret   (1807–1870) Spanish bishop. Born the son of a weaver in Sallent, Spain, Antony (or **Anthony**) Mary Claret became a priest and longed to undertake missionary work, but was declined by the missionary order he sought to join. He settled instead (1837–49) for evangelical work in his home province of Catalonia, earning a reputation as a preacher and writing extensively upon religious matters. He also founded a religious library and established the Missionary Sons of the Immaculate Heart of Mary, popularly dubbed the Claretians, to organize missionary campaigns. In 1850 he began seven years as reforming archbishop of Santiago, Cuba, taking charge of a diocese that had been much neglected for 14 years. He returned to Spain in 1858 and served as chaplain to Queen Isabella II. He spent much of the rest of his life at court, founding a scientific laboratory and music and language schools while still maintaining his links with the Claretians until forced into exile from Spain as a result of the revolution of 1868. By the time of his death he was estimated to have delivered some 25,000 sermons. He was canonized in 1950. *Feast Day: 24 October.*

Antony Zaccaria   (1502–1539) Italian preacher. Born in Cremona in Lombardy, Antony (or **Anthony**) Maria Zaccaria trained initially as a medical doctor at the University of Padua before entering the priesthood. Ordained in 1528, he proved a powerful and uncompromising preacher and in due course emerged as a leading Catholic reformer. He moved to Milan and there, assisted by Louisa Torelli, Countess of Guastella, founded the Clerks Regular of St Paul, a loosely-knit community of priests working together to regenerate the Christian way of life and do good deeds. The community won official recognition in 1533, with Antony as its leader. Subsequently he resigned the post in order to establish a new branch at Vicenza. The Clerks Regular moved to the church of St Barnabas in

Milan in the year of their founder's death and hence became known as Barnabites. Antony Zaccaria was canonized in 1897.
Feast Day: 5 July.

Aphraates of Persia   (*c*.297–*c*.345) Syrian monk. Born in Syria near the Persian border, Aphraates converted to Christianity and lived as a hermit in a cell outside Edessa in Mesopotamia, dedicating himself to a life of penance and fasting. After several years he moved to a new location close to a monastery near Antioch and here began to receive visitors seeking his advice. He also spoke out against Arian heretics and, according legend, impressed the emperor Valens sufficiently to win his protections.
Aphraates is sometimes identified as the otherwise unknown author of the 23 *Demonstrations*, the oldest writings of the Syrian church.
Feast Day: 7 April.

Apollinaris of Ravenna   (dates unknown) Italian bishop and martyr. No details are known for certain about the life and death of this early martyr beyond the fact that he was a bishop of Ravenna in Italy who apparently died for his faith. Another tradition suggests that he lived in Antioch and was a disciple of St PETER who died after being stoned by a mob.
Feast Day: 23 July.

Apollonia   (d.249) Martyr of Alexandria. Tradition has it that Apollonia was an elderly deaconess of Alexandria who was among the Christians put to death by a rioting mob. Her attackers knocked out several of her teeth before moving to burn her alive if she did not renounce her faith. Before they could manhandle her further Apollonia spoke a brief prayer and then walked willingly into the fire. She is honoured today as the patron saint of dentists. Her emblem is a tooth gripped by forceps.
Feast Day: 9 February.

Arnulf of Metz   (582–641) French bishop. Born into a noble family from Nancy, Arnulf (or **Arnoul**) lived at the royal court until the age of 30, playing his part in civic affairs for many years as adviser to Chlotar II. In 614, though a layman, he combined his secular duties with the role of bishop of Metz. He disliked having to play such a prominent part in public life, however, and eventually (629) retired from his official posts and retreated to the Vosges mountains to live as a hermit, settling near the monastery of Habend (later renamed Remiremont) with his friend St **Romaric** (d.653). Through the marriage of his elder son to St Begga, a daughter of Pepin of Landen, he was an ancestor of the Carolingian royal dynasty.

Feast Day: 18 July.

Arsenius   (*c*.354–*c*.412) Roman hermit and monk. He is thought to have served as a deacon in Rome and may have been tutor to the sons of the emperors Theodosius, Arcadius and Honorius in Constantinople before retiring to live with the desert fathers in Alexandria. There he lived in conditions of considerable austerity and became famous both for his outspokenness and for his perceptive understanding of his fellow man. He was also well-known for his emotional nature, liable to break into tears at the slightest provocation. Legend has it that he wore his eyelashes away through copious weeping.

Feast Day: 19 July.

Asaph   (6th century) Welsh bishop. Asaph was a pupil of St KENTIGERN in north Wales who succeeded to the bishopric of Llanelwy (subsequently renamed St Asaph in his honour) late in the 6th century. It may have been Asaph who founded the monastery at Llanelwy rather than Kentigern. Little more is known for certain of Asaph's life, though he is said to have had a charming, pious nature.

Feast Day: 1 May.

Athanasius   (*c*.297–373) Egyptian bishop. Born to Christian parents in Alexandria, Egypt, he received a good education before retiring to the desert in 315 to continue his religious studies with St ANTHONY. In 318 he was ordained as a deacon and subsequently (326) rose to the position of archbishop of Alexandria, in which role he inherited responsibility for all the churches and monasteries in Egypt and Ethiopia. Much of his effort over the ensuing years was dedicated towards resisting the threat posed by Arianism, which questioned the divinity of Christ. In 325 he attended the Council of Nicea which officially condemned the heresy and subsequently formed the alliance of orthodox opinion that at length brought about the defeat of the Arians in 381. Despite his undoubted skills as an administrator, the furore caused by the Arian question resulted in Athanasius being deposed or forced into retreat from Alexandria on several occasions and in total he spent some 17 years in exile from his see. Several of his influential writings survive, although he probably did not write the so-called Athanasian creed. He is honoured as one of the four Greek Doctors of the Church.

Feast Day: 2 May.

Athanasius the Athonite (c.925–1003) Abbot of Mount Athos. Born into a wealthy family of Trebizond on the Black Sea, Athanasius the Athonite served as a teacher in Constantinople before joining the monks at Mount Kyminas in Bithynia. In 958 he moved to Mount Athos in Greece where he organized the hermits and built the first monastery, funded by Emperor Nicephorus II. With the emperor's continued support, he overcame the opposition of some of the hermits there to found a further three monasteries on the mountain, providing a rule by which all the monks ran their lives. He was killed when the cupola of his church collapsed during an inspection of building works. The monasteries founded by Athanasius on Mount Athos still exist today.
Feast Day: 5 July.

Aubert of Avranches (d. c.720) French bishop. Nothing is known for certain of the life of Aubert of Avranches beyond the fact that he was the founder of the church of Mont-Saint-Michel. He is said to have founded the church as the result of a series of visions he had of St MICHAEL THE ARCHANGEL. The church, which became a major centre of religion and culture in France, was dedicated in 709 and subsequently became a Benedictine monastery.
Feast Day: 10 September.

Audoenus *See* OUEN.

Audomarus *See* OMER.

Audrey *See* ETHELDREDA.

Augustine of Canterbury (d. c.605) Italian missionary bishop. Augustine served as a monk at the monastery of St Andrew in Rome, becoming prior there, before being selected by the pope, St GREGORY THE GREAT, to lead a band of 40 missionaries to pagan Britain in 597. Once in England, Augustine won the support of St ETHELBERT, king of Kent, who soon set an example for his subjects by converting to Christianity. Consecrated as archbishop of the English, Augustine established his see at Canterbury and founded the monastery of SS. Peter and Paul (renamed St Augustine's) there. Over the next seven years he went on to organize two further sees, one for the East Saxons and one at Rochester. He had less success spreading the gospel in Wales and more distant parts of Britain, failing to establish the supremacy of Canterbury over other bishops. Other significant contributions included his role in advising King Ethelbert in drawing up the earliest extant Anglo-Saxon written laws. Augustine is remembered today as the most important figure in the early evangelization of Britain. *Feast Day: (England) 26 May, (elsewhere) 27 May.*

Augustine of Hippo (354–430) Bishop and theologian. Born in Tagaste (modern Algeria) in north Africa, the son of a pagan father, Augustine lived a dissolute youth that he subsequently came to repent. He founded a school of rhetoric in Milan in 383 and soon began to feel the need to reform, finally converting to Christianity in 386 while in Milan, Italy (partly through the influence of the teachings of St AMBROSE). He returned to Africa that same year and was ordained a priest at Hippo in 391. He was raised to the rank of bishop in 396 and for the next four decades won recognition as the most prominent figure in the north African church. He founded a number of monasteries and also defended the orthodox position against various heresies. His extensive writings, which included *Confessions*, an account of his immoral early life, and *On the City of God*, a defence of faith written at a time when Rome was under siege by the Goths in 410, had a profound and lasting influence upon Christian theology. He died in Hippo while the city was being besieged by the Vandals. Considered second only to St PAUL as the most influential figure in the early history of the Christian church, Augustine is revered as both Western Father of the Church and Doctor of the Church. He is also honoured as the patron saint of theologians. His emblem is a pierced, broken or burning heart.
Feast Day: 28 August.

Augustine of Trondheim *See* EYSTEIN.

B

Baldhild   *See* BATHILD.

Barbara   (dates unknown) Legendary martyr. According to traditions dating from around the 7th century, Barbara was a beautiful young virgin who lived in the 3rd or 4th century. To remove Barbara from the attentions of her many admirers, her father Dioscurus confined her in a tower but was subsequently enraged to discover she had become a Christian. He attempted to kill her for her temerity, but was miraculously prevented from completing the act. After Dioscurus reported Barbara to the authorities she was tortured and formally condemned to death by beheading, Dioscurus volunteering himself as her executioner. As Barbara expired her father was struck by lightning and burned to ashes. In consequence of this legend St Barbara is invoked as protection against lightning and honoured as the patron saint of gunners, miners and firefighters. Her emblem is a tower.
Feast Day: 4 December.

Barnabas   (1st century AD) Cypriot-born apostle. Although not formally identified as one of the 12 apostles, Barnabas ranks alongside them as one of the champions of early Christianity. Tradition claims that he was born a Jew, originally named Joseph but renamed Barnabas (meaning 'son of encouragement') by the apostles. Although little is known of the details of his life, he won respect for his tireless efforts on behalf of the developing Christian community and is said to have sold all his possessions to help the poor. He was also instrumental in persuading Christians in Jerusalem to give St PAUL a hearing, overcoming their fear of him as a former oppressor. In later years he took charge of the new church at Antioch, where he was assisted by Paul, and accompanied Paul on the first of his missionary journeys through Asia Minor. The two saints subsequently quarrelled, however, and separated, Barnabas returning to Cyprus to pursue his evangelical mission there. The two men were apparently reconciled some time before Barnabas's death, which may have taken place at Salamis in the year 61 (one version of his life suggests he died a martyr, being stoned to death). Today he is honoured as the patron saint of Cyprus.
Feast Day: 11 June.

Barra   *See* FINBAR.

Bartholomew   (1st century AD) apostle. Named as one of the 12 apostles at Mark 3:14–19, he is often identified as being the same person as **Nathanael**, whose meeting with Christ is described at John 1:45–51. No other details are known of his life, but he is credited with promoting the dissemination of Christianity through the Indian subcontinent. Legend has it that he died a martyr at Derbend in Armenia, being flayed alive and beheaded. His body is said to have been taken to an island in the Tiber at Rome and his church there became a famous centre of medical expertise (hence the naming of Barts hospital in London). His emblem is a butcher's knife (as used in flaying the saint alive). He is honoured as the patron saint of tanners and others who work with skins and leather, such as bookbinders, furriers and cobblers.
Feast Day: 24 August.

Basil   (*c.*329–379) Cappadocian bishop. Born into a wealthy Christian family of Caesarea (in modern Turkey), which had already produced several saints, Basil was persuaded by his older sister St MACRINA THE YOUNGER to give up a promising secular career and join the church. Accordingly, in 356 he founded a monastery on the family estate in Pontus (perhaps the first monastery in Asia Minor) and established a monastic rule there that became a model for the development of early monasticism in the East, still the basis of Orthodox monasticism. As bishop of Caesarea from 370, Basil proved a stubborn defender of the church's independence from state influence (openly defying the authority of the emperor Valens) and a flinty opponent of Arianism, which he combatted alongside his friend and ally St GREGORY NAZIANZEN. Together with St GREGORY OF NYSSA, these saints are sometimes known as the 'Three Cappadocians'. Basil's treatise *On the Holy Spirit* ranks high among the most important early writings of the Catholic church. Other surviving writings by his hand include commentaries upon the scriptures, sermons and 366 letters. Because of his profound influence upon the growth of early monasticism and for his undoubted leadership qualities, Basil is identified as one of the Doctors of the Church and is often referred to as **Basil the Great**. He is also honoured as the patron saint of Russia. His emblem is a supernatural fire, sometimes with a dove.
Feast Day: 2 January.

Bathild   (d.680) English queen of the Western Franks. The beautiful Bathild (otherwise called **Balthild** or **Baldhild**) was brought up as a Christian in

England but in 641, while still a girl, was kidnapped by pirates and eventually sold as a slave to Erchinoald, a nobleman at the court of Clovis II, king of the Western Franks. The pleasure-loving Clovis married Bathild in 649 but died in 657, leaving Bathild as regent in the place of their eldest son (who eventually took the throne as Chlotar III). As queen, Bathild strove to end slavery and promoted monasticism, founding monasteries at Corbie and Chelles. More controversial was her alleged involvement in the assassination of Bishop Annemund of Lyons and other high-ranking church officials. She was forced from office in 665 and ordered to retire to the nunnery she had established at Chelles. She spent the rest of her life there living as a humble nun, willingly undertaking the lowliest chores. Her emblem is a ladder reaching towards heaven. She is honoured as the patron saint of children.

Feast Day: 30 January.

Bavo (d. *c*.655) Dutch hermit. Born Allowin, the son of a wealthy landowner in Brabant, he married and fathered a daughter and generally lived an indulgent, unprincipled existence before opting for a more holy way of life, under the influence of St AMAND OF MAASTRICHT, following the death of his wife. Bavo accordingly gave away all his possessions and joined the monastery at Ghent in the hope of redeeming himself for his past wickedness. He undertook missionary work with St Amand in France and Flanders before eventually settling as a hermit in a tree in a wood at Ghent, alongside the monastery that was renamed Saint-Bavon in his honour after his death. Ghent cathedral is dedicated to him.

Feast Day: 1 October.

Beatrice *See* SIMPLICIUS, FAUSTINUS AND BEATRICE.

Beatrice of Assisi *See* CLARE OF ASSISI.

Beatrice da Silva (1424–1490) Portuguese abbess. Born into a noble Portuguese family, Beatrice (or **Beatrix**) spent her childhood in the royal court and accompanied Queen Isabel of Portugal to the court in Spain. Briefly imprisoned on false charges, she abandoned the life of the court and joined the Cistercian convent of Santo Domingo de Silos in Toledo. Ultimately she founded the Congregation of the Immaculate Conception of the Blessed Virgin Mary. She was canonized in 1976 and is honoured as the patron saint of prisoners.

Feast Day: 1 September.

Bede, the Venerable   (*c*.672–735) English monk and historian. Born in Northumberland, Bede was installed at Wearmouth Abbey at the age of seven and studied under St BENEDICT BISCOP there. Subsequently he studied under St CEOLFRITH at the monastery at Jarrow, where he spent most of the rest of his largely uneventful life, dedicating himself to prayer and study. It is thought that he never left his native Northumberland. He became a deacon at the age of 19 and was ordained a priest around 703, aged 30. Bede is remembered today for his hugely influential writings, of which his *Ecclesiastical History of the English People* (729) was the most important. This epic work of history became one of the principal reference sources for the period, often proving the sole fount of knowledge for certain episodes. Bede's other writings included biographies, a martyrology and treatises on the Bible, science, poetry and music. His scripture commentaries in particular were widely used by Anglo-Saxon missionaries. He died shortly after dictating the final sentence of his translation of St John's Gospel. Another legacy of Bede's work was the creation of the term *anno domini* as applied to dates from the period after the birth of Christ. Acclaimed the father of English history, Bede was pronounced a Doctor of the Church in 1899. Today he is honoured as the patron saint of scholars.
Feast Day: 25 May.

Begga   *See* GERTRUDE OF NIVELLES.

Benedict   (*c*.480–*c*.547) Italian patriarch and founder of the Benedictine Rule, considered the father of western monasticism. Beyond the fact that he was born into a prosperous family in Nuroia in Umbria, the twin brother of St SCHOLASTICA, little is known of the details of Benedict's life. Tradition has it that, revolted by the degeneracy of Rome, he opted initially for the life of a hermit, living in a cave near Subiaco. In due course he was asked to assume the leadership of a community of monks nearby, only for them to attempt to poison him when they failed to live up to his high expectations. Subsequently he organized the disciples he had attracted into 12 new communities, including the monastery of Monte Cassino (founded *c*.529). For these communities Benedict formulated the *Regula Monarchorum* or Benedictine Rule, to provide practical and spiritual guidance. This profoundly influential rule placed particular emphasis upon the role of the monastery as a place of sanctuary and education and directed monks to spend most of their time praying, studying, working and living on a communal basis. They were also expected to preach and do charitable work among the local population. The Benedictine Rule provided the foundation for monastic life throughout the Western world and it is still observed in many monasteries today. Legend has it that Benedict died at prayer, standing in his chapel at Monte Cassino with his hands raised to heaven. He is honoured as the patron saint of Europe and also of cave explorers. His emblems are a broken cup (a reference to the failed attempt to poison the saint) and a raven (which carried the cup · away).

Feast Day: 11 July.

Benedict of Aniane (*c.*750–821) French abbot. Born into a noble French family and brought up at the court of the Emperor Charlemagne, he chose the life of a monk and around 780, after some time living the life of a hermit, founded a community on the river Aniane (Corbière) in Languedoc. This group foundered on his insistence that it adhere to a very austere rule of life, but a subsequent community organized under the more flexible Rule of St BENEDICT prospered and became the basis of a large and important monastery. A committed reformer, Benedict himself took on the foundation and reorganization of numerous other communities and in due course was given charge of all the monasteries within Charlemagne's empire, effectively restoring the Rule of St Benedict throughout the Frankish realm. Monks were encouraged to attend mass on a daily basis and also to concentrate upon their clerical studies rather than upon manual labour. In 817 Benedict oversaw an influential council at his headquarters at Aachen, which agreed a code governing all the member houses. This disintegrated after the death of Benedict but lived on as an inspiration for the continuing growth of the monastic tradition, making Benedict of Aniane second only to St BENEDICT himself as an influence upon early Western monasticism.

Feast Day: 11 February.

Benedict the Black (1526–1589) Sicilian laybrother. Born to Black African slaves near Messina in Sicily, he was granted his freedom when he reached the age of 18. As a young man his restraint when insulted because of his colour impressed the leader of a community of Franciscan hermits based near San Fratello and he was invited to join the group. In due course he succeeded to the leadership of the community before it finally broke up around 1564 and he took up the post of laybrother at the Franciscan friary at Palermo, working in the kitchen there. In 1578, though still a laybrother and unable to read, Benedict the Black (otherwise called **Benedict the**

African) was persuaded to take charge of the friary and set about returning the community to a stricter observance of the rule of St FRANCIS. In the years that followed he served the group in various capacities, winning great respect for his sympathy for others and earning a reputation as a miraculous healer of the sick. In his final years he returned to fulfilling humble tasks in the kitchen. He was canonized in 1807 and is honoured today as the patron saint of Palermo.
Feast Day: 4 April.

Benedict Biscop   (628–689) English abbot. Born Biscop Baducing into a wealthy Northumbrian family, he served as a courtier of King Oswy until 653, when he abandoned the secular life with the intention of becoming a monk. Shortly afterwards, in company with St WILFRID, he undertook the first of six pilgrimages to Rome. On his way back from the second of these journeys, while staying at the great monastery of Lérins, he took his vows as a monk and assumed the name Benedict (or **Benet**). After his third trip to Rome he was appointed abbot of St Augustine's in Canterbury under the Archbishop of Canterbury, St THEODORE. Around this time he conceived the idea of founding a monastery of his own and in due course returned to Rome in order to conduct a tour of the greatest monasteries already founded. Once back in England, with the support of King Egfrith, he founded Wearmouth Abbey (the first Romanesque church in northern England) in 674. After a fifth visit to Rome in 678, in the course of which he gathered together a rich treasury of books and relics, a second monastery followed at Jarrow. As well as furnishing his monasteries with the books, paintings and relics he had brought back from Rome (added to after his sixth and final trip in 682), he also introduced the Gregorian style of singing and chanting that he had heard abroad, thus having a profound and lasting impact upon religious practice in England throughout succeeding centuries. He is also credited with the first use of glass windows in English churches. The libraries he founded at Wearmouth and Jarrow played a key role in promoting learning in England's monasteries and provided much of the material upon which Benedict's pupil the VENERABLE BEDE relied in his own writing. Benedict himself was struck down by paralysis in 683 and was bedridden in his remaining years. He is honoured as the patron saint of painters and musicians.
Feast Day: 12 January.

Benedict Joseph Labre   (1748–1783) French mendicant. Born the son of a shopkeeper near Boulogne, he determined to enter the church at a young age and was prepared for the priesthood by his uncle, who was a pastor. In 1766 he applied to enter the Trappist abbey of La Trappe, near Dijon, but was turned down on account of his youth and his evident eccentricity. Attempts to gain admittance to a number of Carthusian monasteries similarly met with disappointment. Finally, in 1769, he was allowed to spend six weeks with the Carthusians at Neuville, only for it to be decided that he was not suited to the monastic life. After the Cistercians also turned him down, Benedict chose instead to undertake a pilgrimage to Rome and on the journey reconciled himself to a future as a wandering holy man. In the years that followed he travelled to numerous sacred sites throughout Europe. He lived in conditions of great austerity, eating food from rubbish heaps, sleeping in the open and never bathing. In 1774 he arrived in Rome, where he spent his days at prayer in the city's churches and his nights sleeping in the Colosseum. By the time of his death he had already achieved the reputation of a saint and huge crowds attended his funeral. Nicknamed the 'Beggar of Rome', he was canonized in 1881. He is honoured today as the patron saint of the homeless and the mentally ill. *Feast Day: 16 April.*

Benet *See* BENEDICT BISCOP.

Bénézet (*c.*1163–1184) French shepherd-boy. Born at Hermillon in Savoy, he moved to Avignon around 1178 and there experienced a vision during an eclipse in which a voice instructed him to build a bridge near Avignon. Although only a teenager, he convinced the local bishop to assist in the project and spent the remaining seven years of his life working on the bridge over the Rhône. It was completed shortly after his death. For many years his corpse was preserved in a chapel built on the bridge (transferred after floods in 1669 to Avignon cathedral and later to the church of Saint Didier). He is honoured today as the patron saint of Avignon. *Feast Day: 14 April.*

Benignus (*c.*3rd century) French martyr. The story of Benignus was inspired by the discovery of an ancient tomb at Dijon early in the 6th century. According to tradition, he was a missionary priest from Lyons who was put to death for his faith during the reign of the Emperor Aurelian (270–275). The site of his grave was subsequently occupied by a large church. *Feast Day: 1 November.*

Berard and Companions (d.1220) Italian martyrs. Berard was born into a noble family in Carbio, Italy, but elected to join the Franciscan order and

in 1219, along with four other friars, was ordered by St FRANCIS to conduct missionary work among the Muslims. The group worked initially with the Moors in Seville before being imprisoned and then forced to leave the city, upon which they journeyed to Marrakesh in Morocco. Here they preached in the market-place but soon incurred the wrath of the locals when they denounced the teachings of Mohammed and were arrested. When they refused their captors' demands to renounce Christ they were beheaded, allegedly by the hand of the sultan himself, thus becoming the first Franciscan martyrs. They were canonized in 1481.
Feast Day: 16 January.

Berin   *See* BIRINUS.

Bernadette   (1844–1879) French visionary. Born Marie Bernarde Soubirous in Lourdes, the daughter of a poor miller, she was considered sweet-natured but backward as a child. In 1858, at the age of 14, she allegedly experienced the first of 18 visions of the Virgin Mary in a cave on the bank of the river Gave. Calling herself Mary of the Immaculate Conception, the vision continued to appear to her over a period of two months, both when she was alone and when she was accompanied by others, although only Bernadette could see her. For years the church authorities declined to take her claims seriously and she was the subject of much scorn. She entered the convent of the Sisters of Charity in Nevers in 1866 and remained there until her death at the age of 35, winning respect for her steadfast refusal to acknowledge her own growing fame. In due course the visions of Berna-dette established Lourdes as a major centre of pilgrimage, renowned for miraculous cures. She was canonized in 1933, chiefly in recognition of the humility she showed in her final years.
Feast Day: 16 April.

Bernard of Clairvaux   (1090–1153) French abbot. Born into a noble family of Fontaines de Dijon in Burgundy, he became a monk in 1113, entering the newly-founded Benedictine abbey of Cîteaux. Intelligent and charming by nature, he earned a reputation for piety and was noted as a preacher and on the strength of his growing reputation was sent with 12 other monks to found a new Cistercian monastery at Clairvaux in Cham-pagne. He went on to oversee the foundation or reformation of 68 more subsidiary houses throughout western Europe, providing the inspiration for a substantial spiritual revival. In 1145 he spoke out publicly in favour of the ill-fated Second Crusade: when it failed he was widely blamed for the disaster although he preferred to place the blame upon the sins of the armies that had participated. He also opposed the teachings of Peter Abelard and promoted evangelical missions among the Albigensian heretics of Languedoc. His many important writings included works on theology, sermons and letters, including the treatise *De consideratione*, a study of the papal office that he wrote for Pope Eugenius III, who had been a monk at Clairvaux. He was canonized in 1174 and is honoured today as a Doctor of the Church and as the patron saint of cancer victims and also of Gibraltar. His emblem is a beehive.

Feast Day: 20 August.

Bernardino of Siena (1380–1444) Italian missionary and preacher. Born at Massa Marittima in Siena, Italy, he trained as a lawyer before becoming a Franciscan friar of the Strict Observance in 1403. He followed his vocation quietly at Fiesole for some 14 years, then, in response to the prophecy of a novice, moved to Milan and pursued his calling as a preacher, earning a wide reputation for his tireless speeches against immorality. He preached to large crowds throughout Italy, always travelling by foot, and became the most famous missionary of his time. He also acquired a reputation as a miraculous healer, curing many lepers and other seriously ill people. He was elected general of the Observants in 1437 and dedicated the remainder of his life to reforming and expanding the order as well as to sending friars on evangelical missions around the world. He also promoted learning within the order, encouraging the study of theology and canon law. His death in Aquila in Abruzzi followed shortly after he resumed his evangelical trips in 1444. He was canonized in 1450.

Feast Day: 20 May.

Bertilla Boscardin (1888–1922) Italian nursing sister. Born Anna Francesca Boscardin into a peasant family near Vicenza, she was considered slow as a child but determined on a life in the church and conceived the ambition of becoming a saint. She was admitted to the convent of the Sisters of St Dorothy in Vicenza in 1904, initially working in the kitchen there but later being allowed to help in the children's ward at Treviso. During World War I she distinguished herself through her dedication to her charges at a military hospital near Como. In 1919 she was appointed head of the children's isolation ward at Treviso and remained there until ill health prevented her from continuing her work. She died during an operation. Much loved for her devotion to her patients and credited with a number of miraculous acts of healing, she was canonized in 1961.

Feast Day: 20 October.

Bertin (d. *c.*700) French abbot. Born near Coutances, Bertin joined the monastery at Luxeuil and worked alongside several companions as a missionary in the waterlogged Pas-de-Calais region of northern France. He was appointed abbot of Sithiu (later renamed Saint-Bertin after his death) and consolidated it as an important evangelical centre. The prosperity of the monastery there inspired the growth of the surrounding settlement, which developed into the town of Saint-Omer. In 663 Bertin and St OMER build the church that in due course became the cathedral of Saint-Omer. The influence of Bertin was further spread to England, where he also inspired a cult following, through visiting English clerics travelling to and from Rome. His emblem is a ship (a reference to the fact that Sithiu could originally only be reached by boat).

Feast Day: 5 September.

Beuno (6th century) Welsh abbot. The story of Beuno was first written down in the 14th century and is largely a matter of legend. Little is known of the details of his life beyond the tradition that he was born in Herefordshire and that his monastery was located at Clynnog Fawr in Caernarvonshire. Such was the reputation for healing enjoyed by Beuno that sick people were still being brought to Clynnog in search of a cure as late as the end of the 18th century.

Feast Day: 21 April.

Beuzec *See* BUDOC.

Birgitta *See* BRIDGET.

Birinus (d. *c.*650) Missionary in England. Possibly of German or Lombard origin, Birinus (otherwise called **Birin** or **Berin**) lived in Rome before being ordered by Pope Honorius I to spread the gospel in England. He duly set about evangelizing the largely pagan population of Wessex, baptizing Cynegils, king of Wessex, in 635 and being permitted to establish his see at Dorchester. He went on to build many churches and to win numerous converts through his work before his eventual death in Dorchester.

Feast Day: 3 December.

Blaan *See* BLANE.

Blaise (dates unknown) Armenian bishop and martyr. Blaise (or **Blase**) is traditionally identified as one of the FOURTEEN HOLY HELPERS who enjoyed cult status in certain parts of medieval Europe. Tradition claims that he was a bishop of Sebastea in Armenia, born into a wealthy Christian family, who died a martyr's death, possibly early in the 4th century during the reign of the Emperor Licinius. In later centuries his name was often invoked in relation to the cure of diseased animals (a reference to a legend that he cured sick animals while in hiding in a cave) and his intervention was also sought in the treatment of throat problems (because he once saved the life of a boy who was choking on a fishbone). His emblem is a wool-comb (referring to the tradition that his flesh was torn with iron wool-combs before he was beheaded).
Feast Day: 3 February.

Blandina (d.177) French martyr. According to legend, Blandina was a slave who was sentenced to death in Lyons by the Romans for her Christian faith. Despite her poor health, she was the last of a group of martyrs (known as the Martyrs of Lyons) to die, patiently enduring various tortures, which culminated in her being tied in a net and tossed before a wild bull and gored to death. At no stage did she show any sign of renouncing her faith. She also won respect for the encouragement she gave to a 15-year-old boy called Ponticus who was put to death alongside her.
Feast Day: 2 June.

Blane (late 6th century) Scottish bishop. Blane (or **Blaan**) was born on the island of Bute and studied for the priesthood in Ireland under St COMGALL and St CANICE before returning to Scotland. He founded a monastery at Dunblane (now the site of Dunblane cathedral, where a bell alleged to be his is still preserved) and also performed missionary work among the Picts. Other details of his life are shrouded in legend.
Feast Day: 11 August.

Boethius *See* SEVERINUS BOETHIUS.

Bonaventure (*c*.1218–74) Italian bishop and theologian. Born at Bagnorea near Viterbo in Italy, he entered the Franciscan order in 1238. As a teacher of scripture and theology at the Franciscan school in Paris he earned a reputation as a leading religious scholar. In 1257 he was appointed minister-general of the Franciscans, in which post he proved a determined reformer and a stalwart defender of the order against the rival claims of

the secular clergy. He also championed academic study among the friars, departing from the less cerebral approach of the order's founder, St FRANCIS. Such was the importance of his influence upon the order that he is often considered its second founder. In 1264 he was also given charge of the Poor Clares and established the Society of the Gonfalone in the name of the Virgin Mary. He was promoted to the rank of cardinal archbishop of Albano by Pope Gregory X in 1273 but died just a year later while engaged in an effort to reunite the churches of the East and West at the Council of Lyons. His writings included several mystical works, numerous sermons and his *Commentary on the Sentences*, which comprised a comprehensive examination of scholastic theology of that period. He was canonized in 1482 and is revered as a Doctor of the Church. His emblem is a cardinal's hat (a reference to the story that when his cardinal's hat was presented to him he asked that it be hung on a nearby branch as his hands were greasy from washing dishes).
Feast Day: 15 July.

Boniface of Crediton (*c*.680–754) English missionary and martyr. Born at or near Crediton in Devon, he was baptized Winfrith and was ordained a priest at the age of 30. Pursuing the quiet life of a monk at Exeter and then at Nursling near Southampton for many years, he earned a reputation as a scholar and won respect as a preacher. In 715, however, he decided to undertake missionary work in Germany, believing this was God's will. Changing his name to Boniface, he received a papal commission from Pope Gregory II to evangelize in Germany and began his mission in Hesse in 718. Such was the success of his work that in 722 he was raised to the rank of bishop and given charge of all the German territories. The pope also secured for him the protection of Charles Martel, leader of the Franks. With this support Boniface won vast numbers of converts and effectively established the church in Germany, founding many monasteries as centres of education and evangelization and staffing them with fellow missionaries from England. He also did much to revive the church in France. In 731 he set up a system of dioceses throughout Germany and appointed bishops to take responsibility for them. He also undertook the reorganization of the Frankish church. In recognition of these achievements Boniface was appointed archbishop of all Germany by the pope in 747 and he established his see at Mainz. He continued his missionary work in his final years, continuing to win converts in Friesland until his murder by a band of pagans on the eve of Pentecost in 754. Many of his letters still survive.

He is honoured as the patron saint of brewers and tailors, as well as Germany.
Feast Day: 5 June.

Boris and Gleb (d.1015) Russian martyrs. Boris and Gleb were half-brothers and sons of St VLADIMIR, the first Christian prince of Russia. After their father's death their elder brother Svyatopolk resolved to kill Boris and Gleb to forestall any challenge to his claim to the throne. Boris and Gleb met their deaths without attempting to resist, refusing to endanger the lives of their servants or to oppose their own flesh and blood. After their demise they were acclaimed as Christian martyrs and they are still revered in Russia and Ukraine. Their treacherous brother Svyatopolk did not prosper long from his misdeeds, being driven out by another brother, Yaroslav of Novgorod, and dying in exile in Poland. In the West, Boris and Gleb are sometimes referred to by the names **Romanus and David**.
Feast Day: 24 July.

Botvid (d.1100) Swedish martyr. Botvid (or **Botwid**) was a layman from Sodermannland who converted to Christianity while in England. He returned to Sweden to help spread the gospel there. To assist him in this work he bought a Finnish slave and gave him religious instruction before agreeing to set him free on the understanding that he would work as a missionary in Finland. The slave, however, murdered Botvid and his companion Asbjorn as they prepared to row him back across the Baltic to his native land.
Feast Day: 28 July.

Brandon *See* BRENDAN THE VOYAGER.

Braulio (*c*.590–651) Spanish bishop. Born into a noble Hispano-Roman family of Zaragoza, he was the son of the bishop of Osma and himself became a monk in 610. A brilliant scholar, however, he subsequently moved to Seville in order to enroll at the school of St ISIDORE, who became a close friend. He was ordained by Isidore and succeeded his brother as bishop of Zaragoza in 631, becoming in due course the most respected bishop in the country after Isidore. Throughout his life he continued to live in the conditions of austerity and simplicity that he had adopted as a monk. A number of his letters have survived and he also edited the encyclopedic *Etymologies* of St Isidore after the latter's death. He is honoured as the patron of Aragon.
Feast Day: 26 March.

Brendan the Voyager (*c*.486–*c*.577) Irish abbot. Little is known for
certain about the life of Brendan (or **Brandon**) beyond the facts that he
was born in Kerry, that he was brought up by St ITA at Killeedy and that
he founded a monastery at Clonfert in Galway around the year 559.
Legend has it that the rule he drew up for use by the monks there was
dictated to him by an angel. Other monasteries, such as those at Anna-
down, Inishdroum and Ardfert, may also have been founded by Brendan.
He is often remembered for the many journeys he made abroad and is said
to have visited St COLUMBA in Scotland, where he founded another monastery, to have crossed to Wales, where he served as abbot of a monastery,
and to have sailed to Brittany in company with St MALO. Another suggestion claims that he may actually have got as far as the Americas. Medieval
legend, recorded in *The Navigation of St Brendan* written around the 9th
century, embellished his life story with further magical voyages across the
Atlantic ocean in the course of which he and his companions braved sea
monsters and other dangers. Also known as **Brendan the Navigator**, he
is honoured today as the patron saint of sailors.
Feast Day: 16 May.

Brice (d.444) French bishop. Brice (otherwise called **Britius** or **Brictio**)
was born in Touraine and studied for the church under St MARTIN OF
TOURS at the monastery of Marmoutier, eventually succeeding St Martin as
bishop of Tours in 397. He appears to have had an unruly nature, having
to apologize to St Martin for rash words on at least two occasions and as
bishop being obliged to vacate his see around 430 and go into exile for
some seven years after he was accused of neglecting his duties and commit-
ting adultery among other misdeeds. After going to Rome and getting
vindication from the pope he returned to his post a reformed man and
dedicated himself to his work, founding several new religious establishments. His status as a saint probably owes much to his links with
St Martin. His emblem is a fire or hot coals.
Feast Day: 13 November.

Bride *See* BRIGID.

Bridget (1303–1373) Swedish foundress. Born in the province of Upland,
Sweden, Bridget (or **Birgitta**) lived as a married woman for 28 years and
bore eight children to her wealthy land-owning husband Ulf Godmarsson
before his death in 1344. During this time she rose to the rank of principal lady-in-waiting to Queen Blanche of Sweden and in this post did her

best to persuade the royal family to give up their immoral way of life. After her husband's death, in defiance of the turbulence and decadence of the contemporary religious establishment, she founded a monastery for men and women at Vadstena, with herself as abbess, and from this institution evolved the Order of the Holy Saviour (popularly known as the Bridgettines). She became well-known not only for her zeal as abbess but also for her prophetic visions, through which she offered guidance to popes and crowned heads. She also worked tirelessly towards the reform of the church and (unsuccessfully) towards the restoration of the papacy to Rome, petitioning three popes and pleading with them to leave Avignon. She also conducted a pilgrimage to Jerusalem in 1371 and died in Rome, where she had done much charitable work, not long after her return. She was canonized in 1391. Today she is honoured as the patron saint of Sweden.

Feast Day: 23 July.

Brieuc (6th century) Welsh-born abbot. Brieuc (or **Brioc**) is thought to have been born in Cardiganshire and to have lived in south-western Britain before moving to Brittany and founding a monastery near Tréguier. Other details of his life are shrouded in legend. His memory is preserved in a number of placenames in Cornwall and Brittany, notably in the town of Saint-Brieuc that developed around his monastery. Because of his legendary generosity to the poor he is honoured as the patron saint of purse-makers.

Feast Day: 1 May.

Brigid (*c.*450–523) Irish abbess. Born the daughter of a slave woman and a Celtic chieftain in the vicinity of Dundalk, Brigid (or **Bride**) was granted her freedom and determined at an early age upon a life in the church. In due course she was accepted as a nun by St MEL, bishop of Armagh, but defied the usual convention of living at home with her family by imitating the example of St PATRICK (by whom she may have been baptized) and founding the first convents for nuns in Ireland. The first of her houses (for both men and women) was established at Kildare in 471 and, with Brigid as its first abbess, this soon became an important religious and academic centre. It also became famous for the fine religious ornaments and manu-scripts that were produced there. Many other convents followed through-out Ireland. Brigid herself was celebrated both for her leadership skills and for her generosity towards the needy and continues to be revered as the chief saint of Ireland, second only to Patrick himself. She was also credited

with many miracles. She died at Kildare, where she was buried before removal to Downpatrick to be reinterred alongside St Patrick. Today she is honoured as the patron saint of Irish women, poets, blacksmiths and healers. She is often depicted in art with a cow resting at her feet.
Feast Day: 1 February.

Brioc   *See* BRIEUC.

Britius   *See* BRICE.

Brother André   *See* ANDRÉ BESSETTE.

Bruno   (*c*.1033–1101) German founder. Born into a noble family of Cologne, he studied at the cathedral school in Rheims before being ordained a priest and taking up a post teaching theology in Rheims around 1056. He remained in this post for 20 years but then incurred the disfavour of his archbishop, whom he accused of simony. Discharged from his office, Bruno and six companions retreated to the mountains near Grenoble and at a location called the Grande Chartreuse erected a modest church that in due course became the first home of the so-called Carthusian monks. From these humble beginnings grew the entire Carthusian order, which placed emphasis upon solitude, fasting, worship, hard work and repentance. Six years later Bruno was summoned (against his will) to Rome by Pope Urban II, who had studied under Bruno, and to take the role of papal adviser. Subsequently he turned down the post of bishop of Reggio and instead, at his own request, established a new monastery at La Torre in Calabria, to be run along similar lines to the house at the Grande Chartreuse. A further house followed at San Stefano-in-Bosco. His emblem is a ray of light.
Feast Day: 6 October.

Budoc   (6th century) French bishop. Budoc (or **Beuzec**) may have been a missionary monk who became bishop of Dol in Brittany. His memory is preserved in a number of placenames in Brittany and Cornwall. The details of his life are shrouded in legend, one of which claims that Budoc was born in a barrel into which his mother Azenor (falsely accused of adultery) had been tossed into the sea at Brest and that they were finally cast ashore in Ireland five months later none the worst for their ordeal. This episode would appear to be a borrowing from Greek mythology.
Feast Day: 8 December.

C

Cadoc (d. *c*.560) Welsh abbot. Cadoc (or **Cadog**) was reportedly of royal birth and was identified as the founder of the monastery of Nant Carfan (renamed Llancarfan) in south Wales. Subsequently he may have lived the life of a hermit on the island of Flat Holm in the Bristol Channel. He had a considerable following both in Wales and in Ireland through his pupil St FINNIAN OF CLONARD. He may also have visited Cornwall and Scotland. Little more is known of his life and the circumstances of his death are shrouded in legend: according to one source, he was carried on a cloud to Italy where he became the bishop of Benevento and ultimately died a martyr's death there during Mass. Today many churches in south Wales remain dedicated to Cadoc.
Feast Day: 25 September.

Caedmon (d. *c*.680) English poet. According to BEDE, Caedmon was a cowherd who lived near the great abbey at Whitby. During a dream one night he was miraculously endowed with a divine poetic gift and was inspired to compose a song in praise of God's creation. This he subsequently performed in front of St HILDA and the monks of the abbey. Suitably impressed, they invited Caedmon to take up religious study and to join them as a monk. He went on to compose various songs based upon the scriptures and in so doing established a lasting reputation as the first great English poet and the father of English sacred poetry. Of all his songs, which were sung to reinforce the faith of Christians throughout northern England, only a few lines from his initial composition survive. He died shortly after prophesying his own demise.
Feast Day: 11 February.

Caesarius of Arles (470–543) French bishop. Born into a noble Gallo-Roman family of Châlons-sur-Saône in Burgundy, he became bishop of Arles in 503 and remained in the post for the next 40 years. A popular preacher, he rarely spoke for more than 15 minutes and had many of his sermons written down and distributed throughout much of western Europe. He also did much to promote worship in the lives of laypeople, adapting the liturgy of the hours so that ordinary people might celebrate their faith as part of their daily routine. Among other significant acts, he

founded a nunnery at Arles (the first known convent for women in the country) and laid down the rules by which it should be run. In some respects these ideas paved the way for the development of the rule of St BENEDICT. During his lifetime Caesarius (or **Cesarius**) of Arles won almost universal admiration and was even respected by such barbarian kings as Theodoric (the king of the Ostrogoths whose armies invaded the Languedoc region), who gave him gifts of silver and gold – which the saint promptly used to ransom Burgundian captives.
Feast Day: 27 August.

Cain   *See* KEYNE.

Cainnech   *See* CANICE.

Cajetan   (1480–1547) Italian cofounder of the Theatine Order. Born into a noble family of Vicenza, he aimed initially at a secular career, becoming a senator in his hometown in 1506. He decided to become a priest, however, in response to his dismay at the corruption and demoralization he perceived in the contemporary church and was ordained in 1516. He went on to dedicate himself to the reform of the church in Rome, Vicenza, Verona and Venice through the foundation of the Oratory of Divine Love, which emphasized the importance of prayer and pastoral work. In 1523, together with Bishop John Peter Caraffa (later Pope Paul IV), he cofounded the Theatine Order in Rome (moved to Naples in 1527) to promote reform. Members of the community dedicated themselves to preaching, tending the sick and encouraging the regular taking of communion. Above all, they sought to return priests to their calling through repentance and spiritual discipline. Cajetan worked tirelessly for spiritual renewal throughout the Christian congregation and, among other important innovations, introduced pawnshops to assist the plight of the Naples poor. The demands of these efforts, coupled with disappointment at the slow progress he felt he was making, probably hastened his eventual demise in Naples. He was canonized in 1671.
Feast Day: 7 August.

Callistus I   (d. *c.*222) Roman pope. Callistus (or **Callixtus**) lived as a high-ranking slave to a Christian master in Rome and at one point in his life experienced the hardships of hard labour in the quarries of Sardinia as punishment for his involvement in a banking controversy. Upon his release he won his freedom from slavery and became a deacon. He was given responsibility for the Christian cemetery on the Appian Way (now

called San Callisto) and after 18 years his abilities ultimately led to him being appointed pope in succession to ZEPHYRINUS. In 217 detractors opposed his appointment on both doctrinal grounds and in the belief that his insistence upon Christian forgiveness made him too tolerant of indiscipline. His period in office, which was marked by a schism in the church resulting from opposition to his relatively lenient views, was short and subsequently the tradition became established that he had died a martyr's death (he was probably killed in a riot). The legend that he was thrown down a well (possibly with a millstone round his neck) appears to have no historical foundation.
Feast Day: 14 October.

Camillus   (1550–1614) Italian priest. Born at Bocchianico in the Abruzzi, he converted to Christianity and became a Capuchin novice only after fighting as a soldier of fortune against the Turks and after overcoming an addiction to gambling. A diseased leg resulting from his military experiences prevented him being admitted to the order so he dedicated himself instead to tending the incurably sick at a hospital in Rome. With the support of St PHILIP NERI, he became a priest in 1584 and founded the Ministers of the Sick to organize staff at eight hospitals throughout Italy. His innovations in the care of the sick included providing a healthy diet, fresh air and isolation of infectious patients. Despite often being sick and in pain himself, Camillus and other members of the order also provided medical help to soldiers wounded in 1595 and 1601 in Croatia and Hungary, thus becoming the first field medical unit in recorded history. Camillus was canonized in 1746. Today he is honoured as the patron saint of nurses and the sick.
Feast Day: 14 July.

Canice   (*c.*525–600) Irish abbot. Canice (otherwise called **Cainnech** or, in Scotland, **Kenneth**) was born the son of a bard in County Derry and studied under St FINNIAN OF CLONARD. A companion of St COLUMBA, whom he visited several times on Iona, he appears to have spent time in the Western Isles, on the Scottish mainland and in Wales before returning to Ireland to found the monastery of Aghaboe in Ossory around 577. He may also have founded another monastery at Kilkenny. Various legends attached to his name also suggest he spent some time living the life of a hermit. He died at Aghaboe. His memory is preserved through several Scottish placenames.
Feast Day: 11 October.

Canute IV   (c.1043–86) King of Denmark. Canute (or **Cnut**) was the illegitimate son of Swein Estrithson (nephew of King Canute of England) and succeeded to the throne of Denmark in 1081. He had already led one unsuccessful attempt at rebellion in England, in 1075, and in 1085 planned a second attack in the hope of seizing the English crown from William the Conqueror. This campaign was abandoned when rebellion erupted at home and Canute had to flee to Odense, where he was captured by rebels in the church of St Alban and put to death while kneeling at the altar. Because he had done much to consolidate the church in Denmark during his reign, building new churches and supporting the clergy, and because of the circumstances of his death Canute came to be venerated as a martyr. His cult was officially endorsed by Pope Paschal II in 1101. He is honoured today as the patron saint of Denmark.
Feast Day: 10 July.

Canute Lavard   (c.1096–1131) Danish nobleman. Born at Roskilde, he was the second son of the Danish king Eric the Good and was brought up at the royal court. As Duke of Schleswig, he was ordered by his uncle King Niels to defend their lands against the Wends. Canute worked for peace and was recognized as king of the Western Wends by Emperor Lothair III. This enraged Niels, who had Canute ambushed and murdered in the forest of Haraldsted near Ringsted. Noted for his pursuit of justice and for the support he offered to evangelical missions led by St VICELIN among the Wends, he was canonized as a martyr on the request of his son Valdemar I in 1169.
Feast Day: 7 January.

Carpus, Papylus and Agathonice   (d. c.170) Martyrs of Pergamum in Asia Minor. Carpus was bishop of Gordus, while Papylus was a deacon of Thyatira and Agathonice was Papylus' married sister. All three were burned alive on the order of the Roman authorities during the reign of Marcus Aurelius for refusing to make sacrifices to the gods. The death of St Agathonice was particularly poignant: encouraged not to follow the example of Carpus and Papylus as her death would leave her children orphans, she refused to cooperate, arguing that she would leave her children in God's care.
Feast Day: 13 April.

Casimir   (1458–1484) Polish prince. Born at Cracow, he was a son of King Casimir IV of Poland and through his relatively short life struggled with

the conflicting demands of his secular role and his strong religious calling. While still a boy, he was embroiled in a foiled plot to put him on the throne in the place of his father, as a consequence of which he was sent into exile for a time. As an adult he wielded power with wisdom and justice and refused to have anything to do with waging war with other Christian countries, thus earning the sobriquet of 'The Peacemaker'. Having vowed to live an austere and celibate life, in 1483 he also turned down a politically advantageous proposed marriage with a daughter of Emperor Frederick III. He died of tuberculosis a year later, aged 26, and, after reports of miracles at his tomb, was canonized in 1521. Today he is honoured as the patron saint of Poland and Lithuania.
Feast Day: 4 March.

Cassian *See* JOHN CASSIAN.

Catherine of Alexandria (*c*.290–*c*.310) Martyr of Alexandria. Legend has it that Catherine of Alexandria (or **Katherine**) was born into a noble family of the city and converted to Christianity at the age of 18. Shortly afterwards she found that neither her high rank nor her beauty protected her when she publicly criticized the worship of pagan idols in front of the Emperor Maxentius. She managed to confound the arguments of 50 philosophers subsequently ranged against her on the orders of the infuriated emperor to point out the flaws in her Christian faith, upon which all 50 were burned alive. Still refusing to recant her Christian belief and turning down an offer of marriage to the emperor on the grounds that she was already 'the bride of Christ', Catherine was thrown into prison, where she was given new strength by visions of Christ in her cell. When she was tortured upon a spiked wheel (from which the circular firework known as a catherine wheel takes its name) the wheel miraculously burst apart and several of her torturers were killed by the splinters. Catherine's courage inspired the conversion of 200 soldiers, who were promptly put to death for their temerity, before she herself was finally beheaded. Angels are said to have carried her body off to Mount Sinai, where a great monastery was subsequently named after her. She became the focus of a widespread cult from the 9th century, although there has always been a strong suspicion that she was an entirely fictional character created by one of the Greek writers. Her emblem is a wheel. Today she is honoured as the patron saint of philosophers, preachers, potters, spinners, hospitals, librarians and young girls.
Feast Day: 25 November.

Catherine of Bologna   (1413–1463) Italian abbess. Born Catherine de' Vigri in Bologna, she was educated at the ducal court at Ferrara but decided to turn down an advanteous marriage and instead to join the Franciscan tertiaries (later the Poor Clares). In 1456 she returned to Bologna to become abbess of a new convent there and soon impressed everyone with her kindness and her devotion to the sick. She also became famous for her many visions, though she disliked discussing these publicly, and attracted admiration as a writer and painter of miniatures. Her body remained uncorrupted after death and her relics have been on display since 1475 seated upright in the church of the St Clares in Bologna. She was canonized in 1712. Today she is honoured as a patron saint of artists.

Feast Day: 9 March.

Catherine of Genoa   (1447–1510) Italian mystic. Born into a noble family of Genoa and described as beautiful and sensitive though lacking humour or wit, she was forced into an unhappy and abusive marriage at the age of 16. Around 1473 she experienced the first of many intense and uplifting mystical revelations during confession, during which she felt she had become one with God, and entered a new life characterized by ecstatic religious contemplation. Her husband underwent a similar spiritual transformation and the couple agreed a new celibate relationship. After a period of withdrawal from the world Catherine, assisted by her husband, selflessly dedicated herself to caring for the poor and the sick at the large hospital of Pammantone, ultimately becoming administrator of the institution in 1490 and providing inspired leadership during a plague epidemic three years later. She wrote two notable works on her mystical experiences, entitled *Spiritual Dialogue Between the Soul, the Body, Self-Love, the Spirit, Humanity and the Lord God* and *Treatise on Purgatory*. Catherine was canonized in 1737. Today she is honoured as the patron saint of Genoa and Italian hospitals.

Feast Day: 15 September.

Catherine of Siena   (1347–1380) Italian mystic. Born Catherine Benincasa into a large family in Siena, she is reported to have experienced visions from her childhood onwards. Her most profound mystic revelation occurred in 1370 when she entered a trance-like state during which she claimed to have been shown hell, purgatory and heaven and to have been ordered to abandon her relatively solitary existence as a Dominican tertiary (she never became a nun) and take a more active role in public life. Upon this experience was based her book *The Dialogue of the Seraphic Virgin Catherine of Siena*. In obedience to her revelation she dedicated herself to a life of poverty and service of others, gathering a group of disciples around her in Siena to offer material and spiritual assistance to the needy both there and on her travels. She also involved herself in diplomatic affairs, attempting to mediate in the hostilities that erupted between Florence and other city-states in 1375. She became one of the most highly respected figures in the church of her time and was consulted by popes, rulers and prominent members of the Italian nobility. She helped Pope Gregory XI make the historic decision to leave Avignon and return to Rome and subsequently supported Pope Urban VI in the Great Schism that resulted from the opposition of a rival pope. Any doubts about Catherine's holy status were dispelled in 1375 when she suffered the pain of the stigmata while at prayer (though without exhibiting the actual wounds). She was canonized in 1461 and with St TERESA OF AVILA shares the distinction of being the only woman to have received (in 1970) the title Doctor of the Church. Today she is honoured as the patron saint of Italy and nursing services.

Feast Day: 29 April.

Catherine of Sweden (1331–1381) Swedish abbess. Catherine of Sweden (sometimes called **Catherine of Vadstena**) was born in Ulfasa, Sweden, the daughter of St BRIDGET through her marriage to the nobleman Ulf Godmarsson. She married an invalid and nursed him devotedly until his death, although the union may never have been consummated. She assisted her mother in Rome and Jerusalem over many years and after her mother's death, as abbess of the convent at Vadstena, completed her work by securing (1376) papal recognition of the Order of the Holy Saviour, known as the 'Bridgettines', that she had founded. Catherine was never formally canonized but her cult was given official recognition by Pope Innocent VIII around 100 years after her death.

Feast Day: 24 March.

Catherine dei Ricci (1522–1590) Italian mystic. Born into a wealthy family in Florence, Catherine dei Ricci was admitted to the Dominican convent of San Vincenzo in Prato, Tuscany, around the age of 14. She exhibited great seriousness in her devotions, living a life of considerable austerity and meditating daily upon Christ's crucifixion. When she was about 20 years old, she began to enter ecstatic trances in which she actually 'relived' rather than just witnessed the events of the crucifixion,

having weekly 28-hour raptures in which she experienced all the events of Christ's Passion and exhibited the stigmata. News of her revelations spread quickly and large crowds gathered to watch her at her meditations, among them bishops, cardinals and crowned heads. Though she claimed to be embarrassed by her ecstasies and eventually prayed for them to cease, which they did some 12 years later, Catherine shared her experiences with many of the most prominent figures in the church of her day, her correspondents including the saints CHARLES BORROMEO and PHILIP NERI. She was elected prioress for life at the age of 30 and was also noted for her work as a teacher and nurse. She was canonized in 1747.
Feast Day: 2 February.

Catherine Labouré   (1806–1876) French visionary. Born into a farming family on the Côte d'Or, she became one of the Sisters of Charity of St Vincent de Paul in Paris and lived a relatively quiet, humble life there, tending to the sick and undertaking routine domestic tasks. In 1830 she reported having visions of the Virgin Mary standing on a globe and commanding her to have medals struck with her image on one side and the hearts of Mary and Jesus surrounded by 12 stars on the other. Many thousands of these so-called 'miraculous medals' were subsequently fashioned according to her vision and have been widely worn by the faithful ever since. The identity of Catherine Labouré as the person who had the original vision was kept secret for 46 years, until shortly before her death, and she spent the rest of her life in obscurity at a convent in Enghien-Neuilly. She was canonized in 1947.
Feast Day: 28 November.

Ceadda   *See* CHAD.

Cecilia   (dates unknown) Roman virgin martyr. The life of Cecilia (otherwise **Cecelia** or **Celia**) is a matter of legend. A devout Christian, she is said to have been forced to marry a non-Christian husband named Valerian. Telling him that she had a guardian angel and that he would be able to see the angel as well if he would consent to be baptized by Pope Urban I, she managed to persuade Valerian to convert and become as committed to her faith as she was herself. Valerian's brother Tiburtius followed their example and also converted. A further legend claims that the two brothers were beheaded after trying to bury the bodies of Christian martyrs and that Cecilia herself was condemned to death for refusing to worship the gods. An attempt to suffocate her failed and when the

executioner tried to behead her he missed his aim and she lingered on for another three days, during which time she made arrangements to leave all her property to the church. It has been suggested that these legends may have been invented to give flesh to the otherwise unknown lady named Cecilia who founded a church in the Trastevere quarter in Rome. Cecilia is honoured as the patron saint of music, musicians and poetry.
Feast Day: 22 November.

Cedd (d.664) English bishop. The brother of St CHAD, he was educated at Lindisfarne under St AIDAN and undertook evangelical work in Essex before being appointed bishop of the East Saxons. He founded numerous churches, as well as monasteries at Bradwell-on-Sea and Tilbury, and acted as interpreter at the Synod of Whitby in 664. He was also founder of Lastingham abbey in north Yorkshire, where he died of the plague and was buried.
Feast Day: 26 October.

Celestine I (d.432) Italian pope. Born in Campania, he succeeded Boniface I as pope in 422 and devoted most of his energy towards combatting Pelagianism, Nestorianism and Manichaeanism among other heresies. He is said to have sent St GERMANUS OF AUXERRE to oppose Pelagianism in England and to have sent St PATRICK as a missionary to Ireland (431). Little is known about Celestine's personal character beyond the fact that he was a close friend of St AUGUSTINE OF HIPPO. He is usually depicted in art with a dove, dragon and flame.
Feast Day: 27 July.

Celestine V (c.1214–1296) Italian pope. Born into a peasant family of Abruzzi, Celestine V was previously known as Peter of Morrone and lived for many years as the head of a community of hermits on Monte Morrone. In 1294, when he was 80 years old, he became the surprise compromise choice for pope after the cardinals failed to agree on any other candidate. Peter of Morrone obediently took office as Celestine V but, despite his personal sanctity, proved totally unsuited to the position. He fell easy prey to the political machinations of King Charles II of Naples and after just five months despairingly resigned the papal office (becoming the only pope to leave the post voluntarily), to be replaced by Boniface VIII. In order that no one should use the old man as a focus of opposition to the new pope, Boniface had him confined in the castle of Fumone near

Anagni, where he died a few months later. Celestine was canonized in 1313.
Feast Day: 19 May.

Celia   *See* CECILIA.

Ceran   *See* CIARAN OF CLONMACNOISE.

Cesarius of Arles   *See* CAESARIUS OF ARLES.

Chad   (d.672) English bishop. Chad (or **Ceadda**) was born in Northumbria and was educated under St AIDAN on Lindisfarne alongside his brother St CEDD. He succeeded Cedd as abbot of Lastingham in north Yorkshire before being appointed bishop of York by King Oswiu of Northumberland's son Alcfrith, but was subsequently removed from the post by THEODORE OF CANTERBURY in favour of the rival claim of St WILFRID, who had been appointed to the same post by Oswiu himself. Chad's dutiful acceptance of the demotion impressed Theodore sufficiently to persuade him to reinstate him some time afterwards, this time as first bishop of Mercia, based at Lichfield. During the remaining three years of his life, Chad continued to be true to his reputation for piety and humility and also founded a monastery in Lincolnshire.
Feast Day: 2 March.

Charbel Makhlouf   (1828–1898) Lebanese monk and hermit. Born Joseph Zaroun Makhlouf at Béka-Kafra in Lebanon, he was the son of a Catholic mule driver. In the face of family opposition, he entered the monastery of St Maron at Annaya, taking the name Charbel in honour of a 2nd-century martyr of that name. He was ordained as a priest in 1859 but continued to live the life of a monk until 1875, when he took up the austere life of a hermit at a hermitage nearby. He remained there for the remaining 23 years of his life, refusing to handle money and surviving on the most meagre diet. He became well-known for his insistence upon the importance of prayer and many people came to consult him in his humble cell. He was canonized in 1977.
Feast Day: 24 December.

Charles Garnier   *See* NORTH AMERICA, MARTYRS OF.

Charles of Sezze   (1613–1670) Italian mystic. Born John Charles Marchioni into a humble family in Sezze, Italy, he learned a love of God from his grandmother but was prevented from entering the priesthood

because of his lack of education. He opted instead for the role of a
Franciscan laybrother at Naziano, subsequently serving in various menial
roles at monasteries near Rome. He became well known for his many
mystical experiences, which he described in an autobiography, as well as
for his simple holiness and was also respected for his wisdom, being
consulted on spiritual matters by three popes and other high-ranking
officials in the church. He was canonized in 1959.
Feast Day: 7 January.

Charles Borromeo   (1538–1584) Italian archbishop. Born into a wealthy
family near Lake Maggiore, he was the nephew of Pope Pius IV and at the
age of 22 was raised to the rank of cardinal and appointed administrator
for the ruinous see of Milan before he had even been ordained a priest.
Further senior posts quickly followed as the pope's favourite consolidated
his reputation as a talented and tireless reformer. He played a prominent
role in the final session of the reforming Council of Trent (1562), was made
bishop of Milan (1563) and became archbishop the following year. After
his uncle's death in 1566 he was able to concentrate upon restoring order
in the disorganized see of Milan and made many important reforms,
including the establishment of seminaries for the instruction of the clergy.
A profound influence upon the progress of the Counter-Reformation, he
showed determination when faced with opposition to his improvements
but also gentle and intelligent in his dealings with individuals. When
plague struck Milan in 1576 he was unstinting in providing resources for
the sick and needy. Ultimately his exertions in so many fields hastened his
premature death at the age of 46. He was canonized in 1610.
Feast Day: 4 November.

Charles de Foucauld   (1858–1916) French hermit. The Viscount Charles
de Foucauld was born into a wealthy family and lived a dissolute youth as
a rake and soldier before turning to the church. He rejoined the church
formally in 1886 and spent the next 10 years in Trappist houses. In 1897 he
entered into the life of a hermit at Nazareth. He was ordained in 1901 and
later resumed his hermit existence in the Algerian desert where he aimed
to evangelize among the desert tribes. Based at Tamanrasset in Algeria
from 1905, he became well-known in the region under the nickname 'Little
Brother Charles of Jesus', continuing his evangelistic mission until his
eventual murder by marauding Muslims.
Feast Day: 16 December.

Charles Lwanga and Companions (d.1885–1886) Martyrs of Uganda. The youthful and mentally unstable King Mwanga of Buganda launched a campaign of persecution against Christians in his country after Joseph Mkasa Balikuddembe, master of the royal pages and a Catholic, criticized the young king for his dissolute behaviour and specifically for the murder of the Anglican missionary bishop James Hannington in 1885. Balikuddembe was beheaded on the orders of the enraged king and replaced by Charles Lwanga, who was also a Christian. Some months later, when one of the pages refused the king's sexual advances, Mwanga had Lwanga and all the other Christians among the royal pages arrested and condemned all 32 of them to death. They were duly burned alive at Namugongo, wrapped in burning reed mats. Despite their youth, the victims of the massacre met their deaths with cheerfulness and with their faith in God intact. They were canonized in 1964.
Feast Day: 3 June.

Chionia   *See* AGAPE, CHIONIA AND IRENE.

Christopher (3rd century) Martyr of Lycia. Nothing is known of the life of St Christopher beyond the belief that he died a martyr's death in Lycia (in modern Turkey) during the reign of the Emperor Decius around the middle of the 3rd century. He was sentenced to be burned to death but when this failed he was shot with arrows and beheaded. The substance of the modern legend of Christopher was invented in the medieval period. According to this tradition, he was a great giant who vowed to serve the most powerful king on earth. He swore loyalty initially to a Christian ruler, but subsequently abandoned him to serve the Devil. When the Devil revealed his terror of Christ, Christopher determined to serve the latter instead. He was told by a hermit that Christ might be found on the other side of a particular river. When Chistopher reached the river he agreed to carry across a child, only to find that the child – which became heavier and heavier – was Christ (proved when the child made Christopher's staff sprout fruit and flowers). Subsequently he obeyed Christ's command to defend the Christians in Lycia at a time of harsh persecution. He converted all those who sought to capture him but was eventually put to death for refusing to sacrifice to the gods. Today Christopher is one of the most popular of all saints, honoured as the patron saint of travellers and motorists, who commonly carry a medallion bearing his image as a good luck charm.
Feast Day: 25 July.

Chrodegang (c.715–766) French bishop. Born near Liège, he played a prominent political role as principal minister to Charles Martel but also had a profound effect as a reformer of the Frankish church of his day, carrying on the work started by St BONIFACE OF CREDITON. Learned and generous in character, he was appointed bishop of Metz in 742 and in this post promoted the education of the clergy and emphasized the importance of monastic living, establishing an influential rule based on that of St BENEDICT. Other significant innovations included the introduction of Roman chant and liturgical usages into the diocese of Metz. He also served King Pepin the Short as ambassador to the pope and effectively consolidated Frankish rule in Italy. Other notable achievements included the foundation of the Metz school of church music and of the celebrated abbey of Gorze in 748.
Feast Day: 6 March.

Chrysogonus (d. c.304) Roman martyr. Nothing is known of the details of the life of Chrysogonus beyond the fact that he died a martyr's death by beheading at Aquileia in northern Italy. Tradition claims he was a Roman official put to death during the reign of Diocletian. His cult seems to have been well established in Rome by the late 5th century.
Feast Day: 24 November.

Ciaran of Clonmacnoise (c.512–545) Irish abbot. Ciaran (otherwise referred to as **Ceran, Kieran** or **Queran**) was born the son of a travelling carpenter in Connacht and educated at the monastery of St FINNIAN OF CLONARD. Subsequently he studied as monk under St ENDA on Inishmore. He settled eventually at Clonmacnoise on the Shannon, in County Meath, and there established a famous monastery. Although he died within a year of the monastery's foundation, aged only 33, it became hugely influential through the many pupils who studied there. He is also remembered for his generosity and through various legends, including one to the effect that the other saints, who had grown jealous of Ciaran's fame, prayed for his premature demise.
Feast Day: 9 September.

Ciaran of Saighir (5th–6th century) Irish bishop. Details of the life of Ciaran of Saighir are sketchy. It is said that he was born in West Cork and carried out missionary work in Ireland prior to the emergence of St PATRICK, establishing a monastery around which grew the town of Sier-Ciaran (Saighir). Revered as the first bishop of Ossory, he is also supposed to have set up a convent, which he entrusted to the leadership of his mother. In his youth he may also have lived as a hermit on the island of Cape Clear in Cork. Legend claims he had a miraculous influence over wild animals.

Feast Day: 5 March.

Citha   *See* ZITA.

Clare of Assisi   (1193–1253) Italian founder of the Franciscan Poor Clares. Born into a noble family in Assisi, she was profoundly influenced by hearing St FRANCIS OF ASSISI preach in 1212 when she was 18 and resolved to imitate his life of poverty and simple faith. In defiance of her family's wishes she ran away from home and, with the blessing of St Francis, joined a Benedictine convent, where ultimately she was joined by her mother (St **Beatrice of Assisi**) and sister (St **Agnes of Assisi**). At the invitation of St Francis, she founded a community of women who wished to live like Franciscan friars near the church of San Damiano in Assisi, calling them the Poor Clares and insisting upon the observance of absolute poverty. Members of the Poor Clares were expected to stick to the most rigorous of lifestyles, giving up their possessions, never eating meat, sleeping on the floor and rarely speaking. The community prospered and inspired the establishment of similar convents throughout Europe. Respected for her great wisdom and also credited with miraculous powers of healing, St Clare was consulted by many prominent figures in both the religious and secular world. She was canonized in 1255, just two years after her death. Today she is honoured as the patron saint of the blind and also of television (a consequence of the legend that she witnessed a Christmas service by means of a vision when illness prevented her attending in person).

Feast Day: 11 August.

Clare of Montefalco   (d.1308) Italian nun. Born at Montefalco in Italy, Clare of Montefalco (or **Clare of the Cross**) became a member of a community of Franciscan hermits who observed the rule of St AUGUSTINE. She was appointed abbess of the convent in 1291 and became widely known not only for her austere lifestyle but also as miracle worker. Legend has it that when her heart was removed after her death it was found to bear symbols of the passion of Christ. Her body and heart are claimed to have remained incorrupt ever since and her blood, carefully

collected in a phial, was for several centuries said to become liquid at times of political crisis. She was canonized in 1881.
Feast Day: 17 August.

Claude La Colombière (1641–1682) French Jesuit. Born in Saint-Symphorizen d'Orzen near Lyons, he became a member of the Jesuit Order at Avignon in 1659 and established a widespread reputation as a preacher, noted both for his articulacy and for his intelligence. He became head of the Paray-le-Monial College in 1675 and a leading supporter of St MARGARET MARY ALOCOQUE, but a year later was appointed chaplain to Mary of Modena, Duchess of York, in London and became a prominent figure among English Catholics. Here he became embroiled in the scandal surrounding the wholly fictitious Popish Plot to assassinate Charles II and, though innocent of any charges, was imprisoned and then (after the intervention of Louis XIV of France) exiled from England. He died of ill-health shortly after his return to Paray-le-Monial. Various writings by Claude La Colombière have survived, among them many letters and sermons. He was canonized in 1992.
Feast Day: 15 February.

Clement I (d. *c*.100) Roman pope. Little is known of the life of Clement I (or **Clement of Rome**) beyond the fact that he was the fourth bishop of Rome and ranks alongside the apostles as one of the fathers of the early church. He was the probable author of an important epistle discussing unrest in the Church of Corinth and may be the colleague mentioned by St PAUL in his letter to the Philippians (at Philippians 4:3). Legend has it that he was lashed to an anchor and drowned on the orders of the Roman Emperor Trajan. His emblem is an anchor.
Feast Day: 23 November.

Clement of Alexandria (*c*.150–*c*.215) Greek theologian and Father of the Church. Probably born in Athens, he converted to Christianity and studied under Pantaenus in Alexandria, eventually succeeding Pantaenus as head of the celebrated catechetical school there around 190. He was forced to flee Alexandria during the persecutions of 202 under the Emperor Severus and moved to Caesarea in Cappadocia, where he was reunited with his old friend and pupil Bishop Alexander. Clement of Alexandria was revered as a saint until the 17th century, but interest in him has revived in recent times through his many writings, the largest body of Christian

writing to survive from the second century. He is also honoured as the patron saint of lighthouses.
Feast Day: 5 December.

Clement-Mary Hofbauer   (1751–1820) Czech priest. Born Jan Dvořák at Tasswitz in Moravia, he worked as a baker before opting for the life of an itinerant hermit. Though barely educated, he eventually became a priest in the Redemptorist congregation of St ALPHONSUS LIGUORI at the age of 34. Over the following 20 years he was prominent in establishing the order in northern Europe, despite opposition from anti-Catholic monarchs, working chiefly at Warsaw in Poland. After 1808, when Napoleon broke up religious orders throughout Poland, he lived in Vienna, establishing a new college there and seeking to defend the church from secular interference. He won great respect both for his wisdom and his humility and effectively inspired a Catholic revival in Austria. He also promoted the Catholic church's interests at the Congress of Vienna in 1814–15 by helping to block a proposal for an independent German church. He was canonized in 1909. Today he is honoured as the patron saint of Vienna.
Feast Day: 15 March.

Cletus   (1st century) Roman pope. Cletus (or **Anacletus**) is traditionally identified as the third bishop of Rome, in succession to PETER and LINUS. Nothing is known of his life beyond the fact that he supposedly died the death of a martyr towards the end of the 1st century. The organization of Rome into 25 parishes is usually dated to his reign.
Feast Day: 26 April.

Clotilde   (*c.*474–545) Burgundian princess. Clotilde (or **Clotilda**) was born in Lyons and in due course became the wife of Clovis, king of the Franks, in 491. The two appear to have enjoyed a strong and possibly loving marriage, the pagan Clovis respecting Clotilde's Catholic faith and, in the face of her cogent arguments, even conceding to her demands that their infant sons be baptized as Christians. Clovis himself resisted his wife's encouragement to become a Christian himself until 496 when the threat of defeat in battle against the Alemanni persuaded him to turn to the Christian god for aid. Upon his subsequent victory he agreed to be baptized at Reims and gave his tacit approval to the evangelization of the Frankish kingdom. This in turn led ultimately to the creation of the first Christian states in northern Europe. After the death of Clovis in 511, Clotilde's final years were marred by feuding within her family and she retreated to the

monastery of Tours, where she died. She is honoured today as the patron saint of adopted children, brides, exiles, queens, bereaved or abused parents and the parents of large families.
Feast Day: 3 June.

Cloud   (*c*.524–*c*.560) Frankish prince. Cloud (or **Clodoald**) was a grandson of Clovis, king of the Franks, and was brought up by his grandmother St CLOTILDE. The murderous feuding that erupted following the death of Clovis claimed the lives of two of his brothers, but Cloud renounced his claim to the throne and survived to take up the life of a hermit, remaining in seclusion for the rest of his life. The commune where he died, near Versailles, was subsequently named Saint-Cloud in his memory.
Feast Day: 7 September.

Cnut   *See* CANUTE IV.

Coemgen   *See* KEVIN.

Colette   (1381–1447) French nun. Born Nicolette Boylet, Colette was the daughter of a carpenter of Calcye in Picardy and joined the Franciscan order on the death of her parents, when she was aged 17. She spent some eight years living as a hermit at Corbie Abbey in Picardy before claiming to have had a vision of St FRANCIS, who allegedly commanded her to set about restoring the order of the Poor Clares to their original austerity. Colette accordingly emerged from her seclusion and set about her mission of reform, initially meeting with much hostility from the Poor Clares themselves. She succeeded, however, in winning the approval of the antipope Benedict XIII at Avignon and was duly given ultimate authority to apply her reforms when she was appointed by him head of the Poor Clares. Assisted by a friar named Henry de Beaume, she set about renewing the community of the Poor Clares at Besançon in 1410 and over the next 30 years or so continued her work at 17 convents throughout Europe. She never flagged in her mission, praying daily for the conversion of sinners and securing many converts to her cause. She died at her convent at Ghent in Flanders. She was canonized in 1807.
Feast Day: 6 March.

Colman of Lindisfarne   (d.676) Irish bishop. Born in Ireland, Colman lived as a monk on Iona before succeeding St FINAN as bishop of Lindisfarne around 661 and consolidating the community's reputation for austerity and religious dedication. Three years later he played a prominent role at the Synod of Whitby, where he argued the Celtic position on the dating of Easter and other issues. When the decision at Whitby went in favour of the Roman position, Colman resigned his bishopric and retired to Iona and ultimately (c.667) to the island of Inishbofin, off the coast of Connacht, together with a party of Irish and English monks. The monks argued among themselves, however, and Colman was obliged to set up a separate community for his English followers on the Irish mainland, at Mayo. This establishment became famous and was praised by St BEDE as a centre of learning.

Feast Day: 18 February.

Columba of Iona   (c.521–597) Irish abbot and missionary. Columba (or **Colmcille**) was born in Donegal the descendant of two royal Celtic houses and was intended for the church from an early age. In due course he became a monk under St FINNIAN OF CLONARD and spent some 15 years preaching and founding monasteries, including those at Derry (546), Durrow (c.556) and possibly Kells. He eventually fell out with Finnian over the issue of a transcript he had made of Finnian's copy of St Jerome's Psalter, which Finnian (with the support of King Diarmaid) claimed was rightfully his. Relations with Diarmaid worsened some time later when some of the king's men killed a man seeking sanctuary with Columba. Columba led members of his clan in a campaign against the king and won a bloody battle at Cooldrevne in which some 3000 warriors died. Through this victory Columba won back his Psalter, but perhaps it was his sense of guilt over the many deaths he had precipitated that persuaded him to go into self imposed exile from his beloved homeland. Accordingly he and a small band of his relatives sailed to the island of Iona off the Scottish coast in 565. There he founded the famous monastery from which he launched various missionary expeditions into Pictish Scotland and northern England. The community at Iona became Columba's most enduring legacy, attracting students from all over Europe and becoming an important centre of religious learning and writing. Its founder never overcame his sense of loss at leaving Ireland, however, and his writings included poetry expressing his homesickness. Considered the central figure in Celtic Christianity, Columba is honoured today as the patron saint of Ireland, as well as of bookbinders and poets.

Feast Day: 9 June.

Columban   (c.542–615) Irish abbot. Born into a noble family of Leinster, Ireland, Columban (or **Columbanus**) dedicated himself to the church at

an early age and studied under St COMGALL. After several quiet years at
the monastery of Bangor in Ireland, he was ordained in 590 and that same
year led a band of 12 missionaries to Burgundy in France. There they established a number of monasteries, including those at Annegray, Luxeuil and
Fontaine. These houses were run in accordance with the Celtic tradition,
observing harsh punishment for even minor infringements of the rules.
Columban and his followers were eventually obliged to leave Burgundy
after making criticisms of King Theodoric II for keeping mistresses. Columban spent the rest of his life on evangelical missions elsewhere in France
and in Germany, Switzerland and Italy, consolidating his reputation as
the most influential of the many missionaries to come out of Ireland. The
severity of the rule imposed at his monasteries was later superseded by
the somewhat more tolerant rule of St BENEDICT. Columban died at the
monastery he had founded at Bobbio near Milan. His emblem is a bear.
Feast Day: (Ireland) 23 November, (elsewhere) 21 November.

Comgall   (517–603) Irish abbot. Born in Ulster, Comgall is traditionally
supposed to have been a warrior in his youth but subsequently to have
been ordained as a priest around the age of 40. After living for a time as a
hermit in Lough Erne, he settled at Bangor around 558. The community
that formed around him there became the famous monastery of Bangor,
which remained a major religious centre until destruction by the Danes in
823. Notable figures attracted to Bangor included St COLUMBAN. Later in
life, Comgall spent some time in the monastery of Tiree in Scotland and
may have undertaken an evangelical mission among the Picts in company
with St COLUMBA. He is remembered today as one of the fathers of the
Irish monastic tradition.
Feast Day: (Ireland) 11 May, (elsewhere) 10 May.

Conrad of Parzham   (1818–94) Capuchin laybrother. Born into a peasant
family of Parzham in Bavaria, he dedicated himself to a life of Franciscan
simplicity as a Capuchin laybrother after the death of his parents in 1849.
He was professed in 1852 and subsequently, as porter of the friary at the
shrine of Mary at Alltotting, dedicated himself to the care of pilgrims
there. Over the years he became widely known for his patient and charitable ways and also earned a reputation for prophecy. He was canonized
in 1934.
Feast Day: 22 April.

Cornelius   (d.253) Roman pope. Nothing is known of the details of
Cornelius's early life before he succeeded St FABIAN as pope in 251. He

faced many challenges as head of a deeply divided church, of which perhaps the most important was the issue of the readmittance to the church of the lapsed faithful. Cornelius, in opposition to his rival Novatian, favoured forgiveness of apostates and repentant sinners, providing they performed suitable penance. His reign ended with a resurgence of persecution of Christians under Emperor Gallus and his exile to Civita Vecchia. He died shortly afterwards, according to one tradition being beheaded and on this account being venerated as a martyr. He is honoured as the patron saint of cattle and domestic livestock.
Feast Day: 16 September.

Cosmas and Damian   (d. *c*.303) Syrian martyrs. Little is known of the lives of these two early saints beyond the tradition that they were both martyred for their faith at Cyrrhus in Syria. They became the focus of a considerable cult from the 5th century onwards, their legend being embellished with such details as their being twin brothers who practiced medicine, performing numerous extraordinary miracles and being nicknamed 'the Moneyless Ones' because they never requested payment for their services. The cult continued to prosper in medieval times under the patronage of the Medici family. Today they are honoured as the patron saints of physicians, surgeons and barbers.
Feast Day: 26 September.

Crescentia   *See* VITUS, MODESTUS AND CRESCENTIA.

Crispin and Crispinian   (d. *c*.285) Roman martyrs. According to legend, Crispin and Crispinian were two Roman brothers of noble birth who brought the gospel to the region of Soissons in France, where they earned their living as shoemakers. Ultimately they were tortured and martyred for their faith. A local English tradition claims that they survived and subsequently settled in Faversham in Kent, which was formerly a site of pilgrimage on their account. Their names are most familiar to modern readers from their mention in the celebrated 'St Crispin's Day' speech before the battle of Agincourt in William Shakespeare's *Henry V*. Today they are honoured as the patron saints of shoemakers and leather workers. Their emblem is a shoe or a last.
Feast Day: 25 October.

Crispina   (d.304) African martyr. Born in Numidia, Crispina (sometimes called **Crispina of Tagora**) was a married noblewoman and mother whose Christian faith brought her into conflict with the Roman authorities during the reign of Diocletian. Demands from Anulinus, the proconsul at Thevaste, that she make sacrifice to the gods met with a stout refusal, upon which her head was shaved and she was executed with a sword. After her death she was selected for special praise by St AUGUSTINE. *Feast Day: 5 December.*

Cuby   *See* CYBI.

Cunegund   (c.978–1033) German empress. The wife of the Holy Roman Emperor St HENRY II, she shared her husband's dedication to the cause of Benedictine monasticism and greatly influenced his foundation of new monastic centres. On her own behalf she founded a nunnery at Kaufungen in Hesse, in which she spent the years of her widowhood living as a Benedictine nun. After her death she was buried alongside her husband in Bamberg cathedral. She was canonized in 1200, and is the patron saint of Lithuania and Luxembourg. *Feast Day: 3 March.*

Cuthbert   (c.634–687) English bishop. Cuthbert was born in Northumbria and brought up by a foster mother after the death of his parents. He spent his youth as a shepherd and soldier before wearying of warfare and, after a vision, entering Melrose Abbey at the age of 15 and becoming a monk. Shortly afterwards he narrowly survived a plague epidemic that claimed many lives and prompted many Christians to revert to pagan practices. In response to this he embarked upon a lifetime of missionary work throughout northern England, tirelessly calling on the faithful to maintain their faith and taking the gospel as far as the Picts of northern Scotland. He eventually became prior at Melrose but from 664 was based at Lindisfarne, acquired a gathering reputation as a worker of miracles and becoming known as the 'Wonder Worker of Britain', being credited with miraculous powers of prophecy and healing. In 676, however, he withdrew from the world and spent the next 10 years living as a hermit in a cell on the isolated Farne islands, only to find that his solitude was frequently disturbed by visitors asking for his advice. In 684 he reluctantly gave up the solitary life when he was elected bishop of Hexham but almost immediately arranged to exchange this position for the see of Lindisfarne. Widely revered for his dedication, compassion and generosity towards his flock, he died in his cell in the Farne islands two years later. The best-loved saint in northern England, he became the focus of a considerable cult and numerous churches were dedicated to him. His remains were later removed from Lindisfarne because of the threat of Viking raids and placed in Durham cathedral. Today he is honoured as the patron saint of sailors. *Feast Day: 20 March.*

Cuthburga   (d. *c.*725) English abbess. Born into the royal family of Wessex, she became the wife of King Aldfrid of Northumbria. After the death of her husband in 704 she became a nun and founded the famous double monastery of Wimbourne. She is reported to have been austere in her manner of life and rigorous in her religious observances, but kindly towards others.
Feast Day: 31 August.

Cuthman   (8th century) English hermit. Little is known for certain about the life of St Cuthman, but he appears to have lived as a shepherd in his youth and to have settled in the area of Steyning in West Sussex, arriving there pushing his elderly mother along in a handcart. Tradition has it that he built a small wooden church at Steyning and lived in a hut beside it for the rest of his days. He became the focus of a considerable cult in pre-Conquest Britain and a small monastic establishment was set up on the site of his church.
Feast Day: 8 February.

Cybi   (6th century) English abbot. Cybi (or **Cuby**) is thought to have been born in Cornwall, possibly the son of St Selevan. He is said to have undertaken extensive journeys through Wales as a missionary, going as far as Anglesey, where he established a monastery in the old Roman fort at what is now Holyhead (called Caer Gybi, or Cybi's town, in Welsh). According to a 13th-century account of his life, he also went on pilgrimage to Jerusalem and visited St ENDA on Aranmore. His memory is preserved in placenames throughout Cornwall and Wales.
Feast Day: 8 November.

Cyprian   (*c.*200–258) Bishop of Carthage. Born Thasius Cecilianus Cyprianus into a wealthy family of Carthage, he became a leading lawyer before converting to Christianity around 246, when he was in his forties. He gave away his wealth, took a vow of chastity and around 248 was elected Bishop of Carthage, though he was obliged to spend much of the rest of his life in hiding. Acknowledged as one of the early Fathers of the Church, he wrote extensively on the scriptures and the church of his day. He also clashed with Pope Stephen I over the issue of the readmittance of

heretics and apostates to the church (Cyprian adopting a fairly moderate position on the matter). Cyprian (sometimes referred to as **Cyprian of Carthage**) is believed to have died a martyr's death, being beheaded during the persecution instituted by Emperor Valerian after he refused to make sacrifice to the gods. He is honoured today as the patron saint of Algeria and North Africa.
Feast Day: 16 September.

Cyprian and Justina (c.300) Martyrs of Antioch. The story of Cyprian and Justina is at heart derived from 4th-century legend. According to this, Cyprian was a sorcerer of Antioch who attempted to win the love of the Christian maiden Justina through his magic. Depressed at his lack of success in this enterprise, Cyprian found himself attracted to the faith his beloved professed and in due course was baptized himself and became a bishop, while Justina became an abbess. They were both martyred at Nicodemia.
Feast Day: 26 September.

Cyricus and Julitta (d. c.304) Martyrs of Iconium in Lycaonia (Turkey). Julitta was a nobleman's widow who was condemned to death as a Christian at Tarsus under the Emperor Diocletian. When the governor Alexander sought to comfort the woman's three-year-old son Cyricus (otherwise called **Cyriacus** or **Quiricus**), the child only scratched his face. The enraged governor threw the child down some steps and the boy was killed. Julitta rejoiced at her son's martyrdom and went uncomplainingly to her own torture and death. The memory of Cyricus is preserved in a number of placenames across Europe and the Near East.
Feast Day: 16 June.

Cyril and Methodius (828–869 and c.815–884) Slav missionaries. Cyril (born Constantine) and Methodius were two brothers born in Salonika who were ordained as priests in Thessalonica and later moved to Constantinople. Around 863 they were sent to Moravia to spread the gospel. Being speakers of the Slavic language they enjoyed great success but also incurred the enmity of rival German missionaries. Cyril died while the brothers were on a visit to Rome in 869. Methodius, meanwhile, was consecrated bishop by the pope, but on his return to Moravia was imprisoned at the will of hostile German bishops. He was released two years later and continued his missionary work until 879, when he was obliged to go to Rome to respond to the criticisms of his enemies. He was confirmed in the post of archbishop of Sirmium (Pannonia) and Moravia and on his return, with the blessing of the pope, introduced the celebration of the liturgy in the Slavonic language. Opposition to the reforms of Methodius continued, however, and after his death many of his followers were driven out of the region. Known as the 'apostles of the Slavs', the two brothers are remembered chiefly for compiling an early version of what became the Cyrillic alphabet and using it to translate the Bible, thus establishing their claim to be the fathers of Slavonic literature. Today they are honoured, alongside St BENEDICT, as the patron saints of Europe, specifically Bulgaria and Romania.

Feast Day: 14 February.

Cyril of Alexandria   (*c.*376–444) Archbishop of Alexandria. Born in Alexandria in Egypt, he supported his uncle Theophilus of Alexandria in the deposing of St JOHN CHRYSOSTOM and ultimately succeeded him as archbishop of Alexandria in 412. Over the next 32 years he did much to defend the church there against the heresy of Nestorianism but also acquired a controversial reputation for stubbornness and volatility in his defence of the orthodox approach, closing churches that were disloyal to him and driving the Jews out of Alexandria. The mob lynching of the respected Neoplatonist philosopher Hypatia (apparently without his knowledge) was a particular cause of resentment towards his rule. In 431 he presided over the Council of Ephesus, which formally condemned Nestorianism, and following this victory he showed a little more tolerance towards who disagreed with his orthodox stance. His status as a Doctor of the Church reflects his undoubted importance as a theologian and scholar who supported the orthodox approach within the early church against the threat of heresy. He is honoured today as the patron saint of Alexandria. *Feast Day: 27 June.*

Cyril of Jerusalem   (*c.*315–*c.*386) Bishop of Jerusalem. Born in or near Jerusalem, he became a priest around 346 and ultimately bishop of the city. A gentle man by nature, he faced sustained opposition from the supporters of the Arian heresy almost throughout his bishopric. He was forced into exile three times by the advocates of Arianism and in all spent some 16 of his 37 years as bishop absent from his see. In 381 he took part in the Council of Constantinople, which finally brought an end to the Arian heresy and ensured that the final years of his bishopric were relatively peaceful. His many surviving writings include the 24 *Catechetical Lectures*, most of which are directed at those who are preparing for baptism or have been recently baptized. He is honoured today both as a Father of the Church and Doctor of the Church.

Feast Day: 18 March.

D

Dado *See* OUEN.

Damasus I (*c*.304–384) Italian pope. Born in Rome the son of a priest of Spanish descent, he rose through the ranks of the church to become pope in 366, despite fierce opposition from the supporters of his rival for the post, Ursinus, which only ended when Ursinus was sent into exile. His papacy witnessed the recognition of orthodox Christianity as the official Roman religion by the emperors Gratian and Theodosius I (380) and the suppression of Arianism and other heretical beliefs. He also commissioned the celebrated translation of the Bible by St JEROME and undertook the restoration of the catacombs of Rome, composing epitaphs for the tombs himself, as well as the preservation of the relics of the early martyrs. He is honoured today as the patron saint of archeology.
Feast Day: 11 December.

Damian *See* COSMAS AND DAMIAN.

Damien de Veuster (1840–89) Belgian missionary. Damien de Veuster left his native Belgium in 1873 after volunteering to go to Hawaii as a missionary to work at Molokai, where an epidemic of leprosy had erupted some eight years previously. Sometimes called **Damien the Leper**, he worked to better the miserable conditions in which the lepers of Molokai lived in isolation, organizing them into groups to do useful work in the community and generally improving facilities in the colony. He went to Hawaii with a presentiment that he too would die of the disease and, perhaps inevitably, he finally contracted leprosy himself and died at Molokai after 16 years of tireless effort, aged 49. He was beatified in 1995.
Feast Day: 15 April.

Daniel *See* DEINIOL.

Daniel the Stylite (409–493) Syrian-born hermit. Born at Maratha, near Samosata, he lived in a monastery from the age of 12 and lived the life of a monk before being inspired to become a hermit by the example of St SIMEON THE STYLITE, whom he twice visited on his pillar at Telanissus. He lived in isolation in a ruined temple at Philempora near Constantinople

for nine years and then, after the death of St Simeon in 459, installed himself permanently there on a platform supported by two pillars. Over the next 33 years he only descended from his platform on one occasion, when he came down to protest against the rule of the Emperor Basiliscus. He became renowned as a prophet and as a source of simple, practical advice, typically counselling faithfulness to God and love of one's fellow man. The countless pilgrims who came to consult him at Constantinople ranged from invalids to emperors. Upon his death at the age of 84 he was buried at the base of his pillar.
Feast Day: 11 December.

David (*c.*520–*c.*601) Welsh bishop. David (or **Dewi**) is traditionally supposed to have been born the son of a local chieftain at Henfynw in Cardigan. Legend has it that he founded 12 monasteries throughout south Wales and southwestern England and that he was consecrated bishop while on pilgrimage to Jerusalem. Subsequently he was acknowledged as head of the church in Wales, establishing his see at Mynyw, now renamed St David's in his honour. Nicknamed 'The Waterman' either because he advised abstinence from alcohol or because he ritually practiced total immersion in cold water, he appears to have insisted that the monks at Mynyw follow a relatively strict rule of austerity and manual labour. Through the many monks who visited his monasteries David is said to have had a profound influence upon the development of monasticism in both Wales and Ireland. He lived to an advanced age, dying at his monastery at Mynyw, where his relics were preserved prior to removal to St David's Cathedral. He was canonized in 1120. Many churches were dedicated to St David and today he is honoured as the patron saint of Wales and of poets. His emblem is a dove. The reasons why people traditionally wear daffodils or leeks on St David's Day are obscure.
Feast Day: 1 March.

David of Scotland (*c.*1085–1153) Scottish king. The son of Malcolm III of Scotland and MARGARET OF SCOTLAND, he was educated at the Norman court in England and in due course succeeded to the throne of Scotland in 1124. As king he proved a fierce defender of Scottish independence from England, leading various armed incursions into northern England before achieving a peace of kinds with the English and subsequently devoting his attentions to religious and social reform in Scotland. He promoted trade, improved the legal system and promoted the Scottish church. He was also praised for his personal piety and generosity and today is remembered as

one of the best of all Scottish rulers. After his death he was buried at Dunfermline and became the subject of a considerable cult following, despite never being formally canonized.
Feast Day: 24 May.

Deiniol   (d. *c*.584) Scottish-born Welsh bishop. Deiniol (or **Daniel**) is supposed to have been a descendant of Celtic royalty and to have come originally from the Strathclyde region. Rising to the rank of bishop of Bangor in Gwynedd, he is reputed to have been the founder of the monasteries at Bangor Fawr on the Menai Strait and at Bangor Iscoed on the river Dee in Clwyd. By the time of the VENERABLE BEDE the latter of these two establishments had become the most important monastery in Britain, with over 2000 monks. Little more is known of Deiniol's life beyond the fact that he was buried on the island of Bardsey.
Feast Day: 11 September.

Demetrius   (early 4th century) Serbian martyr. Details of the life of Demetrius (or **Dmitry**) are obscure, but he may have been a deacon, possibly at Salonika. According to legend, he was put to death without a trial at Sirmium (now Mitrovica in Serbia) during the reign of Emperor Maximian on charges of preaching Christianity. Dubbed 'The Great Martyr', he subsequently acquired the reputation of a warrior saint in the tradition of St GEORGE and others, often being depicted as a soldier and achieving cult status in the East. His popularity spread to the West through his adoption as a patron by soldiers fighting in the Crusades in the 11th century. Today he is honoured as the patron saint of Belgrade.
Feast Day: 8 October.

Denis   (d. *c*.258) French bishop and martyr. Denis (or **Denys**) of Paris is traditionally supposed to have been an Italian missionary originally named **Dionysius** who was sent together with five other bishops to Gaul in 250. According to legend he was beheaded on the orders of the Roman authorities alongside a deacon called **Eleutherius** and another priest named **Rusticus** in Paris on what became known as Montmartre (meaning 'martyrs' hill'). After execution the martyrs' remains were recovered from the river Seine and interred on what became the site of the abbey of Saint Denis. The identification of St Denis with other early saints, notably Dionysius, a disciple of St PAUL, contributed greatly to the saint's popularity around the 9th century and to the spread of his cult throughout Europe. Today Denis is honoured as the patron saint of France.
Feast Day: 9 October.

Devereux   *See* DYFRIG.

Dewi   *See* DAVID.

Diana D'Andalo   (*c.*1201–36) Italian nun. Born into a wealthy family of
Bologna, she played an important role in persuading her father against his
inclination to give St DOMINIC land for the foundation of a friary near the
University of Bologna. Subsequently she took her vows as a nun before
St Dominic and tried to persuade her father to establish a Dominican
convent on his land: when he refused to cooperate she joined an Augustinian community. At length, under gentle pressure from Dominic's
successor as head of the Dominican Order St JORDAN OF SAXONY, the
D'Andalo family made possible the foundation of St Agnes' convent at
Bologna to house Diana and four companions. Diana and Jordan fell
deeply in love, but stubbornly maintained their vows of celibacy and
remained no more than close friends for the next 15 years, writing to each
other regularly to offer spiritual support and ultimately dying within a
year of each other. Often cited as an exemplar of self-discipline and
sacrifice, she was beatified in 1891.
Feast Day: 9 June.

Dino   *See* DONATUS OF FIESOLE.

Dionysius of Alexandria   (*c.*190–*c.*265) Alexandrian bishop. Born in Alexandria, he became bishop of the city in 247. He faced many challenges
during his 17 years as bishop, having to cope with persecution, famine,
plague, schism and recurrent violence. On one occasion, threats to the
personal safety of Dionysius under the persecution instituted by the
Emperor Decius led to his friends forcibly removing him from Alexandria
to seek temporary refuge in the Libyan desert. He soon returned, however,
after the death of Decius in 251 and demonstrated his humanity through
his insistence upon leniency towards those who had lapsed under pressure
from the authorities. Persecution began again during the reign of Emperor
Valerian in 257, resulting in the two-year banishment of the bishop, who
nonetheless returned to the riven city as soon as was practicable. Active as
a preacher and writer upon theological matters, Dionysius was widely
respected for his learning and for his varied personal qualities, while his
fortitude prompted St BASIL to bestow upon him the title **Dionysius the
Great**.
Feast Day: 17 November.

Dionysius of Paris   *See* DENIS.

Dismas   (d. *c.*30AD) The 'Good Thief'. According to St LUKE's Gospel, one
of the two thieves crucified alongside Christ rebuked the other for blas-
pheming against the Saviour. He seems to have accepted Christ's innocence, while also resigning himself to the justice of his own execution for
his crimes, and requested that Christ should remember him when they
arrived in heaven. Christ's reply is reported as 'Truly, I say to you, today
you will be with me in Paradise.' The 'Gospel of Nicodemus' gives him
the name Dismas and a later Arabic text entitled the 'Gospel of Infancy'
elaborates his story with the legend that he robbed but then protected the
Holy Family on the flight into Egypt. He is honoured today as the patron
saint of prisoners, funeral directors, therapists and undertakers.
Feast Day: 25 March.

Dmitry   *See* DEMETRIUS.

Domhnall   *See* DONALD.

Dominic   (1170–1221) Spanish founder of the Dominican Order of
Preachers. Born into a noble family at Calaruega, Spain, he had a quiet
childhood, embarking upon religious study at the University of Palencia
in Castile in 1184 and in due course (1195) becoming a Franciscan canon
regular at the cathedral at Osma. In 1204 he undertook evangelical work
among the Albigensian heretics in Languedoc in southern France, accompanying his bishop Diego, and consolidated his reputation as a formidable
preacher. Although the pope was currently pursuing military action
against the Albigensians, resulting in massacres and civil war, Dominic – a
compassionate and intelligent man – came to the conclusion that a better
way to defend the faith was to establish monastic communities of men and
women dedicated to Christian ideals and concentrate upon peaceful
persuasion of heretics. Accordingly, he set up his first communities for
disciplined men and women at Prouille in France in 1206 and, having
established his base at Toulouse, eventually (1216) won papal recognition
for his new order under the title of the Friars Preachers. Members of the
order – commonly called Dominicans and wearing black and white robes –
took vows of poverty and devoted their lives to preaching and education,
going wherever Dominic ordered them to spread the word. Dominic
himself proved energetic in travelling far and wide to oversee the establishment of new houses throughout France, Spain and Italy. The order
flourished and numbered 60 friaries around Europe by the time of

Dominic's death in Bologna. It played a hugely influential role in the development of the later medieval church and has since achieved worldwide distribution. Dominic himself was canonized in 1234. His emblems include a star, a lily and a black and white dog gripping a torch in its mouth. Today he is also honoured as the patron saint of astronomers.
Feast Day: 8 August.

Dominic Savio (1842–1857) Italian youth. Dominic Savio was born the son of a blacksmith at Riva, near Turin, and showed unusual spiritual awareness at a very young age. At the age of 12 he came under the tutelage of St JOHN BOSCO in Turin and here proved an exemplar of Christian piety and purity for his fellow students. Among other good deeds, he formed the Company of the Immaculate Conception to perform household duties for the community and to assist children who were having trouble settling in at the oratory. He was also credited with prophetic powers. Never in good health but unfailingly cheerful, he died from tuberculosis at the premature age of 15. Dominic Savio was canonized in 1954, becoming one of the youngest individuals ever to be recognized in this manner, and today he is honoured as the patron saint of youth, choirboys and the falsely accused (a reference to a story that he uncomplainingly accepted the blame for a minor infringement of which he was entirely innocent).
Feast Day: 9 March.

Donald (early 8th century) Scottish patriarch. Donald (or **Domhnall**) was supposedly a married man of Ogilvy in Forfarshire, who, following the death of his wife, pursued a devout religious life together with his nine daughters. This quasi-monastic community continued after Donald's death, when the nine women moved to Abernethy. The nine women, sometimes called 'The Nine Maidens', are remembered in the names of various natural features in the Abernethy area.
Feast Day: 15 July.

Donatus of Fiesole (d. *c.*876) Irish bishop. According to legend, Donatus (or **Dino**) was an Irish monk who travelled through Europe before arriving in Fiesole (near Florence) on his return from Rome at a time (*c.*829) when a new bishop was needed. He was miraculously identified as the ideal candidate for the post and was duly installed. A respected scholar and teacher who served under the Frankish kings Lotharius and Louis the Pious, he is said to have been the founder of a hospice for Irish pilgrims at

Piacenza, called St Brigid's, and to have participated in the Roman Council held in 861. His relics are preserved at Fiesole Cathedral.
Feast Day: 22 October.

Donnan (d.617) Irish martyr. Donnan (or **Donan**) lived as a monk on Iona under St COLUMBA before leaving to become the founder and head of a monastic community on the island of Eigg in the Inner Hebrides. Donnan and his companions (52 in number according to one source) were massacred while celebrating Mass on Easter eve, being gathered together in a building that was then set ablaze. The perpetrators may have been Vikings or other brigands sent by a local woman seeking revenge for the loss of her pasture rights on the island. The memory of the martyrs is preserved in the names of a number of churches in Scotland.
Feast Day: 17 April.

Dorothy (d. *c*.303) Cappadocian martyr. The details of the life of Dorothy (or **Dorothea**) are shrouded in legend. The story goes that she was a virgin who lived in Caesarea in Cappadocia and was arrested for her Christian faith during the persecution instituted under the Emperor Diocletian. When two women were sent to obtain a recantation from her she converted them both to the Christian faith and was duly sentenced to death by beheading. On her way to execution she was mocked by a young lawyer named Theophilus, who requested that she send him flowers and fruit from Paradise. A child immediately appeared bearing a basket of apples and roses, which Dorothy handed to her astounded persecutor. The lawyer declared his instant conversion to Christianity and was accordingly martyred as Dorothy was. Dorothy is represented in art with a basket of fruit and flowers. She is honoured as the patron saint of brides, midwives and florists.
Feast Day: 6 February.

Dubricius *See* DYFRIG.

Dunstan (*c*.909–988) English archbishop. Born near Glastonbury and possibly of royal blood himself, he abandoned a secular career in favour of the church after serious illness. He lived for a while as a hermit before being appointed royal adviser during the minority of King Edmund. Around 643 he was given responsibility for monastic reform in Glastonbury and largely from his work there, supported by Edmund and succeeding monarchs, came the revival of Benedictine monasticism throughout Britain. Dunstan founded or refounded numerous abbeys in southwest England and around

970 oversaw a conference for the compilation of a national monastic rule entitled the *Regularis Concordia*. As well as his work on monastic revival and reform of the church, including the reconstruction of many church buildings and the consolidation of church law, Dunstan played a key role in the secular leadership of the country. Appointed Archbishop of Canterbury in 959, he presided over the coronation of Edgar as king of all England in 973: the service he drew up for this event is still essentially the same coronation rite in use today. As well as being the dominant figure in the English church in the 10th century and serving as chief adviser to the kings of Wessex, Dunstan was noted for his varied skills as a writer, metal-worker, bell-founder, harpist and singer. Legend adds the tradition that on one occasion he subdued the Devil by seizing his nose with a pair of tongs (in which act he is often depicted in art). Dunstan continued to teach, to preach and to lead the choristers at Canterbury Cathedral until his death at an advanced age. His shrine in the cathedral was destroyed during the Reformation. Today Dunstan is honoured as the patron saint of goldsmiths, jewellers, locksmiths, blacksmiths, musicians and the blind.
Feast Day: 19 May.

Dyfrig   (d. *c*.550) Welsh bishop. Dyfrig (otherwise called **Devereux** or **Dubricius**) is believed to have been a prominent figure in the 6th-century church of south Wales and Herefordshire, though the details of his life are obscure. He is said to have been born at Madley near Hereford and to have become a founder of the see of Llandaff, where his relics are reported to have been moved from Bardsey Island (where he died) in 1120. According to medieval legend he was the archbishop of Caerleon who crowned King Arthur.
Feast Day: 14 November.

Dympna   (dates unknown) Irish martyr. The story of Dympna (or **Dymphna**) would appear to owe more to folklore than fact. Inspired by the discovery of the ancient skeletons of a man and a woman at Gheel, near Antwerp in Belgium, in the 13th century, the legend grew that they were the bones of an Irish – or possibly British – princess who fled with her chaplain Gerebernus from her pagan father's incestuous desire (supposedly provoked by her physical similarity to her deceased mother). Her father, however, followed the couple to Gheel and slaughtered them both when she refused to return home. Dympna subsequently became associated with the healing of mental disorders and a hospital for the insane (still extant) was established at Gheel by the end of the 13th century.

Today she remains the patron saint of the insane and runaways. In art she is depicted holding a sword and restraining the Devil with a leash.
Feast Day: 30 May.

E

Edburga of Minster   (d.751) English abbess. Edburga (or **Eadburh**) became abbess of Minster-in-Thanet in 716 in succession to St MILDRED. Most of the information that survives about her comes from the letters of St BONIFACE OF CREDITON, to whom she appears to have sent various gifts, including books and gold. Tradition has it that she was a princess of Wessex. She is believed to have built both a church and a monastery at Minster and was eventually buried there herself. Various miraculous cures are said to have taken place at her tomb.
Feast Day: 12 December.

Edburga of Winchester   (d.960) English nun. A grand-daughter of Alfred the Great, Edburga (or **Eadburh**) was educated at the abbey of St Mary in Winchester, which had been founded by her father King Edward the Elder of Wessex. Although she never became abbess, she was renowned far and wide for her pious, humble character. She died at a relatively young age and became the subject of a considerable cult, particularly at Winchester and at Pershore abbey in Worcestershire, where her relics were preserved.
Feast Day: 15 June.

Edith of Wilton   (*c.*961–984) English nun. Born in Kemsing, Kent, the illegitimate daughter of King Edgar and Wulfrida, Edith (or **Eadgyth**) was brought up at the nunnery at Wilton, near Salisbury, and spent her whole life there. She refused all the privileges her connections with royalty could have afforded her and instead became famed for her piety and humility, even turning down offers of the position of abbess at Winchester, Barking and Amesbury in order to remain with the nuns at Wilton. Similarly, in 978, she declined an invitation to become queen on the murder of her half-brother Edward the Martyr. She was particularly noted for her generosity to the poor and for her sympathy with wild animals. After her premature death at the age of 23 she became the subject of a cult, with various miracles of healing supposedly taking place at her tomb.
Feast Day: 16 September.

Edith Stein   (1891–1942) German martyr. Born into a Jewish family in Breslau, Germany (now Wroclaw, Poland), she studied philosophy and

women's issues at the University of Göttingen before enrolling as a nurse during World War I and being decorated for her efforts. She was baptized as a Catholic in 1922 and worked as a teacher before joining the Carmelite nuns in Cologne under the name **Teresa Benedicta of the Cross** in 1933. Internationally respected for her philosophical writings and for her championship of women's rights, she was arrested by the Nazis in 1942 with her sister Rosa after Dutch bishops denounced the massacring of Jews in the concentration camps. She and her sister died in the gas chambers at Auschwitz. She was canonized in 1998.
Feast Day: 10 August.

Edmund   (841–870) English martyr. The adopted heir of Offa of Mercia, he became king of East Anglia as a young man and ruled in peace prior to the arrival of an invading Danish army in 865. He was defeated in battle in 870 and taken prisoner by the Danes, who ordered him to renounce Christianity and agree to pay them tribute. Edmund refused these demands and was subjected to vicious torture before being executed (either tied to a tree and shot with arrows or beheaded). A cult quickly grew around him and the abbey at Bury St Edmunds (where his body was taken) was named after him and became the site of a powerful Benedictine abbey. His emblem in art is an arrow. He was the patron saint of Richard II and in former times his name was often invoked as protection against the plague. He was formerly the patron saint of England.
Feast Day: 20 November.

Edmund of Abingdon   (*c.*1175–1240) English archbishop. Born Edmund Rich into a wealthy merchant family in Abingdon, he was educated at Oxford and Paris before becoming a priest. As a teacher of theology at Oxford, he earned a reputation both for his holiness and his eloquence as a preacher. He was appointed treasurer to Salisbury cathedral in 1222 and ultimately became archbishop of Canterbury in 1233. He steered the church through seven troubled years, preventing war between the king and his nobles and promoting ecclesiastical reform (though he professed to dislike politics). He clashed, however, with Henry III over legal issues and became involved in lengthy argument with the monks at Canterbury, who challenged his authority over them. He was en route to consult the pope over such matters in 1240 when he died at Soissy, near Pontigny in Burgundy. Remembered for his personal virtue, he was the last archbishop

of Canterbury to be canonized (1246). In art he is often depicted praying before the Virgin Mary.
Feast Day: 16 November.

Edmund Arrowsmith (1585–1628) English martyr. Born Brian Arrowsmith, the son of a Catholic yeoman farmer, he was sent by his parents to the English College at Douai, where he could study Catholicism safe from persecution in anti-Catholic England. He returned to England shortly after being ordained in 1612 and spent the next ten years preaching the Catholic faith. In 1622 he was finally arrested for his activities but was released along with other Catholics during a lull in the government's anti-Catholic campaign. Undaunted, Edmund joined the Jesuits in 1624 and it was not long before he was arrested once again and this time put on trial in Lancaster. He refused to deny his Catholic faith and was duly hung, drawn and quartered. He was canonized in 1970.
Feast Day: 25 October.

Edmund Campion (1540–81) English martyr. Born the son of a London bookseller, Edmund Campion established a reputation as a scholar at Oxford before entering the Church of England as a deacon in 1569. He was attracted, however, to the Roman Catholic church and, after a period of time spent in Ireland co-founding Trinity College, Dublin, he travelled to the English College in Douai, France, where he converted to Catholicism (1573), and thence to Rome, where he joined the Jesuit order later that same year. He was ordained as a priest in Prague in 1578 and two years later undertook a mission to promote the Jesuit order in England. In 1580 he landed in England disguised as a jewel merchant and set about supporting English Catholics against the demands of the Protestant establishment through his preaching and writings. Ultimately, after many narrow escapes, he was tracked down and arrested at Lyford Grange in Berkshire and sent to the Tower of London. Despite torture, he refused to recant his views and was tried alongside several confederates in Westminster Hall on charges of plotting rebellion. Though he declared his loyalty to Elizabeth I, he was condemned to death and duly hanged, drawn and quartered at Tyburn. He was canonized in 1970.
Feast Day: 25 October.

Edward the Confessor (1003–1066) English king. The son of King Ethelred II (the Unready), he was educated in Ely until the Danish invasion of 1013, after which he completed his studies in Normandy with

his Norman mother Emma. He remained in Normandy after his widowed
mother married the new king of England, Cnut, and himself succeeded to
the throne on Cnut's death in 1042 (Cnut and Emma's son Harthacnut
having acknowledged Edward's claim to the crown). Edward married
Edith, daughter of the powerful Earl Godwin, but the couple produced
no heir (according to popular but unsubstantiated tradition because of
Edward's godly chastity). Edward's reign was a time of peace and prosperity and the king himself was praised for his generosity to the poor and
for his firmness towards recalcitrant nobles, gradually acquiring a saintly
reputation. History remembers him chiefly, however, for the confusion that
resulted from the conflicting claims to the throne of Earl Godwin's son
Harold and William of Normandy. Both were said to have been promised
the kingship. Other less damaging achievements of Edward's life included
the building of St Peter's Abbey on the future site of Westminster Abbey.
Edward was canonized in 1161 and during medieval times was widely
considered the patron saint of England until eclipsed by St GEORGE. He is
usually depicted in art presenting a pilgrim with a ring (an allusion to the
story that he once gave his ring to an impoverished Westminster beggar).
Feast Day: 5 January.

Edward the Martyr   (c.962–978) English king. The son of King Edgar, he
faced rival claims to the throne but acquired it in 975 largely through the
influential support of St DUNSTAN. Unfortunately, the youthful king's reign
ended just three years later when he was murdered by assassins at Corfe
in Dorset, apparently by supporters of his half-brother Ethelred (popular
rumour assigned much of the blame to Ethelred's mother Aelfthryth).
Stories of miracles surrounding Edward's name quickly accrued and he
was being described as a saint and martyr as early as 1001. Initially
buried at Wareham, his remains were transferred to Shaftesbury on the
instructions of Dunstan in 980.
Feast Day: 18 March.

Edwin   (584–633) English king. Edwin spent much of his youth in exile in
Wales and East Anglia before defeating and killing his rival King Ethelfrith
and claiming the throne of Northumbria for himself in 616. A widower, he
found that his advances to Ethelburga of Kent were initially refused on the
grounds that he was not a Christian. The marriage eventually took place
on condition that Ethelburga should be free to pursue her religion and that
Edwin would consider converting to Christianity as well. Encouraged by
the missionary bishop St PAULINUS OF YORK, he eventually became a

Christian himself at Easter 627 (together with many of his nobles), a key event in the expansion of Christianity in northern England. Edwin presided over a relatively peaceful kingdom and successfully expanded his possessions to the north and west prior to being killed in battle against Penda of Mercia. After his death, Edwin became the focus of a considerable cult based on York and Whitby.
Feast Day: 12 October.

Egbert   (d. 729) English monk. Born into a noble family in Northumbria, he became a monk at Lindisfarne but subsequently continued his studies in Ireland. When he and his companion Aethelhun were struck down by the plague Egbert swore that if he was spared he would go into exile for the rest of his life. Aethelhun died, but Egbert survived and accordingly left Ireland for ever. He went on to organize several evangelical missions to Germany, although he himself remained permanently on Iona from 716, his achievements there including persuading his fellow monks to accept the Roman date for Easter.
Feast Day: 24 April.

Egwin   (d. *c*.717) English bishop. Possibly born into a royal Mercian family, he became bishop of Worcester around 692. Details of his life are uncertain beyond the fact that he was the founder of the great abbey at Evesham, where (so tradition has it) he had been vouchsafed a vision of the Virgin Mary. It appears that he had a reputation for severity towards erring parishioners, whose complaints eventually attracted the sympathy of the archbishop of Canterbury. Unrest reached such a pitch that Egwin was obliged to vacate his diocese and travel to Rome to gain the vindication of the pope. According to legend, to make his point doubly effective, he locked his feet in fetters, throwing the key into the river Avon: on his arrival in Rome he bought a fish at the market and found the key inside. After his death, Egwin's relics were preserved by the monks at Evesham. He is usually depicted in art with a fish and a key.
Feast Day: 30 December.

Eleutherius   *See* DENIS.

Eligius   *See* ELOI.

Elizabeth   *See* ZECHARIAH AND ELIZABETH.

Elizabeth of Hungary   (1207–1231) Hungarian noblewoman. The daughter of King Andrew II of Hungary and wife of Louis IV, Landgrave of

Thuringia, Elizabeth was devoted to her husband and grief-stricken when ultimately he died of plague during the Crusades. Unlike many other saints who sought holiness through chastity and isolation from the world, she was fully committed to her life as a wife and mother (bearing her husband a son and two daughters) but also became widely loved for her generosity in distributing the wealth of her family among the poor. Other acts of kindness included the building of hospitals and, on one occasion, nursing a leper in the royal bedroom. After her husband's death in 1227 she came under the brutal influence of her confessor Conrad of Marburg and, weakened by his cruelties (which included physical chastisement), died an uncomplaining death at the premature age of 24. One of Germany's most beloved saints, she was canonized in 1235 and is honoured as the patron saint of beggars, bakers, charities, lacemakers and the Sisters of Mercy.

Feast Day: 17 November.

Elizabeth of Portugal   (1271–1336) Portuguese queen. The daughter of the King of Aragon, she married King Denis of Portugal aged 12 and lived a pious life of prayer besides fulfilling her responsibilities as queen. Also called **Isabel** or the **Angel of Peace**, she used her influence to reconcile her husband with various rivals, including Pope Nicholas IV and his own brother, and also, on two occasions, to prevent war between Ferdinand IV of Castile and his enemies. When warfare loomed between her husband and one of their children she rode a donkey between the two armies and shamed the two sides into laying down their weapons. It was partly due to her efforts that the reign of King Denis (though unfaithful and inconsiderate as a husband) became a golden age of peace and prosperity. She also founded institutions to help orphans and fallen women as well as refuges and a hospital. Upon her husband's death in 1324 Elizabeth gave away her possessions and went on pilgrimage to Compostela before settling in a house close to a Franciscan convent. She died after a last peacemaking mission between her son Alfonso IV and Alfonso XI of Castile. Canonized in 1626, she is honoured as the patron saint of brides, charities, widows, queens and victims of unfaithful marriages.

Feast Day: 4 July.

Elizabeth of Schönau   (1129–1165) German abbess. Born into a wealthy family in Schönau, Germany, she joined the Benedictine order at the age of 12 and was a pupil and friend of St HILDEGARD. In 1152, during a fit of depression, she had the first of many visions and subsequently became

famous for her visionary and prophetic powers. Her insights were
recorded by her brother Ekbert, who collected her visions and sermons in
such publications as *The Book of the Ways of God* (10 sermons derived from
her mystic experiences), *The Resurrection of the Blessed Virgin* (describing
her visions of Mary) and *The Book of Revelations About the Sacred Company of
the Virgins of Cologne* (recounting the martyrdom of St URSULA). Other
surviving writings include some of her letters.
Feast Day: 18 June.

Elizabeth of the Trinity   (1880–1906) French nun. Born Elizabeth Catez,
she settled on a life within the church at a young age and defied her
parents' wishes by joining the Carmelites at Dijon in 1901. Subsequently
she devoted herself to a life of work and prayer within the Carmelite
order, evidently deriving the greatest happiness from her chosen path.
Impressed by her unfailing love of life, which made her a great favourite
in the convent, she was commanded by her superiors to commit her
somewhat mystical reflections upon the nature of God and the Trinity to
paper, which she did before dying a premature death from illness at the
age of 26.
Feast Day: 8 November.

Elizabeth Bichier des Âges   (1773–1838) French noblewoman. Born at
the Château des Âges near Poitiers, she organized secret worship among
the faithful during the upheaval of the French Revolution and through this
met St ANDREW FOURNET. She went on to establish a group of sisters to
care for the sick and educate young girls and from this developed a chain
of 60 small convents run by the Sisters of St Andrew the Apostle (or, the
Daughters of the Cross). She was much respected for her patient determination to improve the lives of others in the face of many difficulties and
was canonized in 1947.
Feast Day: 26 August.

Elizabeth Leseur   (1866–1914) French housewife. Married to an atheistic
doctor called Felix Leseur, she converted to Christianity after her husband
persuaded her to read Renan's *Life of Jesus*. She recorded her spiritual
development in a secret journal and it was only after her agonizing death
from cancer in Paris (which she typically accepted as a form of prayer)
that the intensity of her faith was revealed. Felix Leseur was so affected by
the journal that he found his own faith renewed and became a Dominican

priest, travelling extensively through Europe to spread the message of his wife's writings.
Feast Day: 3 May.

Elizabeth Seton   (1774–1821) US nun. Born Elizabeth Ann Bayley in New York, Elizabeth Seton bore five children during her nine-year marriage, which ended with her wealthy husband's death in 1803. Having founded the Society for the Relief of Poor Widows, she converted to Catholicism in 1805 and went on to establish a school for girls in Baltimore, Maryland. In 1809 she co-founded a religious community at Emmitsburg, the nucleus of what became the American Sisters of Charity, a pillar of the Catholic church in the USA dedicated to helping the poor and to teaching in parish schools. She was canonized in 1975, thus becoming the first native-born North American saint. She is honoured as the patron saint of widows.
Feast Day: 4 January.

Elmo   *See* ERASMUS.

Eloi   (*c*.588–660) French bishop. Born into a Gallo-Roman family near Limoges, Eloi (or **Eligius**) worked as apprentice to a goldsmith before finding employment making golden thrones and other precious items for the royal treasurer Bobon. Noted for making his raw materials go further than most others, he was recruited by King Clotaire II and in due course he became master of the mint in Paris. As chief adviser to King Dagobert from 629 he carried out important state missions and amassed a personal fortune. He used his wealth to help the poor, buy slaves their freedom and to found churches and other beneficent institutions. He joined the priesthood in 640 and a year later became bishop of Noyon and Tournai. A powerful preacher, he proved an energetic evangelist and reformer and also founded several monasteries, including that at Noyon, where ultimately he died. He was among the most revered saints of the Middle Ages, celebrated as much for his skill as a craftsman as for his undoubted spiritual qualities. His emblems in art are the hammer, the anvil and the horseshoe and he is honoured as the patron saint of blacksmiths and metalworkers.
Feast Day: 1 December.

Elphege   *See* ALPHEGE.

Elzear   (*c*.1285–1323) French nobleman. Born in Provence, he married an heiress and inherited his father's estates at the age of 23. A deeply religious man, like his wife, he treated his servants and neighbours with respect and generosity. Besides running his estates he also served as tutor to the son of King Robert of Naples and worked as a diplomat in Paris, where he resisted all the venal temptations of the French court. He died at the relatively young age of 38 and was canonized by his nephew Pope Urban V.

Feast Day: 27 September.

Emily de Rodat (1787–1852) French noblewoman. Born into a wealthy family near Rodez, she was brought up at the Château de Ginals and as a young woman occupied herself with charitable works, as well as joining local convents for brief periods. In 1815 she established a free school at Villefranche-de-Rouergue, from which evolved the Congregation of the Holy Family of Villefranche, whose activities soon spread to many parts of the world. Emily de Rodat remained at the head of the organization for 30 years, despite prolonged and intense physical suffering resulting from a range of ailments, including cancer of the eye. Some contemporaries were daunted by her determined, even severe manner, while others praised her for her prayerful devotion. She was canonized in 1950.

Feast Day: 19 September.

Emily de Vialar (1797–1856) French foundress. Born near Albi, she spent 20 years looking after her widowed father before coming into enough money to expand her charitable activities in the Languedoc region. She used her money to found charities in Gaillac and, in 1835, in Algeria, braving the opposition of the bishop of Algiers, who in 1842 had Mother Emily excommunicated and returned to France. Undaunted, as head of the Sisters of St Joseph 'of the Apparition', she established numerous similar institutions throughout the world, cementing her reputation both for her shrewdness and her humanity. She was canonized in 1951.

Feast Day: 24 August.

Enda (d. *c.*530) Irish abbot. Tradition has it that Enda (or **Eanna**) was born in Meath and became a monk at Rosnat, an unidentified monastery variously identified as St David's in Pembrokeshire or St Ninian's in Galloway. He is remembered primarily as the founder of the religious community on the island of Inishmore (the gift of King Oengus of Munster), which is considered the first formal Irish monastery. Notable pupils of Enda's on Inishmore included St CIARAN OF CLONMACNOIS. Enda is also said to have founded monasteries in the Boyne valley. There is little evidence available

to support legends that claim that Enda's sister Fanchea played the leading role in pioneering monastic work credited to Enda.
Feast Day: 21 March.

Ephraem (*c.*306–*c.*373) Syrian monk. Born the son of a pagan priest in Nisibis in Mesopotamia, Ephraem (or **Ephrem**) was baptized around the year 324 and in due course, having accompanied his teacher St JAMES OF NISIBIS to the Council of Nicea in 325, became head of the cathedral school at Nisibis. When Rome ceded control of Nisibis to the Persians in 363 he fled to a cave in Edessa, where he spent the last 10 years of his life as a hermit, writing prolifically upon religious matters. His writings, of which only fragments survive, included apologetics, hymns and commentaries upon scripture. He also played a leading role in promoting the use of hymns in public worship, fitting religious lyrics to popular secular tunes, and for that reason is sometimes known as the 'Harp of the Holy Spirit'. He was declared a Doctor of the Church in 1920.
Feast Day: 9 June.

Epiphanius of Salamis (*c.*315–403) Judean bishop. Born into a hellenized Jewish family in Judea, he lived as a monk and hermit in Egypt before returning to Judea and founding a monastery at Eleutheropolis (Beit Jibrin). He remained head of the monastery for 30 years before being appointed bishop of Constantia (Salamis) in 367. He earned a controversial reputation as an impassioned defender of orthodoxy, earning the nickname 'the Oracle of Palestine' but offended many with his forthright, often tactless manner. As an old man, he was vocal in his opposition to St JOHN CHRYSOSTOM but then changed his mind and announced his return to Cyprus, only to die at sea on the journey home. His writings include *Ancoratus* ('The Well-Anchored'), a defence of Christian doctrine, and *Panarion* ('The Medicine Box'), a description of the remedies available to heresies of all kinds.
Feast Day: 12 May.

Erasmus (d. *c.*303) Bishop and martyr. Little is known for certain of the life of Erasmus (also called **Elmo** or **Telmo**) beyond the tradition that he was a bishop in Formiae in the Campagna in Italy who was put to death during the persecutions of Diocletian. Another legend claims that, after many tortures, he was executed at Formiae by having his entrails pulled from his body through the use of a windlass. The name Elmo is best known today from 'St Elmo's Fire', the popular name for the luminous

light sometimes seen on ships' masts during storms, a result of electrical discharges. The patron saint of sailors and also called upon by people suffering from colic or other stomach ailments, he is represented in art by a windlass.
Feast Day: 2 June.

Erconwald   (d. 693) English bishop. Born into a well-connected aristocratic English family, Erconwald (also referred to as **Earconwald** or **Erkenwald**) was appointed bishop of the East Saxons by St THEODORE OF CANTERBURY in 675 and is remembered as one of the most influential figures in the early history of the church in the London area. Although little is known in detail of his life, he is known to have been the founder of a monastery at Chertsey and of a nunnery at Barking, where his sister St ETHELBURGA served as abbess. Erconwald's tomb in St Paul's Cathedral attracted many pilgrims during the medieval period and today he is honoured as the patron saint of London.
Feast Day: 30 April.

Eric   (d. c.1160) King of Sweden. Having ascended to the throne of Sweden in 1156, he sought to convert his neighbours the Finns to Christianity through conquest, but was subsequently killed during a Danish attack upon Uppsala, being wounded in an assassination attempt and then tortured and beheaded. Eric's saintly reputation was largely the invention of his son Cnut, who promoted his father as the patron saint of Sweden. He did, however, found a monastic chapter at Old Uppsala and consolidated the Christian church throughout his country.
Feast Day: 18 May.

Eskil   (d. c.1080) Bishop and martyr. Possibly English by birth, Eskil is supposed to have accompanied his relative St SIGFRID on a mission to reconvert the people of Sweden, who had resumed pagan practices. Once in Sweden, he set about evangelizing the residents of Södermanland, becoming the bishop of Strängnäs. After initial success, he provoked a hostile reaction from his audience when he spoke out against a local pagan festival and, when a violent storm destroyed the altar used at the festival, he was stoned to death by a vengeful mob. He became one of Sweden's best-known saints and Eskilstuna was named in his honour.
Feast Day: 12 June.

Ethelbert of Kent   (560–616) English king. Having married a Christian, the Frankish princess Bertha, he overcame initial doubts and converted to

Christianity himself after welcoming St AUGUSTINE on his arrival in England in 597, thus becoming the first Christian Anglo-Saxon king. He went on to do much to promote Christianity among his subjects through his patronage of St Augustine at Canterbury without actually forcing them to convert. Among other good deeds he also ordered the building of St Andrew's cathedral in Rochester and enabled the establishment of the first St Paul's cathedral in the territory ruled by his neighbour King Sabert of the East Saxons, who had also converted to Christianity with encouragement from Ethelbert. With help from Augustine Ethelbert also drew up the earliest surviving Anglo-Saxon code of law, under which special protection was afforded to the clergy and the church.

Feast Day: 25 February.

Ethelburga of Barking   (d. 675) English abbess. As abbess of a nunnery at Barking in Essex, Ethelburga (or **Aethelburh**) was, according to Bede, much respected for her piety and for the concern she showed towards those came under her care. Various miraculous incidents were credited to her, although little else is known for certain about her life beyond the fact that she was probably of noble, even royal, birth.

Feast Day: 11 October.

Ethelburga of Kent   *See* PAULINUS OF YORK.

Etheldreda   (c. 630–679) English abbess. Born at Exning in Suffolk a daughter of King Anna of the East Angles, she married twice, the second time to Egfrid, son of King Oswy of Northumbria. Both marriages remained unconsummated and, when Egfrid gave her up, Etheldreda (or **Audrey**) became a nun, settling on the Isle of Ely. She founded a double monastery (now the site of the present cathedral) at Ely around 672 and remained abbess there for the rest of her life, devoting herself to penance and prayer. After her death from plague her shrine at Ely attracted numerous pilgrims. Many legends built up surrounding her name and, revered primarily for her long-preserved virginity, she became one of the best loved of Anglo-Saxon saints with many churches dedicated to her. She is honoured as the patron saint of Cambridge University.

Feast Day: 23 June.

Ethelred   *See* AELRED.

Ethelwold   (c.912–984) English monk. Born in Winchester, he served at the court of King Athelstan before becoming a priest. He was ordained on the same day as his friend St DUNSTAN and subsequently the two worked alongside towards the revival of monasticism in England, based at Glastonbury. Around 954 he left Glastonbury and took over the ruinous monastery at Abingdon, building a new church there and establishing a reputation as a capable and committed leader (winning him the nickname Boanerges, meaning 'son of thunder'). After Dunstan's exile (*c.*956) he took over responsibility for the reform movement and acted as teacher to Edgar, heir to the English throne. He was appointed bishop of Winchester in 963 and among other reforms consolidated the principle of the monastic cathedral, reviving several dormant monasteries and replacing secular clerics with Benedictine monks.

Feast Day: 1 August.

Eucherius of Lyons   (d. *c.*450) French bishop. Born into a noble Gallo-Roman family, Eucherius (or **Eucharius**) married a woman named Galla and by her fathered two sons (both of whom became bishops and saints). Around 422 he became a monk, initially at the monastery of Lérins. A brief period spent as a hermit on the island of Lerona (now Sainte-Marguerite) off Cannes was brought to an end (*c.*434) by his appointment as bishop of Lyons, a consequence of his growing reputation for wisdom and piety. He founded a number of religious institutions and was also noted for his generosity towards the needy. His surviving writings include letters and a history of the martyrs of the Theban legion.

Feast Day: 16 November.

Eugenia   (dates unknown) Roman martyr. Little is known about Eugenia's life beyond the legend that she lived in Rome before disguising herself as a man and in that guise eventually becoming abbot of a monastery in Egypt. After various other fanciful adventures she returned to Rome and was there beheaded for her faith. Tradition has it that she was buried in the cemetery of Apronian on the Via Latina.

Feast Day: 25 December.

Eugenius of Carthage   (d. 505) Carthaginian bishop. Eugenius became bishop of Carthage in 481, at a time of persecution by Arian Vandals. He spent many years in exile in Tunisia and elsewhere, suffering considerable privations, and eventually died in exile in southern France. He is remembered not only for his sufferings but also for his undoubted faithfulness and unfailing support for his followers.

Feast Day: 13 July.

Eulalia of Merida   (d. *c*.304) Spanish martyr. Little is known for certain
about the life of Eulalia of Merida beyond the basic fact that she was a
12-year-old girl who was persecuted at Merida in Spain for her Christian
faith. Legend has it that she protested against Maximian's punitive policy
against the Christians and for her temerity was tortured and, when she
refused to recant, burnt to death. A complementary tradition describes
how a white dove flew from her mouth as she died and how her body
was covered by snow. Eulalia's fame spread far beyond Spain's borders
and she remains one of the country's most revered virgin martyrs.
Feast Day: 10 December.

Eulogius of Alexandria   (d.608) Syrian priest. Born in Antioch, he became
patriarch of Alexandria in 580 and established a reputation as a determined champion of orthodox Christianity. He was particularly noted for
his opposition to Monophysism, which denied the humanity of Christ, and
would appear also to have had some role in organizing the evangelical
mission of St AUGUSTINE to England, mentioned in a surviving letter to
Eulogius from GREGORY THE GREAT.
Feast Day: 13 September.

Eulogius of Cordoba   (d.859) Spanish martyr. According to a brief
account of the life of Eulogius of Cordoba by his friend Alvarus, he was a
learned priest who fell foul of his superiors during the Muslim occupation
of the city. Eulogius was thrown into prison but, unlike many other
contemporaries, was later released. He was moved by his experiences to
record the persecution of his fellow Christians in a *Memorandum of the
Saints*. He was then appointed bishop of Toledo (859) but before he could
be consecrated was again thrown into prison on charges of sheltering a
Muslim girl called Lucretia who had converted to Christianity. Refusing to
recant his faith, Eulogius started to preach the gospel to the court, upon
which he was taken out and immediately beheaded. Lucretia herself was
executed four days later. The two victims were subsequently laid to rest
together in Oviedo cathedral.
Feast Day: 11 March.

Euphrasia   (*c*.382–*c*.412) Egyptian nun. Born into a wealthy family in
Constantinople, Euphrasia (or **Eupraxia**) moved to Egypt at the age of
seven with her widowed mother and at her own request, while still a
child, broke off the engagement arranged by her parents when she was
five, gave away all her possessions, set free her slaves and joined a

convent. She remained in seclusion with the community for the rest of her life, countering the temptation to resume her former life by volunteering herself for all the most demanding domestic chores and forcing herself to exist in conditions of the greatest austerity, often with barely enough to eat. Some of the other nuns suspected her of vanity and hypocrisy, but all were gradually won over by her gentle and loving manner as well as her resolute determination to forego the luxuries of her childhood.
Feast Day: 13 March.

Euphrasia Pelletier (1796–1868) French foundress. Born Rose Virginia Pelletier to refugee parents on the island of Noirmoutier off the French coast, she joined the Institute of Our Lady of Charity and Refuge at Tours and became superioress of the community in 1825. In 1825 she founded a new house at Angers and went on to argue for full-scale reform of the order, overriding fierce opposition and eventually (1835) gaining official recognition of the Congregation of the Good Shepherd at Angers. By the time of her death, the organization had opened 110 convents throughout the world and is now renowned for its work with vulnerable and abused children.
Feast Day: 24 April.

Euphrosyne (dates unknown) Alexandrian virgin. According to legend, Euphrosyne fled her home to avoid having to marry and, disguising herself as a man and calling herself Smaragdus, joined a monastery near Alexandria. Her disguise was so perfect even her own father did not recognize her when he consulted her for advice. Euphrosyne eventually revealed her true identity to her father on her deathbed 38 years later, upon which the repentant parent also joined the monastery.
Feast Day: 25 September.

Euphrosyne of Polotsk (d.1173) Belarussian virgin. Born into a titled family in Polotsk, Belarus, Euphrosyne dedicated herself to a life of religious devotion from the age of 12, living in a cell beside the cathedral of Polotsk. As well as raising funds for the needy by copying and selling books, she established a monastery for women and, in 1170, embarked on a pilgrimage to the Holy Land, being received on her journey with great respect by Michael III of Constantinople and by the crusader king Amaury I. She died in Jerusalem and her body was returned to Kiev. Today she is honoured as the patron saint of Belarus.
Feast Day: 23 May.

Eusebius of Vercelli   (d.371) Italian bishop. Born in Sardinia, Eusebius
was educated in Rome and ultimately entered the priesthood there. As
bishop of Vercelli in northern Italy, Eusebius is credited as the first bishop
in the West to live in a monastery with his priests. He is believed to have
taken a particular interest in the selection of his priests and to have
accepted personal responsibility for their training and welfare. In 354 he
was chosen by Pope Liberius to extend his practices to the wider church.
The following year Eusebius persuaded Emperor Constantius to call a
council in Milan in order to settle the Arian controversy, but he was
obliged to go into exile when the emperor took exception to the bishop's
defence of ATHANASIUS. Imprisoned in Palestine, he was subjected to
public humiliation, being dragged naked through the streets, and attempts
were made to prevent him communicating with his supporters. When
Constantius died, Eusebius was released and went on to conduct missions
to Alexandria and Antioch, continuing in his defence of orthodoxy against
Arianism. A noted scholar, he is thought to have collaborated upon the
composition of the Athanasian Creed. On account of his sufferings in exile,
he is often counted among the martyrs.
Feast Day: 2 August.

Eustace   (dates unknown) Roman martyr. There is scant evidence that
Eustace (or **Eustachius**) ever existed, but legend has it that he was a
general serving under the emperor Trajan who, whilst out hunting near
Tivoli, encountered a stag bearing a glowing crucifix in its antlers. As a
result of this vision Eustace is said to have converted to Christianity without delay, despite the disgrace and loss of wealth that this would entail
His superiors demanded that he recant his new Christian faith, but he
refused and was roasted to death in a brazen bull together with his wife
and sons. He is honoured as the patron saint of hunters.
Feast Day: 2 November.

Eustathius   (c.270–c.360) Bishop of Antioch. Born in Side, Pamphylia,
Eustathius served as the first bishop of Beroea in Syria before transferring to
Antioch in 323. There he courted controversy by vigorously opposing the
Arian sect. His enemies eventually secured his exile to Trajanopolis, at which
his supporters threatened to cause a riot. Eustathius, however, calmly
accepted his fate and left the city. Those of his followers who remained in
Antioch organized themselves as Eustathians and continued to reject the
authority of the Arian bishops there (the so-called 'Meletian Schism').
Feast Day: 16 July.

Eustochium   (c.368–c.419) Roman virgin. One of the daughters of St PAULA, she was born in Rome and travelled to Bethlehem with her mother in 385 in order to be near St JEROME, who undertook her religious education over the next 35 years. When Paula died in 404, Eustochium became head of the community of virgins and widows that had formed around Jerome in Bethlehem. She died shortly after this community was attacked by a mob and their house destroyed. Jerome grieved deeply for her and in his letters described her as a woman of great spirit, crediting her with being the inspiration for the writing of many of his biblical commentaries.
Feast Day: 28 September.

Euthymius the Great   (377–473) Armenian-born abbot. Born at Melitene in Armenia, Euthymius entered the priesthood and in due course became head of a group of monastic communities in Armenia. Around the age of 30, however, he felt the need to seek out a solitary life and consequently travelled in Palestine and there lived the life of a nomadic recluse for some five years. Eventually he accepted the leadership of the group of disciples that had been attracted to him and thus became a prominent figure in the early history of Palestinian monasticism, emphasizing the need for discipline but discouraging penances that might encourage pride. Through his influence many Arabs in the area converted to the Christian faith. The fame of Euthymius became such that those who sought out his advice included the Empress Eudoxia, widow of Theodosius II, who consulted him about family problems.
Feast Day: 20 January.

Euthymius the Younger   (c.824–898) Turkish abbot. Born near Ankara, he abandoned his wife and infant child in order to become a monk, living initially with a religious community on Mount Olympus in Bithynia and later, seeking a more solitary life, as a hermit in a cave on Mount Athos. After three years of this life he moved to a tower near Salonika, but eventually gave up the solitary life under pressure from the crowds who came to hear him preach. He went on to re-found (870) the monastery at Peristera, near Salonika, and also established a convent before returning to Athos and ultimately dying on the island of Hiera nearby. Various rumours subsequently circulated attributing to him a range of miraculous powers, including the gift of prophecy.
Feast Day: 15 October.

Ewald   *See* HEWALD THE BLACK AND HEWALD THE WHITE.

Eystein   (d.1188) Norwegian bishop. Born into a wealthy family at Trondheim, Eystein (or **Augustine**) Erlendsson was educated in Paris and on
his return became chaplain to the king. He was appointed archbishop of
Trondheim in 1157 and spent the next 30 years promoting the independence of the Norwegian church from the nobility and establishing
Cistercian and Augustinian monasteries. He also consolidated the church's
links with Rome, as a result of which Pope Alexander III made him a
papal legate. He played an active role in the drawing up of legislation and
in the political life of the country, but in 1181 was forced into exile in
England after supporting King Magnus V against his rival Sverre. While
living at the abbey of Bury St Edmunds he wrote an account of the life of
St OLAF. He returned home in 1183, mending relations with King Sverre
and setting about the rebuilding of his cathedral. He was recognized as a
saint by the Norwegian bishops in 1229.
Feast Day: 26 January.

F

Fabian (d.250) Roman pope and martyr. Fabian was a humble farmer who, according to legend, became pope in 236 when a dove marked him out by settling on his head and thus indicating this unknown stranger in town as God's choice for his representative on earth. Fabian distinguished himself for his holiness and hard work during his 14 years in office, which ended with his martyrdom when he became the first Christian in Rome to be put to death under the persecution ordered by Decius. It was probably Fabian who took the important step of reorganizing the church in Rome into seven deaconries. Today he is honoured as the patron saint of lead-founders and potters.
Feast Day: 20 January.

Fabiola (d.399) Roman noblewoman. The daughter of a Roman patrician, Fabiola was a devout but energetic woman, to whom a life of religious seclusion had little appeal. She married but was subsequently criticized by fellow-Christians for gaining a divorce from her abusive spouse and taking a new husband. She was later readmitted to the fold after the death of her second husband and her completion of public penance. Subsequently she dedicated her wealth to doing good deeds and in 395 visited St JEROME in Bethlehem, before fleeing the Holy Land under threat from invading Huns and returning to Rome via Jaffa. Her most significant achievements including the foundation at Porto of a hospice for needy pilgrims.
Feast Day: 27 December.

Faelan *See* FOILLAN.

Faith (d.3rd century) French martyr. Born into a Christian family in Agen, Aquitania, Faith (otherwise called **Foi** or **Foy**) dedicated her life to Christ as a child. While still a young girl, she refused to leave Agen under the persecution of the Romans and was arrested on the orders of the Roman prefect Dacian. When demands that she make sacrifices to the goddess Diana proved fruitless she was sentenced to be roasted alive on a gridiron. So extreme was her suffering under this torture, however, that her captors took pity on her and she was beheaded instead alongside other fellow martyrs. Her remains were buried in secret by her friends. Veneration of

Faith's name reached a peak throughout England and France in medieval times.
Feast Day: 6 October.

Faustina Kowalska   (1905–1938) Polish nun. Born Helena Kowalska into a peasant family in Glogowiec, Poland, she joined the Congregation of the Sisters of Our Lady of Mercy in Warsaw in 1925. In 1931, while performing domestic service in the convent, she had a vision of Christ commanding her to spread the message of divine mercy around the world. Although virtually illiterate, Faustina went on to make detailed records of her many visions and manifestations of stigmata, later published as *Divine Mercy in My Soul*, and to found the Divine Mercy movement, which soon attracted thousands of adherents throughout Poland and beyond. Under orders received in one of her visions Faustina also commissioned a widely-reproduced painting of Christ, with red and white beams of light emanating from his heart. She was canonized in 2000.
Feast Day: 5 October.

Faustinus   *See* SIMPLICIUS, FAUSTINUS AND BEATRICE.

Faustus of Riez   (*c*.400–*c*.490) French bishop. Probably born in Brittany, he joined the island monastery of Lérins as a monk in 426 and eventually became abbot there, establishing a reputation as an inspiring preacher and steadfast observer of monastic rule. Around 460, having led his monastery with distinction for a quarter of a century, he was promoted to the rank of bishop of Riez in Provence, but – being an outspoken opponent of Arianism and Pelagianism – was subsequently ousted from the post by the Arian Visigoth king Euric. He resumed his pastoral duties after Euric's death and was widely mourned on his own death at the advanced age of 90.
Feast Day: 28 September.

Felician   *See* PRIMUS AND FELICIAN.

Felicity of Carthage   *See* PERPETUA AND FELICITY.

Felicity of Rome   (2nd century) Roman martyr. Felicity is variously identified as the leader, or possibly the sister or even the mother, of a group of seven Christian men martyred for their faith in ancient Rome during the reign of Antoninus Pius. Evidence for the legend of Felicity and the so-called **Seven Brothers** is scant but their veneration became well established in the early Roman church. The story runs that the group refused to recant their faith or to make sacrifices to pagan gods and were consequently put to death, Felicity being the last to die. It has been suggested that the legend may have come about through imitation of the biblical story of the Machabees.

Feast Day: 23 November.

Felix and Adauctus   (dates unknown) Roman martyrs. According to legend, Felix was a Christian priest in Rome who during the persecution of Diocletian was sentenced to death for his faith. As Felix was being led to his execution a stranger in the crowd declared that he was also a Christian and would die alongside Felix. The two men were killed and buried on the Ostian Way. Because no one knew the name of the second man he was dubbed Adauctus (meaning 'additional one').

Feast Day: 30 August.

Felix of Dunwich   (d.648) English bishop. Little is known of Felix's early career beyond the fact that he was born in Burgundy and at some point left Gaul for England. By now a bishop, Felix was ordered by HONORIUS OF CANTERBURY to embark on a mission to promote the Christian church in East Anglia at the request of Sigebert, the Christian king of the region. Felix accordingly settled at Dunwich and did much over the next 17 years to advance the church among the East Angles, his various good deeds including the establishment of a boys' school at Dunwich, staffed by teachers from Canterbury, and the foundation of a monastery at Soham, where Felix was eventually buried. The town of Felixstowe was named in Felix's honour.

Feast Day: 8 March.

Felix of Nola   (d. *c.*260) Italian priest. A priest at Nola, near Naples, which was also his birthplace, Felix was imprisoned and tortured during the persecutions that occurred under the Emperor Decius in 250 but eventually managed to escape, apparently by miraculous means. He went on to shelter his bishop, Maximus, who was also being hunted and in poor health, but when Maximus died declined to accept the post of bishop himself, preferring to pursue the simple life of a lowly priest. Felix was credited with many conversions and miracles, as subsequently related by PAULINUS OF NOLA and by the VENERABLE BEDE. After his death his church at Nola, where he was buried, became a famous centre of pilgrimage.

Feast Day: 15 November.

Felix of Thibiuca (247–303) Carthaginian bishop. Little is known of the early career of Felix of Thibiuca, in northern Africa, prior to him becoming a bishop and in due course becoming one of the more prominent martyrs to die during the persecution of Christians instituted by the Emperor Diocletian. When the bishop was ordered to surrender to the authorities all the Christian writings in his possession, so that they could be burned, he refused and was arrested. He was given three days to reconsider his decision, but undaunted he repeated his defiance of the order before the proconsul at Carthage and was accordingly beheaded for his disobedience, thus becoming one of the first victims of Diocletian's persecutions. *Feast Day: 15 July.*

Ferdinand III of Castile (1199–1252) Spanish king. Born near Salamanca, the son of Alfonso IX of León and Berengaria of Castile, he ascended to the throne of Castile in 1217 and to that of León in 1230, thus uniting the two kingdoms. Under his leadership over the next 27 years his armies seized much of Andalusia from Moorish control and made it Christian. He showed tolerance towards the Muslims and Jews who remained after the ousting of the Moors and his judges were praised for their impartiality. He also founded the university of Salamanca and rebuilt the cathedral at Burgos. He was canonized in 1671, 400 years after his death, and is honoured as the patron saint of local rulers, prisoners and the poor. *Feast Day: 30 May.*

Fergal *See* VIRGIL.

Feuillan *See* FOILLAN.

Fiacre (d. *c.*670) Irish hermit. Fiacre (or **Fiachra**) lived as a monk in Ireland before undertaking voluntary exile in France and living the life of a hermit on a piece of ground near the French town of Meaux. There he established a well-known hospice for needy travellers (now the site of the town of Saint-Fiacre-en-Brie). Although a generous man, tradition has it that he was adamant in forbidding women from entering his hermitage or his chapel – possibly because of or a reason for his role as patron of people suffering from venereal disease. After Fiacre's death his shrine became a place of pilgrimage, particularly favoured by those seeking miraculous cures for haemorrhoids. Because of his skill as a gardener Fiacre is also honoured as the patron saint of gardeners and is usually depicted with a spade. His name is further preserved in the French name

for a taxi cab, *fiacre*, a link that came about because the first four-wheel hackney carriages in Paris set out from the Hôtel Saint-Fiacre.
Feast Day: (France and Ireland) 1 September, (elsewhere) 30 August.

Fidelis of Sigmaringen (1577–1622) German martyr. Born Mark Roy in Sigmaringen (Hohenzollern), he practiced initially as a lawyer, representing the poor and other vulnerable persons, before despairing of the corruption he encountered in secular life and ultimately joining the Capuchin branch of the Franciscans in 1612. Under his new name Fidelis of Sigmaringen, he built a considerable reputation as a preacher and was head of three houses in turn in the years 1618–22. He died a martyr's death in 1622 after he attempted to preach to schismatic Zwinglians in the hope of healing the rift that had opened between them and the Church of Rome. The resentful Zwinglians responded by inciting a mob to murder him in the church at Seewis in Switzerland. He was canonized in 1746.
Feast Day: 24 April.

Fillan (d. *c.*777) Scottish hermit. Fillan (otherwise called **Foelan** or **Fulan**) was born the son of an Irish prince exiled to Scotland and lived the life of a hermit at Pittenweem in Fife prior to becoming abbot of the monastery on Holy Loch in Argyle. He remained there for several years before resigning the post in order to resume his earlier life as a hermit, this time at Glendochart (later Strathfillan) in Perthshire. Here he consolidated his reputation as a miracle-worker and holy man noted for great wisdom, many legends accruing around his name. Centuries after the hermit's death, the Scottish warrior-king Robert the Bruce, who carried a relic of the saint's arm with him, credited his victory at Bannockburn to Fillan's intercession and in gratitude restored the monastery at Strathfillan as an Augustinian priory.
Feast Day: 26 August.

Finan (d.661) Irish bishop. An Irish monk on Iona, Finan earned a reputation for wisdom and prudence and in due course succeeded St AIDAN as bishop of Lindisfarne in 651. With the patronage of King Oswiu of Northumbria he consolidated the church at Lindisfarne, building the wooden church there, and also continued Aidan's missionary campaign in Mercia and East Anglia. Significant achievements in this campaign included the baptism of Peada, king of the Middle Angles, and of Sigebert, king of the East Saxons, events that greatly facilitated the promulgation of Christianity among their peoples. Finan was also noted among his contemporaries as a stalwart defender of the Celtic dating of Easter.

Feast Day: 17 February.

Finbar (d. *c.*610) Irish bishop. Finbar (otherwise called **Finbarr, Findbarr, Barra, Barr** or **Barry**) was born the son of a metal-worker in County Cork but later took up the life of a hermit at Lake Gougane Barra and in time the small religious community that congregated around him there developed into the monastery of Etargabail. This monastery became famous as a centre of religious learning, attracting scholars from all over Ireland. Finbar went on to found many other churches as well as the monastery at Cork, which triggered the growth of the city itself. He is said to have been consecrated first bishop of Cork around the year 600; after his death he became the focus of a considerable cult in Ireland and Scotland and the monastery at Gougane Barra became, and remains, a place of pilgrimage. Tradition claims that Finbar visited St DAVID in Wales and that together they made a pilgrimage to Rome, but there is no historical evidence for this. Today Finbar is honoured as the patron saint of Barra in Scotland and of Cork in Ireland.

Feast Day: 25 September.

Fingar *See* GWINEAR.

Finnian of Clonard (d. *c.*549) Irish abbot. Born in Leinster, Finnian studied the monastic way of life in Wales and subsequently played an influential role in the early monastic movement in Ireland, founding a number of important religious houses, of which the most important was the monastery at Clonard, in Meath. This foundation became well known as a centre of religious learning and attracted thousands of disciples, among them such notable names as St COLUMBA and St BRENDAN THE VOYAGER. There is some doubt over whether Finnian was ever consecrated bishop but he was much respected as a teacher, dubbed the 'Master' or 'Teacher of the Saints of Ireland'. He died during an epidemic of the plague sweeping Ireland, supposedly accepting death from the disease in order to save the rest of his flock from a similar fate.

Feast Day: 12 December.

Finnian of Moville (d. *c.*579) Irish bishop. Allegedly of royal birth, Finnian (otherwise called **Finnio** or **Winin**) studied at Dromore and at the monastery of Whithorn under St NINIAN but had to leave the latter institution after a local girl fell in love with him, threatening a scandal. He

travelled to Rome and while there was ordained as a priest before
returning to Ireland and establishing religious communities at Moville in
Ulster and also at Holywood and Dumfries in Scotland. The religious
school at Moville became famous and Finnian himself, who was well-
known for his love of books, won renown as a teacher and scholar. Among
those attracted to him was St COLUMBA, with whom he is said to have
clashed over the latter's possession of an unauthorized transcription of
St Jerome's psalter.
Feast Day: 10 September.

Fintan of Clonenagh   (d.603) Irish abbot. Born in Leinster, Fintan
was renowned for his austere way of life as head of the monastery of
Clonenagh in Leix, of which he was the founder. Such was the strictness of
his regime that Fintan and the monks in his charge ate only stale barley
bread and muddy water and they denied themselves the assistance of
animals in working their fields, which they tilled with the simplest tools.
When neighbouring monks criticized Fintan for this severity he responded
with such gentleness that the criticisms were soon dropped.
Feast Day: 17 February.

Flannan   (7th century) Irish bishop. The life of Flannan is largely a matter
of legend. Allegedly of royal birth, he is said to have prayed for some
physical deformity to enable him to avoid having to succeed to the throne
and was accordingly afflicted with scars and boils. Free to pursue the life of a
monk, he became a disciple of MOLUA, the founder of the monastery of
Killaloe, and spent much of the rest of his career as an itinerant preacher. He
is reputed to have made a pilgrimage to Rome (one legend claiming that he
floated all the way there on a stone). Churches at Lough Corrib and Inishbofin are supposed to have been founded by Flannan and his memory is
preserved in the name of the Flannan Islands west of Lewis and Harris.
Feast Day: 18 December.

Foi   *See* FAITH.

Foillan   (d. *c*.655) Irish monk. Foillan (otherwise called **Faelan** or **Feuillan**) accompanied his brothers St FURSEY and St ULTAN to East Anglia in
630 and there founded the Benedictine monastery of Cnobheresburg
(Burgh Castle), near Yarmouth. Foillan succeeded Fursey as abbot of the
monastery but subsequently, when driven out by invading Mercians, he
and Ultan joined their brother in Neustria, where they enjoyed the protec-

tion of Clovis II. Foillan spent the rest of his life in France and Belgium, founding a new monastery at Fosses on land given to him by Abbess Itta of Nivelles. Remembered for his missionary zeal among the inhabitants of the Fosses area, he finally met his death at the hands of outlaws on returning from Nivelles and passing through the forest of Seneffe. *Feast Day: 31 October.*

Fortunatus   *See* VENANTIUS FORTUNATUS.

Forty Martyrs of England and Wales   (16th–17th centuries) A group of Roman Catholic martyrs who were put to death for their faith in England and Wales in the 16th and 17th centuries. This period of persecution of Catholics began during the reign of Henry VIII and lasted for some 150 years, during which time it claimed the lives of a wide range of clerics and lay people. In alphabetical order, the 40 individuals singled out were: John Almond, EDMUND ARROWSMITH, Ambrose Barlow, John Boste, Alexander Briant, EDMUND CAMPION, MARGARET CLITHEROW, Philip Evans, Thomas Garnet, Edmund Gennings, Richard Gwyn, John Houghton, Philip Howard, John Jones, John Kemble, Luke Kirby, Robert Lawrence, David Lewis, Anne Line, John Lloyd, Cuthbert Mayne, Henry Morse, Nicholas Owen, John Paine, Polydore Plasden, John Plessington, Richard Reynolds, John Rigby, John Roberts, Alban Roe, Ralph Sherwin, Robert Southwell, John Southworth, John Stone, John Wall, Henry Walpole, Margaret Ward, Augustine Webster, Swithun Wells and Eustace White. Their alleged crimes ranged from refusal to take the Oath of Supremacy to harbouring priests. The so-called Forty Martyrs of England and Wales were canonized in 1970. *Feast Day: 25 October.*

Forty Martyrs of Sebaste   (d.320) A group of 40 Roman soldiers who were put to death for their Christian faith during the persecution of Christians in the East ordered by Emperor Licinius. The soldiers, who were stationed with the 12th Legion at Sebaste (now Sivas) in Turkey, refused pressure from the local governor to give up their religion, resisting all manner of persuasion, including torture. Ultimately the exasperated governor had them all stripped and forced them to spend a whole night naked on a frozen lake outside the city, tempting them with fires and warm baths set up on the bank. All but one of the soldiers stubbornly froze to death without recanting their faith: the single man who surrendered to the governor's demands died after being placed in a hot bath and was replaced by another man who, moved by the courage of the others, also declared himself to be a Christian. He too died, keeping the number of martyrs at 40.

Feast Day: 10 March (suppressed 1969).

Foster   *See* VEDAST.

Four Crowned Martyrs   (d.306) There are two different versions of who exactly the Four Crowned Martyrs (or **Quattro Coronati**) were. According to the first of these, they were actually five Persian stone-carvers who died for their faith in Pannonia during the persecution of Christians instituted by the Emperor Diocletian (the reason why the fifth man, named Simplicius, was left out is obscure, although one suggestion is that he only adopted Christianity because he thought this was the key to the fine work of his companions). The legend describes how Simplicius, together with his colleagues Simpronian, Claudius, Nicostratus and Castorius, refused to make a statue of Aesculapius for Diocletian and, when they further refused to make sacrifices to the god, were sealed in lead coffins and thrown into the river to drown. As a result of their martydom they were particularly revered by stonemasons in medieval times. The second version of the story identifies the Four Crowned Martyrs as four Roman soldiers who were beaten to death during the reign of Diocletian after refusing to show respect for the image of Aesculapius in the Baths of Trajan in Rome.

Feast Day: 8 November.

Fourteen Holy Helpers   (15th century) A group of saints who were commonly called upon for divine protection in the 15th and 16th centuries. The Fourteen Holy Helpers (or **Fourteen Auxiliary Saints**) first acquired cult status in the years 1346–49 when the Black Death was raging through Europe. In the 1440s a shepherd boy of Bamberg, Bavaria, claimed to have met apparitions of the Fourteen Holy Helpers and been instructed by them to build a chapel in their honour: the chapel that was eventually constructed became a popular site of pilgrimage, attracting pilgrims from several countries, and was eventually replaced by a great cathedral (completed in 1772). The saints in question are usually identified as Achatius, BARBARA, BLAISE, CATHERINE OF ALEXANDRIA, CHRISTOPHER, CYRICUS, DENYS, ERASMUS, EUSTACE, GEORGE, GILES, MARGARET OF ANTIOCH, PANTALEON and VITUS, all having their own individual feast days.

Foy   *See* FAITH.

Frances of Rome   (1384–1440) Italian noblewoman. Born into a wealthy family in Rome, she married at the age of 13 and bore her husband several children but really longed for the life of a nun. She dedicated herself to charitable activities, helping to alleviate the distresses of the poor and those suffering due to epidemics of plague and the outbreak of war and, to further these efforts, in 1425 established a society to organize such good works. In 1433 she founded a Benedictine community of devout women called the Oblates of Tor de' Specchi, into which she retreated herself after the death of her husband in 1436. Apart from her good works, Frances of Rome was also said to have had many mystical experiences, including visions and visitations by angels. She was canonized in 1608.
Feast Day: 9 March.

Frances Xavier Cabrini   (1850–1917) Italian-born US foundress. Born Frances Cabrini into an Italian farming family in Lombardy, she dreamed as a child of becoming a missionary and adopted the additional name Xavier in honour of the great missionary leader FRANCIS XAVIER. She was twice turned down as a nun on health grounds but was instead recruited to help run an orphanage in Codogno. When this failed, she went on to found (1880) the Missionaries of the Sacred Heart to organize schools and orphanages for the poor. Kindhearted but practical and morally strict, she oversaw the rapid growth of this organization before, in 1889, leading a group of her assistants to New York to undertake work with needy Italian immigrants there. Such was her success that soon the society had opened branches in many other cities around the world, with some 68 houses dedicated to the care of poor orphans by the time of Cabrini's death in 1917 (although her rigid moral code forbade allowing illegitimate children into the homes). Honoured as the patron saint of immigrants, Frances Xavier Cabrini became (1946) the first US citizen to be canonized.
Feast Day: 13 November.

Francis of Assisi   (1181–1226) Italian founder of the Franciscan order. Born Francesco Bernadone into a wealthy family of Assisi in Italy, he had a dissolute youth and fought as a soldier before being taken prisoner in 1202 and ultimately returning home because of poor health. After experiencing a vision, he decided to dedicate himself to the service of God, taking a strict vow of poverty and adopting a simple, faithful lifestyle. He began by restoring the dilapidated church of San Damiano, but later saw the restoration of the church in a more general sense as his duty. Subsequently he travelled extensively in central Italy as an itinerant preacher, attracting many disciples and going on to found the highly influential order of the Friars Minor for men and, with his friend St CLARE, a parallel religious community called the Poor Clares for women. Members of these orders were encouraged to give up all their possessions and to imitate the simple lifestyle of Francis himself. In 1219 Francis led a group of his friars east in the hope of converting the enemies of Christianity in Palestine and Egypt, but he failed to have much success in this and soon returned home to tackle the issues raised by the burgeoning expansion of the movement he had started. In 1224, while praying in retreat on Mount Alvernia, Francis is said to have seen a vision of an angel nailed to a cross and to have received the stigmata of Christ's wounds. The pain of these persisted until his death two years later, at the premature age of 45, by which time his order numbered several thousand (though he himself was never ordained as a priest). Francis is especially remembered today for his gentleness and for his readiness to see God's presence in all aspects of nature, as evidenced by his love of animals. The Franciscan order (as the movement founded by Francis became known) spread throughout Europe and the world and Francis himself became one of the most celebrated and best-loved of all the saints. He was canonized in 1228 and is honoured today as the patron saint of ecologists, animals, Assisi and Italy. His emblem is a bird.

Feast Day: 4 October.

Francis of Comporosso   (1804–1866) Italian laybrother. Born Giovanni Croese into a farming family in Liguria, he joined the Franciscan friary at Sestri Ponente near Genoa but subsequently left them to become a member of the more rigorous Capuchin order. In due course he rose to the rank of questor in Genoa, his duties including the begging of food for the other brothers and himself. When cholera broke out in Genoa in 1866 he was unflinching in setting about ministering to the ill and went so far as to offer his own life to God in exchange for a halt in the epidemic. He soon contracted the disease himself and died, upon which the epidemic ceased. He was canonized in 1962.

Feast Day: 17 September.

Francis of Paola   (1416–1507) Italian founder of the Franciscan Minim Friars. Born in Paola, Calabria, he joined the Franciscan Friars Minor at the age of 13 and undertook pilgrimages to Assisi and Rome before adopting the life of a hermit in a cave near his birthplace. In time he attracted a number of disciples and from these beginnings developed the community

known as the Minim Friars, whose lifestyle was based on humility and austerity. Francis himself established a reputation as a miracle-worker and prophet and, after moving to France, was summoned in 1482 by Louis XI on his deathbed in the hope that he would prolong the monarch's life. Instead he reconciled Louis to death and subsequently served as tutor to the future king Charles VIII. After his own death (at Tours in France) he became the subject of a cult in France, Italy and Mexico among other countries and was canonized in 1519. In 1943 he was named patron saint of sailors (a reference to a legend that he used his cloak as a boat and other miraculous seafaring stories connected with his name).
Feast Day: 2 April.

Francis Borgia   (1510–1572) Italian nobleman. Born the great-grandson of the notorious Pope Alexander VI, Francis Borgia became Marquis of Lombay and a trusted advisor of Emperor Charles V, who eventually rewarded his service by making him viceroy of Catalonia. He finally abandoned the court in 1539 and came under the influence of PETER OF ALCANTARA and PETER FAVRE. He succeeded his father as Duke of Gandia in 1543 but four years later, after the death of his wife, he fulfilled his long-term ambition to live a religious life by passing all his wealth to his children and joining the Jesuits. Despite his hopes of a life of contemplative seclusion, his talents as an administrator led to his appointment by St IGNATIUS as the order's commissary for Spain, where he founded numerous seminaries and other institutions. In 1565 he became father-general of the Jesuit order worldwide and won recognition as the second founder of the society. He did much to consolidate and reorganize Jesuit activities in many countries and also furthered the expansion of Jesuit influence in the Americas, maintaining close contact with the order's missionaries in the New World. He died in Rome shortly after returning from a papal mission to strengthen an international alliance against the Turks. He was canonized in 1671 and is today honoured as the patron saint of Portugal. His emblem is a skull wearing an emperor's crown.
Feast Day: 10 October.

Francis Caracciolo   (1563–1608) Italian founder of the Lesser Clerks Regular. Born Ascanio Caracciolo, he became a priest and adopted the name Francis in honour of St FRANCIS OF ASSISI. In 1588 fellow-priest John Augustine Adorno conceived the idea of a new order of priests and wrote to Ascanio Caracciolo to ask for his help: as it happened he wrote to the

wrong Ascanio Caracciolo, but the two nevertheless became firm friends and the resulting order prospered. He was canonized in 1807.
Feast Day: 4 June.

Francis de Sales (1567–1622) French bishop. Born into a noble family in Thorens, Savoy, he worked as a lawyer but defied his parents' expectations of a prominent secular career by becoming a priest, being ordained in 1593. He performed missionary work throughout the Chablais region, attracting many converts from Calvinism, and in time (1602) rose to the rank of bishop of Geneva, establishing himself as a leading figure of the Counter-Reformation. He was noted both as a priest and as an administrator and educator, numbering among his disciples St JANE DE CHANTAL, with whom he founded the Order of the Visitation in 1610. His many writings included the influential *Introduction to the Devout Life* and *Treatise on the Love of God*. He was canonized in 1665 and today is honoured as the patron saint of writers and of the Catholic press.
Feast Day: 24 January.

Francis di Girolamo (1642–1716) Italian Jesuit. Born near Taranto, he became a priest in Naples but at the age of 28 decided to join the Jesuit order. After his request to be sent as a missionary to Japan was declined, he spent the rest of his life working as a commissioner for the order in the Naples area, earning a reputation as a preacher among the oppressed and deprived members of the community, including the lowest of criminals and paupers. He won many converts to Christianity among Turkish and Moorish prisoners and became particularly well-known for his work among needy children. Dubbed the 'Apostle of Naples', he acquired iconic status among the poor of the city and he was credited with many miraculous cures. He was canonized in 1839.
Feast Day: 11 May.

Francis Solano (1549–1610) Spanish Franciscan missionary. Born in Montilla in Andalusia, he was educated by the Jesuits and at the age of 20, inspired by the example of St FRANCIS OF ASSISI, entered a Franciscan monastery. He became a priest in 1576 and distinguished himself for his selflessness in treating victims of black typhus during an epidemic a few years later. On being sent on a mission to Peru and northern Argentina in 1589, he determined first to learn the language of the local population – a feat he accomplished in just 14 days – and went on to have a huge impact upon the native inhabitants of the region through his sermons, winning thousands of converts to the Catholic church. He also became well-known, in imitation of St Francis of Assisi, for his gentleness towards animals. He spent the last years of his life among sinners in Lima and became known popularly as the 'Miracle-Worker of the New World'. He was canonized in 1726. He is the patron saint of Argentina, Bolivia, Paraguay and Peru. *Feast Day: 14 June.*

Francis Xavier   (1506–1522) Spanish Jesuit missionary. Born into a well-connected Spanish Basque family at the castle of Xavier near Sanguesa, Navarre, in Spain, he was educated in Paris and initially taught Aristotelian philosophy at the University of Paris. There he came under the influence of St IGNATIUS OF LOYOLA and became one of the small group of disciples who took a vow of chastity in 1536 and in due course co-founded the Society of Jesus. He was ordained as a priest in 1537 and spent most of the rest of his life doing missionary work abroad on behalf of the Jesuit order, mostly in India and the Far East, with his base being established in Goa. Over the years he won many thousands of converts (30,000 in India alone) and effectively laid the foundations for the Christian church in that part of the world. In doing so he earned a lasting personal reputation as the most influential missionary since St PAUL. He died while planning to enter China and was canonized in 1622. Today he is honoured as the patron saint of foreign missions, India and Pakistan. *Feast Day: 3 December.*

Frederic Ozanam   (1813–1853) Italian founder of the St Vincent de Paul Society. Born in Milan, he studied at the Sorbonne in Paris and while there established a reputation as a steadfast defender of the Catholic faith at a time when there was much criticism of the Catholic church. He also became known for his charitable work on behalf of the poor, often providing for them out of his own pocket, and attracted a number of sympathetic followers, who in due course formed the nucleus of the first conference of the St Vincent de Paul Society. The society grew rapidly and by 1837 boasted some 2000 members. Ozanam himself married and became a professor of literature at the Sorbonne, remaining a prominent figure in French public life until his premature death in Marseilles at the age of 40. *Feast Day: 8 September.*

Frideswide   (c.680–727) English abbess. Legend has it that Frideswide (or **Fridiswede**) was of royal blood but as a young woman got into trouble after attracting the amorous attentions of the youthful King Aethelbald of

Mercia, who wished to marry her. She fled to Oxford seeking refuge from his forceful advances, only to find her lover hot on her heels. In desperation she prayed to God for help and the young king was instantly struck blind. Aethelbald subsequently repented his pursuit and his sight was immediately restored. Frideswide for her part founded a convent on the site where she had uttered her prayer and remained there for the rest of her life. Historians have suggested that Frideswide was in fact the daughter of King Dida of Eynsham and served as the first abbess of a monastery for men and woman founded at Oxford by her father (now the site of Christ Church). Frideswide is best known today as the patron saint of the city and university of Oxford.
Feast Day: 19 October.

Fructuosus of Tarragona   (d.259) Spanish bishop. The details of the life of Fructuosus of Tarragona are obscure beyond the story of his martyrdom. Legend claims that he was arrested by the Romans together with his deacons Augurius and Eulogius and charged by the Roman governor Aemilianus with being a Christian, in defiance of an imperial order insisting upon the worship of the pagan gods. When the three men refused to recant, they were taken to the amphitheatre in Tarragona and burned to death, saying prayers to the last.
Feast Day: 21 January.

Frumentius   (d. *c*.380) Tyrian-born bishop. Details about the life of Frumentius are uncertain, but it would appear that he arrived in Ethiopia in company with fellow-Tyrians Aedisius and Meropius (a philosopher). Meropius was murdered but the remaining two were granted the protection of the royal court of Axum. Frumentius promoted the opening of chapels throughout Ethiopia and also undertook missionary work on his own account. When he visited Alexandria to request the sending of a bishop to Ethiopia, he was chosen to fulfil this role himself and he returned to Ethiopia to win many converts to the church.
Feast Day: 27 October.

Fursey   (d.650) Irish abbot. Fursey (or **Fursa**) lived as a monk in Ireland before migrating to East Anglia around 630, where he and his companions (who included St FOILLAN) enjoyed the protection of King SIGEBERT, establishing a monastery at Cnobheresburg (Burgh Castle), near Yarmouth. After the death of Sigebert he moved to France and founded a new monastery at Lagny-sur-Marne. He was credited with having various visions of the afterlife, including glimpses of heaven and hell. As recorded by BEDE, who testified to Fursey's holiness, these revelatory experiences remain one of the earliest such visions of which records survive. After the saint's death at Mézerolles in the Somme region, he became the subject of a substantial cult and his shrine at Péronne became a site of pilgrimage.

Feast Day: 16 January.

G

Gabriel the Archangel   The biblical angel of the annunciation of the birth of both John the Baptist and Jesus Christ. Gabriel is identified in the Old Testament (at Daniel 8:15 and 9:21) as the angel who appears to Daniel, and in the New Testament reappears (at Luke 1:11–20) to Zachariah, father of the unborn John the Baptist, and to Mary (Luke 1:26–38) to announce the coming birth of Christ. He is known to have been revered by early Roman Christians and was included among the saints from at least the 7th century, if not much earlier. Subsequently he appeared frequently in religious art of the medieval period. In reference to his role as a messenger of God, Gabriel has been honoured as the patron saint of the post office and of telecommunication workers since 1921. His emblems in art are a spear and a shield emblazoned with a lily.
Feast Day: 29 September.

Gabriel Francis Possenti   (1838–1862) Italian cleric. Born Francis Possenti, the son of a prominent lawyer in Spoleto, Italy, he showed little interest in religion as a child until he reached his teenage years, when he resisted an impulse to become a priest. He considered the possibility on a further two occasions when he lay seriously ill but it was not until the death from cholera of a beloved sister that he finally entered a religious community called the Passionist Order under the name Gabriel of Our Lady of Sorrows. Although he lived only another four years, dying of tuberculosis at the age of 24, before reaching ordination, he established a reputation for patience and kindness and a cheerful determination to enjoy even the humdrum routines of daily life. He was canonized in 1920 and is honoured today as the patron saint of clerics and youth.
Feast Day: 27 February.

Gabriel Lalement   *See* NORTH AMERICA, MARTYRS OF.

Gall   (d. *c*.630) Irish monk. Probably a native of Leinster, Gall came under the influence of St COLUMBAN after joining the monastery at Bangor in northern Ireland. In 590 he accompanied Columban on his missionary journey to the mainland of Europe and went on to assist him in the

foundation of monasteries at Annegray and Luxeuil. The monks were forced to leave the area in 610 after offending the local rulers and moved to Switzerland, where they settled beside Lake Constance. Gall became well-known as a preacher but was forbidden by Columban to celebrate mass in his absence after Gall failed to accompany him to Italy because (he claimed) of illness. In Columban's absence Gall established a hermitage on the Steinach River, preferring to live a simple, solitary life with a small number of companions and refusing all invitations to take up the post of abbot or bishop. The site of this hermitage was later occupied by a famous monastery and town bearing his name. Gall is honoured today not only as the patron saint of Sweden and Switzerland but also as the patron saint of birds (a linkage of uncertain origin).
Feast Day: 16 October.

Gaudentius of Brescia   (d. *c*.410) Italian bishop. Gaudentius was a humble but popular priest in Brescia, Italy, who preferred not to court public attention. While he was on pilgrimage to Jerusalem in 386, however, the bishop of Brescia died and in his absence Gaudentius was acclaimed the people's choice as his successor. When the local populace refused to contemplate any other candidate, Gaudentius reluctantly accepted the post. He was respected as a teacher and especially noted for his sermons, of which 21 survive. In 406 he was among the bishops selected by Pope Innocent I to support St JOHN CHRYSOSTOM before Emperor Arcadius in Constantinople. The bishops' representations were ignored, however, and they narrowly escaped for home with their lives.
Feast Day: 25 October.

Gelasius I   (d.496) Roman-born pope. The exact details of the life of Gelasius before his election as pope in 492 are unclear. Allegedly of African descent, the son of a man named Valerius, he was apparently born in Rome and may have served as a priest in the city before being raised to the pontificate. According to some, he may have acted as secretary to Pope St SIMPLICIUS and Pope St FELIX. During his relatively brief papal reign of just four and a half years he proved himself an effective pontiff, working (with mixed success) to establish the supremacy of the Roman church over Constantinople and promoting ecclesiastical discipline. He died penniless after giving all his money to the poor and was buried in St Peter's. Various of his writings have survived.
Feast Day: 21 November.

Gemma Galgani   (1878–1903) Italian laywoman. Gemma Galgani was
born into a poor family at Borgo Nuovo di Camigliano near Lucca and
dedicated herself to Christ as a child. While still a girl she decided upon a
life as a nun, but was denied the possibility of joining the Passionist
Congregation by chronic illness. She spent many hours in prayer and
professed to have had many visions of Christ, the Virgin Mary and a
guardian angel. Though such declarations made her an object of ridicule
among her family and friends, she insisted upon the truth of these experiences. Harder to pour scorn on, however, were the displays of Christ's
stigmata that appeared on her body periodically in the years 1899–1901,
as described by various witnesses. Wounds resembling those suffered by
Christ bled freely on her hands, feet and side every Thursday evening
and did not heal over until Sunday, causing Gemma much pain. She died
of nephritis and tuberculosis of the spine at the age of just 25. She was
canonized in 1940 and is honoured today as the patron saint of
tuberculosis sufferers and pharmacists.
Feast Day: 11 April.

Genesius of Arles   (d. *c*.303) French martyr. Genesius worked as a notary
whose job it was to make a written record of judicial proceedings in Arles.
When he was faced with the task of writing down an imperial edict
promoting the persecution of Christians he threw aside the register and
refused to continue, declaring himself to be a Christian. He fled the town
and sought shelter with a local bishop, hoping that he might be formally
baptized. The bishop declined to baptize him, fearing a trap, and he
was turned away, captured and beheaded, thus being baptized 'by his
own blood'. After his death he became the object of a considerable
cult following extending beyond France to Spain and ultimately Rome
itself.
Feast Day: 3 June.

Genesius the Actor   (dates unknown) Roman martyr. According to
tradition, Genesius was an actor in ancient Rome who took part in an
entertainment staged before the emperor Diocletian. The entertainment
comprised a parody of Christian baptism, but when Genesius was
subsequently presented to the emperor the actor explained that during the
performance he had undergone a revelatory conversion to the Christian
faith himself. He was promptly arrested and tortured. When he refused to
recant he was beheaded. There is little historical evidence in support of the

legend of Genesius, although similar stories are also linked to at least three other Roman actors.
Feast Day: 25 August.

Geneviève (*c.*422–*c.*500) French laywoman. Born in Nanterre, France, Geneviève (or **Genovefa**) was singled out for future holiness by St GERMANUS OF AUXERRE who spotted her in 429 when she was only seven years old in a crowd that had gathered to hear him speak as he passed through Nanterre on his way to Britain. In answer to his questions the girl told him that she was going to dedicate her life to God and accordingly, at the age of 15, she took a vow of virginity. She decided, however, to remain a laywoman and went to live with her godmother in Paris, where she busied herself praying and working on behalf of the poor (despite hostility from some quarters). When the Franks besieged Paris, Geneviève saved the city from starvation by leading a convoy of ships up the Seine to find supplies and thus became a national heroine. Similarly, in 451, when Attila the Hun's invading army unexpectedly skirted Paris the credit was placed on the prayers of Geneviève that the city might be spared. Long after her death her relics were carried in procession at times when the safety of the city was in question. Today Geneviève is honoured as the patron saint of Paris as well as of sufferers from drought and other disasters. Her emblem is a candle.
Feast Day: 3 January.

Gennaro *See* JANUARIUS.

Geoffrey of Amiens *See* GEOFFREY OF AMIENS.

George (d. *c.*303) Legendary dragon-slayer and martyr. The details of the life of St George (otherwise known as **George of Lydda**) have been the subject of considerable debate, but it would appear he may have been a Roman soldier who was martyred for his Christian faith during the reign of the emperor Diocletian. Some accounts identify him as a son of the Roman governor of Palestine who trained as a soldier in the Roman army and rapidly rose to the rank of general. He allegedly took part in a campaign against Persia and may even have participated in an expedition to Britain (although there is little evidence for this). He left the army around 298 when only those who worshipped the gods of Rome were allowed to remain in the armed forces but he subsequently spoke up on behalf of beleaguered Christians before the imperial court at Nicomedia. As punishment for his temerity, he was savagely tortured and beheaded at

or near Lydda. The familiar story of George and the dragon is a much later addition to his story, probably conceived some 900 years after his death. According to this, George was a knight from Cappadocia who happened upon a young woman who was about to be sacrificed by the people of Silene in Libya to a fierce dragon in order to appease its fury. George wounded the creature and brought it to the town but only killed it after the terrified local populace consented to be baptized as Christians. Today St George is honoured as the patron saint of England, Portugal, Genoa, Spain and Venice. His flag, a red cross on a white ground, was carried by knights fighting in the Crusades and is now considered the national flag of England. His emblem is a dragon.
Feast Day: 23 April.

Gerald of Aurillac   (*c*.855–909) French nobleman. Born the son of the count of Aurillac in Auvergne, he inherited the family estates and, despite poor health, distinguished himself for his fairness and competency as count in his turn. He was particularly respected for his piety, spending many hours in prayer, and considered becoming a monk himself, but was persuaded he could do more good as a layman. Around 890 he founded the celebrated monastery at Aurillac, which later became the home of the Cluniac order. His personal fame was ensured by a biography written by St ODO OF CLUNY.
Feast Day: 13 October.

Gerard of Csanad   (*c*.980–1046) Venetian-born bishop and martyr. Gerard of Csanad lived initially as a monk at San Giorgio Maggiore in Venice, also studying in Bologna, and in due course became abbot of the monastery. Some time later, however, he resigned his post in the hope of adopting a more solitary life in the Holy Land. When his journey to Palestine was disrupted by bad weather he sought shelter with an abbot in Hungary and remained there, in time being appointed tutor to the son of St STEPHEN OF HUNGARY, the king of the country, and subsequently living as a hermit in the forest of Bakony for seven years. In 1030 he accepted the role of first bishop of Csanad and performed much influential missionary work. In the upheaval following the death of King Stephen he was attacked and murdered by the former monarch's enemies while travelling from Csanad to Szekesfehervar and his remains thrown into the River Danube.
Feast Day: 24 September.

Gerard Majella   (1726–1755) Italian laybrother. Born at Muro Lucano in Italy, he worked in his youth as a tailor's apprentice and bishop's manservant and opened his own tailor's shop in 1745 but gave it up in 1752 in order to become a Redemptorist laybrother at the monastery of Caposele, Avellino. He never became a priest but worked instead in such lowly posts as porter and gardener at the monastery. Generous and pious in character, he soon became well known both for his penitential practices and for his extraordinary gifts, which included powers of healing and prophecy as well as the ability to be in two places at the same time in order to do God's work with greater efficiency. Such was his eagerness to spend every hour of the day in prayer that he had to use violence against himself in order to keep himself out of church all the time. He died prematurely at the age of 29 as a result of the combination of long-standing ill-health and of the exertions he made on behalf of the poor, upon which his superiors identified him as a model for all other laybrothers. Many miracles were attributed to him both during and after his lifetime and he was canonized in 1904.
Feast Day: 16 October.

Gereon   (d. *c.*304) Legendary martyr. Gereon (or **Geron**) is one of the haziest figures in the canon of saints, tentatively identified as the leader of a group of 50 Roman soldiers of the Theban Legion who were martyred in Cologne for their Christian faith in the late 6th century. A variant account suggests there were 330 martyrs in all. Gereon and his companions were venerated at the church of St Gereon in Cologne and in medieval times various tales were told of miracles associated with their supposed relics.
Feast Day: 10 October.

Germaine of Pibrac   (1579–1601) French peasant woman. Germaine Cousin was born in Pibrac near Toulouse the daughter of a poor French farmer and endured a short life full of disease and suffering. Afflicted with scrofula and crippled in the right hand, she lost her mother as a child and was cruelly treated by her stepmother, who made her live in a stable and live off kitchen scraps. She found some consolation in her religious faith and was well-known locally for her kindness to others. When she died, at the premature age of 22, she was allegedly witnessed ascending to heaven on a beam of light, accompanied by angels. Various miracles of healing were reported happening at her grave, which became a site of pilgrimage, and she was canonized in 1867.
Feast Day: 15 June.

Germanus of Auxerre   (c.378–448) French bishop. Born in Auxerre of
Gallo-Roman parents, he pursued a career as a lawyer in Rome and
married before returning to Gaul to take up the office of governor of
Amorica. In 418, however, he was forced against his will to accept the
position of bishop of Auxerre. Once in his post, he dedicated himself to his
Christian faith, taking a vow of poverty and foregoing all his previous
privileges and luxuries. He used his former wealth to support churches
and cathedrals within his diocese and founded a monastery at Auxerre. In
429 he and LUPUS OF TROYES were sent on a mission to bolster Catholicism
in England against the Pelagian heresy, doing much to consolidate the
church throughout Britain through their preaching and stories of miracles
associated with their names. While there he also played a key role in ward-
ing off a threatened raid by Picts and Saxons. He paid another visit to
Britain in 440 to complete the defeat of Pelagianism. He died in Ravenna
while attempting to prevent the sending of an imperial army to quash a
revolt in Amorica.
Feast Day: 31 July.

Germanus of Constantinople   (c.634–732) Patriarch of Constantinople.
Born into a wealthy patrician family, Germanus of Constantinople was the
son of a high-ranking government official. He served initially as a cleric at
the cathedral in Constantinople before becoming bishop of Cyzicus. An
orthodox, he clashed with the emperor Philippicus on theological issues
but returned to imperial favour with the succession of Anastasius to the
imperial throne. In 715 he was officially approved as patriarch of Constantinople by Pope Constantine. When he disagreed with Emperor Leo III the
Isaurian in 730 over the issue of the veneration of sacred images he sought
the support of Pope Gregory II but was ordered to prohibit the use of such
images in worship. Germanus refused to obey and was forced to resign his
post and spent the remainder of his very long life in retirement with his
family. Some of his writings have survived.
Feast Day: 12 May.

Germanus of Paris   (c.496–576) French bishop. Born near Autun in
Burgundy, he served as abbot of the monastery of St Symphorian in Autun
before his appointment as bishop of Paris around 556. He proved steadfast
in his efforts to end civil conflict when Burgundy was invaded by the
Franks and developed a constructive relationship with the Frankish kings
Theodebert and Childebert but had difficulty restraining the excesses of
Childebert's successor Charibert, whom he felt obliged to excommunicate.

He is also remembered as the founder of a monastery in Paris, later renamed Saint-Germain-des-Prés in his memory, and for the miracles of healing that became associated with him. Today he shares with St GENEVIÈVE the honour of being the patron saint of Paris.
Feast Day: 28 May.

Geron   *See* GEREON.

Gertrude   (1256–1302) Benedictine nun. The details of Gertrude's family background are obscure, but she was probably born near Eisleben in Saxony. At the age of five she began her education in the Benedictine nunnery of Helfta, becoming a pupil of St MECHTILD OF HELFTA. She took her vows as a nun at the age of 25 and remained at the nunnery for the rest of her life, dedicating herself to the veneration of the Sacred Heart and to the study of the scriptures. Sometimes called **Gertrude the Great**, she became perhaps the most renowned of all medieval visionaries, claiming to have undergone a profound spiritual conversion aged 26 and subsequently to have experienced numerous mystic revelations while at her devotions. Details of these visions were recorded in the *Revelations of St Gertrude*, the best-known of the writings of Gertrude and her mentor Mechtild that have survived. Though Gertrude was never formally canonized, her name was added to the canon of saints by papal command in 1677. She is honoured today as the patron saint of the West Indies.
Feast Day: 16 November.

Gertrude of Nivelles   (626–659) Abbess and visionary. Born at Landen in the Low Countries, she was the daughter of parents noted for their piety and the sister of St **Begga**. While still a young woman she was appointed abbess of the monastery at Nivelles founded by her mother in 640 and despite her youth proved very capable in the post, showing great wisdom in her decisions and offering hospitality to St FOILLAN and other Irish monks when they arrived in the area on missionary duty. She resigned from her position shortly before her premature death and became the subject of a considerable cult following. She is honoured as the patron saint of travellers, gardeners and the recently deceased. Her emblem is a pastoral staff with a mouse running up the shaft.
Feast Day: 17 March.

Gervase and Protase   (dates unknown) Roman martyrs. Nothing is known about the circumstances of the martyrdom of these two supposed early Christians, whose remains were discovered in Milan in 386. The

search for their decapitated bodies had been ordered by St AMBROSE, following some kind of dream or revelation in which he was alerted to their presence. Various miracles accompanied the retrieval of the bodies, which were transferred to the newly-completed cathedral of Milan and when Ambrose himself died he decreed that his own corpse should lie beside them. Historians have suggested a link between Gervase and Protase and the legend of Castor and Pollux.
Feast Day: 19 June.

Gilbert of Sempringham   (*c*.1085–1189) English founder of the Gilbertine Order. The son of a Norman nobleman, he was physically disabled and thus considered unsuitable for a military career. Instead he was appointed parson of Sempringham, which was part of his father's manor in Lincoln-shire, and – after being ordained as a priest and turning down the rank of archdeacon – settled there into an austere, devout way of life. In 1131 he founded his own order, assembling a religious community of young women on the Benedictine model in a house next to the church. The order prospered with the addition of laybrothers and sisters and, in 1148, with the introduction of chaplains to guide the nuns. In the years that followed the order spread with new monasteries being established throughout Lincolnshire and Yorkshire, complete with hospitals and orphanages. As an old man, Gilbert experienced political difficulties, being arrested by Henry II on charges of providing shelter to his recalcitrant archbishop St THOMAS BECKET (he eventually managed to obtain a royal pardon). He also had to cope with a rebellion among the laybrothers of his order, whose complaints about overwork and underfeeding were taken to Rome before the affair was settled in Gilbert's favour. He was over 100 years old when he died and was canonized in 1202. The Gilbertine Order (the only wholly English order ever founded) itself ceased to exist during the reign of Henry VIII, when the 20 or more houses that had been established by then were closed.
Feast Day: 4 February.

Gildas   (*c*.500–570) British monk. Details of the life of Gildas are scant, including the place of his birth, which may have taken place in the Clydeside region of Scotland. He is remembered chiefly as the author of *De excidio et conquestu Britanniae,* in which he delineates the many prob-lems facing Britain in the wake of the Roman occupation and indignantly criticizes the corruption of contemporary rulers, clergymen and people. Sometimes dubbed **Gildas the Wise**, he would appear to have been a

well-educated man with extensive biblical knowledge and, while a monk at Llaniltud in south Wales, is traditionally supposed to have contributed to the development of the church in Ireland through his teaching and many writings. He may also have lived at one time as a hermit on Flatholm Island in the Bristol Channel and is thought to have spent his last years living in Brittany, founding a monastery at Rhuys.
Feast Day: 29 January.

Giles   (d. *c.*710) French hermit. Giles (or **Aegidius**) is thought to have lived as a hermit at Saint-Gilles, near Arles, and to have founded a monastery there but the rest of his life is shrouded in legend. The most celebrated story concerning him describes how he was accidentally wounded by an arrow fired by the Visigoth king Wamba while protecting his pet deer, upon which the king's hunting hounds were miraculously rooted to the spot. Other tales describe how he received the confession of the emperor Charlemagne and how he received two beautiful doors as a gift from the Pope while on a visit to Rome. Giles ranked among the most popular of all saints during the medieval period, when he was considered the patron saint of cripples, beggars and blacksmiths. Many English churches were dedicated to him, as were such localities as St Giles Cripplegate in London and St Giles Street in Oxford. His emblem in art is an arrow.
Feast Day: 1 September.

Gleb   *See* BORIS AND GLEB.

Godelive   (*c.*1045–70) French martyr. Born in Boulogne, Godelive (otherwise called **GodelIva** or **Godeleine**) was the young deserted wife of a Flemish nobleman who suffered not only from her abandonment by her husband but also from cruel treatment at the hands of her mother-in-law. The bishop of Tournai-Noyon eventually obliged the husband, Bertulf of Ghistelles, to return to his wife, only for her to be strangled to death by two family retainers not long afterwards and attempts made to make her death appear to have resulted from natural causes. Although Bertulf was never convicted of the murder suspicions of his guilt were intensified by reports of miracles associated with Godelive's name and she soon acquired the status of a saint throughout Flanders. Her shrine in the church of Ghistelles became a site of pilgrimage.
Feast Day: 6 July.

Godfrey   (d.1115) French bishop. Godfrey (or **Geoffrey**) of Amiens was born near Soissons and attracted attention through his success in reviving the run-down monastery at Nogent-sous-Coucy, which prospered under his disciplined leadership. In 1104 his talents were officially recognized when he was appointed bishop of Amiens. He proved a stern master in this role, however, stamping out corrupt practices among the local clergy and in the process acquiring many enemies. In 1114 opposition to his reforms had become so fierce that he was obliged to retreat to the monastery of the Grande Chartreuse. He died a year later, before he could return to his troubled diocese. His name appears to have been first included in the canon of saints around the 16th century.

Feast Day: 8 November.

Godric   (c.1065–1170) English hermit. Born at Walpole near King's Lynn in Norfolk, Godric lived as a pedlar before establishing a career as a successful sea merchant. He sailed to many distant lands and in the course of these travels made several pilgrimages to holy sites in Jerusalem, Rome and elsewhere. By all accounts little more than a rogue in his early adulthood, his adventures included assisting King Baldwin I of Jerusalem's escape after the battle of Ramleh in 1102. Ultimately he settled down to the life of a scholar in Durham, eventually choosing the life of a hermit in a hut on the banks of the River Wear at Finchale, just outside Durham (now the site of Finchale Priory). Here he dedicated himself to a life of piety and penance to atone for the sins he had committed in his former life. Dressed in a hair shirt and metal breastplate, he became well-known for his gift of prophecy and was also noted for his sympathy with wild animals, even treating vipers as pets. Today he is chiefly remembered as the earliest lyrical poet in English, his surviving works being four scraps of verse together with tunes for these (earning him the extra distinction of being the first man to set words in English to music).

Feast Day: 21 May.

Gothard   (c.960–1038) German bishop. Born in the Bavarian village of Reichersdorf, Gothard (or **Godehard**) became a Benedictine monk and in due course rose to the rank of abbot. He went on to distinguish himself through his reform of several monasteries in Bavaria and in 1022 was appointed bishop of Hildesheim, in which role he proved very capable, winning lasting praise for his charitable activities. His most important achievements included the foundation of a hospice at Sankt Moritz just outside Hildesheim to provide shelter for the needy of the city. Although the sick and the poor were warmly welcomed here, those deemed to be professional tramps were not permitted to stay for more than a few days.

Gothard was canonized in 1131 and his memory is preserved today in the name of the St Gothard pass and railway tunnel connecting Switzerland and Italy.
Feast Day: 4 May.

Gregory I   *See* GREGORY THE GREAT.

Gregory II   (*c*.669–731) Roman pope. Born into a wealthy family in Rome, he became a Benedictine monk and in due course was raised to the rank of subdeacon under Pope Sergius. Subsequently he became treasurer of the Roman church and then librarian before accompanying Pope Constantine to Constantinople as deacon. He played a prominent role in securing Emperor Justinian II's acceptance of papal supremacy and when Constantine died in 715 was elected his successor as pope. An able pontiff, he repaired the walls of Rome, recaptured territories from the Lombards, warded off a Lombard invasion of the city, defended the church's independence from interference by the Greek emperor Leo III the Isuarian, and received many notable pilgrims in Rome. He also gave his support to the monastic movement, restoring the ruined abbey of Monte Cassino and even converting his family home into a monastery.
Feast Day: 11 February.

Gregory III   (d.741) Syrian-born pope. As a priest in Rome, Gregory became well-known both for his scholarship and for his piety. In 731 he was elected pope by acclamation while accompanying the funeral procession of his predecessor as pope, St GREGORY II. His ten-year papacy opened with the intensification of the dispute with Emperor Leo III on the subject of iconoclasm (the use of sacred images in worship) and led to the holding of two councils at which Gregory excommunicated those who destroyed such images. Subsequent events included the forging of an alliance with the Frankish king Charles Martel in order to defend the independence of the church and the promotion of missionary activity in Germany and elsewhere. In Rome itself Gregory built the oratory of Our Lady in the Vatican basilica of St Peter's to house the relics of the saints and ultimately was buried there himself.
Feast Day: 28 November.

Gregory VII   (*c*.1021–85) Italian pope. Born into a relatively humble family in Ravaco, Tuscany, and baptized Hildebrand, he became a Benedictine monk and in due course was appointed secretary to Pope Gratian (1045). Within a few months, however, Gratian was deposed and Gregory was obliged to accompany him into exile. In 1047 Gratian died and Gregory returned to monastic life. In 1049 he was summoned to Rome by Pope Leo IX, who made him a cardinal-subdeacon and administrator of the Patrimony of St Peter's. He went on to establish himself as the power behind the throne during the reigns of Popes Victor II, Stephen, Nicholas II and Alexander II before becoming pope himself in 1073. His 12-year reign witnessed many reforms and further efforts to maintain the church's independence from secular control, leading to confrontation with various kings and emperors who resisted Rome's supremacy. Among other reforms, he commanded that in future bishops could no longer be selected by secular rulers. This particular measure outraged Henry IV of Germany, resulting in his excommunication and, in retaliation, the besieging of Rome by a German army. Gregory called on Robert Guiscard of Sicily to break the siege, only for the city to be sacked by this second force and Gregory himself being forced into exile in Salerno, where he died. He was canonized in 1606.

Feast Day: 25 May.

Gregory of Nazianzus (*c*.329–*c*.390) Cappadocian patriarch. Born in Nazianzus, Cappadocia (in modern Turkey), Gregory of Nazianzus (or **Gregory Nazianzen**) was the son of wealthy Christian converts, his father being the bishop of Nazianzus. He was educated in Caesarea, Alexandria and Athens and was planning a career as a lawyer or rhetorician before being persuaded by his father to enter the church as a monk. Known as one of the three Cappadocian Fathers, alongside BASIL THE GREAT and GREGORY OF NYSSA, Gregory became patriarch of Constantinople in 380. A year later, though he longed for a solitary life, he presided over the Council of Constantinople, which condemned Arianism. He also produced some highly influential writings, among them sermons, poems and the five *Theological Discourses*.

Feast Day: 2 January.

Gregory of Nyssa (*c*.330–*c*.395) Cappadocian bishop. The younger brother of St BASIL THE GREAT and St MACRINA THE YOUNGER, he was born in Caesaria, trained for a career as a rhetorician and married before entering the church. Identified as one of the three Cappadocian Fathers, alongside St Basil and GREGORY OF NAZIANZUS, he became bishop of Nyssa in 371 and supported the orthodox position against the Arian heresy. A somewhat rash, tactless man, he was deposed by Arian opponents in 376 but was reinstated in 378 and appointed bishop of Sebaste in 380, playing a

prominent role at the Council of Constantinople the following year and becoming a greatly respected figure in the Eastern church. Many of his writings, including treatises and letters, survive. Dubbed the 'Father of Fathers', he is remembered as one of the greatest theologians of the early church.
Feast Day: 9 March.

Gregory of Sinai   (*c.*1290–1346) Mystic and monk. Born near Smyrna in Asia Minor, he survived the trauma of being taken prisoner with his family by Turks in his youth and subsequently became a monk on Cyprus. From there he moved to the monastery of St Catherine on Mount Sinai in Palestine, where he dedicated himself to a life of contemplative prayer. He went on to undertake a pilgrimage through the Holy Land and later visited monasteries and other religious establishments in Crete, Mount Athos in northern Greece, Constantinople and Thrace, communicating his ideas about prayer. He also established in Macedonia three communities devoted to contemplative prayer and a monastery on Mount Paroria in Bulgaria, where he died. His influential writings include *The 137 Chapters or Spiritual Meditations*.
Feast Day: 27 November.

Gregory of Tours   (*c.*538–*c.*594) French bishop and historian. Born Georgius Florentius into a wealthy Gallo-Roman family at Clermont-Ferrand, he became bishop of Tours in 573. Despite poor health, he showed great energy in meeting the many challenges he faced as bishop, including civil war and opposition from highly-placed political figures. On the whole, he succeeded in avoiding getting enmeshed in political issues and concentrated upon alleviating the suffering of the people. He also oversaw the rebuilding of Tours cathedral. Today, however, he is remembered chiefly as a historian. His most important writings included the *History of the Franks* and various biographical works concerning the lives of the martyrs, among them *Glory of the Martyrs* and *Life of the Fathers*.
Feast Day: 17 November.

Gregory the Enlightener   (*c.*240–*c.*326) Armenian bishop. The circumstances of the early life of Gregory the Enlightener (or **Gregory the Illuminator**) are obscure, though one story has it that he was the son of a Parthian who assassinated King Khosrov I of Armenia. He is said to have been brought up as a Christian at Caesarea in Cappadocia and to have married and fathered two sons before returning to Armenia. Here he is

supposed to have suffered persecution on the orders of King Tiridates
but eventually to have succeeded in converting the king to Christianity.
Subsequently he became bishop at Caesarea and spent most of the rest
of his life promoting the church throughout Armenia, being called the
'Enlightener' because he shed the light of Christ upon the lives of the
people. Shortly before his death he retired to a hermitage on Mount
Manyea, leaving his son Aristakes to succeed him as bishop. Today he is
honoured as the patron saint of Armenia.
Feast Day: 30 September.

Gregory the Great (*c*.540–604) Roman pope. Beyond the fact that he
was born into a noble family in Rome, the son of a senator, and was
attracted to the religious life from a young age, little is known of the
details of Gregory's early life. He was appointed prefect of Rome in 573
but a year later gave up this prestigious secular post in order to become a
monk and then a deacon and an abbot, turning his own home and his six
estates in Sicily into monasteries. Subsequently he was appointed ambassador to the court of Byzantium in Constantinople and became adviser to
Pope Pelagius II in Rome. He was elected to the papacy himself in 590
(thus becoming the first monk to become pope) and, ruling as **Gregory I**
over the next 13 years, assumed the leadership of the city, which was in a
ruinous state after barbarian invasions. As Rome's political leader he
provided spiritual and practical support as the population of Rome
struggled against famine, floods and plague, made peace with threatening
invaders and rebuilt the ravaged city, opposed slavery and withstood the
pressure of the rival Byzantine empire. As head of the church he instituted
sweeping reforms, promoted the Benedictine monastic movement, spon-
sored the Christianization of England and effectively laid the basis for the
political power of the medieval papacy. As well as being remembered as a
gifted orator and the originator of Gregorian chant, he also wrote prolifically upon religious matters, his books including the *Liber Regulae
Pastoralis*, which formulated the rules for religious observance, four
Dialogues, letters and biographies of the saints. He is honoured today as
the patron saint of musicians, singers and teachers.
Feast Day: 3 September.

Gregory the Wonderworker (213–*c*.270) Cappadocian bishop. Born into
a prominent pagan family of Neocaesarea, Pontus (in modern Turkey), he
converted to Christianity and ultimately was elected bishop of Neocaesarea
around 238. As bishop he had a profound impact upon the people of

Neocaesarea, converting virtually the entire population to Christianity. He was respected as an orator and also established a reputation for miracle-working, hence his title **Thaumaturgus** (meaning 'Wonderworker'). Among other celebrated deeds, he was alleged to have diverted rivers, dried up a lake, moved a mountain and assumed the form of a tree in order to deceive his pursuers during the persecution of Christians instituted by Decius in 250. His writings included the books *Oratio Panegyrica*, *Exposition of the Faith* and *Epostola Canonica*. He is sometimes identified as the patron saint of people in desperate situations, especially those threatened by floods or earthquakes.
Feast Day: 17 November.

Gregory Palamas   (*c.*1296–1359) Athonite archbishop. Probably born in Constantinople into a noble Anatolian family, he entered the monastery on Mount Athos together with two of his brothers following the death of his father and lived in solitude there under the rule of St BASIL for around 20 years. A respected pastor and teacher, he became a prominent defender of hesychasm (a form of prayer based on controlled breathing and posture, possibly influenced by Buddhist techniques) and was excommunicated for these beliefs in 1344, but three years later was nonetheless made bishop of Thessalonica after the imperial throne changed hands. Hesychasm (alternatively called Palamism in tribute to Gregory himself) was officially adopted by the Orthodox Church at Constantinople in 1351. He was canonized in 1368.
Feast Day: 14 November.

Gudule   (*c.*648–712) Belgian laywoman. Gudule (or **Cudula**) was of noble birth and received her religious education in the convent of her cousin St GERTRUDE OF NIVELLES. She settled in Brabant after the death of St Gertrude and became renowned for her pious way of life, travelling two miles early every morning to pray at the church at Moorsel. Much loved for her charitable deeds, she became the subject of a considerable cult following. When she died she was buried initially in front of the church door at Moorsel, although her remains were later moved to the magnificent church of St Gudule and St Michael in Brussels. Today she is honoured as the patron saint of Brussels.
Feast Day: 8 January.

Guénolé   *See* WINWALOE.

Guthlac   (*c.*673–714) English hermit. Born in Mercia of royal blood,

Guthlac fought as a soldier for King Ethelred of Mercia for several years before choosing the life of a monk at the monastery of Repton when he was 24. Guthlac's adoption of an austere way of life that prohibited the consumption of all alcohol met with some hostility at first but gradually his devotion to Christ won over his critics. Around 701 he decided upon a life of seclusion, moving into a hermitage on the bank of the River Welland in Lincolnshire, where he could confront the inner temptations and torments that troubled him (as well as the threat of attack by refuge Britons hiding in the Fens). He also became known for his sympathy with the birds and wild animals that frequented the area. After his death some 15 years later, his hermitage became the site of the abbey of Crowland and his shrine there became a site of pilgrimage.
Feast Day: 11 April.

Guy   *See* VITUS, MODESTUS AND CRESCENTIA.

Guy of Anderlecht   (*c*.950–1012) Belgian layman. Born into a peasant family in Brabant, he became sacristan of the church at Laeken, near Brussels. According to legend, he invested everything he had in a shipping prospect but lost it all when the ship concerned sank. Having thus lost all his savings and with them his post as sacristan, Guy decided to embark on a seven-year pilgrimage, eventually reaching Jerusalem. He died at Anderlecht not long after his return. Centuries later his grave had become the focus of a cult that had slowly developed around his name, inspiring numerous additional fantasies based on his life.
Feast Day: 12 September.

Gwenfrewi   *See* WINIFRED.

Gwinear   (6th century) Irish or Welsh martyr. According to medieval accounts of the life of Gwinear (otherwise referred to as **Fingar** or **Guigner**), he was the leader of a party of missionaries who arrived in Cornwall in the hope of converting the heathen inhabitants. Instead Gwinear and some of the others were captured by Theodoric, king of Cornwall, and put to death. Some members of the party managed to escape and continued with their evangelistic mission. Today they are commemorated in the names of certain towns and villages. Another version of the Gwinear legend suggests he survived and subsequently continued his missionary work in Brittany, where he also had a considerable cult following.
Feast Day: 23 March.

Hadrian   *See* ADRIAN.

Hallvard   (d.1043) Norse martyr. Born into a noble Viking family in Husaby, Norway, Hallvard is known from a legend according to which he sought to protect a woman who was falsely accused of stealing. When the woman appealed to the young man for protection from her pursuers by taking her with him in his boat across the Drammenfiord, he became convinced of her innocence and acceded to her request, refusing to surrender the woman to her enemies. Both he and the woman were then put to death with a shot from a bow. Attempts to dispose of Hallvard's body by throwing it into the water weighed down with stones miraculously failed and it rose to the surface, upon which it was recovered and placed with reverence in a church in Oslo. He is honoured today as the patron saint of Oslo.
Feast Day: 4 May.

Hedda of Peterborough   (d.870) English abbot and martyr. Hedda (or **Haeddi**) was head of the 84 members of a monastic community at Peterborough who were massacred, supposedly for their religious beliefs, by the Danes in 870. His name was revered in medieval times, when mass was regularly said over the grave of the victims, marked by the so-called Hedda Stone.
Feast Day: 10 April.

Hedda of Winchester   (d.705) English bishop. Educated in Whitby, Hedda (or **Haeddi**) was consecrated by St THEODORE in 676 and became the first bishop of Winchester after it was separated from the Dorchester diocese. Little is known of the details of Hedda's life beyond the fact that he assisted in organizing the law under King Ina, had the remains of St BIRINUS brought to Winchester and was widely respected for his virtuous and prudent advice (as acknowledged by BEDE). After his death, his tomb in Winchester became the site of numerous alleged cures of a miraculous nature.
Feast Day: 7 July.

Hedwig (c.1174–1243) Silesian noblewoman. Born into a noble family in
Bavaria, Hedwig (or **Jadwiga**) was brought up in the monastery of
Kitzingen and was married to Henry, heir to the dukedom of Silesia, at the
age of 12. As well as bearing seven children by Henry, she played an
active role in the governing of the country and used her wealth to benefit
the poor through the foundation of various religious houses and hospitals,
including (at Trebnitz) Silesia's first convent. When her husband was
captured by his enemy Conrad of Masovia, she acted as peacemaker and
restored good relations between the two states. After Henry's death in
1238 she spent the rest of her life in residence at the Cistercian convent at
Trebnitz, where the abbess was her daughter Gertrude (the only one of her
children to survive her), devoting herself to charitable work. A variety of
miracles were attributed to her and she was canonized in 1267.
Feast Day: 16 October.

Helen (c.250–330) Roman empress. Helen (sometimes identified as
Helena or **Ellen**) was born the daughter of an innkeeper at Drepanum
(later renamed Helenopolis in her honour) in Bithynia (Turkey) and in due
course became the wife of the Roman general Constantius Chlorus. She
bore him a son (later Constantine the Great, the first Christian emperor)
but was divorced by her husband when he became emperor. In 312, the
year in which she was named empress by her son Constantine, she
converted to Christianity and became well-known for her piety and for her
generosity to good causes, building churches and doing much to promote
the Christian faith throughout the Empire. As an old woman she also
made a pilgrimage to the Holy Land and according to legend played a key
role in the finding of the True Cross upon which Christ was crucified.
After her death, probably in Nicomedia in Turkey, her body was returned
for burial in Rome. Because of her son Constantine's links with Britain (he
was in York when he succeeded to the imperial throne) Helen was once
supposed to be British herself and her name is preserved in various
placenames in northeast England. The cross is her emblem in art.
Feast Day: 18 August.

Helier (6th century) Belgian-born martyr. Probably born at Tongres,
Belgium, he was converted to Christianity as a youth by his tutor, a man
named Cunibert, but fled his home when his outraged pagan father killed
Cunibert for this act. Helier eventually settled in a cave in Jersey in the
Channel Islands and there lived the life of a hermit with another man

named Romard. After 15 years he was murdered by some brigands to whom he had attempted to preach. The town of St Helier on Jersey was named in his honour.
Feast Day: 16 July.

Henry II (973–1024) Holy Roman emperor. Born in Bavaria, he succeeded to the dukedom of the country in 995 and became emperor of the Holy Roman Empire in 1014. He devoted himself to the consolidation of the empire, chiefly through waging war with various neighbours, but he also reformed and reorganized the church as a subordinate part of the imperial structure. According to unsubstantiated legend, he really wished to become a monk and agreed a celibate marriage with his wife St CUNEGUND. As emperor he restored the wealth of the church and also founded the see of Bamberg, where he built a monastery and the cathedral in which he was eventually buried. He was canonized in 1146.
Feast Day: 13 July.

Henry of Finland (d.1156) English-born bishop and martyr. Also known as **Henry of Uppsala**, he was born in England but appointed bishop of Uppsala in Sweden *c*.1152. He accompanied the army of the Swedish king St ERIC against the Finns in 1154 and subsequently set about baptizing the defeated Swedish warriors, remaining in Sweden after Eric had returned home. He built a church at Nousis but fell foul of a convert Finn, who had taken exception at Henry excommunicating him after he had murdered a Swedish soldier and consequently felled the bishop with an axe. Henry's body was moved to Abo cathedral in 1300 and he became the centre of a substantial cult. He is honoured today as the patron saint of Finland.
Feast Day: 20 January.

Henry Suso (*c*.1295–1366) Swiss mystic and author. Born Heinrich von Berg into a noble family in Constance, Switzerland, he was cared for by the Dominicans as a frail child and underwent a mystical revelation at the age of 18, subsequently dedicating himself to a life of penance and prayer. Around 1334, overcoming doubt and depression with the assistance of the German mystic Johann Eckhart, he embarked on a career as a preacher and religious adviser, braving persecution and in due course winning renown throughout Europe. He was also known for his books *The Little Book of Truth* and *The Little Book of Eternal Wisdom*. He ended his life as prior of the Dominican monastery at Ulm in Germany and was canonized in 1831.
Feast Day: 2 March.

Hermes (3rd century) Roman martyr. The details of the life of Hermes (or **Erme**) are not known beyond the facts that he may have been a slave of Greek origin and was put to death for his faith during the persecution of early Christians. An unsubstantiated tradition identifies him as a prefect of Rome who was condemned to death as a Christian under the emperor Hadrian. Whatever, the case, his cult flourished in the 4th century and many churches were dedicated to him. Buried initially in the cemetery of Basilla on the Old Salarian Way in Rome, his supposed relics are now preserved at Renaix in Belgium where they have long been a focus of pilgrimage and the alleged agent of apparently miraculous cures of lunatics.
Feast Day: 28 August.

Hewald the Black and Hewald the White (d. *c.*695) Anglo-Saxon priests. Sharing the name Hewald (variously given as **Ewald** or **Herwaldus**), the two men were called 'Black' and 'White' after the colour of their hair. Born in Northumbria, they are reputed to have lived in exile in Ireland before joining St WILLIBRORD in Frisia and eventually meeting their deaths in the vicinity of Dortmund at the hands of pagan Old Saxons. Hewald the White was killed by a blow from a sword, while Hewald the Black was tortured to death. According to St BEDE their corpses were thrown into the River Rhine but later retrieved after a series of miraculous incidents and placed in a church in Cologne. They remain the patron saints of Westphalia, the region in which they were slain.
Feast Day: 3 October.

Hilarion (*c.*291–371) Egyptian hermit. Born into a pagan family in Gaza, Hilarion converted to Christianity as a student in Alexandria and travelled into the desert to visit St ANTONY. Finding, on his return around 306, that his parents had died, he gave always all his possessions and devoted himself to a life as a hermit, living in the most austere circumstances in a rude shelter at Majuma in Palestine. A monastic community of disciples gradually formed around him, distracting him from contemplation of God, and after 50 years at Majuma he moved in search of solitude to Egypt and thence to Sicily, Epidaurus in Dalmatia and Cyprus, eventually dying in remote seclusion near Paphos at the age of 80. His steadfast denial of physical comforts and reputation for miracle-working inspired a lasting cult following, prompting many converts to Christianity, and came to be presented as a model for monastic discipline.
Feast Day: 21 October.

Hilary of Arles (*c*.400–449) French bishop. Talented and well-educated, he was uncertain whether to pursue a secular career or a religious vocation but was persuaded by his elder relative St HONORATUS OF ARLES to train as a monk at the island monastery of Lérins. In 429, aged just 29, he became bishop in succession to Honoratus, of whom he wrote a celebrated memoir. The youthful bishop became well-known for his energetic approach to his post, even undertaking manual labour himself in order to earn money for the poor and selling off church possessions to raise ransoms for captives. He was, however, less tactful in his dealings with other bishops and twice provoked the wrath of Pope Leo I for acting beyond his responsibilities, although they were subsequently reconciled. *Feast Day: 5 May.*

Hilary of Poitiers (*c*.315–367) French bishop and theologian. Born into a wealthy pagan family in Poitiers, he converted to Christianity in 350 and in due course (despite being a married man with a daughter) became the city's bishop by popular demand, earning a reputation both for his religious zeal and for his gentle manner. He was unswerving in his passionate but controversial opposition to Arianism (the denial of the divinity of Christ) and as a consequence was eventually exiled to Phrygia by the Arian emperor Constantius II. He continued to defend orthodoxy and discipline against the Arians in the East and four years later was returned by his exasperated hosts whence he had come. His many influential writings on the subject of Arianism included *De Trinitate* and *De Synodis*. Sometimes called the 'Athanasius of the West', he is also remembered for his innovative use of metrical hymns in teaching Christian doctrine and through the Hilary term in the calendar of law courts and some universities, which was named after him. He was made a Doctor of the Church in 1851 and is honoured as the patron saint of retarded children and of cures for snakebites. In art he is often depicted with a child in a cradle at his feet.
Feast Day: 13 January.

Hilda (614–680) English abbess. Born in Northumbria, she was a grand-niece of King Edwin of Northumbria and was baptized by St PAULINUS OF YORK at the age of 13. She lived a secular life until the age of 33, then became a nun and in 649 was made abbess of a convent in Hartlepool. She is usually remembered, however, for the work she did at the monastery she founded (or re-founded) at Whitby in 657. Men and women lived separately but prayed together at this establishment, among them such

luminaries as the religious poet Caedmon and St JOHN OF BEVERLEY. Under her guidance, the monastery became an important centre of religious learning with a fine library and it was there that the highly influential Synod of Whitby took place in 663–664, Hilda supporting the Celtic position over the dating of Easter and other issues but in the event acceding to the wishes of Rome. Much admired for her wisdom and compassion in the writings of St BEDE, she was highly respected in her lifetime, being consulted by rulers and peasants alike, and after her death several churches were dedicated to her.
Feast Day: 17 November.

Hildebrand   *See* GREGORY VII.

Hildegard of Bingen   (1098–1179) German abbess and visionary. Born in Bokelheim, she was educated by a reclusive aunt and with the Benedictines at Disabodenberg and became a nun herself at the age of 18. In 1136, at the age of 38, she was appointed prioress at Diessenberg. She had claimed to have visions since the age of five but in 1141, at the age of 42, she underwent a profound spiritual transformation and her prophecies became increasingly intense. She went on to record her visions in a book entitled *Scivias*, which comprised a series of 26 revelations, many of them describing the Day of Judgement and warning against sinful ways. Transferring her expanding community to a new convent at Rupertsberg, near Bingen, around 1147, she became widely renowned for her prophetic powers and took it upon herself to offer advice and reproofs to several popes and crowned rulers. She also conducted lengthy correspondences with such luminaries as St BERNARD OF CLAIRVAUX (although other contemporaries accused her of being self-deluded or a fraud). Other writings included commentaries on the gospels, books on natural science and medicine, poems, hymns and a morality play. She was canonized in the 15th century and today is remembered as much for her role as a prototype feminist and for her output as a composer as for her religious revelations.
Feast Day: 17 September.

Hippolytus   *See* PONTIAN AND HIPPOLYTUS.

Holy Innocents   (1st century AD) The children of Bethlehem who were massacred on the orders of Herod in his attempts to eliminate the threat posed by the newborn Christ (as related at Matthew 2:1–18). Their number is given in different sources as being anything from six to 25. They were

identified as martyrs as early as the 4th century and their memory was once celebrated in the English feast of Childermas. They are considered the protectors of dead children and comforters of their grieving parents.
Feast Day: 28 December.

Homobonus   (d.1197) Italian merchant. Born Homobonus Tucingo into a wealthy merchant family in Cremona, Lombardy, he succeeded his father as head of a prosperous tailoring business but dedicated the greater part of his wealth to alleviating the suffering of those less fortunate than himself. A married man, he often looked after those in need in his own home, attending personally to all their wants. Dubbed the 'Father of the Poor', he spent much time at prayer in his local church and ultimately breathed his last while participating in mass there. He was canonized by popular demand in 1199, just two years after his death, and is honoured as the patron saint of tailors and clothworkers, as well as the patron saint of Cremona.
Feast Day: 13 November.

Honoratus of Arles   (c.350–429) French monk and bishop. Born into a high-ranking Gallo-Roman family, he and his elder brother Venantius converted to Christianity and, against his pagan father's wishes, conducted a pilgrimage to Greece and Rome looking for a site to found a monastic hermitage before ultimately settling on a bleak island off Cannes. Here, after his brother's death, Honoratus established what was destined to become the famous monastery of Lérins, whose early members included St EUCHERIUS OF LYONS, St HILARY OF ARLES and St LUPUS OF TROYES. St PATRICK is also thought to have spent several years there. Though troubled by illness himself, Honoratus was greatly respected for his hard work within the community and for his attentions to the welfare of those attracted to him. He was elected bishop of Arles in 427, just two years before his death. The religious community he founded continues today as a Cistercian monastery.
Feast Day: 16 January.

Honorius   (d.653) English bishop. Honorius arrived in England in 627 as a Roman missionary, possibly accompanying St AUGUSTINE, and that same year succeeded St JUSTUS as the fifth archbishop of Canterbury. Little detail is known of his reign over the next 25 years, although it appears he consolidated the position of the church in England, his most influential decisions including the sending of St FELIX OF DUNWICH on an evangelical mission to

East Anglia. Other key moments in his episcopate included the appointment in 644 of the first Englishman (Ithamar) to the rank of bishop. On his death, he was buried alongside his predecessors as archbishop in the monastery of SS. Peter and Paul (renamed St Augustine's) in Canterbury.
Feast Day: 30 September.

Hormisdas   (d.523) Italian pope. Born in Frusino, Italy, he married and fathered a son prior to entering the priesthood. In due course he was appointed archdeacon under Pope St SYMMACHUS and eventually pope himself after Symmachus' death in 514. The most important event to occur during his reign was the healing of the schism between the Eastern and Western churches, which had divided them since 484, with the signing of the Formula of Hormisdas in Constantinople. The Formula confirmed the supremacy of the Roman see and condemned the heresies that had led to the schism 35 years previously. Honoured as the patron saint of grooms and stable-boys, Hormisdas is often portrayed in art as a young man with a camel.
Feast Day: 6 August.

Hubert   (c.656–727) French bishop. The circumstances of St Hubert's youth are obscure though it has been suggested he was the son of the Duke of Guienne and, according to 14th-century legend, converted to Christianity whilst out hunting on Good Friday after encountering a stag that bore a cross in its antlers and called upon him to repent. He served as a priest under St LAMBERT and succeeded him as bishop of Maastricht, promoting missionary work in the Ardennes district. In 716 he built a church in Liège to house the relics of St Lambert, subsequently transforming this church into a cathedral and becoming first bishop of the new see of Liège. Injuries he sustained in a fishing accident in 726 hastened his death the following year. His emblem is a stag and he is honoured as the patron saint of hunters and trappers in the Ardennes. Perhaps because of the use of dogs in hunting, his help may also be called upon by the faithful in cases of rabies.
Feast Day: 30 May.

Hugh, Little Saint   (d.1255) English martyr. The discovery of the body of a nine-year-old boy in a well in Lincoln in 1255 led to accusations that he had been ritually crucified by local Jews (as in the parallel case of WILLIAM OF NORWICH). Some 19 Jews were tortured and hanged on charges of involvement in the boy's death; others were thrown into prison or heavily

fined. The legend of Little Saint Hugh is perhaps best-known today from an allusion to it in Chaucer's *Canterbury Tales*.
Feast Day: 27 August.

Hugh of Cluny   (1024–1109) French abbot. Born into a prominent noble family of Burgundy, he defied the expectations of his rank to become a monk at the monastery of Cluny while still just 16 and entered the priest-hood aged 20. He was appointed abbot of Cluny in 1049 at the age of 25 and over the next 60 years exercised a powerful influence over the Benedic-tine order throughout Europe. Respected both for his diplomatic skills as well as for his piety and personal integrity, he was responsible for wide-spread ecclesiastical reform and became a trusted adviser to succeeding popes, acting as a papal legate in Hungary, Toulouse and Spain and help-ing to launch the first Crusade in 1095. He also did much to unify the Cluniac congregation, which enjoyed a peak in influence under his leader-ship, and as a consequence of Hugh's policies the monastery at Cluny became the largest abbey in the Christian world. He was canonized in 1120.
Feast Day: 29 April.

Hugh of Grenoble   (1053–1132) French bishop. Born at Châteauneuf near Valence, he overcame natural shyness to rise quickly through the ranks of the church and was appointed bishop of Grenoble at the age of 27. As bishop he carried through widespread reform of the disorganized and disreputable diocese and also offered shelter at the Grande Chartreuse estate to the first Carthusian monks under St BRUNO (formerly his teacher), thus establishing a lasting reputation as co-founder of the Carthusian order. Other notable deeds included the founding of a market-place and three hospitals in Grenoble as well as the building of a stone bridge over the Isère river. Revered both by the people of Grenoble and by the Carthusian monks he had encouraged, he was canonized just two years after his death.
Feast Day: 1 April.

Hugh of Lincoln   (c.1135–1200) French-born bishop. Born into a noble family at Avalon in Burgundy, Hugh of Avalon (as he was originally styled) received a convent education and while still a young man was appointed prior of a monastery at Saint-Maxim. He joined the Carthusian order in 1160 and was made a procurator at the Grande Chartreuse in 1175. His reputation for piety, combined with his proven administrative

abilities, led to him being invited by Henry II of England to become prior of Charterhouse in Witham, Somerset (founded by Henry in 1178 in penance for the murder of Thomas Becket). The monastery flourished under Hugh, who was duly appointed bishop of Lincoln (the largest diocese in the country) in 1186. Under his leadership Lincoln became a prominent centre of religious learning and the great cathedral there was considerably extended. Relations between Hugh and the king were some-times tempestuous as the bishop did not flinch to oppose the monarch when he felt this was right, but Hugh's unfailing good humour always healed the rift, both with Henry and his successor Richard I. He also showed courage in opposing single-handed a mob threatening the Jews of Lincoln during the persecution of 1190–91. In 1199 he visited France in a diplomatic role on behalf of King John, but died shortly after his return to London. He was canonized in 1220 and is honoured as the patron saint of sick children. In art he is usually depicted with his pet swan or with a chalice carrying the image of the infant Christ.
Feast Day: 17 November.

Humbert of Romans (*c.*1200–77) French Dominican leader. Born at Romans, near Valence in France, he trained as a lawyer before becoming fifth master-general of the Dominican Order of Preachers in 1254. He worked hard to unify the far-flung and disorganized order and instituted widespread reform of the community, revising the liturgy, promoting disci-pline and defending the Dominicans against the hostile attentions of the secular clergy. He also mended relations between the Dominican and Franciscan orders. As a result of his efforts, he is sometimes honoured as the second founder of the Dominican order. His writings included the influential treatise *On the Formation of Preachers.*
Feast Day: 14 July.

Hyacinth *See* PROTUS AND HYACINTH.

Hyacinth of Cracow (1185–1257) Polish friar. Born into a noble Silesian family in Kammien (Grosstein), Hyacinth (originally Jacob) was the nephew of the bishop of Cracow and followed him into the church, accom-panying his uncle as a canon on a trip to Rome in 1220. While in Rome, he was received into the Order of Preachers led by St DOMINIC. On his return to Cracow he went on to establish the first of five Dominican houses in Poland; friaries at Danzig and Kiev followed. Hyacinth earned a reputation for his work as an apostle and educationalist and also played a key role in extending the Dominican order through northern and eastern Europe. After his death many miraculous episodes were credited to his name and ultimately he was canonized in 1594.

Feast Day: 15 August.

Ia (8th century) Irish maiden revered in Cornish and Breton tradition. According to Cornish legend, she sailed across the Irish Sea on a leaf and once in Cornwall persuaded the chieftain Dinan to found a church. Little else is known of her life, although Breton tradition identifies her as a convert of St PATRICK who was put to death with her followers in Armorica in 777. Also called **Hya** or **Ives**, she is remembered today as the patron saint of St Ives (formerly called Porth Ia) in Cornwall, where she is supposed to have landed after her voyage from Ireland. *Feast Days: 3 February and 27 October.*

Ide *See* ITA.

Ignatius of Antioch (d. *c.*107) Syrian bishop and martyr. Little is known about his life beyond the fact that he became bishop of Antioch around AD 69 and as an elderly man was arrested by the Romans and sent with a military escort to Rome under a sentence of death imposed by the emperor Trajan. After a long journey, during which he was feted by Christians at many of the places that he passed through, he was thrown to wild beasts in the public arena. During his final journey he wrote seven celebrated letters, in which he variously urges unity within the Christian community, expresses his consolation in being able to demonstrate his devotion to Christ by dying for his faith, and makes his farewells to St POLYCARP, whom he had met in Smyrna on his way to Rome. Legend identifies Ignatius of Antioch as the child set down by Christ among his disciples (as related at Matthew 18:1–6 and Mark 9:36–37), although he is also named elsewhere as a disciple of St PETER and St PAUL or of St JOHN. *Feast Day: 17 October.*

Ignatius of Laconi (1701–1781) Capuchin lay brother. He was born Ignatius Vincent Peis into a poor family in Laconi, Sardinia, and remained in the area all his life, living as a lay brother with the Capuchin Franciscans at Buoncammino near Cagliari from the age of 20 after suffering a severe shock when his horse bolted. As a middle-aged man of 40, after 20 years devoted to prayer and silence, he embarked on some 40 years of begging for alms on behalf of the community, becoming widely revered for his devout, gentle ways and for his kindness towards the poor, the sick and the young. Local tradition describes how he travelled barefoot whatever the weather and also recounts various remarkable incidents associated with his name, including miracles of healing. He was canonized in 1951. *Feast Day: 11 May.*

Ignatius of Loyola   (1491–1556) Founder of the Jesuit order. Born Iñigo de Recalde de Loyola into a noble Basque family at Loyola Castle near Azpeita in Spain, he trained as a soldier and fought against the French in Castile. In 1521 he sustained a severe leg wound from a cannon shot at the siege of Pamplona (the badly reset break leaving him with a permanent limp) and subsequently underwent a spiritual conversion after reading the life of Christ during his convalescence. He retreated for 10 months to a cave at Manresa, spending his time in prayer and penance and later recording his experiences in his celebrated book *Spiritual Exercises* (published in 1548). He went on pilgrimage to Jerusalem in 1523 but was dissuaded from his intention of evangelizing among the Muslims there and went on to spend several years in academic study in Spain. Living a life of piety and austerity, he was treated with suspicion by the Spanish authorities and was imprisoned for a time on charges of heresy before electing to continue his studies in Paris. In 1534 he combined with St FRANCIS XAVIER and five others in taking vows of poverty and chastity, with the ultimate aim of converting Muslims in Palestine. When journeying to Palestine proved impossible, the group met once more in Venice in 1537 and resolved to found a new religious order called the Society of Jesus in Rome. The society, which espoused spiritual discipline as well as obedience to Christ and the pope, won official papal approval in 1540, with Ignatius (now ordained as a priest) as its superior general from 1541. The Jesuits, as members of the order became known, went on to play a prime role in the Catholic Reformation throughout Europe, countering the Protestantism of Luther and Calvin, and in succeeding centuries undertook missionary work on behalf of the Catholic church all over the world. Renowned for his piety as much as for his qualities of leadership, Ignatius spent the remainder of his life directing the society's activities from Rome, but also found time to establish a foundation for Jewish converts to Catholicism and a home for reformed prostitutes. He died in Rome in 1556, was canonized in 1622, and is variously honoured as the patron saint of the Jesuit order, soldiers, retreats and spiritual exercises. His emblems are a book, a chasuble, the Holy Communion and the apparition of the Lord. *Feast Day: 31 July.*

Ildephonsus of Toledo (*c*.606–667) Spanish archbishop. Born at Toledo into a noble family, he entered the priesthood *c*.637, became the abbot of the monastery in Toledo *c*.650 and ultimately archbishop of the city (657). He was widely admired both for his administrative capabilities and for his piety and was also respected as a musician and writer. It was under his guidance that a council of 653 agreed the right of secular leaders to participate in ecclesiastical decision-making (an early pattern for the medieval relationship between church and state throughout Europe). Surviving writings by Ildephonsus (or **Ildefonsus**) include a treatise on baptism, another on the Virgin Mary – who according to legend once appeared to the archbishop, seated on his episcopal throne – and brief biographies of the worthies of the Spanish church in his time.
Feast Day: 23 January.

Illtyd (d.early 6th century) Welsh abbot. Variously identified as **Illtud, Iltut, Eltut** or **Hildutus**, Illtyd lived in southeast Wales, where he founded the celebrated monastic school of Llanilltyd Fawr (Llantwit Major in modern South Glamorgan) and earned a reputation for being the most learned Briton in philosophy and scriptural studies. His school became a centre for religious learning and supposedly numbered among its students St SAMSON, among other notables. Little else is known about Illtyd's life, beyond stories that he took corn to Brittany to relieve famine there and that he prophesied his own death, but his school is known to have remained in existence until the Norman Conquest. Many Welsh churches are dedicated to him.
Feast Day: 6 November.

Innocents *See* HOLY INNOCENTS.

Irenaeus of Lyons (*c*.130–200) Bishop and theologian, probably born at Smyrna. Allegedly a pupil at Smyrna of St POLYCARP, by whom he was profoundly influenced as a child, Irenaeus subsequently studied in Rome and entered the priesthood at Lyons, eventually becoming bishop there (*c*.178) and earning a reputation as a peacemaker during a time of persecution of minority sects. Little more is known of the details of his life, although there is an unsubstantiated tradition that ultimately he died a martyr's death. He is remembered as a prominent theologian of the second century, whose most important writings included a treatise warning against the ideas of the Gnostics (the *Adversus Haereses*) and arguments in

favour of Christian unity and in defence of the traditions of the Church (translated as the *Demonstration of Apostolic Preaching*).
Feast Day: 28 June.

Irenaeus of Sirmium   (d.304) Bishop and martyr. A native of the town of Sirmium (near Sremska Mitrovica in modern Serbia), he was imprisoned by the Romans after refusing to sacrifice to their gods on the order of the prefect Probus during the persecution of Christians under the emperor Diocletian. He continued to resist the prefect's demands even after torture and was eventually condemned to death by drowning. Irenaeus, however, protested that this was too ignominious a death for one who was to die in such a noble cause and instead, with a final prayer to Christ, he was beheaded and his corpse thrown off a bridge into the river Sava.
Feast Day: 6 April.

Irene   *See* AGAPE, CHIONIA AND IRENE.

Isaac Jogues   (1607–1646) French missionary and martyr. Born in Orléans, he joined the Society of Jesus in 1624 and was sent out to Canada as a missionary some 12 years later, spreading the gospel among the Mohawks. He was captured by Iroquois Indians at Ossernenon (modern Auriesville, New York) in 1642 and over the following year of imprisonment was exposed to brutal torture, during which he lost several fingers. He escaped with the help of the Dutch but subsequently, after disease broke out among the Bear clan, he was blamed for this misfortune and when he and another priest named John Lalande entered a longhouse supposedly for a peace banquet, they were set upon with knives in the belief that they were sorcerers. Both men were beheaded with tomahawks and their bodies thrown in the Mohawk river.
Feast Day: 26 September.

Isabel   *See* ELIZABETH OF PORTUGAL.

Isidore of Pelusium   (d. *c*.450) Egyptian abbot. Probably born in Alexandria, Isidore left his family to become a monk at the monastery of Lychnos near Pelusium and in due course is believed to have become abbot of the monastery. He was widely respected for his pious and austere way of life, dressing in skins and eating only herbs. Remembered as one of the Fathers of the Church, he offered guidance to St CYRIL OF ALEXANDRIA and wrote numerous letters on spiritual matters, of which some 2000 survive. He was a strong supporter of monastic discipline and steadfast in his opposition to heresy.

Feast Day: 4 February.

Isidore of Seville (*c.*560–636) Spanish archbishop. Variously known as **Isidore the Bishop** or the **Schoolmaster of the Middle Ages**, he was born into a noble family of Cartagena in Spain and in due course succeeded his elder brother St LEANDER as archbishop of Seville in 601. He established a wide reputation as a scholar, writer and teacher and did much to organize and strengthen the Spanish church, presiding over the influential councils of Seville (619) and Toledo (633). He promoted the conversion of the Visigoths from Arianism and established the cathedral schools from which developed the great universities of the medieval period. Under Isidore's guidance the schools provided instruction in a wide range of subjects, including medicine, law, Hebrew and Greek. Noted for his austere lifestyle and generosity to the poor, Isidore was also the author of many books, among them the encyclopedic *Etymologies*, a history of the world, a dictionary of synonyms and biographies of famous men. Canonized in 1598, he is the patron saint of students and computer users.

Feast Day: 4 April.

Isidore the Farmer (d. *c.*1080) Spanish farmer. Born Isidore Merlo Quintana into a peasant family in Madrid, he worked as a farm labourer all his life, combining his love of the land with devotion to God. Various legends tell how the angels, impressed by his faithfulness, assisted him with his ploughing and replaced the gifts he divided amongst the needy, heedless of his own poverty. In one story he distributes half the contents of a sack of corn among some starving birds, in spite of the jeers of his neighbours, and is rewarded by the remaining corn miraculously providing twice the usual amount of flour. After his death, his grave became the site of numerous miracles of healing and his cult spread quickly throughout Spain. Also known as **Isadore the Farmer**, **Isidro Labrador** and **Isidoro Labrador**, he was canonized in 1622 at the request of King Philip III of Spain, who credited Isidore with his recovery from illness. He is the patron saint of farmers, livestock, dead children and also of Madrid. His emblem is a spade, sickle or plough.

Feast Day: 15 May.

Istvan *See* STEPHEN OF HUNGARY.

Ita (d. *c*.570) Irish abbess and teacher. Ita (or **Ide**) is traditionally supposed to have been born under the name Deirdre near Waterford, possibly of royal descent. She spent most of her life in the nunnery she founded at Killeedy in Limerick, dedicating herself to prayer and fasting and to helping the sick. She also ran a school for young boys, her pupils allegedly including the youthful St BRENDAN. She remains Ireland's best-known female saint after St BRIGID, with many churches dedicated to her, and is fondly credited with the authorship of an Irish lullaby for the baby Jesus. *Feast Day: 15 January.*

Ives *See* IA.

Ivo of Brittany (*c*.1235–1303) French lawyer. Born into a noble family at Kermartin near Tréguier in Brittany, and hence also known as **Ivo of Kermartin**, he studied law and theology in Paris and Orléans and was ultimately appointed judge of the church courts at Rennes and Tréguier. He quickly established a reputation for impartiality and honesty and as a champion of the poor, but, having been ordained in 1284, resigned his legal posts in 1287 in order to devote himself to the welfare of his parish, working initially with the people of Tredez and subsequently (from 1292) at Lovannec. His many good deeds included the building of a hospital at Lovannec and selfless acts of generosity towards the poor. He was canonized in 1347 and remains one of Brittany's most popular saints. *Feast Day: 19 May.*

James   *See* MARIAN AND JAMES.

James the Greater   (d.44) Apostle. James (called **James the Greater** to distinguish him from another apostle, JAMES THE LESS) lived as a fisherman alongside his brother St JOHN before being called to serve as one of Christ's disciples. Hard physical labour had made him very tough and on account of this (and possibly his fiery temper) he and John were nick-named Boanerges (meaning Sons of Thunder). James became one of the leaders among the disciples and was present at several of the key episodes of Christ's life, including the agony in the Garden of Gethsemane. Christ warned James that he would have to suffer considerably before he could take an honoured place in heaven and accordingly, after Christ's cruci-fixion, he became one of the first victims of persecution of the Christian community. Arrested in Jerusalem on the orders of King Herod Agrippa I, he was beheaded and thus became the first of the apostles to die. After James's death his body is said to have been removed to Spain (where he is also supposed to have preached) and his shrine at Compostela in Galicia became one of the most important centres of pilgrimage in the medieval period. James the Greater is honoured as the patron saint of pilgrims, blacksmiths and labourers and also of the countries Spain, Chile, Guate-mala and Nicaragua. His emblems are a scallop-shell and a pilgrim's hat. *Feast Day: 25 July.*

James the Less   (d. *c.*61) Apostle. James the Less (so called to distinguish him from another apostle, JAMES THE GREATER) was the son of a man named Alphaeus and is traditionally identified either as a brother or first cousin of Christ. If the identification as Jesus' brother is correct, he is the one to whom the risen Christ appeared and subsequently he became the first bishop of Jerusalem, in which post he presided over a meeting of the apostles to decide whether Gentile converts had to become Jews. He supported the eventual conclusion that Gentiles and Jews could worship God alongside one another within the church. James was eventually hauled before the Sanhedrin in Jerusalem and then stoned or beaten to death with a fuller's club. James is traditionally identified as the author of the Epistle of St James in the New Testament. As well as being the patron

saint of Uruguay, he is honoured as the patron saint of apothecaries, fullers, hatters, milliners, pharmacists and the dying. His emblem is a fuller's club.
Feast Day: 3 May.

James of the March   (1394–1476) Italian missionary. James of the March (or **James of the Marches**) was born into a poor family at Montebrandone (Marches of Ancona) and was ordained a Franciscan priest in 1423. He established a reputation as a powerful preacher and spent much of his life engaged in missionary work in Bosnia, Hungary and elsewhere. He was noted for his sympathy towards the poor and oppressed but was also a somewhat controversial figure who played a prominent role in controversies within the Franciscan order. He was also criticized for his harsh attitude towards heretics and others he felt were behaving incorrectly. He succeeded St JOHN CAPISTRANO as papal legate to Hungary in 1456 but subsequently declined the offer of the bishopric of Milan, preferring to live the life of an itinerant preacher. After a serious confrontation with the Inquisition in 1462 over his views upon the blood of Christ he was moved to Naples, where he died. He was canonized in 1726.
Feast Day: 28 November.

Jane Frances de Chantal   (1572–1641) French foundress. Born Jane Frances Frémyot in Dijon, she was the daughter of the president of the parliament of Burgundy. When she was 20 years old she married Baron Christophe de Rabutin-Chantal of Bourbilly, to whom she was devoted, and went on to bear him seven children before he was killed in a hunting accident in 1601. Jane took a vow of celibacy and for a time endured harsh treatment at the hands of her tyrannical father-in-law before hearing St FRANCIS DE SALES preaching in 1604 and being inspired to serve as one of his disciples. She became a nun in 1610 and that same year, in collaboration with her close friend and spiritual adviser St Francis, founded the Order of the Visitation of the Virgin Mary, establishing the first house at Annecy in Savoy. This order took in widows and others who were not eligible to enter other orders or through sickness or old age were unable to endure the rigours imposed at other convents. The order prospered accordingly, even after the death of St Francis in 1622, until by the time of her own demise Jane Frances de Chantal stood at the head of some 86 convents. Many of her letters survive. She was canonized in 1767.
Feast Day: 12 December.

Januarius (d. *c*.305) Italian bishop and martyr. Details of the life of St Januarius (or **Gennaro**) are sketchy and uncertain. Tradition has it that he was a bishop of Benevento who died a martyr's death with six companions at Pozzuoli during the persecutions carried out under the Emperor Diocletian. He is best known through a relic kept in Naples cathedral, comprising a phial of what is alleged to be his dried blood: three times a year the phial is presented to the faithful to witness its contents miraculously becoming liquid once more. On the rare occasions that the blood does not liquefy there is much concern locally that the city of Naples will suffer some calamity. Scientists have so far failed to account convincingly for the phenomenon, although sceptics point out that there is no historical record of the phial prior to the year 1389, many centuries after the saint's death. As well as being patron saint of Naples, Januarius is also honoured as the patron saint of blood banks.
Feast Day: 19 September.

Japan, Martyrs of *See* PAUL MIKI AND LAWRENCE RUIZ.

Jarlath of Tuam (d. *c*.550) Irish bishop. Relatively little is known of the life of Jarlath of Tuam, who is believed to have been born into a noble family of Galway and to have become a disciple of St ENDA. Tradition has it that he was the founder of a monastery at Cluain Fois, near Tuam, and that he subsequently became the first bishop of Tuam. His disciples are said to have included BRENDAN OF CLONFERT and COLMAN OF MUNSTER.
Feast Day: 6 June.

Jeanne de Lestonnac *See* JOAN DE LESTONNAC.

Jerome (*c*.341–420) Italian biblical scholar. Born Eusebius Hieronymus Sophronius into a wealthy family of Strido, near Aquileia in Dalmatia, he established a reputation as a scholar while living in Rome, inspired by classical literature and the rhetoric of Cicero, before being baptized by the pope at the age of 18. Subsequently he rejected the distractions of the material world and lived as a monk near Aquileia for some years. In 374, having left Aquileia and travelled to Antioch, he contracted a serious illness during which he experienced a vision of Christ, who berated him for his failings as a Christian. Upon his recovery Jerome spent the next four years as a hermit in the Syrian desert before eventually returning to his scholastic studies in Constantinople under the guidance of St GREGORY OF NAZIANZUS. Though ordained a priest against his wishes at Antioch, he concentrated solely upon his calling as a biblical scholar and never conducted a mass. As a person, Jerome was by all accounts a bad-tempered and difficult man who embodied the ascetic ideal, fasting for weeks at a time, praying incessantly and condemning the failings of both himself and others. He made many enemies and after returning to Rome to serve as secretary (382–85) to Pope St DAMASUS I was so unpleasant to both pagans and fellow-Christians that he was obliged to leave the city after three years and to go back to the Holy Land, where he made a new home in Bethlehem. Despite his tactless and unfriendly nature, he attracted many disciples (chiefly women) to Bethlehem, among them St PAULA. With her he founded a monastery, a convent, a hospice for pilgrims to the Holy Land and a free school. Of Jerome's many influential writings his translation of the Bible from Greek and Hebrew into Latin was the most important, the resulting Latin Vulgate Bible remaining the authoritative translation until around the middle of the 20th century by virtue of its clarity and accessibility. Other notable writings included his continuation of the *Historia Ecclesiastica* begun by Eusebius of Caesarea, *De Viribus Illustribus*, which discussed important ecclesiastical writers, translations of Origen, treatises upon some of the controversies of the contemporary church and many letters. Considered one of the greatest of all biblical scholars, Jerome is honoured today both as a Doctor of the Church and as the patron saint of biblical scholars and librarians. His emblem is a lion. *Feast Day: 30 September.*

Jerome Emiliani   (1481–1537) Italian priest. Born in Venice, Jerome Emiliani served as a officer in the army of the city-state of Venice but underwent a spiritual transformation after being captured as commander of the fortress of Castelnuovo and confined in a dungeon, where he had time to re-examine his life. After his escape from imprisonment he abandoned his career in the army and joined the priesthood, being ordained in 1518. He survived an attack of the plague in 1531 and devoted the rest of his life to the care of the sick and other needy people. He was particularly concerned to protect Italy's orphans. To further this aim he founded the Somaschi order of clerks regular to run orphanages. He was canonized in 1767 and is honoured as the patron saint of orphans and abandoned children.
Feast Day: 8 February.

Joachim and Ann   (1st century) The parents of the Virgin Mary. There is no biblical source for information about the parents of Mary, but tradition (drawing upon an ancient and unreliable document entitled the

Protevangelium of James) identifies them as Joachim and Ann (or **Anne**). According to this, Joachim was born in Nazareth while his wife Ann came from Bethlehem. The couple showed sincere religious faith, donating two-thirds of their income to the temple and to helping the poor. They failed, however, to conceive any children for some 20 years, prompting them to promise God that if they did have a child they would consecrate the child to him. When Joachim was forbidden to approach the altar in the temple because of his sterility he was overcome with shame and hid himself away, causing Ann much anxiety. At this point an angel appeared to Ann to announce that their prayer had been heard and the couple were joyfully reunited. Ann duly conceived and gave birth to Mary. Joachim is supposed to have died some time after the presentation of Christ at the temple in Jerusalem. Ann is honoured as the patron saint of Canada, Brittany, housewives, women in labour and cabinetmakers. *Feast Day: 26 July.*

Joan of Arc (*c*.1412–1431) French heroine otherwise known as the Maid of Orléans. Born into a poor peasant family of Donrémy in Champagne, she underwent a revelatory experience in 1425 when, at the age of 13, she heard what she identified as the voice of St MICHAEL. She went on to hear his voice, and that of various other angels, many more times and in 1428 reported that St Michael had instructed her to raise the English siege of Orléans and achieve the crowning of the Dauphin Charles at Rheims. Believing this to be the will of God, the illiterate 16-year-old Joan embarked on her mission, initially provoking scorn and admiration in equal measure among the French soldiery and general populace. Stories quickly accumulated of miracles she had performed and the Dauphin, suitably impressed, recruited her assistance, providing her with a suit of armour and forces. She became the inspiration of the French army, which with Joan at its head successfully drove the English besiegers from Orléans. She enjoyed further victories at Patay and Troyes. In 1429 she saw Charles crowned king of France in Rheims cathedral, as she had dreamed. Within a year, however, while attempting to relieve Compiègne, Joan was captured by the Burgundian rivals of Charles and, abandoned by the Dauphin, handed over to their allies the English. After nine months in prison she was hauled before an ecclesiastical court presided over by the bishop of Beauvais, Peter Cauchon, on charges of heresy. Joan's spirited defence failed to persuade the court against imposing the death penalty, although there was a delay when she seemed to recant but then resumed

her defiant stance. She was burned at the stake in the market square in Rouen on 31 May 1431 and her ashes thrown into the Seine. Joan was declared innocent of heresy by papal decree in 1456 and was canonized in 1920, not for dying a martyr's death but for living the life of a pious Christian virgin. Her story has inspired countless works of art and literature. She is honoured as the patron saint of France, soldiers, prisoners and virgins.
Feast Day: 30 May.

Joan of France   (1464–1505) French queen. Born Joan of Valois, she was the daughter of King Louis XI of France and Charlotte of Savoy. Unfortunately she was born physically deformed and was never accepted by her family, a sad situation that she typically endured with patience and understanding. In 1476 she was married off to Louis, Duc d'Orléans, who took no interest in her. When Louis himself became king in 1498 he secured an annulment of the marriage, allowing Joan to enter fully into the religious life she had always craved. She became a nun in 1504 and spent the rest of her life in prayer and performing acts of charity at Bourges. Aided by the Franciscans, she founded a small order for women called the Annonciades of Bourges, which became part of the Franciscan community. She was canonized in 1950.
Feast Day: 4 February.

Joan de Lestonnac   (1556–1640) French foundress. Born in Bordeaux, the niece of the essayist Montaigne, Joan (or **Jeanne**) de Lestonnac married the noble-born Gaston de Montferrand in 1573 and bore him four children before his death in 1597. In 1603 she defied family opposition to become a Cistercian nun at Les Feuillantes in Toulouse. Under the influence of the Jesuits, she perceived the need for the organized religious education of girls and accordingly founded the Sisters of Notre Dame of Bordeaux to pursue such work. Despite various divisions within the sisterhood (one of which resulted in Joan being deposed as superioress and humiliated) further foundations followed and the schools earned a considerable reputation. Her order continues in existence today. She was canonized in 1949.
Feast Day: 2 February.

Joan Thouret   (1765–1826) French foundress. Born Joan Antida Thouret near Besançon, she was the daughter of a tanner. In response to her strong religious vocation, she joined the Sisters of Charity of St Vincent de Paul in Paris at the age of 22, but was obliged to return home in 1793 after the community was broken up during the French Revolution to assume the role of schoolmistress. When the political climate improved she was invited by the vicar general of Besançon to open a new school, which accepted its first pupils in 1799. This gradually expanded with the addition of a kitchen and dispensary and in due course developed into the congregation of the Sisters of Charity. Overcoming formidable opposition, this organization prospered and new schools and hospitals were established in Switzerland, Savoy and Naples, where Joan herself ran a hospital. The order was officially approved by the pope in 1819 under the title Daughters of Charity. Joan's final years, which saw the foundation of many more schools and other institutions throughout Italy, were clouded by arguments with the archbishop of Besançon, who deprived her of control over the convents she had established in France. She was canonized in 1934. *Feast Day: 24 August.*

Joaquina (1783–1854) Spanish foundress. Born Joaquina de Vedruna in Barcelona, she dreamed of becoming a Carmelite nun but instead married a lawyer at the age of 16. She bore her husband eight children before he was killed during the French occupation of Spain while Joaquina was in her early thirties. Joaquina responded by dedicating herself to prayer, penitence and works of charity and, when her children were grown up, by setting about the foundation of her own religious order. The Congregation of the Carmelite Sisters of Charity was established at Vich in Catalonia in 1826 and, aided by St ANTONY MARY CLARET and others, prospered and rapidly spread, concentrating upon nursing and teaching. The order received papal approval in 1850 and now operates worldwide. Illness forced Joaquina herself to give up control of the order in her final years. She was canonized in 1959 and is honoured as the patron saint of victims of abuse, exiles and widows.
Feast Day: 28 August.

John (d. *c*.100) Apostle. Variously called **John the Apostle**, **John the Evangelist** or **John the Divine**, he was one of the most trusted of Christ's disciples as well as the youngest, and the only one of them to witness the Crucifixion. A fisherman of Galilee alongside his brother St JAMES and his father Zebedee, he was rarely separated from Christ after his recruitment as a disciple. Other key biblical moments at which John was present included the Last Supper, at which he was permitted to recline against Christ, and the discovery of Christ's empty tomb. At the Crucifixion it was to John that Christ entrusted the future care of his

mother Mary. Following the deaths of St PETER and St PAUL John stayed
with the church at Ephesus. According to one tradition he was taken from
there to Rome on the orders of the Emperor Domitian, but miraculously
escaped execution and was subsequently exiled to the island of Patmos,
where he wrote the Book of Revelation, before returning to Ephesus in 96.
It may have been at Ephesus that he wrote the Gospel that carries his
name and finally died at a very advanced age, becoming the only disciple
to die a natural death. When he became too old and feeble to preach he
simply exhorted the faithful to love one another. He is the patron saint of
theologians and writers. His emblem is an eagle.
Feast Day: 27 December.

John and Paul   (dates unknown) Martyrs. Nothing is known of the details
of the life and death of John and Paul, who are named as martyrs in early
lists of the saints. Their story is often associated with that of two Roman
officers named **Juventinus and Maximinus**, who were martyred for
their Christian faith at Antioch in 363.
Feast Day: 26 June.

John I   (d.526) Italian pope and martyr. Born in Tuscany, he rose to the
rank of archdeacon in Rome and assumed papal office in 523, though by
then he was elderly and in poor health. As pope he had to defend the
interests of the Catholic church against the sometimes unsympathetic
attitude of the Arian Emperor Theodoric the Goth. Using the threat of
reprisals against Catholics in the West, Theodoric obliged John to go to
Constantinople as his ambassador to the Roman Emperor Justinian and
there to plead for greater toleration of Arians in the East. John appears to
have been fairly successful in this mission, but back in Italy Theodoric had
grown increasingly suspicious of the Catholic hierarchy and ordered a
number of executions. When the ailing John returned to Theodoric's capital
Ravenna he was immediately thrown into prison, where he died after just
a few days.
Feast Day: 18 May.

John XXIII   (1881–1963) Italian pope. Born Angelo Giuseppe Roncalli in
Sotto il Monte, near Bergamo, he was ordained priest in Rome in 1904. He
served in the medical corps in the Italian army during World War I but in
1917 was invited by the current pope to undertake the reorganization of
the Congregation for the Propagation of the Faith. He was raised to the
post of archbishop in 1925 and was then appointed Apostolic Visitor to

Bulgaria and Apostolic Delegate to Greece and Turkey. In 1958 he was elected pope, in which role he made considerable use of his diplomatic experience (notably during the 1962 Cuban missile crisis) and also promoted social reform and communication between different faiths. In 1962 he convened the influential Second Vatican Council to approve such liberalizing measures as the introduction of the mass spoken in the vernacular instead of Latin, but died before these changes were finally passed. He was beatified in 2000.
Feast Day: 3 June.

John of Avila   (1500–1569) Spanish priest and missionary. Born into a wealthy family of Almodovar del Campo in Castile, he studied law at the University of Salamanca and theology at Alcala before renouncing his studies in favour of the religious life. He was ordained a priest in 1525 and steadily built a reputation as a speaker, in due course winning recognition as the most charismatic preacher of his generation. Denied his wish to evangelize in Mexico, he spread the gospel through Andalusia, attracting congregations numbering thousands. He also wrote copiously to his converts and many of his letters survive, together with some of his sermons. In 1531 his success attracted the opposition of the Inquisition, who imprisoned him on various charges but subsequently let him go. John continued his missionary work through Spain and acted as spiritual adviser to many notable figures, including St IGNATIUS LOYOLA, St JOHN OF THE CROSS, St PETER OF ALCANTARA and St TERESA OF AVILA. Remembered today chiefly for his writings on spiritual matters, he was canonized in 1970.
Feast Day: 10 May.

John of Beverley   (d.721) English bishop. Born at Harpham, he studied at Canterbury under St ADRIAN before serving as a monk at the monastery at Whitby during the time of St HILDA. He was consecrated bishop of Hexham in 687 and earned a reputation both as a teacher and for his sympathy towards the poor and handicapped. He was also well known for his love of solitude, often retiring to a hermitage to pray. In 705 he became bishop of York, in which post he founded the monastery of Beverley (then a secluded location in a forest). He retired to Beverley in 717 and remained there until his death. John of Beverley was much honoured in medieval and post-medieval England and it was to his influence that Henry V credited the great victory of Agincourt in 1415.
Feast Day: 7 May.

John of Bridlington   (d.1379) English monk. Born at Thwing near Bridlington, he studied at Oxford before joining the canons of St Augustine's monastery at Bridlington. In due course he rose to the rank of prior, acquiring a reputation for piety and wisdom. After his death many miracles were reported at his tomb and he was canonized in 1401.
Feast Day: 21 October.

John of Capistrano   (1386–1456) Italian missionary. Born at Capistrano in the Abruzzi, he studied law in Perugia, married and became governor of Perugia before responding to his religious vocation and giving everything up to become a Franciscan friar. He was ordained in 1420 and spent most of the rest of his life preaching as a missionary throughout the length and breadth of Italy, attracting huge crowds wherever he went. His closest associates in this work included St BERNARDINO OF SIENA and St JAMES OF THE MARCH. John of Capistrano also played a prominent role in reconciling rivals within the Franciscan brotherhood and travelled abroad on several occasions as a representative of the pope. Appointed inquisitor-general to Vienna in 1451, he proved a vigorous opponent of the Hussites (a cause of criticism in after years). In 1453 he was ordered to preach a crusade against the Turks and was present at the Hungarian victory at Belgrade in 1456. He died shortly afterwards, however, after being struck down with plague. He was canonized in 1724.
Feast Day: 23 October.

John of God   (1495–1550) Portuguese founder. Born at Monte Mor il nuovo in Portugal, he lived the life of a mercenary soldier for many years, fighting against the French and the Turks in Hungary, and generally abandoned himself to a dissolute, immoral existence. On his return to Spain he spent some time as a shepherd before, at the age of 40, suddenly repenting his past life and deciding to dedicate himself to God. Such was the violence of his conversion that his behaviour (including tearing out his hair and running wildly in the streets) was mistaken for that of a madman and he was hospitalized. Under the guidance of St JOHN OF AVILA he devoted himself to the care of the sick and needy and set up a house in Granada to provide shelter for prostitutes and other outcasts. His dedication to his charges, combined with his humility and piety, gradually won him great respect and after his death the organization he had begun evolved into an order of hospitallers called the Brothers of St John of God (also known as the Brothers Hospitallers). He was canonized in 1690 and is honoured as

the patron saint of nurses, the sick and booksellers (a reference to a brief period he spent as a religious bookseller).
Feast Day: 8 March.

John of Kanti (1390–1473) Polish priest. Born into a fairly prosperous family of Kanti near Oswiecim, John of Kanti (otherwise called **John Cantius**) won respect both for his scholarship and for his generosity towards the poor in his post as professor of sacred scripture at the University of Cracow, where he had been a student himself. He also served a brief period as a parish priest, but proved relatively ineffective in this role and soon returned to his university, where he encouraged students to behave with moderation and himself lived in conditions of extreme austerity. He was canonized in 1767.
Feast Day: 23 December.

John of Nepomuk (*c.*1345–1393) Bohemian priest and martyr. Born at Nepomuk in Bohemia, he entered the priesthood and became a canon of Prague. The details of the martyrdom of John of Nepomuk (or **Nepomucene**) are disputed: according to tradition he was murdered on the orders of King Wenceslas IV after he refused to repeat what he had heard during the queen's confession, but in reality his murder appears to have been the consequence of a bitter difference of opinion between the king and the archbishop of Prague over ecclesiastical rights and property. His murder would appear to have been precipitated by acts he took to prevent the king taking possession of the abbey of Kladruby upon the death of the abbot there, specifically by announcing the appointment of a new abbot at the same time that he announced the death of his predecessor and thus preventing any opportunity for the king to declare the post vacant and confiscate the abbey. Whatever the cause, John of Nepomuk was seized by his murderers, bound, gagged and thrown into the river Vltava to drown. He was canonized in 1729 and is honoured today as the patron saint of Bohemia.
Feast Day: (locally) 5 January.

John of Sahagun (d.1479) Spanish friar. Born into a wealthy family of Sahagun in Spain, he entered the priesthood and through his influential connections enjoyed the possession of no less than five benefices. A favourite of the bishop of Burgos, who perceived his emerging talent, he eventually gave up four of his benefices and used the remaining one to pay for him to study theology at the University of Salamanca. After completing his studies he preached reconciliation to the divided population of the city, becoming known as the apostle of Salamanca. In 1463 he became an Augustinian friar and in due course assumed the post of prior of the community. Though greatly loved by many, he was not without his enemies and his death may have been precipitated by poisoning at the hand of a rich man's mistress after he intervened to end the affair. He was canonized in 1690. *Feast Day: 12 June.*

John of the Cross (1542–1591) Spanish theologian and mystic. Born John de Yepes into an impoverished noble family of Fontiveros near Avila, he was educated by the Jesuits and at the age of 21 entered the Carmelite monastery of Medina del Campo. Given the name John of St Matthias, he was sent to the Carmelite monastery near the University of Salamanca. He was ordained a priest at the age of 25 but, together with his friend St TERESA OF AVILA, was dismayed by the lack of rigour in the order and in collaboration with St Teresa went on to organize the reformed Discalced (meaning barefooted) Carmelite Order, founding its first house at Duruelo in Spain. These reforms stirred up a great deal of opposition during John's own lifetime. Rivals within the Carmelite order kidnapped John of the Cross (a name he assumed in 1568) in 1577 and for nine months confined him in a cell in Toledo, where he was tortured, beaten and starved. While in prison he wrote one of many celebrated poetical works on religious matters, *The Spiritual Canticle.* He eventually managed to escape his captors (supposedly with the help of a vision of the Virgin Mary) and went on to describe the mystical journey of the soul to God in such famed works as *The Ascent of Mount Carmel, The Living Flame of Love* and *The Dark Night of the Soul.* His final months were clouded by rebellion amongst his reformed friars, who took exception to his moderate position and removed him from his post, forcing him to adopt the life of a simple friar and treating him with considerable brutality. He was canonized in 1726 and declared a Doctor of the Church in 1926. *Feast Day: 14 December.*

John the Almsgiver (*c.*560–619) Cypriot-born bishop. Born into a wealthy family of Amathus in Cyprus, he is thought to have married and lived with his family in Cyprus or Egypt. He worked as a public administrator until the age of 50 when, all his family having died, he accepted the post of patriarch of Alexandria. The church in Alexandria was then in a

state of collapse as a result of the controversy engendered by the Mono-physite heresy, but John reinforced the orthodox camp by undertaking widespread reform, setting an example through his own virtuous behaviour and through his unparalleled generosity to the poor. As well as distributing alms on a lavish scale, he also established hospitals and shel-ters for travellers, strove to combat bribery, insisted upon the use of accu-rate weights and measures and adjudicated in disputes between people of the city, however trivial these might be. In 614 he provided money and other aid for refugees from Jerusalem after it was sacked by the Persians. In 619, when Alexandria was similarly threatened with invasion by the Persians, he was forced to retreat to Constantinople and from there to Cyprus, where he died. His reputation for unstinting generosity to the poor and needy long outlived him and he was the original patron of the Order of St John of Jerusalem (though later replaced in this by St JOHN THE BAPTIST).
Feast Day: 11 November.

John the Baptist   (d. *c*.30) Biblical prophet and martyr. Described in the Bible as the forerunner of Christ, John the Baptist was (according to Luke) the child of the elderly Zechariah and his hitherto barren wife Elizabeth, who conceived after the angel Gabriel appeared to her and told her that she would bear a child who would prepare the way for the Messiah. Noth-ing is known of John's early life until, in his early thirties, he retreated to the desert to fast and pray, dressing in skins and eating only locusts and wild honey. After emerging from the desert he preached the word of God and baptized converts in the river Jordan as a sign of their purification, ultimately baptizing Christ (sometimes identified as John's cousin) himself. Subsequently John was arrested on the orders of King Herod Antipas who feared his preaching might spark a rebellion. Unfortunately John had previously incurred the displeasure of Herod's wife Herodias by condemn-ing their marriage (on the grounds that Herodias had been the wife of Herod's half-brother) and Herodias now plotted revenge against him. Accordingly, she told her daughter Salome to dance before the king and, when as a reward Herod promised Salome anything she desired, told her to ask for John the Baptist's head on a platter. John was duly beheaded and his head served up as proof of his death. He is honoured as the patron saint of farriers, tailors, the Knights Hospitallers and also of Turkey. His emblem is a lamb.
Feast Day: 24 June.

John the Egyptian   (c.304–394) Egyptian hermit. Born at Asyut (Lycopolis), John the Egyptian (or **John of Egypt**) worked as a carpenter before
taking up the life of a hermit in his middle age. He set up his retreat on a
mountain near Asyut and remained there for the next 50 years, living on a
diet of dried fruit and vegetables. He became widely respected for his holiness and also for his prophetic gifts. Those who consulted him included
such notable figures as Emperor Theodosius I, who visited him on two
occasions.
Feast Day: 27 March.

John-Baptist de La Salle   (1651–1719) French educator. Born into a noble
family of Rheims, he became a canon at Rheims cathedral and was
ordained a priest in 1678 but changed course when he became interested
in furthering Christian educational reform. Founding two schools for poor
boys, he used his wealth to pursue his aims of improving the quality of
teachers (who on his instructions were not permitted to be priests) and of
reclaiming delinquent children by offering education to those who would
otherwise never go to school. Despite resistance from the Jansenists and
also from professional schoolteachers, he went on to open further schools
for working-class children and teacher-training colleges in Rheims, Paris
and Saint-Denis. Out of these organizations evolved a religious community
dedicated to Christian education, called the Brothers of the Christian
Schools. In due course the order opened schools throughout France as well
as in Rome and today the order has many thousands of members around
the world. Important innovations put in place by the order included the
foundation of Sunday schools, the use of the vernacular instead of Latin in
lessons and an insistence upon silence from the pupils while teaching was
going on. La Salle was canonized in 1900 and is sometimes identified as
the father of the teaching profession. He is honoured today as the patron
saint of teachers.
Feast Day: 7 April.

John Baptist Rossi   (1698–1764) Italian priest. John Baptist Rossi served
for some 40 years as a priest in Rome, earning a reputation for his
unselfish devotion to the sick and needy. Among many other good deeds,
he established shelters for homeless women and prostitutes, cared for the
sick and dying and even donated his own house to his religious order, the
Capuchins. Considered a model of charitable Christian behaviour, he was
canonized in 1881.
Feast Day: 23 May.

John-Baptist Marie Vianney (1786–1859) French preacher. Born into a peasant farming family of Dardilly, he had little education and did not thrive at the ecclesiastical school in Ecully that he attended from the age of 20. He left the school to go into hiding when he was drafted into the army. He escaped punishment when his brother took his place. On his return, he resumed his studies and in 1817 was appointed parish priest for the village of Ars-en-Dombes, near Lyons. While in this post he established a reputation as an impassioned preacher whose sermons attracted huge audiences and he became widely respected for his wisdom, piety and moral intelligence. Hundreds of people came to Ars-en-Dombes each day in order to have their confessions heard by its famous curé who observed the strictest austerity in his personal life and spent up to 18 hours a day in his confessional. On three occasions he planned to leave the village in order to enjoy a quieter life in a monastery, but on each occasion allowed himself to be persuaded to stay. He was canonized in 1925 and is honoured as the patron saint of parish priests.
Feast Day: 4 August.

John Berchmans (1599–1621) Belgian Jesuit. Born in Brabant, Belgium, John Berchmans was the son of a master shoemaker who was too poor to send his son to school. He was educated instead by a local priest and soon determined upon a life as a priest himself and dreamed of achieving sainthood. At the age of 17, defying the wish of his parents, he decided to join the Jesuit order and in 1617 entered the Jesuit novitiate. While studying at the Jesuit College in Rome he showed great promise as a scholar priest and impressed others with both his piety and his characteristic cheerfulness. He completed the course in 1621 but was then struck down by dysentery and died aged only 22. A highly popular figure in his native Flanders, he was canonized in 1888. He is honoured as the patron saint of youth, altar boys and altar girls.
Feast Day: 13 August.

John Bosco (1815–1888) Italian visionary and founder of the Salesians. Born into a peasant family of Becchi in Piedmont, he had the first of many prophetic dreams at the age of nine, believing he was being instructed by the Virgin Mary to dedicate his life to the care of poor boys. He studied for the priesthood from the age of 16 and was ordained a priest in 1841, aged 26. After moving to Turin, he worked selflessly on behalf of homeless children in the city and set about providing religious services for them as well as other resources. Over the years that followed he gathered around

him a considerable community of street youths and, overcoming the opposition of civil authorities, provided them with various facilities, including
schools and a church dedicated to St FRANCIS DE SALES. Among his pupils
were such notable figures as St DOMINIC SAVIO. The priests who were
attracted to John Bosco and his work formed the basis for what in 1854
became the Society of St Francis de Sales, often referred to as the Salesians,
which now has foundations in countries all round the world. The order
provides schools of various kinds as well as hospitals and foreign
missions. In 1872, conscious of the need to help poor girls, he co-founded
with St **Mary Mazzarello** (d.1881) the Daughters of Our Lady, Help of
Christians. He recorded some of his many dreams and visions at the
request of Pope Pius IX and was widely credited with prophetic powers.
Many of his letters survive. Commonly called one of the Apostolic Fathers,
John Bosco was canonized in 1934. He is honoured as the patron saint of
apprentices and labourers.
Feast Day: 31 January.

John de Brébeuf (1593–1649) French martyr. Born in Condé-sur-Vire in
Normandy, he became a Jesuit priest and in 1625 volunteered to be one of
the first three Jesuit missionaries to be sent to Canada. Despite suffering
from tuberculosis, he spent the next 25 years converting the Hurons in
Quebec, even writing a catechism for their use. In 1649, however, he was
captured at Sault Ste Marie, along with several others, by the Iroquois,
who were the enemies of the Hurons. The priests were exposed to the
most brutal tortures, including the wearing of necklaces of red-hot lance
blades, but John de Brébeuf never ceased preaching. The faces of the
missionaries were then torn to shreds and they were finally put to death
by being plunged into boiling water in a mock baptism. The Iroquois were
much impressed by John de Brébeuf's courage and after they had killed
him they drank his blood in order to inherit his bravery. A number of
letters by John de Brébeuf have survived. He was canonized in 1930.
Feast Day: 26 September.

John de Britto (1647–1693) Portuguese martyr. Born in Lisbon, he joined
the Jesuits and was sent as a missionary to southern India in 1673. As
head of the mission at Madurai, he strove to immerse himself in the lives
of the local population and thereby had considerable success in converting
them. Unfortunately, after one convert repudiated his many wives under
the influence of his Christian advisers, the outraged raja of Marava singled

John de Britto out for blame and instigated persecution of all Christians in the region. John de Britto himself was beheaded at Oriur. He was canonized in 1947.

Feast Day: 4 February.

John Cassian (*c.*360–*c.*435) Abbot and Father of the Church. Possibly born in Romania, John Cassian served as a monk in Bethlehem from around 380 and then spent time in the Egyptian desert in company with the desert fathers, keeping records of the discussions he had with them. He moved on to Egypt and Constantinople and was then sent to Rome to argue the case of St JOHN CHRYSOSTOM. Having been ordained a priest while in Rome, he spent the rest of his life in France, living in Marseilles and there founding (415) two monasteries, one for men and one for women. His influential writings included the *Institutes* and the *Conferences*, which exerted a profound effect upon the monastic tradition in both the East and the West. Among the notable figures much influenced by his work were St BENEDICT, St AUGUSTINE and St GREGORY.

Feast Day: 23 July.

John Chrysostom (*c.*347–407) Syrian patriarch of Constantinople. Born into a wealthy family of Antioch in Syria, the son of an officer in the imperial army, he was baptized as a Christian at the age of 20 and, giving up his law studies, spent six years living the life of a hermit in the wilderness before returning to the city and being ordained a priest in 385. Known as 'the golden-mouthed' because of his eloquence as a preacher, he was appointed patriarch of Constantinople by Emperor Arcadius in 397 and is remembered as one of the most celebrated and influential churchmen of his time, whose sermons typically emphasized the greatness of God's mercy. His outspoken manner and his campaign against the immorality and extravagance of the imperial court of Empress Eudoxia, however, made him many enemies and the empress was twice persuaded to order the patriarch into exile. On the second occasion he died of exhaustion while on his way to a remote location on the Black Sea. His extensive and influential writings included *On the Priesthood*, which comprised a dialogue between himself and St BASIL, sermons, homilies and letters. John Chrysostom is considered one of the four great Greek Doctors of the Church and is honoured today as the patron saint of preachers and of Turkey. His emblem is a beehive (a symbol of eloquence).

Feast Day: 13 September.

John Climacus   (c.570–c.649) Syrian abbot. Born in Syria, John Climacus (otherwise called **John the Scholastic**) entered the monastery of Mount Sinai at the age of 16 and lived as a monk there for some years, possibly as a pupil of St GREGORY OF NAZIANZUS. When his mentor Abba Martyrius died he left the monastery to live the life of a hermit in a cave at Tholas at the foot of the mountain and remained there for 20 years, in conditions of great austerity. He also paid visits to the monasteries of Egypt and at the age of 70 was appointed abbot of the monastery back at Sinai. As abbot, he wrote the celebrated *The Ladder of Divine Ascent*, a book in 30 chapters that detailed the steps to be taken in climbing the spiritual ladder (*klimakis* in Greek) to God. It is for this book, which introduced the metaphor of the ladder to heaven, that he is usually remembered.
Feast Day: 30 March.

John Damascene   (c.657–c.749) Damascus-born monk and theologian. The son of a prominent Christian official at the khalif's court in Damascus, John Damascene (otherwise known as **John of Damascus**) succeeded his father as chief financial officer of the court before retiring in order to take up the life of a monk at the monastery at Mar Saba near Jerusalem, where he was to remain for the rest of his life. He emerged as the leading opponent of the heresy of Iconoclasm (which denounced the veneration of images), writing three influential treatises against such beliefs, and won recognition as a major theological scholar of his time. He was also the author of *The Fountain of Wisdom*, a series of three books in which he summarized the teaching of the Greek Fathers of the Church. Other works by his hand included books on philosophy and religious education as well as several enduring hymns. He was himself declared a Doctor of the Church in 1890.
Feast Day: 4 December.

John Eudes   (1601–1680) French founder. Born the son of a farmer at Ri in Normandy, John Eudes attended the Jesuit College at Caen before entering the Congregation of the Oratory of France in 1623 and emerging as an energetic and enthusiastic preacher and parish missionary who in due course did much to promote the renewal of the faith throughout the country. He also won great respect for his selfless service of victims of two plague epidemics. In 1643 he left the Oratory and founded a seminary called the Community of Jesus and Mary (known as the Eudists) at Caen to support the campaign for renewal of the priesthood. Although this order failed to win papal approval, he did win papal recognition of his later creation, the

order of the Sisters of Our Lady of Charity of the Refuge, which offered
shelter to reformed prostitutes. John Eudes spent his final years comple-
menting the work of St MARGARET MARY ALACOQUE towards promoting
devotion of the Sacred Heart, specifically by contributing a doctrinal basis
for such worship. He was canonized in 1925.
Feast Day: 19 August.

John Fisher (1469–1535) English bishop and martyr. Born the son of a
textile merchant of Beverley in Yorkshire, John Fisher was educated at
Cambridge and in due course became master of Michaelhouse College
there and in 1501 vice-chancellor of the university. In 1504 he became chancellor of Cambridge University and bishop of Rochester and set about
revitalizing both the university (founding several new colleges) and his
diocese, in so doing earning the praise of Henry VIII among many others.
However, relations between the bishop of Rochester and the king soured
when Fisher emerged as the leading critic of his planned divorce from
Catherine of Aragon (whom Fisher served as confessor) and assumption of
independence as head of the Church of England. In 1535 Fisher refused to
take the Oath of Succession to Henry and was consequently arrested and
imprisoned in the Tower of London. The pope responded by sending
Fisher a cardinal's hat, but Henry had the rebellious bishop tried on
charges of high treason and condemned to death. Already in ill health,
Fisher was beheaded on 22 June 1535, several days before his friend
St THOMAS MORE. He was canonized in 1935.
Feast Day: 22 June.

John Gabriel Perboyre (1802–1840) French missionary and martyr. Born
in LePeuch, Cahors, John Gabriel Perboyre became a Lazarist priest at
Montauban in 1826 and at his own insistence was eventually sent as a
missionary to China in 1835. After four years' dedicated work there, caring
for abandoned children and winning converts to Christianity, he was
arrested during a renewed wave of persecution against Christians and
subjected to brutal torture over the course of a year. Refusing stubbornly
to inform on his companions or to stamp on a crucifix, he was eventually
strangled to death alongside five criminals. He was canonized in 1996.
Feast Day: 11 September.

John Gualbert (*c*.995–1073) Italian abbot and founder. According to
tradition, John Gualbert (the son of a nobleman of Florence) determined
upon a life as a monk after experiencing a religious revelation that

occurred when he had his brother's murderer at his mercy and was suddenly moved by the thought of the crucified Christ to spare the man's life. He lived as a monk at San Miniato in Florence for some years before leaving and in due course founding a Benedictine community at Vallombrosa in Tuscany. Supporting the monks with lay-brothers (his own innovation) the community prospered and in turn inspired the establishment of a whole series of similar monasteries, complete with hospices for the care of the poor and the sick. The success of the order did much to promote reform in the wider church. John Gualbert was canonized in 1193. *Feast Day: 12 July.*

John de Lalande   *See* NORTH AMERICA, MARTYRS OF.

John Henry Newman   (1801–1890) English cardinal. Born in London, he was brought up as an Evangelical in the traditions of the Anglican church before becoming a fellow at Oxford University. In 1833 he became leader of the so-called Oxford Movement, which favoured the reformation of the Anglican church and a return to the more Catholic character of early Christianity. Newman himself finally resigned from Oxford University and converted to Roman Catholicism in 1845. Subsequently he gradually won recognition as a leading Catholic theologian through such books as *An Essay on the Development of Christian Doctrine* and *A Grammar of Assent*. Other celebrated writings included his autobiography, *Apologia pro Vita Sua*. He was raised to the rank of cardinal in 1879. *Feast Day: 11 August.*

John Joseph of the Cross   (1654–1734) Italian friar. Born Carlo Gaetano on the island of Ischia, off Naples, he determined upon a life as a monk at a young age and accordingly joined the Franciscans at Santa Lucia del Monte at Naples at the age of 16. He quickly established a reputation for the austere life he led and when he became head of the monastery at Piedimonte di Alife at the tender age of 21 he encouraged his charges to practise similar self-denial. He also constructed hermitages around the monastery so that he and others could go into retreat for prayer and penance from time to time. Such was the reverence in which he was held by the populace of Naples that whenever he walked in the streets he would be followed by a crowd hoping to snip off a piece of his friar's habit. He was canonized in 1839 and is honoured today as the patron saint of Naples. *Feast Day: 5 March.*

John Leonardi (c.1542–1609) Italian founder. Brought up in Lucca, he lived the life of a laybrother for some years before being ordained a priest in 1572. Dedicated to the cause of reform in the Catholic church, he was appointed to inspire the renewal of faith in Lucca after the turmoil of the Reformation and quickly won respect for his tireless work in the hospitals and prisons of the city. In due course he attracted a considerable number of other priests who shared the same ideals and he decided to organize them into a new religious order, later named the Clerks Regular of the Mother of God. This congregation of diocesan priests was dedicated to reform, education and charitable works and ultimately won papal approval (though surprisingly the organization was driven out of Lucca itself). John Leonardi himself died of plague while ministering to the sick. He was canonized in 1938.
Feast Day: 9 October.

John Nepomucene Neumann (1811–1860) Bohemian bishop and founder. Born the son of a German businessman of Prachatitz in Bohemia, he was named after St JOHN OF NEPOMUK and determined to enter the priesthood while attending Prague University. He settled in the USA in 1836 and, after being ordained a priest by the bishop of New York, was sent to work among the German-speaking immigrants of the Niagara Falls area. After four years he joined the Redemptorist novitiate in Pittsburgh and in due course, after a period as a parish priest in Baltimore, became provincial superior of the order across the USA. In 1852 he was appointed bishop of Philadelphia, in which post he oversaw the building of 100 churches and 80 schools and paid particular attention to the plight of the poor. He also founded the School Sisters of Notre Dame, who undertook religious education and the maintenance of an orphanage. Exhausted by his labours, he died suddenly in a Philadelphia street. He was canonized in 1977, thus becoming the first US bishop to achieve sainthood.
Feast Day: 5 January.

John Ogilvie (1579–1615) Scottish martyr. Born at Drum-na-Keith in Banffshire, the son of a Scottish nobleman, John Ogilvie became a Catholic at the age of 17 while studying on the continent of Europe and subsequently entered the Jesuit order, living until 1610 at Rouen. Defying the ban on priests in the British Isles, he returned secretly to Scotland in 1613 to undertake missionary work in Edinburgh, Renfrew and Glasgow. Perhaps inevitably he was eventually betrayed to the authorities and arrested, tortured and tried on a charge of high treason. In the hope of

extracting a confession from him, as well as the names of other Catholics, John Ogilvie's captors deprived him of sleep for eight days, but this and torture by means of the notorious 'boot' (which crushed the victims' legs) proved futile. John Ogilvie was duly condemned to death and hanged in Glasgow. He was canonized in 1976.
Feast Day: 10 March.

John Regis   (1597–1640) French missionary. Born the son of a wealthy merchant of Narbonne, he entered the Jesuit order and following his ordination in 1631 spent the rest of his life as a missionary worker in the Auvergne and Languedoc regions, which had been ravaged by prolonged civil war. He became greatly loved for his work on behalf of outcasts and the poor and after his premature death his grave in the village of La Louvesc in Dauphiné became an important site of pilgrimage. He was canonized in 1737. He is honoured as the patron saint of medical social workers.
Feast Day: 16 June.

John Ruysbroeck   (1293–1381) Belgian founder and writer. Born in Ruysbroeck near Brussels, he became a priest in Brussels and emerged as a prominent figure in the influential *Devotio Moderna* movement that encouraged the faithful to make a personal commitment to follow Christ. He concentrated upon prayer and writing on spiritual matters (in Flemish instead of the usual Latin) between the years 1317 and 1343 but then engaged more directly with the world around him by co-founding a monastery at Groenendael in Belgium. Under his leadership the monastery became famous as a centre for the ideals of the *Devotio Moderna* movement, attracting huge numbers of pilgrims seeking spiritual advice.
Feast Day: 2 December.

Jordan of Saxony   (d.1237) German Dominican leader. Jordan's considerable leadership qualities were recognized early in his career as a member of the Dominican order. Having joined the order in 1220 he took part in the first general chapter at Bologna and when the order's founder St DOMINIC died just two years later he was the natural choice to become the Dominicans' second master-general. A kindly and charming man, he presided over a massive expansion in the Dominican order, winning many converts at the universities where he preached. His disciples included St ALBERT THE GREAT. He sent friars to distant parts of Germany, Switzerland and Denmark to further the Dominican cause and also promoted the foundation of institutions for the Dominican sisters, forming a long and enduring friendship with St DIANA D'ANDALO and writing numerous letters to her, of which many survive. His other writings included a celebrated biography of St Dominic. His death came when he and two other friars drowned in a shipwreck off Syria while sailing to the Holy Land. *Feast Day: 15 February.*

Josaphat   (c.1580–1623) Bishop and martyr of Lithuania. Born Josaphat Kunsevich into a wealthy merchant family of Vladimir, he served as a monk at a monastery in Vilna, in time becoming abbot there, before being appointed bishop of Vitebsk and then archbishop of Polotsk in Belarus in 1617. As bishop he instituted many reforms of clerical and lay life throughout his diocese and also dedicated himself to the reunion of the Byzantine Orthodox church with Roman Catholicism. A noted preacher, he managed to attract much support for his cause, but also encountered fierce opposition from those who feared the loss of independence in their church. Josaphat's opponents managed to persuade the chancellor of Lithuania to place a charge of using violent methods against him: when Josaphat visited Vitebsk in a bid to calm the atmosphere he was met with seething anger and was ultimately attacked by a mob and murdered. His mutilated body was thrown into the Dvina river. He was canonized in 1867, thus becoming the first person from the Eastern church to be officially recognized by the Vatican as a saint.
Feast Day: 12 November.

Josemaría Escrivá   (1902–1975) Spanish founder of Opus Dei and the Priestly Society of the Holy Cross. Born the son of a businessman of Barbastro in Aragon, he was ordained a priest at the Logrono seminary in 1925. He moved to Madrid to study law in 1927 and a year later founded Opus Dei to promote the spreading of the word of God throughout the world. In 1930 he extended the scope of Opus Dei to include women as well as men. When the Spanish Civil War broke out Josemaría Escrivá was obliged to go into hiding and eventually relocated to Burgos. He returned to Madrid with the end of the war and went on to found the Priestly Society of the Holy Cross to support the evangelical work of Opus Dei through the ordination of lay members of Opus Dei. Josemaría Escrivá moved to Rome in 1946, where he was granted senior posts at the Vatican, and subsequently he visited many countries around the world to encourage the activities of Opus Dei, which boasted over 60,000 members by the time of its founder's death. His organization was formally renamed the

Prelature of the Holy Cross and Opus Dei in 1982. Josemaría Escrivá was canonized in 2002.
Feast Day: 30 June.

Joseph   (1st century) The husband of the Virgin Mary. According to the Bible, Joseph was distantly descended from King David, thus linking Christ with the royal line of the Jews. He came from Bethlehem and lived the life of a poor carpenter. In character he is described as just, kindly and obedient. Having become betrothed to Mary, the revelation of Mary's pregnancy appears to have troubled Joseph considerably as the child was evidently not his, but after praying and being visited by an angel in his dreams he resolved to accept the situation and not to divorce Mary as the law allowed him but instead to place his trust in God and make her his wife. He appears to have proved a caring husband to Mary and foster-father to Christ in the years that followed, trying to protect them from Herod by leading them into exile in Egypt and eventually settling in Nazareth. He disappears from the biblical story of Christ's life before his crucifixion. Reverence of Joseph as a saint reached a peak in the medieval period. Today he is honoured as the patron saint of fathers, carpenters, manual workers and travellers and also of the countries Peru and China.
Feast Day: 19 March, 1 May.

Joseph of Arimathea   (1st century) Disciple. The only source of information about the life of Joseph of Arimathea is the Bible, which identifies him as a wealthy member of the Jewish council who became a disciple and retrieved Christ's body from Pilate and had it placed in the tomb he had had prepared for himself (Mark 15:42–46). Medieval legend added the tradition that Joseph was sent by St PHILIP as a missionary to England, where he founded the first church at Glastonbury. A thorn tree on Glastonbury Tor is said to have sprouted from his staff and to flower each year at Christmas. Joseph of Arimathea also appears in Arthurian legend.
Feast Day: 31 August.

Joseph of Cupertino   (1603–1663) Italian priest. Born Joseph Desa into a poor family of Cupertino (or Copertino) near Brindisi, he was considered slow-witted as a child and nicknamed 'the gaper'. As a young man he was admitted as a servant and ultimately as a friar at the Franciscan friary of La Grottella and went on to be ordained a priest in 1628. Around the same time he experienced the first of many apparently miraculous experiences, which included ecstasies, acts of healing and levitation. It was concluded that these happenings were manifestations of divine influence, though Joseph was generally obliged to live in seclusion because of the disruption he caused to the daily routine of La Grottella and the other friaries to which he was moved over the years. He was canonized in 1767 in recognition of the patience and humility with which he accepted his apparent gifts and is honoured today as the patron saint of students and air travellers.

Feast Day: 18 September.

Joseph Cafasso   (1811–1860) Italian priest. Born in Castelnuovo D'Asti in Piedmont, he was ordained in 1833 and became well-known for his great wisdom and piety. Disabled from birth because of curvature of the spine, he defied prejudice to win respect as a preacher, confessor and teacher, eventually being appointed professor and, in 1848, rector of the Institute of St Francis in Turin, providing guidance for numerous young priests in their future lives. He also dedicated himself to ministering to prison inmates and accompanied some 60 condemned men to their executions. Notable figures who came under his influence included the youthful St JOHN BOSCO, who held him in great reverence and in the fullness of time preached at his funeral. Joseph Cafasso was canonized in 1947 and is honoured today as the patron saint of prisoners.

Feast Day: 23 June.

Juan Diego   (1474–1548) Mexican visionary. Born into a poor Aztec family near Mexico City and for most of his life scraping a living as a farmer and weaver, Juan Diego (or Cuauhtlatoatzin as he was originally known) converted to Christianity in 1625. Quiet and religious in nature, he is reported to have had his first vision of the Virgin Mary at the relatively advanced age of 57. The Franciscan bishop of Mexico remained unimpressed until, on Mary's instructions, Juan gathered roses from the top of a nearby hill and presented them in his cloak to the bishop, upon which her image appeared on the cloth enclosing the flowers. Juan Diego's cloak, still bearing the image of the Virgin Mary, hangs to this day in the Basilica of Our Lady of Guadalupe.

Feast Day: 9 December.

Juan Macías   (1585–1645) Spanish monk. Born in Rivera de Fresno near Badajoz, he claimed even as a child to have experienced visions of the Virgin Mary, Christ and other saints. In 1619 he emigrated to the New World and eventually settled near Lima, Peru. There he worked on a cattle

ranch before moving into the city of Lima and, having given away his earnings, entering the Dominican monastery of Santa Maria Magdalena in 1622. As a monk he became well-known for his prayerfulness and generosity. He undertook the duties of doorkeeper and became a familiar face to those in need of spiritual guidance and more practical help. Such was his reputation for wisdom that he was even consulted by the Spanish viceroy and the nobility of Lima. He was canonized in 1975.
Feast Day: 18 September.

Jude (1st century) Apostle. Often identified with **Thaddaeus**, the brother of JAMES and the author of the Epistle of Jude in the New Testament (not to be confused with Judas Iscariot, the betrayer of Christ). Tradition has it that after Christ's death Jude was martyred in Persia alongside SIMON for preaching the gospel, but nothing else is known about his life. He is honoured today as the patron saint of hospitals and of lost causes (an association that may have arisen through the similarity between his name and that of Judas, as a result of which he is thought less likely to be approached by many petitioners and thus ready to answer even the most hopeless prayer). His emblem is a club (a reference to the weapon with which he supposed to have been killed).
Feast Day: 28 October.

Julian of Norwich (c.1343–c.1423) English mystic. Little is known about this 14th-century female recluse, including even her name – she is called Julian of Norwich simply because she lived in a cell adjoining the Benedictine church of St Julian in Conisford, Norwich. Having narrowly survived death from illness at the age of 30 (purportedly through prayer) she fell seriously ill once more in 1373 and experienced a series of 16 revelatory visions, mostly concerning the passion of Christ. After her recovery she meditated on these visions and, being apparently a well-educated woman, went on to record her thoughts in *Revelations of Divine Love*, which was widely read in later centuries and also appeared in a shortened form entitled *Showings*.
Feast Day: 13 May.

Julian the Hospitaller (dates unknown) Nobleman. Historical evidence for the existence of Julian the Hospitaller appears to be non-existent and it would seem that he was the creation of medieval romance, making possibly his first appearance in a story written in the 13th century by Vincent de Beauvais, subsequently elaborated in the *Golden Legend* by Jacobus de

Voragine. Julian is identified in these tales as a nobleman who mistakenly kills his own mother and father when he finds them in his bed (thinking they are his wife and her lover). He is driven by remorse to give up his wealth and live humbly with his wife beside a ford across a river, where he may do penance by tending to the needs of travellers and offering shelter to the poor. When the couple offer a dying leper their own bed to sleep in they are finally assured that Christ has forgiven them and they are promised a place in heaven. Julian and his wife duly die soon after. Whatever the origins of the legend, many hospitals, churches and other institutions now go by the name of Julian the Hospitaller. He is also honoured as the patron saint of ferrymen and innkeepers as well as circus performers and other wandering folk.
Feast Day: 12 February.

Juliana (4th century) Italian martyr. The life of Juliana is largely a matter of legend. She is supposed to have engaged in a long contest with the devil, who sought to persuade her to give up her vow of virginity and marry as her father and suitor (sometimes identified as a Roman prefect) wished. She is thought to have been tortured and beheaded for her stubborn faith at Cumae (or possibly Naples), still a virgin.
Feast Day: 16 February.

Juliana Falconieri (1270–1341) Italian foundress. Born the daughter of wealthy parents in Florence, she declined to marry and instead entered the Servite order as a tertiary. She remained at home, living a pious existence and doing good deeds, for some 20 years before her mother died in 1304 and she moved into a convent of nuns called the Mantellate and became their superior. She eventually secured full recognition for the sisters as members of the Servite order and is consequently remembered as the effective foundress of the Servite nuns. Few other details of her life are known. She was canonized in 1737.
Feast Day: 19 June.

Julie Billiart (1751–1816) French foundress. Born into a wealthy family of the village of Cuvilly in Picardy, she saw her family gradually slip into poverty but still found time to teach others in religious matters. In 1774, however, her life changed dramatically when someone fired a shot at her father through the window of their house. The shot missed but triggered a mysterious nervous illness in Julie that rendered her a bedridden invalid. Undaunted, she continued her religious studies and, with the outbreak of the French Revolution, emerged as a prominent and outspoken opponent of the new state church. She was obliged to go into hiding from those who would silence her but, with the support of a viscountess named Frances Blin, worked tirelessly to renew the faith in France, founding the Institute of Notre Dame in Amiens to care for and instruct girls of poor families. In 1804 a visiting priest commanded her to pray to the Sacred Heart and soon after she found herself able to walk again. She spent the last years of her life continuing her collaboration with Frances Blin, establishing a chain of 15 Notre Dame convents throughout the country. She was canonized in 1969.

Feast Day: 8 April.

Julitta   *See* CYRICUS AND JULITTA.

Julius I   (d.352) Italian pope. Born in Rome, he succeeded St Marcus as pope after a gap of four months in 337. As pope, he presided over the early church during one of its most turbulent periods, having to cope with much dissension between his bishops, who levelled charges of heresy at one another, and theological controversy. He gave his support to St ATHANASIUS against the adherents of Arianism and helped secure his return to his see at Alexandria and in so doing asserted the authority of the papacy over the church. He also oversaw the expansion of the Christian community, ordered the building of two basilicas and churches and introduced the first lists of saints' days.

Feast Day: 12 April.

Julius of Durostorum   (d. c.302) Roman martyr. Otherwise known as **Julius the Veteran**, he is supposed to have been a respected Roman soldier of 27 years' experience who was beheaded with a sword along with several others for his Christian faith at Durostorum in Lower Moesia (in Bulgaria).

Feast Day: 27 May.

Junípero Serra   (1713–1784) Spanish friar. Ordained as a Franciscan friar in 1738, he established a reputation as a scholar and occupied the Duns Scotus chair of philosophy at Lullian University in Majorca before being sent to the Apostolic College of San Fernando in Mexico City in 1749. In order to further his missionary work in the area he founded nine missions in Upper California (beginning with the mission at San Diego in 1769) after its conquest by Spain and travelled extensively, despite the fact that he was in continual pain throughout much of his life as the result of a venomous bite by an insect or snake. He devoted much of his energy towards converting the native American population of the region and is said to have baptized some six thousand of them into the Christian faith. He also did much to improve living conditions for the indigenous population, improving agricultural practice and defending their interests against their Spanish conquerors.

Feast Day: 1 July.

Justin (*c.*100–165) Greek philosopher and martyr. Born of Greek parentage in Neopolis, the capital of Samaria, he established a reputation as a pagan philosopher before converting to Christianity around 135, finding it a more satisfactory system than those he had previously studied. He went on to devote his considerable gifts as a philosopher to Christian theology, addressing himself in particular to Jews and pagans in the conviction that he could attract many more converts to the faith. He arrived in Rome around 150 and established a school of philosophy in the city, as well as writing books on Christian philosophy, but was soon attacked by pagan critics for his outspoken views and was eventually arrested and beheaded for refusing to make sacrifices to the gods. He is remembered as the first Christian philosopher and is accordingly honoured as the patron saint of philosophers.

Feast Day: 1 June.

Justina *See* CYPRIAN AND JUSTINA.

Justus of Beauvais (dates unknown) French martyr. Legend has it that Justus of Beauvais was a nine-year-old boy who was put to death by the authorities after he helped to hide two fellow-Christians (his father and his uncle) from their Roman pursuers during the persecution carried out in the reign of the emperor Diocletian. The location of these events is traditionally placed at Saint-Just-en-Chaussée between Beauvais and Senlis. No reliable historical basis for the legend has yet been found.

Feast Day: 18 October.

Justus of Canterbury (d. *c.*627) English bishop. Justus of Canterbury arrived in England with the second group of Roman missionaries sent by St GREGORY THE GREAT in 601. He became the first bishop of Rochester in 604 and in this post sought (with little success) to bring the practice of Irish and British Christians into line with that of Rome. He was obliged to flee to Gaul after the death of King Ethelbert but soon returned and in 624,

in recognition of his piety and loyalty to Rome, was appointed fourth archbishop of Canterbury, with the power to consecrate his own bishops.
Feast Day: 10 November.

Juventinus and Maximinus   *See* JOHN AND PAUL.

K

Kateri Tekawitha (1656–1680) Native American convert. Born in Osser-
non (renamed Ariesville) in New York, Kateri (or **Katherine**) Tekawitha
was the daughter of a Mohawk chief and a Christian Algonquin. Badly
affected by smallpox while still a child, she became estranged from her
family when she took a vow of chastity and chose to be baptized as a
Catholic by a Jesuit missionary in 1676. She was forced to flee 200 miles to
the Christian village of Caughnawaga near Montreal and here dedicated
herself to an austere life of prayer and penance, fasting and torturing
herself by various means, including beatings and going without sleep, in
imitation of the suffering of Christ at his crucifixion. She was eventually
dissuaded from her more extreme penitential practices by the Jesuits, but
still insisted upon sleeping on a bed of thorns after the example set by
St ALOYSIUS GONZAGA. Exhausted by illness and this latest torment she
died a few days later at the age of 24. She is remembered as the first
native American to achieve sainthood and her grave at Caughnawaga
became a place of pilgrimage. She is honoured as the patron saint of
ecology and the environment.
Feast Day: 14 July.

Katharine of Alexandria   *See* CATHERINE OF ALEXANDRIA.

Katharine Drexel (1858–1955) US foundress. Born into a famous banking
family of Philadelphia, she inherited a share in a multi-million dollar estate
and used her wealth to pursue her religious vocation. She was particularly
dedicated to the education of native American children and provided the
funds for numerous church schools where they could be taught. Dissuaded
by others from becoming a nun herself, in 1891 she founded the Sisters of
the Blessed Sacrament to minister chiefly to native Americans and African-
Americans. The order boasted over 100 sisters by 1904. Over her lifetime
Katharine Drexel paid some 20 million dollars to establish 145 Catholic
missions, 12 schools for native Americans, 50 schools for African-
Americans and Xavier University in New Orleans for Black Catholics. She
was forced to go into retirement after a heart attack in 1935 but lived
quietly for another 18 years before her death at the age of 97. She was

canonized in 2000, thus becoming the second American-born person to achieve sainthood.
Feast Day: 3 March.

Katherine Tekawitha   *See* KATERI TEKAWITHA.

Kenelm   (d. *c*.811) English prince. The life of St Kenelm is shrouded in obscurity, but tradition has it that he was the son of King Coenwulf of Mercia and was murdered on the orders of his sister Quoenthryth as soon as he succeeded to the throne. Quoenthryth allegedly suffered punishment for the deed when her eyes fell out. Historians suggest that in reality Kenelm probably predeceased his father, possibly dying in battle against the Welsh. He has a shrine at Winchcombe Abbey in Gloucestershire and was revered as a martyr in medieval times.
Feast Day: 17 July.

Kenneth   *See* CANICE.

Kentigern   (*c*.518–d.612) Scottish bishop. Otherwise called **Mungo** (meaning 'darling'), Kentigern is traditionally supposed to have been born in Lothian, possibly of royal birth. He became a monk, adopting the Celtic practices of self-denial and solitude, and in due course founded a church at Glasgow and was appointed the city's first bishop. He is also said to have worked as a missionary in Cumbria or Wales, possibly founding the monastery at Llanelwy. Various legends have accrued around Kentigern's name, including one in which he agreed to assist a queen who had passed a ring the king had given her to her lover, only for the king to retrieve the ring, throw it in the sea and then challenge his wife to present it to him. Kentigern went fishing, found the ring in the stomach of a salmon he caught and was able to return it to the remorseful queen. This tale is thought to be the reason why a ring and a fish appear on the coat of arms of Glasgow, of which he is the patron saint.
Feast Day: 13 January.

Kevin   (d.618) Irish abbot. Born in Leinster, Kevin (or **Coemgen**) was brought up at the monastery of Kilmanach before living the life of a hermit at Glendalough, picturesquely situated in Wicklow. Here he attracted many disciples and out of this community evolved the famous abbey of Glendalough, which also boasted a celebrated school. Kevin is also said to have made a pilgrimage to Rome, from which he brought back various relics. Though weakened by a life of great austerity, he is said to have lived to the age of 120. He is honoured as the patron saint of Dublin. *Feast Day: 3 June.*

Keyne (6th century) English maiden. Little is known of the details of the life of St Keyne (or **Cain**) who is said to have lived somewhere in south-west England or south Wales. According to 14th-century legend, she was a beautiful virgin who took a vow of chastity and variously lived the life of a recluse or worked as an evangelist. St CADOC, whom she met on St Michael's Mount in Cornwall, is said to have been her nephew. *Feast Day: 8 October.*

Kieran *See* CIARAN OF CLONMACNOISE.

Korea, Martyrs of (1839–1867) Group of martyrs who died for their faith in Korea. The Roman Catholic church arrived in Korea towards the end of the 18th century despite a strict prohibition on foreigners in the country and the outlawing of Christianity. In 1839, as the number of converts grew and Bishop Laurent Imbert slipped surreptitiously into the country, the authorities instigated the first of a series of organized persecutions of Christians, which over the next 30 years were to claim the lives of some 10,000 people. Many of the victims were brutally tortured before being put to death. In 1984 a total of 103 saints were canonized as martyrs for their faith. They included 10 French missionaries, Andrew Kim Tae-gon, who was the first Korean-born priest, a 13-year-old boy called Peter Yi Tae-chol and, among the women, Mary Yi Yon-hui and Anne Pak A-gi. *Feast Day: 20 September.*

Lambert (*c.*635–*c.*705) Bishop and martyr of Maastricht. Born into a noble family of Maastricht, he was educated by the local bishop and eventually succeeded to his post upon the latter's murder in 670. Political opponents forced Lambert into exile in a monastery at Stavelot between 675 and 682 but after his restoration as bishop under Pepin of Herstal he went on to earn an enduring reputation as an energetic missionary, working chiefly in Kempenland and Brabant, which were then largely unconverted to Christianity. He was eventually murdered at Liège, possibly on the orders of Pepin after he took exception to the bishop's criticisms of his adultery with his sister-in-law.
Feast Day: 17 September.

Laurence *See* LAWRENCE.

Lawrence (d.258) Roman martyr. Lawrence (or **Laurence**) is traditionally identified as one of the seven deacons of Rome and is believed to have been martyred for his faith in 258, four days after Pope SIXTUS II. Legend has it that he was put to death by being roasted on a grid after defying an order from Emperor Valerian to surrender the riches of the church, offering him only the poor and the sick of the city. He is supposed to have been buried on the site of the future church of St Lawrence-outside-the-Walls on the road to Tivoli. Lawrence is honoured as the patron saint of cooks, cutlers, glaziers and of Rome and Sri Lanka. His emblem is a grid-iron (although historians contend that he was probably executed with a sword).
Feast Day: 10 August.

Lawrence of Brindisi (1559–1619) Italian theologian and preacher. Born Cesare de' Rossi into a wealthy family of Brindisi, he joined the Capuchin Franciscans and completed his education at the University of Padua. Subsequently, aided by his mastery of several languages, he established a considerable reputation as an evangelical preacher, speaking before congregations throughout Europe. Lawrence (or **Laurence**) represented his order on a number of important diplomatic missions and in 1601 became chaplain of the army of Emperor Rudolf II, then engaged in fighting the

Turks in Hungary, even leading the soldiers of the German princes into battle, carrying a crucifix. He became minister-general of the Capuchin order in 1602 and from 1605 acted as papal nuncio to the court of Bavaria. He died in Lisbon while on a diplomatic mission to Philip III. His writings include sermons, treatises and commentaries upon the Bible, notably one upon Genesis. He was canonized in 1881 and declared a Doctor of the Church in 1959.

Feast Day: 21 July.

Lawrence of Canterbury   (d.619) English archbishop. A Roman Benedictine monk who arrived in England on the orders of Pope GREGORY THE GREAT in 597, he was a close ally of AUGUSTINE OF CANTERBURY and was trusted by him to return to Rome with Augustine's reports on evangelical progress in Britain. He made the journey back to Britain in 601 and was nominated Augustine's successor as archbishop of Canterbury by Augustine himself. Lawrence accordingly took over the see on the death of his friend and continued in the post in the face of opposition from the pagan king Eadbald (which ended with Eadbald's conversion), but failed to achieve union with the rival Anglo-Saxon bishops. Legend has it that he resisted the temptation to flee into exile in Gaul after being criticized for his cowardice by a vision of St PETER as he slept.

Feast Day: 13 February.

Lawrence Giustiniani   (1381–1455) Italian archbishop. Born into a noble family of Venice, he became a canon of the Augustinian monastery of San Giorgio on the island of Alga and there lived the life of a devout but penniless beggar. Admired both for his energy and for his generosity and humility, he was eventually made general of the congregation (1424) and then appointed bishop of Castello (1433). Subsequently he dedicated himself entirely to the welfare of his flock, delegating his administrative responsibilities to others. In 1451 he was moved (against his own wishes) to Venice, where he undertook extensive reform and consolidated his reputation for generosity with gifts of food and clothing (but rarely money, which he feared might be misused). He was also the author of a number of works intended to improve standards among fellow clerics. He was canonized in 1690.

Feast Day: 5 September.

Lawrence O'Toole   (c.1128–1180) Irish bishop. Born Lorcan ua Tuathail near Castledermot, Lawrence (or **Laurence**) was the son of a chieftain and at the age of 10 began two years as a hostage of the rival McMurrough clan. Having been accepted as a monk at Glendalough, he distinguished himself by his simple and austere ways and through his devotion to his fellow-man. He was noted especially for his generosity to the poor. In due course he was appointed abbot at Glendalough and subsequently (1161) archbishop of Dublin. After the English invaded Ireland in 1170 Lawrence played a prominent part firstly in the resistance movement and then in negotiations between Rory O'Connor, king of Connacht, and Henry II of England. He also attended the third Lateran Council held in Rome in 1179 but his work as papal legate in Ireland incurred the enmity of Henry II and he was obliged to remain in exile from his homeland until the opportunity finally came for him to meet the king in Normandy and to persuade him to raise the prohibition. Unfortunately Lawrence died in Normandy shortly after setting out on the journey back to Dublin. He was canonized in 1226.

Feast Day: 14 November.

Lazarus   (1st century) Biblical character who was raised from the dead by Christ. Identified at John 11:1–44 as the brother of Martha and Mary, Lazarus of Bethany (just outside Jerusalem) died after a brief illness and was laid to rest in his tomb. He had been dead for four days when Christ finally arrived. In response to Martha's criticisms of his tardiness, Christ had the tomb opened and called Lazarus out, upon which the dead man emerged, restored to life. Legend has it that after his resurrection Lazarus and his sisters sailed to southern France, where Lazarus became the first bishop of Marseilles and ultimately died a martyr's death. Other traditions variously claim that he settled in Cyprus or Syria. The story of his resurrection remains one of the most celebrated of all Christ's miracles.

Feast Day: 29 July.

Leander   (*c*.550–600) Spanish bishop. Born the son of the Duke of Cartegana, he was the elder brother of St ISIDORE and preceded him as bishop of Seville, to which post he was appointed *c*.584. A confidante of GREGORY THE GREAT, whom he first met on a mission to Constantinople in 583, he won admiration for his conversion of the Spanish Visigoths from Arianism. Another legacy was his introduction of the singing of the Nicene Creed at Mass. His only surviving writings comprise a homily and a monastic rule for women.

Feast Day: 27 February.

Lebbaeus *See* JUDE.

Leger (*c*.616–679) Bishop of Autun. Born near Arras, Leger (or **Leodegar**) was educated at court of King Clotaire II and became a deacon at the age of 20. As abbot of Saint-Maixent (653) he reformed the abbey on Benedictine lines and was subsequently appointed bishop of Autun (663). In later years he became embroiled in political struggles and ultimately fell into the hands of Ebroin, the Neustrian palace-mayor, when he chose to surrender himself rather than risk bloodshed among his supporters. His eyes were put out on the orders of his enemies and he was deposed as bishop before finally being beheaded. He was revered as a martyr after his death, his cult spreading throughout France and England.
Feast Day: 2 October.

Leo I *See* LEO THE GREAT.

Leo III (d.816) Roman pope. Of humble birth, Leo rose through the ranks of the church to succeed Hadrian I as pope in 795. His 20-year reign witnessed opposition from supporters of a rival claimant to the papacy, which became so bitter that he was obliged to seek protection from the court of Charlemagne in Paderborn. On one occasion it was only narrowly that he managed to escape from youths who planned to blind him and cut out his tongue. The trouble continued even after Leo secured Charlemagne's blessing, but undeterred he worked steadily to consolidate the links between the papacy and Charlemagne's empire and personally crowned Charlemagne emperor in 800, thus establishing the foundation of medieval Christendom. He did, however, prove capable of resisting imperial demands with which he disagreed. His other achievements included confirming Canterbury as the seat of the church in England and restoring order after a Saracen invasion of parts of Italy in 814. He was canonized in 1673.
Feast Day: 12 June.

Leo IX (1002–1054) Italian pope. Born into a noble family of Alsace, he distinguished himself as a military leader on behalf of the bishop of Toul and in 1027 succeeded to the bishopric himself. Ultimately he rose to the rank of pope (1048) and over the next six years did much to restore the battered reputation of the papacy through extensive reform of the church. He combated simony and other abuses among the clergy and also sought to free the church from secular influence. He promoted monasticism and declared that future popes should be elected by the cardinals alone. He

did, however, stir up controversy by leading the papal army to defeat against the Normans in southern Italy (attracting criticism for involving himself directly in a military campaign), and also failed to prevent the resulting breach between Rome and Constantinople, which eventually led to complete schism within the church. After his death his reforms were continued and developed by his successor as pope, GREGORY VII. He was canonized in 1087.
Feast Day: 19 April.

Leo the Great   (d.461) Roman pope. Probably born in Rome, possibly of Tuscan parents, Leo served as a deacon in the city before being elected pope in 440. As Leo I, he established a reputation as perhaps the greatest of the successors of St PETER, widely respected for consolidating the strength of the church at a time of crisis. In 451, at the Council of Chalcedon, he wrote a profoundly influential letter that established the orthodox approach on the dual nature of Christ, accepting him as both divine and human. A year later he dissuaded Attila the Hun from attacking Rome while, in 455, he prevented a massacre when the Vandals occupied the city. After the Vandals left he supervised the rebuilding of Rome and promoted the welfare of its citizens, as well as sending aid to Roman prisoners held in Africa. He never wavered in emphasizing the authority of Rome over the rest of the church, extending his influence through Spain, Gaul and elsewhere, and set an example for later pontiffs through his piety and determination. Upon his death in Rome he was laid to rest in St Peter's. He was declared a Doctor of the Church in 1754. His emblem in art is a dragon.
Feast Day: 10 November.

Leoba   *See* LIOBA.

Leodegar   *See* LEGER.

Leonard   (dates unknown) French hermit. Nothing is known for certain of the life of St Leonard, who may have lived around the 6th century, but legend claims that he was a hermit who founded a monastery at Noblac (later renamed Saint-Léonard) near Limoges. Various miracles were ascribed to him and he became a popular saint in France, England and Germany. He is honoured as the patron saint of prisoners and pregnant women.
Feast Day: 6 November.

Leonard of Port Maurice (1676–1751) Italian missioner. Born Paul Jerome Casanuova at Port Maurice on the Italian Riviera, he was educated by the Jesuits in Rome and joined the strict Franciscan order known as the Riformella, soon emerging as its charismatic leader. Based in Rome and Florence, he established a reputation as an evangelizing preacher throughout northern Italy, attracting huge crowds and making thousands of converts over some 40 years (though late in life he had less success in bringing peace through his preaching to lawless Corsica). His sermons, typically held outdoors to accommodate his vast audiences, often referred to the Stations of the Cross and in due course he set up 571 sets of stations throughout the country. He also served as religious adviser to Clementina Sobieska, whose husband was the son of the deposed English king James II. He was canonized in 1867 and is honoured today as the patron saint of popular missionaries.
Feast Day: 26 November.

Leopold III (1075–1136) Austrian duke. Leopold III (otherwise known as **Leopold of Austria** or **Leopold the Good**) was born at Melk and inherited the dukedom of Austria in 1095. Very little is known of his reign, but he acquired the reputation of a wise and generous ruler who won the love of his people and did much to promote the church. He also contributed towards the First Crusade and presided over the founding of various religious foundations, of which several survive. He demonstrated his humility, however, in 1125 when he declined to be nominated for the imperial crown. He was canonized in 1485. In 1663 he was named patron saint of Austria. His emblems are a crown and a model of a church.
Feast Day: 15 November.

Linus (d. *c*.80) Roman pope. Possibly born in Tuscany, Linus is remembered as the second pope, following St PETER as bishop of Rome. Nothing more is known of the details of his life beyond the tradition that, after about 12 years as pope, he died a martyr's death and was buried beside Peter at the foot of Vatican Hill in Rome. He is sometimes tentatively identified with the Linus referred to at II Timothy 4:21.
Feast Day: 23 September.

Lioba (*c*.700–780) English abbess. Born into a noble family of Wessex, Lioba (or **Leoba**) became a nun at the abbey of Wimborne in Dorset and, in 748, was chosen as leader of a party of 30 nuns from Wimborne sent to

do missionary work in Germany at the request of St BONIFACE OF CREDI-
TON. Based at Bischofsheim in Franconia, with Lioba as abbess, the group
became well-respected for the support they gave to the missionary priests.
Lioba herself was described as beautiful, patient and charming as well as
wise, generous and devout. She was widely consulted for advice and in
her last years became a close companion of Hildegard, wife of Charlemagne. After 28 years as abbess, she retreated to the nunnery of Schöner-
scheim in 776 and remained there until her death.
Feast Day: 28 September.

Liudger   *See* LUDGER.

Louis IX   (1214–1270) King of France. Born in Poissy, the son of Louis VIII,
Louis succeeded to the French throne at the age of 12 in 1226. He married
Margaret of Provence seven years later and took over the government
of the country in 1235. Louis proved a wise and capable ruler with a
profound religious faith and a sincere belief in the ideals of medieval
chivalry. As well as winning respect as a military leader, defeating the
English at Taillebourg in 1242, he built the Sainte-Chapelle in Paris and
established a reputation both as a statesman and defender of the rights of
the individual. He was noted for his impartiality in dispensing justice. He
was also noted for his dislike of profane or blasphemous language. In 1248
he led a crusade. He captured Damietta in Egypt but then was routed at
Mansurah and briefly taken prisoner. He embarked on another similarly
ill fated crusade in 1270 but died of typhoid fever not long after his army
arrived in Tunis. He was canonized in 1297 and is honoured as the patron
saint of barbers, builders, distillers, embroiderers, the French monarchy,
grooms, haberdashers, hairdressers, kings, masons, needleworkers,
prisoners, sculptors, the sick and soldiers, among others.
Feast Day: 25 August.

Louis Bertrand   (1526–1581) Spanish friar. Born at Valencia and related to
St VINCENT FERRAR, he joined the Dominicans and is remembered chiefly
for the missionary work he undertook in Colombia in the years 1562–1568.
He is credited with having secured thousands of converts among the
native inhabitants of the area during this period, despite the fact that he
could not speak their language and had to communicate through an
interpreter. He also sought to counter the abuses then practised by the
Spanish in the Americas and, back in Europe, helped St TERESA in her

reform of the Carmelite order. He was canonized in 1671 and is honoured today as the patron saint of Colombia.
Feast Day: 9 October.

Louis Grignion de Montfort   (1673–1716) French missioner. Born in Montfort in Brittany, Louis studied at the Jesuit College of St THOMAS BECKET in Rennes before starting training as a priest at the Seminary of St SULPICE in Paris in 1692. He was ordained in 1700 and appointed chaplain at the hospital in Poitiers. Recruiting the women administrators of the poorhouse in Poitiers, he went on to found a congregation known as the Daughters of Divine Wisdom before moving to Paris and there similarly devoting himself to the care of the inmates of a poorhouse. A fiery and difficult man, he was loved by the poor but provoked considerable criticism from his superiors and eventually left Paris for Rome, where he became a missionary apostolic under Pope Clement XI. He spent the last 10 years of his life before his premature death at the age of 43 as an itinerant preacher and the year before he died founded the Missionaries of the Company of Mary. His surviving writings include the books *True Devotion to the Blessed Virgin* and *The Love of Eternal Wisdom*, sermons, letters and hymns. He was canonized in 1947.
Feast Day: 28 April.

Louise de Marillac   (1591–1660) French foundress of the Sisters of Charity. Born into a wealthy aristocratic country family, probably at Ferrières-en-Brie, she hoped to become a Capuchin nun but instead, in 1613 at the age of 22, began 12 years of married life to a royal official. After her husband's death from illness she resumed her religious inclinations and came under the influence of St VINCENT DE PAUL, who was then recruiting assistants with his charitable work from among the wealthy women of Paris. Impressed by Louise above all his other recruits, Vincent put her in charge of the Ladies of Charity, which he had founded. Modest yet practical, Louise proved the perfect choice for this work and a highly capable administrator. In 1633 she opened her own home for the training of social workers and from this evolved the Sisters or Daughters of Charity of St Paul, who within 25 years boasted some 40 convents throughout Europe. Throughout, she continued in close alliance with Vincent de Paul and hundreds of letters exchanged between the two saints survive. She was canonized in 1934 and is honoured as the patron saint of social workers.
Feast Day: 15 March.

Loup   *See* LUPUS OF TROYES.

Lucian of Antioch   (d.312) Syrian-born martyr. Born at Samasata in Syria, he became a priest of Antioch, where he founded an influential theological school. He revised the Greek versions of the Old Testament and of the four gospels before being imprisoned at Nicomedia during the persecution ordered by the emperor Diocletian. Refusing to deny his faith, he spent nine years behind bars and was eventually executed with a sword (though some say he was starved to death). Another tradition has it that he was drowned in the sea and his body was brought to shore by a dolphin. *Feast Day: 7 January.*

Lucius   *See* MONTANUS AND LUCIUS.

Lucy   (d. *c*.304) Sicilian virgin martyr. The substance of the life of St Lucy is largely a matter of legend, according to which she was a virgin put to death in Syracuse after being exposed as a Christian by her rejected suitor. When she was ordered into a brothel it proved impossible to shift her and she was similarly miraculously protected from execution by fire. She was eventually put to death by a sword thrust through the throat. Because there is a story that her eyes were miraculously restored after being torn out she is associated with diseases of the eyes and her emblem is two eyes in a dish. She is honoured as the patron saint of the glaziers, salesmen, writers and the blind, among others. *Feast Day: 13 December.*

Ludger   (744–809) Frisian missionary. Ludger (or **Liudger**) was born near Utrecht, where he was a pupil of St GREGORY OF UTRECHT, but also spent some years as a young man studying in England under Alcuin. On his return to the Low Countries, he rebuilt the ruined church at Deventer and then dedicated himself to evangelical work among the Frieslanders. He was ordained a priest in 777 and built several new churches before being hounded out by invading Saxons in 784. Forced from the region, Ludger travelled to Rome and Monte Cassino, where he determined to found his own Benedictine monastery. In 786 he returned to Westphalia and, with the blessing of Charlemagne, went on to established a monastery at Werden. From his base at what is now called Münster, where he built a monastery for canons, he embarked upon a lengthy campaign to convert the Saxons and had considerable success through his gently persuasive approach to the pagan population. He was made bishop of Münster around 803. *Feast Day: 26 March.*

Ludmilla *See* WENCESLAS.

Luke (1st century) Biblical evangelist. Possibly born in Antioch of Gentile Greek parentage, he practised medicine according to the few details of his life given in the New Testament. He accompanied St PAUL on his missionary journeys and was with him when their ship was wrecked off Malta. Paul describes Luke as his only companion in Rome and another source claims he eventually returned to Greece and died unmarried there, aged 84. Another tradition suggests he died a martyr's death. He is credited as the author of the third Gospel and of the Acts of the Apostles. He is honoured as the patron saint of physicians, surgeons, butchers and artists. His emblem is a winged ox.
Feast Day: 18 October

Lull (d.786) English bishop. Probably born in Wessex, he studied as a monk at Malmesbury before going to Germany and there becoming the right-hand man of his cousin St BONIFACE OF CREDITON. He eventually succeeded Boniface as bishop of Mainz in 752 and proved himself an energetic missionary who was particularly interested in promoting learning. His bishopric was not without its problems, however, and he became embroiled in a lengthy argument with St STURM over Lull's right to jurisdiction over Sturm's monastery at Fulda. Lull himself founded monasteries at Bleidenstadt and Hersfeld.
Feast Day: 16 October.

Lupus of Troyes (*c*.383–478) French bishop. Born at Toul, Lupus (or **Loup**) was briefly married to a sister of St HILARY OF ARLES but then chose the religious life and became a monk at Lérins. Legend has it that as bishop of Troyes from around 426 he did much to protect the local population when Gaul was invaded by the Huns under Attila in 451, offering himself as a hostage. Another tradition has it that he was the companion of St GERMANUS OF AUXERRE when he came to Britain in 429.
Feast Day: 29 July.

Lutgard (1182–1246) Belgian nun. Born in Tongres, Brabant, Lutgard (otherwise called **Lutgarde** or **Lutgardis**) was placed in the Benedictine convent of St Catherine's at St Trond near Liège at the age of 12 and determined to become a nun after experiencing a vision of Christ. She was made prioress of St Catherine's in 1205 but resented having to interrupt her prayers to fulfil her administrative duties. In 1206 she transferred to a French-speaking Cistercian convent at Aywières near Brussels, knowing that because she only spoke Flemish she was unlikely to be given a similar post there. She became well-known for her many visions and mystical experiences.

Feast Day: 16 June.

Lyons, Martyrs of   (d.177) Group of martyrs who died for their faith at Lyons and Vienne. At least 48 in number, the Martyrs of Lyons were put to death during the persecutions ordered by Marcus Aurelius. Mostly Greeks, they included church officials, among them the bishop St POTHINUS, slaves, including St BLANDINA and children. Some died in prison while others were tortured and executed in front of a mob incensed by the charges of cannibalism, incest and other atrocities that had been levelled at the accused. Those who had Roman citizenship were beheaded; the remainder were torn apart by wild beasts in the public arena. Their bodies were burned and their ashes were thrown into the river Rhône.

Feast Day: 2 June.

Macarius the Great (*c*.300–*c*.390) Coptic monk. Also known as **Macarius the Elder** or as **Macarius of Egypt**, he assumed the life of a hermit living in the desert of Sketis in upper Egypt after being falsely accused of rape. Here he attracted a large number of other hermits and in time became one of the most celebrated of the desert fathers whose words of wisdom were recorded for posterity as the *Sayings of the Desert Fathers*. Considered a founder of Egyptian monasticism, he was widely respected for his wise advice and has also been identified as the author of the homilies collected as the *Markarian Homilies*, though there is no substantial evidence backing this identification. Many legends sprang up around his name, including one in which he confronted Satan and reclaimed one of his most faithful servants. In his old age he was banished to an island in the Nile delta, where he made many converts before being allowed back to his desert fastness.
Feast Day: 15 January.

Maccul *See* MAUGHOLD.

Maclou *See* MALO.

Macrina the Elder (d.340) Cappadocian matron. Born in Neocaesarea in Pontus, Cappadocia (now in Turkey), she became a disciple of GREGORY THE WONDERWORKER and with her husband was forced to go into exile in the wilderness of Pontus during the persecution of the Christian community under Galerius. She is identified as the grandmother of the saints BASIL, GREGORY OF NYSSA and MACRINA THE YOUNGER and is said to have exerted a profound influence upon their religious upbringing.
Feast Day: 14 January.

Macrina the Younger (*c*.327–379) Cappadocian virgin. Born at Caesarea in Cappadocia, she was the older sister of the saints BASIL, GREGORY OF NYSSA and Peter of Sebastea, over all of whom she had a profound influence, having dedicated herself to the upbringing of her nine younger siblings after the death of the man to whom she was engaged to be married. While her siblings became prominent figures in the early Christian community, Macrina the Younger spent most of her adulthood living

quietly with her mother in a religious community by the river Iris in Pontus, ultimately succeeding her mother as its leader. Her selfless service of her family was recorded for posterity by her brother Gregory, who based his book *On the Soul and the Resurrection* largely upon his sister's deathbed reflections.
Feast Day: 19 July.

Madeleine Sophie Barat   (1779–1865) French foundress. Born the daughter of the owner of a vineyard in Joigny in Burgundy, she received early religious instruction from her brother, who was studying for the priesthood. She planned to become a Carmelite lay-sister but instead, in 1801, followed advice from Joseph Varin, superior of the newly-founded Society of the Sacred Heart of Jesus, to become a teacher at a convent school in Amiens. She soon rose to the position of superioress of this first house of the Society of the Sacred Heart, dedicated to the education of girls, and remained in the post for the next 63 years. She worked tirelessly upon the expansion of the order, which spread steadily through Europe and America and gradually won recognition as one of the most influential and well-organized educational institutes run by the Roman Catholic Church. The order, of which Madeline Sophie Barat is usually considered a co-founder, won papal recognition from Leo XII in 1826. She was canonized in 1925.
Feast Day: 25 May.

Maedoc of Ferns   (d.626) Irish bishop. Also known as **Aedh** or **Aidan of Ferns**, he was probably born in Connacht and distinguished himself as a pupil studying in Wales under St DAVID. Upon his return to Ireland, he founded a monastery at Ferns in County Wexford and served as the community's first bishop. He also founded monasteries at Drumlane and Rossinver. Various miraculous stories associated with his name celebrate his austere lifestyle, his dedication to religious observance and his fabled generosity and kindness towards others.
Feast Day: 31 January.

Mael Maedoc   *See* MALACHY.

Mafalda of Portugal   (d.1257) Portuguese foundress. The daughter of King Sancho I of Portugal, she was sister to Sts SANCHIA and TERESA. In 1215 she became the wife of her cousin Henry I, king of Castile, but the marriage was annulled a year later and she returned to Portugal. In 1222

she became a nun at Arouca and was instrumental in the nunnery becoming a Cistercian house. She was revered for the austerity of her lifestyle and for her generosity in providing funds for the restoration of the cathedral at Oporto. She also founded a hospice for pilgrims and paid for a hospital for widows and for a bridge over the river Talmeda.
Feast Day: 2 May.

Magnus (c.1075–1116) Martyr king of Orkney. The son of the joint king of the Orkney islands, he lived in exile in Scotland after the invasion of Orkney by the Vikings, taking refuge in the house of a bishop. He eventually returned to Orkney to share the throne with his cousin Haakon but was ultimately betrayed and murdered on Haakon's orders on the island of Egilsay, resigning himself to death after a final prayer for his murderers. Revered for his devout nature, he was buried in Kirkwall cathedral and acquired the status of a Christian martyr (although apparently he was killed on political rather than religious grounds). He is honoured as the patron saint of Norway.
Feast Day: 16 April.

Maieul *See* MAYEUL.

Malachy (c.1094–1148) Irish archbishop. Also known by the name **Mael Maedoc**, he was born the son of a schoolteacher at Armagh and ordained a priest in 1119. A committed and energetic Gregorian reformer, he progressed rapidly from the rank of priest to that of bishop of the diocese of Connor and Down (1124). He proved a dedicated servant of the church and in 1129 was rewarded with the archbishopric of Armagh, which had formerly been a hereditary position. This appointment provoked fierce opposition from those who had expected the post to be inherited in the traditional way and it was only with difficulty that Malachy was persuaded to assert his authority over the see. Under his wise and patient leadership peace was gradually restored to the diocese and in 1137 he agreed a compromise with his opponents, handing over control of Armagh to the abbot of Derry. Two years later he travelled to Rome to obtain papal approval of the reforms he had instituted and there was made papal legate to Ireland by Pope Innocent II. On his return he co-founded the first Cistercian abbey (at Mellifont in Louth) in the whole of Ireland and also oversaw the introduction of the canons regular. He remained in the post of papal legate for eight years before setting out once more for Rome. He became ill on the journey and died in the arms of his friend St BERNARD at

Clairvaux, where he was buried. In his biography of Malachy, Bernard of Clairvaux praised him warmly for his spiritual strength and also described various acts of miraculous healing connected with his name. Malachy was canonized in 1190.

Feast Day: 3 November.

Malo   (d. *c.*640) Missionary monk of Brittany. Possibly born in south-west Wales, Malo (or **Maclou**) is supposed to have studied under St BRENDAN before being forced into exile in Brittany. He is said to have founded the church of Aleth (Saint-Servan) and to have made the town now called Saint-Malo the base for his ministry in the area. Tradition has it that his apostolic zeal made Malo many enemies and he was eventually driven out of the region and obliged to settle at Saintes. Pleas for his return were silenced by his death at Archingeay. After Malo's death his cult thrived both in Brittany and in southern England.

Feast Day: 15 November.

Marcella   (325–410) Roman matron. Born in Rome, she dedicated herself to the religious life after the death of her husband shortly after their marriage. As founder and head of a religious community of women on the Aventine Hill in Rome she offered shelter to her mentor St JEROME and attracted a substantial following among the wealthy women of the city, becoming known both for her personal charm and for her redoubtable character. Jerome himself admired the energetic manner in which she debated religious matters with him, insisting upon proper reasons for his answers. She died shortly after being misused by the Goths when Rome was sacked in 410, having refused to surrender to them the wealth she had long since distributed among the poor.

Feast Day: 31 January.

Marcellian   *See* MARK AND MARCELLIAN.

Marcellinus and Peter   (d. *c.*304) Roman martyrs. Little is known of the details of the lives of these two martyrs beyond the bare facts that Marcellinus was a priest and Peter an exorcist and that both were put to death during the persecution of Christians under Diocletian. Legend has it that while awaiting execution they secured the conversion of the gaoler and his family. They are supposed to have been buried on the Via Labicana. Pope St DAMASUS I wrote an epitaph for their tomb.

Feast Day: 2 June.

Marcellus I (d.309) Roman pope. He was elected pope in 308 in the wake of the turmoil following the persecutions of Christians instituted under Diocletian and faced a major challenge in regrouping the church. During his short papacy he set about reorganizing the church in Rome into parishes, establishing a hierarchy of parish presbyters and only welcoming lapsed Christians back into the fold after they had completed exacting penances, which he enforced with great severity. These measures provoked substantial opposition and Marcellus was ordered out of Rome by Emperor Maxentius. He died in exile shortly afterwards. An unsubstantiated tradition claims that he died the death of a martyr.
Feast Day: 16 January.

Marcellus the Centurion (d.298) Roman martyr. Marcellus was a Roman centurion who declared his Christian faith when ordered to participate in his legion's celebrations of the birthday of Emperor Maximian. Throwing down his badges of allegiance to the emperor he swore that he would refused to obey any orders but those of God. He was immediately arrested and brought before the deputy prefect at Tangier. Marcellus declined to deny his faith and was sentenced to be put to death by the sword. Tradition has it that one of the officials at his hearing was so impressed by the centurion's demeanour that he too declared his conversion to Christianity and was similarly put to death.
Feast Day: 30 October.

Margaret of Antioch (dates unknown) Virgin martyr. Margaret (or **Marina**) of Antioch probably never existed but was included among the popular saints of the medieval period. According to legend, she was the Christian daughter of a pagan priest of Antioch during the reign of Diocletian. After spurning marriage to the Roman prefect Olybrius, she was denounced by him as a Christian and subjected to horrific torture (which included being swallowed by Satan in the form of a dragon) before finally being beheaded. In many respects her story appears to share much in common with that of CATHERINE OF ALEXANDRIA. Over 200 churches throughout England were dedicated to her and she was also revered as the patron saint of childbirth. Her emblem is a dragon.
Feast Day: 20 July.

Margaret of Castello (1287–1320) Italian Dominican tertiary. Margaret of Castello was born a hunchbacked dwarf who was also blind and lame. Her parents took her to a shrine in hope of a miraculous cure and after this failed they abandoned her and she was taken in at a local convent. At the age of 15 she became a Dominican tertiary and dedicated herself to work on behalf of the sick and dying, as well as providing religious instruction for village children. She was credited with various miraculous gifts, which included the powers of prophesy and levitation. She was much respected for her intense religious sentiment and many miracles were attributed to her after her premature death at the age of 33.

Feast Day: 13 April.

Margaret of Cortona   (1247–1297) Italian penitent. Born into a peasant family of Laviano in Tuscany, she became the mistress of a young nobleman, bearing him a son before he was brutally murdered by an enemy. Margaret was convulsed with guilt, blaming herself for her lover's death, and sought shelter with the Franciscans at Cortona. Here she abandoned her former luxurious lifestyle and became widely known for the severity of the penances to which she subjected herself. She was eventually dissuaded from pursuing the most extreme of these penances, which included beating and scarring herself, and (though she never gave up her habits of strict self-discipline) was permitted to join the order. She went on to distinguish herself through her selfless service of the sick poor and founded a hospital in Cortona, though in her later years she lived as a virtual recluse. Considered an ideal of the penitent sinner, she was canonized in 1728 and is revered as the patron saint of the falsely accused, the homeless, midwives, single laywomen and tertiaries.

Feast Day: 22 February.

Margaret of Hungary   (1242–1270) Hungarian nun. The beautiful daughter of Bela IV, king of Hungary, she entered a convent for Dominican nuns founded by her father on an island in the Danube near Budapest and determined to remain there for the rest of her life, even defying her father's wishes that she accept the hand of Ottokar, king of Bohemia. She variously impressed and appalled all who knew her with her dedication to her life of prayer and penance, always volunteering for the most menial and unpleasant work about the convent and paying scant regard to feeding or cleaning herself. Being a princess, the other nuns were unable to persuade Margaret to moderate her habits and the austerities of her existence probably contributed to her premature death at the age of 28. She was canonized in 1943.

Feast Day: 18 January.

Margaret of Scotland   (c.1045–1093) Scottish queen. The granddaughter of the English king Edmund Ironside, she was probably born in exile in Hungary and did not come to England until 1057. When the Normans invaded in 1066 she retreated to Scotland and there married (1070) the Scottish king Malcolm III. At the time of their marriage Malcolm was coarse and uncouth in nature, but long exposure to Margaret's refined and educated character gradually reformed him and he is remembered as one of Scotland's most respected rulers. Margaret was also intensely religious and showed considerable generosity towards orphans and others in need as well as exerting a reforming influence upon the Scottish church, founding a number of churches and other religious houses. She bore her husband eight children and saw to it that they were well brought up: one of them, DAVID OF SCOTLAND, similarly acquired the status of saint, while their daughter Matilda married Henry I of England and thus became an ancestress of the present British royal family. The long and happy marriage of Margaret and Malcolm ended in violence with the king's murder at the hands of his enemies near Alnwick; the ailing Margaret died four days later. She was buried alongside her husband at the abbey of Dunfermline, which they had co-founded. Canonized in 1250, she is the only Scottish saint in the Roman calendar to be universally venerated and is also honoured as a patron saint of Scotland, queens, widows and parents of large families.
Feast Day: 16 November.

Margaret Clitherow   (1556–1586) English martyr. Born into a Protestant family of York, Margaret Clitherow married a wealthy Protestant butcher in 1571 but three years later, while the country was convulsed with Post-Reformation anti-Catholic feeling, converted to Catholicism and soon became one of the most prominent Catholics in the city. Regularly fined for refusing to attend her local Protestant church, she was imprisoned for two years for her Catholic faith but upon her release continued in her beliefs, even sheltering priests in a secret room in her own house. In due course the hiding-place was discovered and Margaret was once again arrested and imprisoned. When she refused to plead at her trial she was sentenced to be pressed to death under heavy weights. Reportedly a vivacious and attractive woman, Margaret Clitherow is remembered as perhaps the most famous of the Forty Martyrs of England and Wales. She was canonized in 1970.
Feast Day: 25 October.

Margaret Mary Alacoque   (1647–1690) French mystic. Born in L'Hautec-
our in Burgundy the daughter of a royal notary, Margaret Mary Alacoque
displayed great religious feeling as a sickly child and entered the religious
life at the age of 15. She refused to marry and instead entered the Visitation convent at Paray-le-Monial in 1671 where, between 1673 and 1675, she
reportedly experienced four visions of Christ in which he instructed her to
urge devotion to his Sacred Heart and to found a Feast of the Sacred
Heart. Initially scorned by the other nuns who were inclined to disbelieve
her revelations, Margaret Mary attracted the support of her influential
Jesuit confessor St CLAUDE DE LA COLOMBIERE as well as that of St JOHN
EUDES and others and devotion to the Sacred Heart of Jesus was eventually
granted papal approval by Pope Clement XIII in 1765. Her surviving
writings include an autobiography and letters. Patient in the face of much
opposition during her lifetime, she was canonized in 1920.
Feast Day: 16 October.

Marguerite Bourgeoys   (1620–1700) French foundress of the Sisters of
Notre Dame, the first unenclosed missionary order for women. Born in
Troyes, at the age of 19 Marguerite Bourgeoys was turned away by both
the Carmelites and the Poor Clares and opted instead to establish her own
uncloistered community. Her attempts to found such an order in Troyes
did not succeed, however, and in 1653 left France to become a teacher and
carer of the sick in Ville-Marie (now Montreal) in Canada. She founded the
uncloistered Sisters of Notre Dame to further such work in 1672 and in
due course the order spread throughout Canada, with many missions established to promote the welfare of the native American population. The early
history of the order was much disrupted by war and opposition from
within the church, obliging Marguerite Bourgeoys herself to cross the
Atlantic several times to protect the interests of her order. The first American branches of the sisterhood were opened in 1889. At her death Marguerite left behind an autobiography and a number of letters. She was
canonized in 1982 and is honoured as the patron saint of those who are
rejected by religious orders.
Feast Day: 12 January.

Marguerite d'Youville   (1701–1771) Canadian foundress of the order
popularly known as the Grey Nuns. Born Marie Margaret Dufrost de la
Jemmarais d'Youville into a poor family of Varennes in Quebec, she
studied for a time at an Ursuline convent boarding school before being
obliged to return home to help her widowed mother. She married at the

age of 21 but the union was not happy and ended after eight years' with her unfaithful husband's death. She then ran a store in order to stave off the debts left by her husband and to provide funds to bring up her two sons. She also undertook charitable work on behalf of the poor of Montreal and in 1737 joined with three friends in dedicating herself to caring for the indigent in God's name, thus founding what became known as the Sisters of Charity of Montreal, or the Grey Nuns (after the colour of the habits the sisters wore). The order spread steadily and won official recognition in 1755. It included among its achievements the establishment of the first home for abandoned children in the Americas as well as the foundation of numerous schools and hospitals. Marguerite d'Youville was canonized in 1990 and is honoured as a patron saint of widows and victims of adultery. *Feast Day: 16 October.*

Maria Goretti   (1890–1902) Italian martyr. Born into a poor peasant family of Ancona, Maria Goretti proved a happy, unselfish child with a devout nature. When she was 12 years old, however, her beauty attracted the attention of a young man named Alessandro Serenelli who threatened to kill her if she would not submit to his sexual advances. When Maria continued to resist him he stabbed her 14 times, causing her death 24 hours later. As she lay dying the girl prayed fervently that her attacker would eventually repent. Maria's murderer did indeed come to repent his terrible deed and following his release after 27 years in prison he sought forgiveness from Maria's mother and supported calls for his victim's canonization as a Christian martyr, which won official approval in 1950. Both Serenelli, who himself went on to join the Franciscan Third Order, and Maria's mother attended the ceremonies that made her a saint. She is honoured as the patron saint of teenaged girls.
Feast Day: 6 July.

Marian and James   (d.259) African martyrs. According to tradition, Marian was a church reader and James a deacon who were among the many Christians put to death for their faith at Cirta Iulia in Numidia during the persecutions instituted during the reign of Valerian. Both resisted torture and demands that they recant their faith and were eventually sentenced to death by the sword. The number of convicted Christians was so large that they were simply lined up in rows and executed in swift succession by the executioner as he ran past them with sword levelled.
Feast Day: 6 May.

Mariana   (1614–1645) Peruvian penitent. Born Mariana Paredes y Flores
into an aristocratic family of Quito (now in modern Ecuador), she
displayed a deeply religious nature as a child, her penances including
going without food, drink and sleep. When her attempts to enter a convent
failed she resolved to live the life of a recluse, praying and caring for the
needy, including native American children, and continuing to exist in
conditions of great austerity. When Quito was hit by earthquakes followed
by a serious epidemic she prayed that her life be taken in exchange for the
forgiveness of the sins of others and died soon afterwards, to universal
lamentation. Known as the Lily of Quito, she was canonized in 1950. In
many respects her story resembles that of ROSE OF LIMA.
Feast Day: 26 May.

Marie of the Incarnation   (1599–1672) French missionary. Born Marie
Guyard, she was the daughter of a baker in Tours and in due course
became the wife of a silk manufacturer, bearing him a son. After her
husband died she entered (1629) the Ursuline convent in Tours under the
name Marie of the Incarnation and 10 years later embarked as a missionary to Canada. She founded the first Ursuline convent in Quebec in 1641
and oversaw its rebuilding after its destruction by fire in 1650. Also known
as **Marie of the Ursulines**, she was particularly active in instructing
native American converts in the area and even compiled dictionaries in the
Algonquin and Iroquois languages for their benefit. She also became well-
known for her various mystical visions.
Feast Day: 30 April.

Marie Marguerite d'Youville   *See* MARGUERITE D'YOUVILLE.

Marina   *See* MARGARET OF ANTIOCH.

Marinus   (d. c.262) Roman soldier. Of noble birth, he did well in the army
and while serving in Palestine, based at Caesarea, was about to be raised
to the rank of centurion when a rival denounced him as a Christian. When
brought before the magistrate he was presented with a choice between his
sword and the Bible: he refused steadfastly to denounce his faith and willingly went to execution, being put to death by the sword.
Feast Day: 3 March.

Marius and Martha   *See* VALENTINE.

Mark   (1st century) Biblical evangelist. The author of St Mark's gospel (the
oldest and shortest of the Gospels), he is often identified as the Mark who

is described as a close companion of PAUL and PETER and as being present at Gethsemane when Christ was arrested by the Romans, narrowly escaping arrest himself by slipping out of his robe when the soldiers laid hold of him. He is usually also considered synonymous with the John Mark who appears in the Acts of the Apostles. According to various passages in the Bible, Mark was born in Jerusalem and it was in the house of his mother that the 12 disciples gathered at her invitation. He subsequently accompanied Paul and his own cousin BARNABAS on their first missionary journey. Mark, however, offended Paul when he turned back after a short time and was consequently not invited to go with Paul on his second missionary journey. Instead, he travelled with Barnabas to Cyprus to spread the gospel there. He was later reconciled with Paul and accompanied him to Rome, where he visited Paul in prison following the latter's arrest. It was probably in Rome that Mark wrote his Gospel, much of it based upon the recollections and teachings of PETER (it remains unclear whether Mark ever actually met Jesus himself). He ended his life evangelizing in Alexandria, where one tradition has it that he became the city's first bishop and was ultimately martyred for his faith during the reign of the emperor Trajan. He is honoured today as the patron saint of glaziers, notaries, prisoners and of the city of Venice (where his relics are supposed to have been taken in the 9th century and preserved in the first church of San Marco). His emblem is a winged lion.
Feast Day: 25 April.

Mark and Marcellian (d. *c.*290) Roman martyrs. Details about the lives and deaths of Mark and Marcellian are scant. Tradition has it that they were twin brothers born into a noble Roman family who, during the reign of the emperor Diocletian, were arrested on charges of being Christian converts. They resisted the pleas of their wives and families to recant their beliefs and willingly went to their execution and were beheaded. They were buried in the cemetery of Balbina.
Feast Day: 18 June.

Martha (1st century) The sister of LAZARUS. According to the biblical account at Luke 10:38–42 Martha and her sister Mary (sometimes identified as MARY MAGDALENE) were once visited in their home at Bethany by Christ. While Mary sat listening to Christ's words, Martha busied herself preparing a meal. Martha became angry when her sister did not offer to help, upon which Christ observed that she was so busy with trivial things that she was losing sight of what was more important in life (apparently

commending the contemplative over the active life). She reappears at John 11:1–46 at the raising of her brother Lazarus from the dead and at John 12:1–2 it is suggested that once again she served Christ a meal six days before the Passover. Medieval legend added the tradition that Martha and Lazarus later evangelized the region of Provence, where their relics are supposed to have been discovered in 1187. She is honoured as the patron saint of housewives, servants and lay sisters. Her emblems range from a dragon to a ladle, a broom and a bunch of keys.
Feast Day: 29 July.

Martha   *See* VALENTINE.

Martin I   (d.655) Roman pope and martyr. Born into a noble family of Todi in Umbria, he rose swiftly through the ranks of the church and for a period served as papal nuncio in Constantinople, the capital of the Byzantine empire. He was elected pope in 649, in which year he presided over a council at Rome denouncing the Monothelite heresy (which denied that Christ had a human will) and two imperial decrees defending it. In response the Byzantine emperor Constans II had Martin arrested and brought to Constantinople, where he was thrown into prison. In 655, after further ill-treatment, he was sent into exile at Kherson in the Crimea where, weakened by illness and the abuses he had suffered from the emperor, which included starvation and flogging, he died within a short time. His last letters reveal his sadness at his apparent abandonment by his friends. After his death he became the last pope to be recognized as a martyr.
Feast Day: 13 April.

Martin of Braga   (c.520–579) Hungarian-born bishop. The early life of Martin of Braga is shrouded in obscurity, but it appears that he was of Hungarian birth and conducted a pilgrimage to the Holy Land before arriving in the Iberian peninsula. He played a significant role in introducing the monastic tradition to Galicia (now northern Portugal) around 550, founding the abbey of Dumium (Mondoñedo). Some 20 years later he was made archbishop of Braga, in which role he combated rural paganism and promoted missionary work among the Suevi tribe living in Galicia, even winning the conversion of their king. Considered one of the great scholars of his age, he wrote a number of moral treatises and collected the sayings of the Desert Fathers for the benefit of his monks.
Feast Day: 20 March.

Martin of Tours (c.316–397) Hungarian-born bishop who became the
founder of French monasticism. Born the son of a soldier at Sabaria in
Pannonia (in modern Hungary), he was educated in Italy and followed his
father into the Roman army, becoming an officer. After splitting his military cloak in two to share it with a freezing beggar in Amiens, where he
was stationed, he experienced a religious revelation and was soon afterwards baptized as a Christian. As his faith now conflicted with his military
duties he requested a discharge from the army in 339 and on securing
this (after a term of imprisonment) elected to live the life of a recluse on
an island off the coast of Liguria for several years. In 360 he undertook
religious study under St HILARY OF POITIERS and went on to found a
monastery at Ligugé (the first such institution to be established in western
Europe). He was appointed bishop of Tours by popular acclamation
around 370 and founded a second monastery nearby, at Marmoutier.
Further monasteries soon followed. While engaged upon evangelical work
in pagan areas of his diocese he proved a formidable opponent of pagan
leaders, even destroying their shrines, but at the same time disapproved of
the death penalty being imposed against pagans and other heretics and
thereby provoked much opposition within the church from the likes of
St BRICE. St Martin's unflinching commitment to holiness and compassion,
together with the many tales of miracles associated with his name, made
him one of the most celebrated figures of his age and his memory is
preserved in the names of numerous churches, towns and villages throughout Europe and beyond. Tours itself became a popular centre of pilgrimage. St Martin is honoured today as the patron saint of France, soldiers,
beggars and innkeepers. His emblems are either a ball of fire suspended
over his head or a goose.
Feast Day: 11 November.

Martin de Porres (1579–1639) Peruvian laybrother. Born of mixed
Spanish and Indian parentage in Lima, he became a laybrother at the
Dominican friary in Lima and remained there for the rest of his life, working in a variety of mundane roles. He became a fully professed brother
there in 1603. Spending much of his time in prayer or observing various
penances, he became famous for his many kindnesses to the sick and
needy and was particularly renowned for his sympathy with animals. As
his great wisdom became known he was consulted for advice by many of
the most important figures of Lima and various miraculous stories became
associated with his name, though he himself was always dismissive of his

own achievements and capabilities. Many witnesses described how they had seen him levitating at the altar or credited to him miraculous healing gifts. Immediately upon St Martin's sudden death from a fever reports circulated of miracles occurring at his tomb and the process of canonization began (finally completed in 1962). Reflecting his status as the first black South American saint, he is venerated as a patron saint of social justice and race relations.
Feast Day: 3 November.

Mary   (1st century) The virgin mother of Christ. According to the Bible, Mary (or **Miriam** in Hebrew) was descended from the house of King David, although no information is offered about her immediate parents or her place of birth. Having become betrothed to St JOSEPH, a carpenter of Nazareth, she was visited (at the so-called 'Annunciation') by the angel Gabriel, who informed her that through the power of the Holy Spirit she would bear the Messiah, Jesus Christ. Submitting to the will of God, she duly became pregnant. Joseph did not reject her because of the pregnancy and the marriage went ahead. Mary's baby was born while the couple were in Bethlehem to have their names recorded in the official census, after which they evaded the murderous soldiers of Herod seeking out the new-born Saviour and fled to Egypt. The holy family later returned to Nazareth and little is known of their lives over the next few years. Mary reappears, however, at the Feast of Cana (as related at John 2:1–10), during which Christ changed the water into wine at his mother's prompting, and finally at the Crucifixion (John 19:25–27), after which she seems to have been entrusted by Christ to John's care. She prayed with the other apostles at the time of Christ's ascension to heaven (Acts 1:12–14) but is not mentioned again afterwards. Conflicting traditions claim that she died either in Jerusalem or in Ephesus. Roman Catholics believe that Mary was herself born without sin, the product of an 'Immaculate Conception', and that she remained a virgin throughout her marriage. At the end of her life she did not die in the usual way but was transported body and soul to heaven in what is usually dubbed her 'Assumption'. As the foremost intercessor between humanity and Christ, Mary has been singled out for special devotion since the early history of the Roman Catholic church and many orders, churches and other organizations have dedicated themselves specifically to her. Countless individuals have claimed to have experienced visions of Mary or to have benefited from her divine intervention. Mary is variously honoured as the patron saint of numerous countries and

organizations and was named patron saint of the entire human race in 1944. Her Annunciation is celebrated on 25 March and her Immaculate Conception on 8 December, while her part in the Incarnation and Redemption is commemorated on 1 January and the Visitation is remembered on 31 May. The feast of Our Lady of Sorrows falls on 15 September. She is also celebrated in numerous local festivals and commemorated in countless placenames.
Feast Day: 15 August.

Mary of Egypt   (5th century) Egyptian penitent. According to the bare facts known about her life, Mary of Egypt was a prostitute of Alexandria who underwent a sudden conversion to Christianity while in Jerusalem through the intercession of the Virgin MARY. Finding herself prevented by an unseen force from entering a church, she realized the error of her ways and called upon Mary to bring her to repentance. In response to this experience she elected to live the life of a hermit in the wilderness on the other side of the River Jordan and remained there for the next 18 years. Her story, which resembles that of MARY MAGDALEN, was particularly popular during the medieval period as an ideal of repentance and a proof of the limitless quality of God's forgiveness. Her emblem in art is three loaves (which she carried with her into the wilderness).
Feast Day: 1 April.

Mary of the Angels   (1661–1717) Italian nun. Born Mary Fontanella at Baldinero near Turin, she entered the Carmelite convent of St Cristina in Turin and there, in response to frequent deep spiritual melancholia, acquired a reputation through her adoption of the most severe forms of penance, which included binding her tongue with an iron ring and suspending herself with ropes. She became novice mistress at the age of 30 and three years later was appointed prioress, in which role she was treated with much respect by all who knew her.
Feast Day: 16 December.

Mary di Rosa   (1813–1855) Italian foundress. Born in Brescia, she dedicated herself to charitable work among the sick and needy while still a teenager and in defiance of her own physical weakness, seeing this as the best way of serving Christ. In 1840 she undertook the foundation of the Handmaids of Charity of Brescia to promote such work in the region. The charity played a prominent role in alleviating suffering during the war with Austria that subsequently convulsed northern Italy and was also

active in treating those infected in the cholera epidemic that followed. Exhausted by her efforts on behalf of others, Mary di Rosa herself died at the age of 42. She was canonized in 1954.
Feast Day: 15 December.

Mary MacKillop   (1842–1909) Australian foundress. Mary Helen Mac-Killop was born in Melbourne of Scottish descent and, having decided at an early age to pursue a religious life, was encouraged to found a new charitable community to assist the poor of South Australia. Assisted by Father Julian Woods, she founded the Sisters of Saint Joseph of the Sacred Heart (commonly known as the Josephites) and oversaw the establishment of many schools, orphanages and other charitable institutions. Elected mother-general of the order in 1875, she continued in such work for the rest of her life, often having to show considerable determination and courage in the face of fierce opposition from within the church (which went as far as a short period of excommunication). She won official papal approval for her work in 1888. Considered Australia's first native-born saint, she was canonized in 1995.
Feast Day: 25 May.

Mary Magdalen   (1st century) Biblical follower of Christ. According to Luke 8:1–2, Mary Magdalen (or **Mary of Magdala**) was a sinner – by tradition a prostitute – who was tormented by seven devils until Christ drove them from her. Henceforth she served him faithfully wherever he went, even attending at the Crucifixion, and became an ideal of the repentant sinner. She was one of the three people who discovered that Christ's tomb was empty and, according to John 20:11–18, it was to her that Christ appeared after his Resurrection with a message for the faithful. She is sometimes assumed to be the same person as the otherwise unidentified sinner mentioned at Luke 7:37–50 who anointed Christ's feet with expensive ointment and washed them with her tears and also sometimes as synonymous with Martha's sister Mary of Bethany. Later legend claims she settled in Provence to live the life of a hermit until her death at Saint Maximin. Her emblem is a jar of ointment. She is honoured as the patron saint of sinners and as a symbol of the contemplative life.
Feast Day: 22 July.

Mary Magdalen dei Pazzi   (1566–1607) Italian nun. Born Maria Maddalena de' Pazzi into a wealthy family of Florence, she was educated by the Jesuits and at the age of 16 gave up all the advantages of her rank and

beauty to enter a Carmelite convent. Shortly after taking the veil in 1584, she was struck down by a combination of life-threatening illness and severe emotional disturbance resulting from temptation and depression. She interpreted these experiences as a sign that she had been allowed to share in the suffering of Christ himself and went on to have daily visions of Christ and regular conversations with him, sometimes retreating into a deep prayerful trance for months at a time. These conversations, which continued until Mary reached the age of 41, were recorded in seven volumes by the other nuns. After five years of these extraordinary experiences Mary seems to have achieved some resolution to her spiritual turmoil and rose in due course to the positions of novice mistress and subprioress. Her mystical revelations remained unreported outside the convent during her lifetime. Like many other saints, her body is said to have remained incorrupt since her death. She was canonized in 1669.
Feast Day: 25 May.

Mary Mazzarello   *See* JOHN BOSCO.

Matt Talbot   (1856–1925) Irish penitent. Born into a poor family of Dublin, Matt Talbot was the son of an alcoholic and himself became addicted to drink while still a child and working at a wine-bottling store. Beaten by his father, he abandoned himself to drink until 1884, when, at the age of 28, he suddenly resolved to give up alcohol completely, with the spiritual support of the Virgin Mary. To the amazement of all who knew him, he remained sober for the next 41 years and became a stalwart of the Catholic community, praying frequently and assuming a life of strict discipline and penance. Ultimately, in 1891, he became a member of the Franciscan Third Order. His life is often cited as an example to others seeking to give up an addiction of some kind.
Feast Day: 7 June.

Matthew   (1st century) Apostle. According to Matthew 9:9, Matthew was a Galilean tax collector working for the Romans in Capernaum until Christ summoned him to become one of his disciples, upon which he immediately abandoned his desk and went with him (despite the fact that tax collectors were universally despised by the Jews). Also referred to by the name **Levi** in the Gospels of Mark and Luke, the rest of his life is shrouded in obscurity. He is credited, however, with writing the first Gospel between the years 60 and 90 and with becoming one of the first Christian evangelists. One tradition claims he died the death of a martyr

in Ethiopia or Persia. He is honoured as the patron saint of accountants, bookkeepers, tax collectors, customs officers and security guards. His emblem is a winged man.
Feast Day: 21 September.

Matthias   (1st century) Apostle. According to Acts 1:15–26 and 2:1–4, Matthias was the man chosen by lot to take the place of Judas Iscariot as one of the 12 apostles after the ascension of Christ and Judas' death. Having witnessed the Resurrection, he was among the apostles to receive the gift of the Holy Spirit at Pentecost, but little is known about his subsequent life and death, though there is a tradition that he preached in Judaea, Cappadocia and even Ethiopia before being himself crucified. A gospel said to have been written in his name is now lost. His emblem is an axe or halberd (supposed to have been the instrument of his martyrdom).
Feast Day: 14 May.

Maudez   *See* MAWES.

Maughold   (d.498) Bishop of the Isle of Man. According to legend, Maughold (or **Maccul**) was born in the Orkneys and lived the life of a pirate until he was converted to Christianity in Ireland by St PATRICK. Subsequently he undertook missionary work in the Isle of Man and became bishop of the island, where he earned great respect for his holiness. His memory is preserved in the Isle of Man through several placenames.
Feast Day: 27 April.

Maurice   (d. c.287) Roman martyr. Legend has it that Maurice was the name of the Roman officer commanding the so-called Theban Legion comprising Christian soldiers from Egypt who were put to death to a man for their faith while serving in Gaul. The legion is supposed to have mutinied at Agaunum (now renamed Saint-Maurice-en-Valais in Switzerland) either upon being ordered to participate in pagan sacrifices or to repress the Christian population living nearby. As a result every tenth man was executed: when the remainder still refused to obey their orders they, too, were put to death. Historians suggest that the legend may be based upon a real incident that took place around the end of the 3rd century but that the number of men involved is unlikely to have been as many as an entire legion. The place where the executions were carried out is now the site of an abbey of canons regular.
Feast Day: 22 September.

Maurus   (6th century) Italian monk. According to tradition, Maurus
was the son of a Roman nobleman but was brought up in the care of
St BENEDICT and opted for the life of a monk at the monastery of Subiaco,
fulfilling the role of Benedict's personal aide. Nothing is known of the
details of his subsequent life apart from a story that he once performed a
miracle by walking on water in order to save St PLACID from drowning.
There is, however, a longstanding claim that he was sent by St Benedict to
Gaul and there founded the abbey of Glanfeuil and served as its abbot
(although this was probably concocted simply to attract pilgrims to
Glanfeuil).
Feast Day: 5 October.

Mawes   (*c.*5th century) Cornish bishop. Details of the life of St Mawes (or
Maudez, as he is known in Brittany) are scant. It is thought that like
St BUDOC, with whom he is usually associated, he was Welsh in origin
and probably travelled to Brittany and Cornwall as a missionary monk. In
Brittany he is particularly revered as a teacher. In Cornwall his memory is
preserved in the name of a fishing village near Falmouth, which he is said
to have founded.
Feast Day: 18 November.

Maximilian   (d.295) African martyr. The son of an army veteran living
somewhere in the vicinity of Tebessa (in Algeria), Maximilian was
instructed to join the Roman army by a court order when he was aged 21
(the sons of army veterans being obliged by law to serve as soldiers).
Being a Christian, he refused to obey, however, arguing that he could
serve no one but God. Maximilian's father was told to persuade his son
to yield to the court's demands but his father simply replied that he was
powerless to change his son's mind. Even the threat of execution had no
effect and Maximilian was accordingly condemned and beheaded with a
sword. His father returned home, rejoicing in his son's entry into heaven.
Feast Day: 26 August.

Maximilian Kolbe   (1894–1941) Polish martyr. Born in Zdunska-Wola, he
joined the seminary of the Conventual Franciscans in Lvov in 1910. He
continued his studies in Rome and there earned doctorates in philosophy
and theology. Having returned to Poland in 1917, he published the first
issue of his influential monthly review *Knight of the Immaculate* in a bid to
defend the importance of spirituality in a threatening modern world.
Within 20 years the magazine had a worldwide circulation of one million.

He contracted tuberculosis in 1920 but undeterred went on to found (1927) the first 'City of the Immaculate' community, named Niepokalonow, at Teresin, comprising a Franciscan friary, a printing house, a Roman Catholic newspaper, a radio station and other amenities. Further similar communities followed in Japan and elsewhere before he returned to Poland in 1936. After the German invasion of Poland the community of Niepokalanow was itself turned into a concentration camp. Its members dedicated themselves to helping refugees, including Jews, but the Nazis responded in 1941 by having Kolbe arrested and sent to Auschwitz concentration camp. When 10 men were selected for confinement in an underground starvation cell Kolbe willingly volunteered to take the place of a man with a family and did his best to keep up the spirits of the others as they wasted away. When he and three others lingered on they were killed with lethal injections. He was canonized in 1982 and is honoured today as the patron saint of drug addicts.
Feast Day: 14 August.

Maximus of Turin   (c.350–415) Italian bishop. Little is known of the life of Maximus beyond the facts that he was born in Vercelli, served as bishop of Turin from around 390 until his death and in 398 presided over a gathering of Gaulish bishops. He was apparently much respected for his abilities as a preacher and over 100 of his evangelizing sermons, many of which sought to repress pagan rituals and beliefs, survive.
Feast Day: 25 June.

Maximus the Confessor   (c.580–662) Roman abbot. Born into a noble family of Constantinople, he was well educated and served as chief secretary to the emperor Heraclius but then resigned the post after three years in order to assume the life of a monk at Chrysopolis (Scutari). He soon became abbot of the community but, when it dispersed before a Persian invasion, he sought refuge in Alexandria, Carthage and finally Rome. Here he supported Pope MARTIN I against Monothelitism, thus incurring the wrath of Emperor Constans II, who had the two men hauled before him in Constantinople. After six years' imprisonment, the 82-year-old Maximus was condemned to be flogged, have his tongue cut out and his right hand removed. Thus maimed, he was confined at a remote spot on the Black Sea, where he died within a short time. He is remembered as a prominent theologian of the early church and left behind a number of important writings, including a much-admired compilation of thoughts and aphorisms

entitled *Four Centuries of Charity*. Also known as **Maximus of Constanti-nople**, his title 'Confessor' refers to the sufferings he endured for his faith.
Feast Day: 13 August.

Mayeul   (906–994) French abbot. Mayeul (or **Maieul**) was born at Avignon and after studying at Lyons attained the rank of archdeacon at Mâcon at a relatively young age. He was unwilling to progress to the rank of bishop, however, and instead became a monk at Cluny. Here, against his own wishes, he succeeded to the post of abbot in 965. A noted scholar, he proved a capable if self-deprecating leader and further extended the influence of Cluny over other monastic institutions as well as playing an active role in reforming the monasteries at Ravenna and Pavia. He won the confidence of the emperors Otto I and Otto II but resisted their attempts to put him forward as a candidate for the papacy. He died at Souvigny while travelling to Paris, where he had been asked by King Hugh Capet to undertake the reform of the abbey of Saint-Denis.
Feast Day: 11 May.

Mechtilde of Helfta   (*c*.1241–1298) German mystic. Mechtilde von Hackborn entered the monastery of Rodarsdorf in Saxony, where her sister was abbess, at the tender age of seven and immediately determined upon a life as a nun, refusing to leave. She accompanied the other nuns when they moved to Helfta, also in Saxony, in 1258 and in due course took charge of their school there. Her pupils included a five-year-old girl who was destined to be remembered as St GERTRUDE OF HELTA and as St Mechtilde's closest friend and supporter. As well as being a fine singer, Mechtilde had many mystic experiences in which she believed herself to be in conversation with Christ. These conversations were recorded by Gertrude and published after Mechtilde's death at the age of 57 as *The Book of Special Grace*.
Feast Day: 19 November.

Méen   (*c*.6th century) Welsh abbot. St Méen (or **Mewan**) probably accompanied St SAMSON from south Wales to Brittany in order to conduct missionary work in the Brocéliande region. He is credited with founding the monastery of Saint-Méen near Paimpoint. After his death his cult spread throughout France and Cornwall.
Feast Day: 21 June.

Meinrad   (d.861) German martyr. Little is known about the life of Meinrad beyond the fact that he was born into a peasant family near Wurtemberg

and became a monk at Reichenau. He left the monastery to take up the life of a hermit at Einsiedeln beside the Lake of Zurich in Switzerland around 836. Here he remained until 861, when he was set upon by robbers who beat him to death when they found he had no treasures they could steal. His hermitage gradually evolved into the Benedictine abbey of St Meinrad. He was canonized in 1039.
Feast Day: 21 January.

Melania the Younger   (383–439) Roman foundress. Born into a wealthy Roman family, Melania aimed from her childhood to pursue a religious life, probably influenced by the ideals of her paternal grandmother St Melania the Elder. Her father, however, obliged her to marry a rich young Roman nobleman named Valerius Pinianus and it was only after the premature death of their two children that she finally persuaded her husband to embrace celibacy and to retreat with her and her mother to a country villa and there to live an austere Christian life as part of a growing community, devoting most of their wealth to the church. When the Visigoths invaded she and her husband sought refuge in Thagaste in Africa, where they established a monastery for men and another for women. The couple later settled in Palestine and, following the death of her husband in 432, Melania occupied a hut on the Mount of Olives and there founded a further community for women dedicated to prayer and charitable work. During her travels she met and influenced many of the leading religious figures of her time, including the saints AUGUSTINE, JEROME and PAULINUS OF NOLA.
Feast Day: 31 December.

Melchiades   *See* MILTIADES.

Mellitus   (d.624) Italian bishop. Of noble Roman birth, Mellitus was among the monks sent by Pope GREGORY I to England in 601 to assist St AUGUSTINE OF CANTERBURY in his missionary work there. In 604 he was appointed first bishop of the East Saxons, based in London. He managed to secure the conversion of Sabert, king of the East Saxons, but was subsequently driven out by his two sons, who remained unbaptized and took exception when he excluded them from taking communion. After a year in exile in Gaul Mellitus returned to England and in 619, being still unable to reclaim his see in London, he succeeded to the post of archbishop of Canterbury. Though suffering from gout, he proved an effective

archbishop, his achievements in his remaining years including the foundation of the church of St Mary's in Canterbury.
Feast Day: 24 April.

Mennas (d. *c*.300) Egyptian martyr. The story of Mennas (or **Menas**) is
largely a matter of legend. Born in Egypt, he served with the Roman army
in Phrygia and was eventually martyred for his faith at Cotyaeum during
the reign of Diocletian. Later tradition added various miraculous episodes
and his shrine at Karm Abu Mina near Alexandria became a popular place
of pilgrimage until the seventh century. He was honoured as the patron
saint of merchants and caravans of the desert and in 1943 was credited
with interceding to secure Allied victory in the battle of El Alamein. His
emblem is a pair of camels.
Feast Day: 11 November.

Meriasek (*c*.6th century) Cornish bishop. A shadowy figure, Meriasek (or
Meriadoc) may have been of Welsh origin and is variously commemorated as a bishop in Brittany and Cornwall, and is credited with founding a
number of monasteries. He is known primarily from a medieval miracle
play called *Bewnans Meryasek* written by a Cornish priest in 1504. He is
honoured as the patron saint of Camborne in Cornwall.
Feast Day: 7 June.

Methodius *See* CYRIL AND METHODIUS.

Methodius of Olympus (d. *c*.311) Bishop of Olympus. A noted preacher
and scholar, Methodius is thought to have served as a bishop of Olympus
in Lycia (in modern Turkey) and of Tyre, or possibly of Patara in Lycia.
He is believed to have died the death of a martyr at Chalcis in Greece. An
opponent of the Alexandrian theologian Origen, he is remembered chiefly
for his writings in praise of orthodoxy, notably the *Symposium*, which drew
on the dialogues of Plato and was written in celebration of virginity.
Feast Day: 18 September.

Mewan *See* MÉEN.

Michael the Archangel The biblical angel who is identified (at Daniel
10:13–21 and 12:1) as the protector of the Israelites and (at Revelation
12:7–9) as the conqueror of the satanic dragon. Together with GABRIEL and
RAPHAEL, Michael is one of only three angels who are also venerated as
saints. As chief of all God's angels, he was singled out for special praise by
the Jews and early Christians and in due course was taken up as a divine

protector of the entire Christian congregation. Numerous churches are dedicated to him and he is also celebrated in countless placenames, the most notable of which include Mont-Saint-Michel in France and St Michael's Mount in Cornwall, both of which are linked with stories of visions of St Michael witnessed locally. He is also honoured as the patron saint of soldiers, the sick and the city of Brussels.
Feast Day: 29 September.

Miguel Pro   (1891–1927) Mexican martyr. Born Miguel Agustin Pro into a middle-class family of Guadalupe, Mexico, he joined the Jesuit order at the age of 20 and was subsequently ordained in Belgium. Despite the fact that priests of any description risked being arrested and prosecuted in contemporary Mexico following the revolution of 1910, he returned to his native country and successfully avoided capture for nearly a year, fulfilling all the usual duties of a Catholic priest. He was eventually betrayed by a young boy and executed by firing squad on charges of being a priest and plotting against the president, meeting his death with great courage. A decision to allow press photographs to record the execution in order to expose the cowardliness of Catholics thus backfired and ensured Miguel Pro's status as a martyr for his faith.
Feast Day: 23 November.

Milburga   (d.715) English foundress. The elder sister of St MILDRED and the daughter of Merewald, king of Mercia, Milburga (or **Mildburga**) is remembered as the foundress of the nunnery of Wenlock in Shropshire around 670. She was credited with various healing powers and was well-known for her pious and saintly way of life.
Feast Day: 23 February.

Mildred   (d. *c*.700) English abbess. Like St MILBURGA, St Mildred (or **Mildthryth**) was a daughter of Merewald, king of Mercia, and had a convent education in France before becoming a nun herself, entering the convent her mother had founded at Minster-in-Thanet. As abbess there she became widely respected for her kindness and generosity to the poor and after her death her tomb became a noted place of pilgrimage.
Feast Day: 13 July.

Miltiades   (d.314) Roman pope. Relatively little is known of the life and brief papacy of Miltiades (or **Melchiades**). He may have been born in Africa and is usually remembered for the fact that it was during his reign, which began in 311, that Emperor Constantine formally ended persecution

of Christianity and other religions throughout the Roman Empire. The church received back confiscated buildings and possessions and was granted new land upon which to erect new places of worship. In character Miltiades was reputed to be both peace-loving and moderate. Miltiades may have been the first pope to live in the Lateran Palace, which remained the residence of the bishops of Rome for the next 1000 years.
Feast Day: 10 December.

Modestus *See* VITUS, MODESTUS AND CRESCENTIA.

Modwenna (*c.*7th century) English hermit. Few details are known of the life of Modwenna beyond the fact that she settled as a hermit on an island at Andressey near Burton-on-Trent, where she became famous for performing miracles. After her death her shrine at Burton became a focus of local veneration. She is sometimes confused with the Irish MONINNE and the fact that she was supposedly born in Ireland, lived in Scotland and died in England led to conflicting claims to her relics.
Feast Day: 6 July.

Monenna *See* MONINNE.

Monica (*c.* 331–87) Mother of St AUGUSTINE. Possibly born at Tagaste in North Africa, she bore her violent-tempered and unfaithful husband Patricius three children before she was widowed when Augustine, her eldest child, was 18. Augustine was unruly as a young man, living with his mistress (who bore him a child) and failing to share his mother's commitment to Christianity, despite the fact she had already managed to secure the conversion of both her husband and her mother-in-law. This intransigence caused St Monica great distress, but her son proved impervious to her prayers as well as to her ceaseless cajoling and weeping on his behalf. In 383 she stubbornly followed Augustine to Italy, going first to Rome and then to Milan and there came under the influence of St AMBROSE. Three years later Augustine finally responded to his mother's unflagging pressure and agreed to be baptized by St Ambrose, to his mother's great joy. Mother and son subsequently decided to return to Africa together, but Monica fell ill and died at the port of Ostia on the Tiber before their departure. She is honoured as the patron saint of alcoholics (having had a serious drinking habit herself in her youth), difficult marriages, mothers, widows and victims of unfaithfulness.
Feast Day: 27 August.

Moninne   (d. *c*.518) Irish foundress. Moninne (or **Monenna**) is said to
have become a nun under the influence of St PATRICK and subsequently
to have founded her own nunnery at Killeevy in County Armagh with
eight virgins and one widow, herself serving as abbess for this small
community. She was credited with a number of miracles but her story has
over the centuries become entangled with that of the otherwise unconnec-
ted St MODWENNA.
Feast Day: 6 July.

Montanus and Lucius   (d.259) Carthaginian martyrs. Montanus and
Lucius were prominent members of a group of martyrs who were arrested
during the reign of Valerian on charges of plotting rebellion against the
procurator at Carthage. During their lengthy imprisonment, Montanus had
visions that revealed to him the extent of his human frailties, revelations
which he shared with the others. After several months the group all
confessed their Christian faith and were duly condemned to death. Lucius
went first, being in poor health, while the sturdier Montanus spoke on
behalf of them all when he vigorously attacked all heretics and those who
made sacrifices to the gods and pleaded with those present to repent their
sinful ways. He and the others were then beheaded.
Feast Day: 23 May.

Moses the Black   (*c*.330–*c*.405) Ethiopian monk. Born in Nubia, Moses the
Black (otherwise known as **Moses the Ethiopian**) served as the slave of
a government official in Egypt prior to being dismissed from the household on suspicion of theft and murder. Subsequently, strong and fierce, he
became notorious as the leader of a gang of robbers whose crimes spread
terror throughout the Nile Valley. When, ultimately, he was forced to go
into hiding among the desert monks of Petra monastery at Sketis near Alexandria, he underwent an apparently miraculous conversion and decided to
exchange his life of crime for one of religious devotion. Though always
rough in nature, he was eventually admitted into the priesthood and in
due course became leader of a colony of hermits at Sketis. He is sometimes
credited with introducing the paschal fast that became today's Lenten fast.
He died refusing to defend himself when his colony was attacked by a
Berber raiding party and is today considered an exemplar of nonviolence.
Feast Day: 28 August.

Mungo   *See* KENTIGERN.

Nathanael *See* BARTHOLOMEW.

Neot (9th century) English monk. The life of St Neot is a matter of legend, which identifies him as a monk of Glastonbury who adopted the life of a hermit on Bodmin Moor in Cornwall. He is supposed to have visited the tombs of Peter and Paul in Rome and to have been a compatriot of Alfred the Great, who is said to have consulted him. On his death he was laid to rest at a monastery at Eynesbury in Cambridgeshire. His memory is preserved in such placenames as Saint Neot in Cornwall and Saint Neots in Cambridgeshire.
Feast Day: 31 July.

Nereus and Achilleus (*c.*2nd century) Roman martyrs. According to one tradition, Nereus and Achilleus were two Roman soldiers who were put to death after converting to Christianity and refusing to perform any further military service. Another version of their story, however, describes them as servants of Flavia Domitilla, a relative of the Roman emperor Domitian, who shared their mistress's Christian faith, accompanying her into exile and eventually being beheaded for refusing to make sacrifices to idols, while she was burned to death.
Feast Day: 12 May.

Nicetas of Remesiana (d. *c.*414) Serbian missionary. Little is known for certain about the life of Nicetas of Remesiana beyond the fact that he became bishop of Remesiana (now Bela Palanka in Serbia) around 370. He is celebrated for his missionary work among the wild pagan peoples living south of the Danube, including the Goths. Various examples of his writing survive, among them a treatise in praise of singing in church. He was also admired by his friend PAULINUS OF NOLA as a writer of poetry and has been tentatively identified as the author of the Latin hymn *Te Deum*.
Feast Day: 22 June.

Nicetius of Trier (d. *c.*566) French bishop. Born at Auvergne, he lived as a monk at Limoges before being appointed bishop of Trier around 527. Ministering to a barely Christianized population, he proved an unflinching critic of all ranks of society when they failed to live up to Christian ideals.

His criticisms resulted in his exile by Clotaire I, whom he had excommunicated, but after the king's death he was restored to his post by his successor Sigebert I and over the years he impressed many with his indomitable courage in the face of fierce opposition. Other highly-placed recipients of his criticisms and advice included the Emperor Justinian at Constantinople, whom he warned against the Monophysite heresy. He also founded a school for the clergy and presided over a number of important councils held at Trier.
Feast Day: 1 October.

Nicholas (4th century) Bishop of Myra. Little is known of the life of St Nicholas beyond the tradition that he was bishop of Myra in Lycia (in modern Turkey) in the 4th century. He is most familiar today as the origin of the modern Santa Claus or Father Christmas, an association derived from his status as patron saint of children. He was revered by Christians as early as the 6th century and there was a church of St Nicholas in Constantinople dating from around that time. In succeeding centuries he became one of the most popular of all Christian saints and the central figure in a number of well-known stories. The legend that he saved three girls from prostitution by tossing bags of gold through their open window into the stockings hanging beside their beds is often cited as the source of the present-giving customs of modern Christmas. Another story describes how he restores to life three children who had been murdered and pickled in a barrel of brine. An unsupported legend about his death claims he was eventually martyred for his faith. What are claimed to be his relics are kept at Bari in Italy, hence the occasional reference to him as 'Nicholas of Bari'. As well as being honoured as the patron saint of children, he is also identified as the patron saint of sailors, merchants, pawnbrokers, brides, travellers, Greece, Russia and Moscow among other cities. His emblem is three gold balls (as displayed outside pawnbrokers' offices in times gone by).
Feast Day: 6 December.

Nicholas I (*c.*820–867) Roman pope. Born into a noble family of Rome, he served a number of popes before being elected bishop of Rome himself in 858. The nine-year papacy of Nicholas I (sometimes called **Nicholas the Great**, one of only three popes to earn the appellation 'the Great') witnessed turmoil variously resulting from conflict with the bishop of Constantinople, with Archbishop John of Ravenna and with Lothair II of Lorraine, who incurred papal wrath by contracting a bigamous marriage.

Nicholas believed strongly in the primacy of the church over earthly rulers and sought to consolidate the authority of his office over both the secular and religious worlds. He felt moved on different occasions to depose two German archbishops and also had to fend off the threat of the invasion of Rome by Lothair's army. A wise and diplomatically astute pope, he managed to defend Rome by making strategic alliances and won the love of his own people through his reputation for fair-dealing and generosity. By the time of his death he had won the respect of many contemporaries, particularly for his steadfast defence of the church from interference by secular rulers.

Feast Day: 13 November.

Nicholas von Flue   (1417–1487) Swiss hermit. Born into a farming family of Flueli near Sachseln, he became a farmer, soldier and respected public official and earned a reputation both for his wisdom and for his sincere religious faith, belonging to a lay association known as the Friends of God. While serving in the Swiss army at Katharinental, he played a crucial role in winning protection for a nunnery threatened with destruction. He married and became the father of 10 children, but in 1465 surprised everyone by renouncing his public role and subsequently, with his wife's consent, leaving home to take up the life of a hermit. Calling himself 'Brother Klaus', he occupied a cottage near his former home in Ranft and, though illiterate himself, was here sought out by many visitors from all ranks of society asking for his advice. The belief grew up that he never ate or drank but devoted all his waking hours to contemplation and prayer. In 1481, towards the end of his life, he established a permanent place as one of the most celebrated personalities in Swiss history when he negotiated a compromise between the rural and urban cantons whose disagreements threatened civil war. The so-called Compromise of Stans effectively prevented the disintegration of the Swiss state. He was canonized in 1947. He is honoured as the patron saint of Switzerland.

Feast Day: 21 March.

Nicholas of Tolentino   (c.1245–1305) Italian friar. Born at Sant' Angelo near Fermo in Italy, he was named after St NICHOLAS and ordained as an Augustinian friar in 1269. From 1275 he lived at the monastery in the town of Tolentino, where he earned a wide reputation as a preacher and doer of good deeds. He was particularly noted for his sympathy with the poor and sick and became famous for the many miracles associated with his name. His habit of blessing pieces of bread before giving them to the sick led to

the custom of 'St Nicholas Breads' in which blessed pieces of bread are distributed at his shrine. He was canonized in 1446.
Feast Day: 10 September.

Nicodemus of the Holy Mountain   (c.1748–1809) Greek monk. Born on Naxos, Nicodemus became a monk at Dionysiou on Mount Athos in 1775. He is remembered as the most revered of the monks on Mount Athos (also known as the Holy Mountain) and as one of the most respected religious writers of his time. His works included meditations, a Greek version of Lorenzo Scupoli's *Spiritual Combat* and the *Philokalia*, his most famous and influential book, which was based upon the writings of the Greek fathers.
Feast Day: 14 July.

Nicomedes   (dates unknown) Roman martyr. Nothing is known of the details of the life and martyrdom of Nicomedes beyond the tradition that he was a priest who was put to death after affording a Christian burial to another martyr called Felicula. He is supposed to have been buried in the catacomb on the Via Nomentana and to have inspired a cult following.
Feast Day: 15 September.

Nilus of Ancyra   (d. c.430) Turkish writer. Born at Ancyra (modern Ankara), Nilus fell under the influence of JOHN CHRYSOSTOM while studying at Constantinople. He went on to found a monastery at Ancyra and to write numerous influential works intended as spiritual guidance for the monks there. Many of his spiritual writings, as well as many of his letters, have survived.
Feast Day: 12 November.

Nilus of Rossano   (c.910–1004) Greek abbot. Born at Rossano in Calabria, he worked as a treasury official and fathered an illegitimate child before entering a Byzantine monastery at Palma in Campania in 940. A deeply compassionate man, he became widely known both for his virtuous ways and for his great wisdom and was eventually made abbot of St Adrian's at San Demetrio Corone. When the Saracens attacked southern Italy Nilus led the monks to safety on Monte Cassino around 981. He is supposed to have finally installed his monks in a permanent home at Grottaferrata near Rome in 1004, shortly before his death, and also to have argued for lenient treatment of the overthrown antipope John Philagathus.
Feast Day: 26 September.

Nine Maidens   *See* DONALD.

Ninian (d. *c*.432) British missionary bishop. Details of the life of Ninian (otherwise known as **Ninnidh** or **Nynia**) are hazy, but the usual version of his story has him born in Britain and receiving religious training in Rome. According to Bede, he became a bishop and worked among the southern Picts, in the process becoming the first significant Christian leader to spread the gospel in Scotland. His base was traditionally identified as a white painted church at Whithorn in Galloway, which subsequently became a site of pilgrimage during the medieval period. This tradition has been supported by archaeological finds in the area. Ninian's memory is preserved in a number of placenames in Scotland and northern England. *Feast Day: 26 August.*

Noël Chabanel *See* NORTH AMERICA, MARTYRS OF.

Norbert (*c*.1080–1134) German archbishop and founder. Born into a noble family of Xanten in the duchy of Cleves, Norbert served as a canon at the cathedral of Xanten but generally lived a carefree life of pleasure at the imperial court until 1115, when he underwent a sudden and profound conversion after narrowly escaping death on being thrown from his horse during a storm. He became a priest and, determined to live as austerely as possible, adopted the life of an itinerant preacher in northern France. In 1120 he gathered a small group of followers about him and, in the valley of Prémontré near Laon, founded the Canons Regular of Prémontré (known as the Premonstratensians or Norbertines). Having founded eight abbeys and two convents, he was eventually obliged to hand over the leadership of the Premonstratensians when he was raised to the post of archbishop of Magdeburg in 1126. He remained in this position until his death, dedicating himself to the reform of corrupt clergy and to the recovery of church property. He gave his support to Pope Innocent II against the antipope Pierleone and was appointed chancellor for Italy by Emperor Lothair II shortly before his death. He was canonized in 1582 and is honoured as the patron saint of Magdeburg and Bohemia. His emblem is a monstrance.
Feast Day: 6 June.

North America, Martyrs of (d.1642–1649) A group of French martyrs who died while spreading the gospel among the Mohawks of North America. All eight of them were born in France and all were members of the Jesuit order. Their leader was ISAAC JOGUES, who died in 1646; the others were **René Goupil** (1606–1642), **John de Lalande** (d.1646),

Antony Daniel (1601–1648), JEAN DE BREBEUF (d.1649), **Gabriel Lalement** (1610–1649), **Charles Garnier** (1606–1649) and **Noël Chabanel** (1613–1649). Celebrated as the first Catholic martyrs in North America, they were canonized in 1930 and are honoured as patron saints of the Americas.

Feast Day: 26 September.

Notburga (*c*.1265–*c*.1313) Tirolese kitchen servant. Born the daughter of a peasant of Rattenberg in the Tirol, Notburga worked in the kitchens of Count Henry of Rattenberg until she was dismissed by the count's wife after being caught distributing leftovers to the poor instead of taking them to the castle pigsties. Undaunted, she continued to do what she could to help the poor while working on a local farm, even giving them the food from her own plate. After the death of his wife, Count Henry took Notburga back and she remained in his service until her death. She is honoured as the patron saint of hired hands in the Tirol and Bavaria. Her emblem is a sickle (a reference to a legend that she refused to reap corn on a Sunday, in response to which her sickle remained miraculously suspended in the air out of her reach).

Feast Day: 13 September.

Nynia   *See* NINIAN.

O

Oda (d.958) English bishop. Oda (or **Odo**) was born in East Anglia of Danish descent and adopted Christianity while still young. He became a priest and around 925 was appointed bishop of Ramsbury. He went on to win the trust of King Athelstan and in 936 served as his representative in France, seeking the restoration of Louis to the French throne. He was professed a monk at the abbey of Fleury in 942, in which year he was appointed to the see of Canterbury. As archbishop he supported the monastic movement led by St DUNSTAN and became chief adviser to the kings Edmund and Edred. His reputation for charitable works and his efforts towards the restoration of the church and the raising of standards among the clergy earned him the epithet Oda the Good during his own lifetime.
Feast Day: 2 June.

Odilia (660–720) Abbess of Alsace. Odilia (otherwise known as **Odile** or **Ottilia**) was the daughter of the Duke of Alsace but, being born blind, was initially rejected by him and was brought up in a monastery. It was only after she miraculously recovered her sight on being baptized that father and daughter were eventually reconciled. Odilia went on to found a nunnery at Hohenburg (now Odilienberg) in the Vosges mountains and to serve as abbess there. Little more is known of the details of her life beyond the fact that she founded a second convent at Niedermünster and died there. After Odilia's death her shrine became a popular place of pilgrimage, particularly for those suffering with eye complaints. Among the more illustrious visitors to pay homage to her memory was the emperor Charlemagne. Today Odilia is honoured as the patron saint of Alsace and of the blind.
Feast Day: 14 December.

Odilo (*c*.962–1049) French abbot. Born into a noble family in Auvergne, he became a Benedictine monk at Cluny and rose to the position of abbot there in 994, remaining in the post for the next 54 years. Though gentle in character and physically weak, he made Cluny one of the most important abbeys in Europe as well as founding many new Cluniac houses. He did much to promote and reform the monastic movement as a whole. Among his most significant innovations were the introduction of periodic truces in military conflicts (achieved through his close association with various crowned heads of Europe) and the observance of prayers for the dead on what became known as All Souls Day, as practiced today throughout the western church. Odilo was also much respected for his generosity to the needy during times of famine, even selling or melting down the treasures held at Cluny to pay for their relief. He died at an advanced age while engaged upon a tour of inspection of Cluniac houses and was canonized in 1063.

Feast Day: 1 January.

Odo   *See* ODA.

Odo of Cluny   (879–942) French abbot. Born at Tours, he was brought up in the household of Duke William of Aquitaine, the founder of the abbey at Cluny. He served as a Benedictine monk at Baume-les-Messieurs for 18 years before being raised to the position of abbot at Cluny in 927. As abbot he oversaw the rapid expansion of Cluny and also exerted the Cluniac influence over the monastic movement through three visits to Rome at the pope's invitation, promoting observance of the Benedictine rule of prayer, manual labour and community life and encouraging stricter spiritual discipline among the monks. By the time of Odo's death Cluny was already among the most influential houses in Europe and his work was continued by his successors.

Feast Day: 18 November.

Oengus the Culdee   (d. c824) Irish martyrologist. Born into the royal family of Ulster, he was brought up at the monastery of Clonenagh in County Laois and subsequently adopted the life of a hermit at Disertbeagh and then Dysert Enos. Observing a life of considerable austerity, he pursued his scholarly studies and set about compiling the first Irish martyrology. When he went on to enter the monastery of Tallacht he attempted to conceal his identity and scholarly background and accepted only menial work but was eventually recognized and encouraged to complete his martyrology. He may also have served in the posts of abbot and bishop before his death.

Feast Day: 11 March.

Olaf   (995–1030) King of Norway. The son of a Norwegian noble, Olaf (otherwise referred to as **Olave**, **Ola** or **Tola**) lived the life of a seafaring pirate raider before converting to Christianity in Normandy and fighting for the English king Ethelred II against the Danes in 1013. He returned to Norway two years later and there drove out the Swedes and the Danes before claiming the throne of Norway. As king, he promoted the conversion of Norway to Christianity, inviting priests and monks from England to conduct missionary work among his people. With the advice of his bishop Grimkel, he outlawed many pagan laws and rituals and set in place new laws to assist in the promulgation of the gospel. Although just, Olaf proved a stern ruler: whenever he met with any resistance from those he wished to convert he was not above threatening to fight with them, a threat that usually secured the desired result. Olaf was eventually overthrown by his enemies in league with King Canute and he was forced into exile in 1029. He died in battle while trying to reclaim his crown a year later and the cathedral of Trondheim was built over his shrine. He was canonized in 1164 and is honoured today as the patron saint of Norway. *Feast Day: 29 July.*

Olga (*c.*879–969) Russian noblewoman. The widow of Prince Igor of Kiev, she assumed power following her husband's assassination and hunted down his murderers. She converted to Christianity in Constantinople around 957 and did much to spread the gospel among her people. These efforts met with mixed success, but the work she had begun was eventually picked up and continued by her grandson, St VLADIMIR. *Feast Day: 11 July.*

Oliver Plunket (1625–1681) Irish martyr. Born into a noble family of Loughcrew, County Meath, Oliver Plunket was educated by the Jesuits and became a priest in Rome in 1654. He remained in Rome for 12 years before being appointed archbishop of Armagh and primate of all Ireland. Plunket arrived in an Ireland suffering from disorder and long neglect and immediately set about renewing the church along the lines laid down by the Council of Trent, securing the confirmation of some 10,000 of the faithful. Under his leadership the Catholic church in Ireland was substantially revived, though still much riven by internal disputes. Over the next 10 years he worked to raise standards among the clergy, to enforce papal authority over the country and to maintain friendly relations between the rival Catholic and Protestant populations. In 1678, however, disaster struck when his name was linked to the so-called Popish Plot supposedly uncovered by Titus Oates in a bid to bring the Catholic community into further disrepute by suggesting its leaders were involved in planning the assassination of Charles II. Plunket was arrested and put on trial in

London, where anti-Catholic feeling was intense. After he was found guilty on concocted evidence, he was condemned to death and duly hanged, drawn and quartered at Tyburn, throughout displaying great courage. He was canonized in 1975.
Feast Day: 1 July.

Olympias   (*c*.366–*c*.408) Widow of Constantinople. Born into a wealthy family of Constantinople, Olympias grew into a beautiful woman and became the wife of the prefect Nebridius, only to be widowed after a short time. Under the influence of her close friend St JOHN CHRYSOSTOM she determined henceforth to pursue a celibate life, refusing all suitors and even turning down a favourite of the emperor Theodosius, for which offence her estate was briefly placed under public administration. Olympias subsequently gave generously to charitable causes and supported the work of, among others, St GREGORY OF NYSSA, in recognition of which she was herself appointed a deaconess of the church. After John Chrysostom was exiled in 404 Olympias and her followers suffered severe persecution from the authorities and Olympias herself was even accused of attempting to burn down the cathedral at Constantinople. She was fined heavily and spent her remaining years being hounded from place to place. St Chrysostom (who valued Olympias above all his other women supporters) continued to write to Olympias and several of his letters, in which he paid tribute to her dignity and wisdom, have survived.
Feast Day: 17 December.

Omer   (d. *c*.699) French bishop. Omer (otherwise known as **Audomarus**) was born near Coutances and spent 20 years as a monk in the monastery of Luxeuil. Around 637 he became a bishop and embarked upon missionary work among the pagan Morini, based at Thérouanne in the Pas-de-Calais, earning a considerable reputation as a preacher. Little else is known of his life beyond the facts that he founded the abbey of Sithiu, now the site of the town of Saint-Omer, and became totally blind in his last years.
Feast Day: 9 September.

Osanna of Mantua   (1449–1505) Italian mystic. Born into a noble family of Mantua, St Osanna experienced her first visions when just five years old. During her trances and ecstasies, which carried on throughout her lifetime, she had repeated visions of Mary and Christ and also displayed the stigmata, which evidently caused her great pain. Osanna's family were inclined to be dismissive of her revelatory experiences but, undeterred, she entered the novitiate of the Dominican Third Order when she was 14,

although she was not professed as a full member of the order until 1500. She became well-known for her prophetic powers as well as for her charitable work and for her outspoken criticisms of the corrupt condition of the state and church in Italy. Such was the respect she commanded that she became spiritual adviser to Duke Francis II of Mantua, even being given charge of his family while he was away on military campaign.
Feast Day: 20 June.

Osburga (d. *c*.1018) English abbess. The details of the life of St Osburga are obscure. She is said to have served as abbess of a convent at Coventry and her shrine there became a popular place of pilgrimage and the scene of many alleged miracles.
Feast Day: 30 March.

Osith *See* OSYTH.

Osmund (d.1099) English bishop. Born into a noble Norman family, Osmund followed William the Conqueror to England and there served as royal chaplain and, from 1072, as chancellor. In 1078 he was appointed bishop of Salisbury, in which role he completed construction of the cathedral at Old Sarum and is credited (probably incorrectly) with drawing up the version of the Latin liturgy known as the Sarum Use, which became a pattern for other churches throughout the country. Osmund was a stern bishop but also showed great dedication to his duties and attempted to mediate between William II and St ANSELM when they disagreed. He was also noted for his love of books, copying and binding many volumes personally (he is also thought to have participated in the compilation of the Domesday Book). His canonization was finally completed after many delays in 1457.
Feast Day: 4 December.

Oswald of Northumbria (*c*.605–642) English martyr king. Oswald was the son of the King Ethelfrith of Northumbria and converted to Christianity while in exile on Iona after his father's murder. He recovered the kingdom of Northumbria after defeating and killing the Welsh king Cadwallon of Gwynedd in battle near Hexham in 633 and at once invited missionaries from Iona to conduct evangelizing work among his people and presided over the building of churches and monasteries. These efforts prospered under the leadership of Oswald's close friend and ally St AIDAN and for a time Oswald's Christianizing influence spread beyond the borders of Northumbria by virtue of his marriage to Cyneburga of Wessex. After

eight years, however, Oswald's reign ended with his death in battle against the pagan King Penda of Mercia. As he died he is said to have prayed for the souls of the soldiers who died with him. He was widely recognized as a Christian martyr during the medieval period. His emblem is a raven with a ring in its beak.
Feast Day: 9 August.

Oswald of Worcester (*c.*925–992) English bishop. Born of military Danish descent, he was related to two archbishops of Canterbury and educated under one of them, his uncle St ODO OF CANTERBURY. He served as a canon in Winchester before becoming a Benedictine monk and completing his education at the Cluniac abbey of Fleury in France and being professed a priest. He was appointed bishop of Worcester by his close friend King Edgar in 962 and, with the king's committed support, worked alongside St DUNSTAN and St ETHELWOLD towards the restoration of monastic life in England. He went on to found the monastery of Westbury-on-Trym (near Bristol) in 962 and subsequently to establish the major monastery of Ramsey in Huntingdonshire in 971. Through these foundations and their daughter houses (such as Pershore and Evesham) he greatly promoted education and higher standards among the clergy. In addition to the see of Worcester, he was appointed archbishop of York in 972, although his reforms had little effect north of Wessex and Mercia. Much loved by the general populace for his humility, his holiness and his gentle manner, he died in Worcester, where he had done much of his most significant work, shortly after completing the ritual washing of the feet of twelve poor men at the beginning of Lent.
Feast Day: 28 February.

Oswin (d.651) English king. Cousin to St OSWALD OF NORTHUMBRIA, Oswin succeeded Oswald as ruler of northern Northumbria, while another cousin Oswiu assumed control of southern Northumbria. Oswin proved a popular king, much loved for his handsome appearance, pleasant demeanour and great generosity. He was also a close friend and supporter of St AIDAN. Unfortunately, it proved impossible for Oswin and Oswiu to live peaceably side by side and in 651 Oswin (who had disbanded his army in a bid to avoid bloodshed) was treacherously murdered on Oswiu's orders. After the killing, a repentant Oswiu had a monastery built at Gilling, the site of Oswin's murder. Oswin was subsequently venerated as a martyr, although his death was not primarily a consequence of his Christian beliefs.
Feast Day: 20 August.

Osyth (d. *c*.700) English queen. Few details are known about the life of St Osyth (or **Osith**) beyond the facts that she became queen of the East Saxons through her marriage to King Sighere and founded a nunnery at Chich in Essex, where she died. Various legends subsequently accrued around her name, including one to the effect that she met her death at the hands of pirates who took exception when she refused to worship their idols. The village of Saint Osyth, also in Essex, was named after her.
Feast Day: 7 October.

Ottilia *See* ODILIA.

Otto of Bamberg (1062–1139) German bishop. Born in Swabia, Otto was ordained a priest and served at the court of Emperor Henry IV, being raised to the rank of chancellor in 1101 and ultimately to that of bishop of Bamberg. He proved an efficient and diligent administrator of his diocese, taking a particular interest in promoting the monastic movement and proving adept in reaching compromises – balancing the sometimes conflicting interests of church and state – over such issues as the appointment of senior church officials. In 1124 he was invited to undertake a missionary campaign in Pomerania and there established a number of churches and secured the conversion of some 20,000 people. He made a second visit to the region in 1128 to consolidate his first mission. He was canonized in 1189.
Feast Day: 30 September.

Ouen (*c*.600–684) French bishop. Ouen (otherwise variously known as **Audoenus** or **Dado**) was born at Sancy near Soissons and spent his childhood and much of his adulthood at the Frankish court, rising to the post of chancellor under Dagobert I and Clovis II. His wish to dedicate himself to the religious life expressed itself through his foundation of the abbey of Rebais and eventually in him taking holy orders and being appointed (641) bishop of Rouen. As bishop he proved determined to secure the conversion of as many pagans within his diocese as possible and also busied himself founding new monasteries and fighting corruption within the clergy. He remained in demand, however, for his political skills and continued as adviser to Queen BATHILD and to the controversial mayor of the palace Ebroin.
Feast Day: 24 August.

Pachomius (*c*.292–346) Egyptian founder. Born near Thebes in Egypt, Pachomius served as a conscript in the Roman army before converting to Christianity and opting for the life of a hermit under the guidance of an anchorite named Palemon. After seven years of this solitary existence, praying and studying the Bible, he decided to gather others around him and accordingly, around 320, organized a group of monks into a community in the desert at Tabbennesi, providing them with a simple written rule to live by. Members of the community were allowed to eat or fast as they chose, but were otherwise expected to show complete obedience to the laws laid down by Pachomius himself. By the time of his death near Thebes, from plague, Pachomius presided over nine such monasteries and two convents comprising some 3,000 monks and nuns. Through these early experiments Pachomius is often identified as the founder of Christian communal monasticism.
Feast Day: 9 May.

Pacian of Barcelona (d.390) Spanish bishop. Born into a wealthy family living in or near Barcelona, Pacian (or **Pacianus**) married and fathered a son before being elected bishop of Barcelona around 365. He was widely respected for his great learning and was the author of numerous influential treatises upon ecclesiastical discipline and other topics. His most celebrated work was an attack upon the Novatian heresy in which he defended the ability of the church to remit sins committed after baptism. His defiant statement "My name is Christian, but my surname is Catholic" is often quoted.
Feast Day: 9 March.

Padre Pio (1887–1968) Italian friar. Otherwise known as **Pius of Pietrelcina**, he was born Francesco Forgione in Pietrelcina in southern Italy, the son of a peasant farmer, and became a Capuchin novice in Morcone at the age of 16. He took the habit in 1903 and, though suffering from tuberculosis, was ordained in 1910. He was drafted briefly into the army in 1915 but was soon discharged on the grounds of ill health and spent the rest of his life in the monastery of San Giovanni Rotondo. In 1910 he exhibited the wounds of the stigmata on his hands, an apparent miracle that

recurred periodically over the following eight years. In 1918 his mystical experiences culminated in a vision of an angel, who subjected him to the agony of a transverberation (in which his soul was pierced by a sharp-pointed steel blade). A month later all five wounds of the stigmata erupted on his body and these continued to bleed for the rest of his life, defying explanation by the many doctors who examined them. This manifestation, coupled with his growing reputation for miracles of healing, made Padre Pio famous and in 1923 his superiors forbade him preaching or writing letters in an attempt to suppress the threat of widespread religious hysteria. In 1940 Padre Pio used the money donated by the thousands who flocked to see him to establish a Home for the Relief of Suffering at San Giovanni Rotondo (now a public hospital under Vatican ownership). He was canonized in 2002 in recognition of his charitable works rather than primarily for his reputation as a stigmatist and miracle-worker and ranks among the most popular saints of recent times.
Feast Day: 23 September.

Palladius (5th century) Irish bishop. Relatively few details are known of the life of Palladius, who may have been a deacon from either Rome or Auxerre and who emerged as an influential leader of the church in Rome under Pope CELESTINE I. In 429 he appears to have played a prominent role in persuading Celestine to send GERMANUS OF AUXERRE to Britain to combat the Pelagian heresy there. In 431 Palladius was himself ordered to Ireland to serve as the country's first bishop, working chiefly in Wicklow before moving to Scotland not long afterwards. Although Palladius is accepted as the first bishop in the history of the Irish church, his pioneering role has been somewhat eclipsed by the fame of his successor St PATRICK.
Feast Day: 7 July.

Pammachius (*c.*340–410) Roman senator. Through his marriage to a daughter of St PAULA, Pammachius became acquainted with St JEROME and, despite the evident differences in their lifestyles and characters (Pammachius was forthright in nature, while Jerome was notoriously bad-tempered), they became friends and correspondents. A wise and learned man, Pammachius devoted much of his life to religious study and twice wrote to Jerome to warn him against the violence of his language. After his wife died in 397, Pammachius dedicated himself to good works, collaborating with St FABIOLA in the foundation of a hospice and hospital for

pilgrims at Porto and constructing a church in his own house in Rome.
Feast Day: 30 August.

Pamphilus   (*c.*240–309) Martyr of Beirut. Born into a wealthy family of
Beirut, Pamphilus (sometimes called **Pamphilus of Caesarea**) studied in
Alexandria before settling in Caesarea in Palestine, where he took over the
great library established by Origen and was ordained a priest. He pursued
his biblical studies and established a school of theology there before being
arrested and imprisoned for his faith in 307 during the Diocletian persecution. While thus confined Pamphilus collaborated with St EUSEBIUS upon
a five-volume apology in defence of the teachings of Origen but was then
subjected to torture and ultimately put to death alongside Eusebius and
several other companions.
Feast Day: 1 June.

Pancras   (d. *c.*304) Roman martyr. Details of the life of St Pancras (otherwise known as **Pancritas** or **Pancratius**) are sketchy. Legend claims that
he was a 14-year-old orphan boy from Phrygia who came to Rome with
his uncle and there was converted with him to Christianity. Pancras is said
to have suffered a martyr's death for his faith in Rome alongside NEREUS
AND ACHILLEUS, but there is no evidence for this. A church dedicated to
his memory was erected over his tomb on the Aurelian Way in Rome and
his name was also given to the first church to be founded in England (by
St AUGUSTINE in Canterbury). His relics were reportedly sent to that
country to promote the evangelical effort there and the cult of St Pancras
consequently became particularly strong there. His name is now best
known through the parish and railway station of St Pancras in London.
He is honoured as a patron saint of children.
Feast Day: 12 May.

Pantaleon   (d. *c.*305) Martyr of Bithynia. According to legend, Pantaleon
(or **Pantelcimon**) trained in medicine and was appointed court physician
to Emperor Galerius in Nicomedia. The son of a pagan father and Christian mother, he eventually denounced his luxurious lifestyle on reaffirming
his Christian faith and was subsequently arrested during the persecutions
instituted by Diocletian. After six attempts to execute him miraculously
failed, he was ultimately successfully beheaded. A phial of his blood
preserved at Ravello in southern Italy is reported to become liquid from
time to time. Pantaleon became the subject of a widespread cult and was
honoured as a patron saint of medical workers.
Feast Day: 27 July.

Paphnutius   (d. *c*.350) Bishop. The location of Paphnutius' birth is unknown, but it appears he became a monk and lived the life of a hermit under the rule of St ANTONY before being appointed bishop in Upper Thebaid. During the persecution of Christians that was carried out under the emperor Maximinus he was arrested and cruelly tortured, with the result that he lost the sight of an eye and suffered severe injuries to his legs. Paphnutius survived these abuses, however, and as a consequence was treated with special respect at the first general council at Nicaea in 325. Here he is said to have argued successfully against the proposal that all married clergy should give up their wives. He was also a committed supporter of St ATHANASIUS and in 335 appealed to Maximus of Jerusalem not to lend his support to those he considered the enemies of the Christian faith. He died in Egypt.
Feast Day: 11 September.

Papylus   *See* CARPUS, PAPYLUS AND AGATHONICE.

Paschal Baylon   (1540–1592) Spanish laybrother. Born at Torre Hermosa in Spain, Paschal Baylon lived the life of a shepherd before joining the Friars Minor in Loreto at the age of 24. He distinguished himself for his devotion to the Eucharist, remaining at prayer on his knees before the Blessed Sacrament for many hours at a time. Paschal Baylon was also noted for his gentle and patient nature while working humbly as door-keeper and was credited with a number of miracles. He died at the moment of consecration during high mass on a Whitsunday (also his birth-day) and is honoured as the patron saint of Eucharistic congresses and confraternities.
Feast Day: 17 May.

Patrick   (*c*.389–461) Irish archbishop. Born to Christian Roman parents in Bannaventa (or Bannavem Taburniae), an unidentified location somewhere on the west coast of Britain, Patrick was kidnapped by Irish sea raiders at the age of 16 and forced to spend the next six years as a slave tending his master's pigs in northern Ireland. Eventually, according to legend, he managed to escape on a cargo ship and travelled widely before returning to Britain by 415. As the result of a vision while he slept he undertook the challenge of taking Christianity to Ireland. He went on to spend several years in preparation for this campaign, undertaking many years of religious study, possibly under St GERMANUS OF AUXERRE in Gaul, and in due course being ordained deacon and then bishop. He finally arrived in

Ireland in 432 and, having obtained the support of local chieftains, began his evangelical work among the pagan peoples there, making thousands of converts and founding monasteries and churches from his episcopal see in Armagh. Having countered the influence of the Druids and established the Christian church throughout Ireland, he was appointed archbishop in 441. Among the many legendary tales recorded of Patrick is one to the effect that he banished all snakes from Ireland. His other works included a number of writings, of which three manuscripts survive. These comprise the *Letter to the Soldiers of Coroticus*, a *Confession* and the popular poetic prayer entitled the *Lorica* and otherwise known as 'Patrick's Breastplate' or the 'Deer Cry'. The effective founder of the church in Ireland, Patrick is thought to have died at Saul on Strangford Lough in County Down. Called the **Apostle of Ireland**, he surpasses both BRIGID and COLUMBA as the country's patron saint and his feast day is a national holiday observed both in Ireland and among expatriate Irish communities all round the world. His emblems include snakes and the shamrock.
Feast Day: 17 March.

Paul   (d. *c*.67) Apostle. Born a Jew and a Roman citizen of Tarsus in Cilicia (in modern Turkey), he was known originally as Saul and was brought up as a strict Pharisee and as a zealous opponent of the first Christians. By trade a maker of tents, he participated enthusiastically in the persecution of Jews who had converted to Christianity, participating in the stoning to death of St STEPHEN and subsequently seeking and obtaining permission to arrest all the Jewish converts in Damascus. While on his way to Damascus to persecute the Christians around the year 35 AD he had a vision of the risen Christ, as a result of which he was rendered temporarily blind and became convinced that Christ wished him to be a witness among the Gentiles on his behalf. On his recovery he converted wholeheartedly to Christianity, assuming the name Paul, and spent three years in prayer and solitude in Arabia. Subsequently he dedicated the rest of his life to spreading the Christian gospel to non-Jews, embarking upon the first of three epic missionary journeys around the year 45. Over the years that followed he pursued his evangelical mission throughout the Mediterranean and Asia Minor and in the process became the first great missionary in the history of the Christian church. He also wrote extensively and 13 of his hugely influential letters, which helped shape Christian theology for centuries to come, are recorded in the New Testament. He was twice arrested for his faith, the first time in Jerusalem and the second time in

Rome, and was ultimately beheaded on the orders of the emperor Nero. Considered the most important figure in the early history of the Christian church after Christ himself, Paul is honoured as the patron saint of Greece (where he preached), Malta (where he was shipwrecked on his way to Rome) and Rome, as well as of tent-makers and saddlers. His emblems are a sword and a book.
Feast Day: 29 June.

Paul   *See* JOHN AND PAUL.

Paul of Léon   *See* PAUL AURELIAN.

Paul of the Cross   (1694–1775) Italian priest. Born Paul Francis Danei into a middle-class family of Ovada in Piedmont, Italy, he served in the Venetian army before being ordained a priest in Rome alongside his brother and best friend in 1727. After experiencing a vision he went on to found his own order, called the Passionists (dedicated to observing the strictest poverty and preaching to the poor), establishing the first house in Tuscany on the Monte Argentario peninsula. Passionist missions were established throughout Italy and Paul earned a reputation as a powerful preacher, often taking the Cross and the Passion of Christ as his subject. Shortly before his death he presided over the foundation (1771) of the first convent of cloistered Passionist nuns at Corneto. The order has since spread to other parts of the world. Paul of the Cross was also credited with miraculous healing powers and with the gift of prophecy. He was canonized in 1867.
Feast Day: 19 October.

Paul the Hermit   (d. *c.*345) Hermit of Thebes. Otherwise known as **Paul the First Hermit** or **Paul of Thebes**, he is said to have fled into the Theban desert during the persecution instituted in the reign of Decius and there resolved to live in solitude in a cave for the rest of his life. Shortly before his eventual death at the age of over 100, he was visited by St ANTONY, who personally buried Paul after he died (allegedly with the help of two lions). Paul, whose life story was written (and much embellished) by St JEROME, is remembered as the first of all Christian hermits.
Feast Day: 15 January.

Paul Aurelian   (6th century) British bishop. The son of a British (probably Welsh) chieftain, Paul Aurelian (otherwise known as **Paul of Léon** or **Pol**

de Léon) studied at the monastery of St ILLTYD and in due course became
a monk and priest. With 12 companions he subsequently settled in Brittany, where he founded a number of churches and became bishop of what
became known as Saint-Pol-de-Léon. He established a substantial reputation as an evangelist, around whose name a number of legends accumulated. He died at an advanced age at his monastery on the island of Batz.
He is usually identified with the Welsh St **Paulinus**, who lived the life of
a hermit at Llandovery and established a monastery at Llanddeusant.
Feast Day: 12 March.

Paul Miki and Lawrence Ruiz   (d.1597) Japanese martyrs. The young
Japanese Jesuit priest and preacher Paul Miki and the missionary Lawrence
Ruiz were prominent figures among a group of 26 Christians martyred for
their faith in Nagasaki in 1597. Japanese ruler Hideyoshi, who feared the
increasing influence of Christianity among his people, ordered their deaths.
The method of their execution was particularly brutal. Each had part of
their left ear cut off and, after being publicly paraded as a warning to
others, were crucified near Nagasaki. Paul Miki, who hailed from an
aristocratic background, and several of the others were canonized in 1862,
Ruiz and the remainder in 1987. Today these first Japanese martyrs are
honoured as representatives of many others subsequently put to death in
Japan over the centuries.
Feast Day: 6 February.

Paula   (347–404) Roman foundress. Born into a wealthy Roman family,
Paula married well and bore her husband five children before being
widowed at the age of 32. Subsequently she dedicated herself to a Christian life and assumed the leadership of a small group of similarly-minded
Christian women then living in Rome. They became patrons and disciples
of St JEROME after he arrived in the city and when Jerome eventually left
for Jerusalem in 385, Paula and her daughter EUSTOCHIUM went with
him, joining him on pilgrimages to various sacred sites in the Holy Land.
Jerome and Paula went on to found a monastery for men in Bethlehem, as
well as a convent for women and a hospice for pilgrims. Under Paula's
guidance the sisters lived in conditions of great poverty and performed
charitable work on behalf of the poor and needy. She also established a
reputation as a biblical scholar, even learning Hebrew in order to sing the
psalms as they were originally written. By the time of her death in Bethlehem she was entirely penniless, having given away all her great wealth.
Feast Day: 26 January.

Paulinus   *See* PAUL AURELIAN.

Paulinus of Aquileia   (*c.*730–802) Italian bishop. Born near Cividale in
Friuli, Paulinus became a priest and earned a reputation as a scholar
before being invited (776) to the court of the emperor Charlemagne. After
working as a grammarian at the court school for several years he was
appointed bishop of Aquileia in 787. He achieved much as bishop, presiding over important church councils, sending missionaries into pagan areas
and opposing the compulsory baptism of heathens. He was also active in
condemning the heresy of Adoptianism and was respected for his many
writings, which included poems and hymns.
Feast Day: 11 January.

Paulinus of Nola   (*c.*355–431) French bishop. Born Pontius Meropius Paulinus into a wealthy family of Bordeaux, the son of a Roman patrician, he
served as governor of Campania before settling down to a comfortable life
in Spain with his Spanish wife. In 389, however, after the death of their
only child, he and his wife both converted to Christianity and decided
to dedicate themselves to a life of prayer and charitable work. Paulinus
was ordained a priest and went on to establish a monastery at Nola, near
Naples, in 395, providing care for pilgrims visiting the tomb of St FELIX OF
NOLA. In 409 he became bishop of Nola and over the following 20 years is
reputed to have used his influence wisely and to have given generously to
the needy. Ultimately he died at his monastery in Nola. His work had a
profound influence upon the development of monastic life in Gaul and his
surviving letters constitute a valuable historical record of early monasticism at the time of the collapse of the Roman Empire. He was also much
admired as a writer of poems and hymns.
Feast Day: 22 June.

Paulinus of York   (d.644) Roman missionary bishop. Paulinus was among
the second group of missionary monks sent from Rome to England by
GREGORY THE GREAT in 601. He was consecrated bishop in Canterbury by
St JUSTUS and in 625 accompanied the princess St ETHELBURGA as her chaplain when she travelled north to marry St EDWIN of Northumbria, in the
process becoming the first apostle of Northumbria. On Easter eve 627 he
baptized King Edwin and many of his nobles at York. He went on to
conduct evangelizing tours throughout the region, securing numerous
converts and helping to maintain an extended period of peace and order.
Paulinus was raised to the archbishopric of York by Honorius I but in 632

was obliged to retreat south to Kent with the widowed Ethelburga and her children, entrusting the care of his see to others. He spent his last years serving as bishop of Rochester.
Feast Day: 10 October.

Pega (d. *c*.719) English anchoress. The sister of the hermit St GUTHLAC, Pega lived at Peakirk in Northamptonshire close to her brother's hermitage at Crowland. She was present at Guthlac's funeral and is also said to have conducted a pilgrimage to Rome, where she is supposed to have died. She was also credited with a number of miraculous cures, some of them associated with her relics after her death.
Feast Day: 8 January.

Pelagia of Antioch (d. *c*.311) Martyr of Antioch. Pelagia of Antioch was a 15-year-old virgin whose arrest was ordered by the authorities after she was reported for being a Christian. In order to escape dishonour at the hands of the soldiers sent to seize her she threw herself to her death from the top of her house. Ever since she has been ranked high among the virgin martyrs honoured in the canon of the mass. She should not be confused with the legendary PELAGIA THE PENITENT, who was also believed to have lived in Antioch.
Feast Day: 9 June.

Pelagia the Penitent (dates unknown) Penitent of Jerusalem. The story of Pelagia the Penitent appears to be largely legendary. Tradition identifies her as a beautiful actress or dancing-girl who pursued an immoral life in 5th century Antioch, becoming very wealthy and attracting many admirers. Everything changed after an accidental meeting with Bishop Nonnus of Edessa, whom she encountered in the street one day. The bishop was immensely impressed with the efforts that Pelagia evidently made to ensure her beauty was always perfectly displayed and in comparison found his own efforts and those of his companions to achieve holiness lacking. On the next day, however, Pelagia, moved by the bishop's sermon, repented her past life and expressed her wish to convert to Christianity. She went on to be baptized and, giving away all her wealth, adopted the life of a hermit on the Mount of Olives, successfully disguising herself as a man and calling herself Pelagius. Her story became a popular example of repentance in the pre-Reformation church.
Feast Day: 8 October.

Peregrine Laziosi *See* PHILIP BENIZI.

Perpetua and Felicity   (d.203) Carthaginian martyrs. Perpetua and
Felicity were prominent among a group of martyrs who were executed as
Christians in Carthage on the orders of Septimus Severus. Vibia Perpetua
was a young married noblewoman with a baby, while Felicity was a
pregnant slave-girl. They and seven men were arrested as Christians
and thrown into prison, where Perpetua had the first of several visionary
dreams in which she saw a ladder reaching to heaven. She and other
members of the group had further similarly miraculous dreams (including
one in which Perpetua wrestled and overthrew the Devil) and interpreted
them as divine reassurances that they would be raised to heaven at their
deaths. When they were consigned to the arena to be torn apart by wild
beasts they showed no fear and assisted one another when mauled by the
savage creatures put in with them. Ultimately they were put to death with
a sword thrust in the throat. When the initial blow failed to kill Perpetua
she personally guided the blade to her throat.
Feast Day: 7 March.

Perran   *See* PIRAN.

Peter   (d. *c*.64) Apostle. According to the Bible, Peter (originally named
Simon) was a fisherman of Bethsaida on the Sea of Galilee when he and
his brother St ANDREW were recruited as disciples by Christ. Renamed
Peter (meaning 'rock') by Christ, he was one of the three disciples who
were closest to Jesus (the others being James and John). Jesus described
him as the rock upon which the Christian church would be built – though
in character he was clearly headstrong and often rash. He was also given
charge of the keys of the kingdom of heaven. Despite his leading role
among Christ's followers Peter notoriously denied knowing Christ three
times when questioned by the authorities (as related at Matthew 26:35 and
69–75). After the Crucifixion and Resurrection Christ recommissioned Peter
(John 21:15-19) Peter spent the rest of his life organizing and guiding the
burgeoning Christian community and was also credited with performing
numerous miracles in Christ's name. He was arrested and imprisoned on
the orders of Herod Agrippa but escaped through a miracle and continued
his evangelical work throughout the Middle East, showing a particular
sympathy for Gentiles who desired to be baptized. Tradition claims that
Peter ultimately travelled to Rome and there laid the basis of the papacy,
often being described today as the first pope. He is said to have died the
death of a martyr for his faith during the reign of Nero, being crucified
head downwards at his own wish (although this part of his life is not

recorded in the New Testament). The altar in the Vatican basilica (known as St Peter's) is supposed to be located directly over his burial-place. Peter has traditionally been identified as the author of the two New Testament letters that bear his name and Mark's Gospel is thought to be largely based upon his teachings. He is honoured as the patron saint of fishermen, clock-makers, bridge-builders, masons, shipbuilders, the papacy and Rome. His emblem is two crossed keys.

Feast Day: 29 June.

Peter   *See* MARCELLINUS AND PETER.

Peter of Alcántara   (1499–1562) Spanish priest and reformer. Born Peter Garavito, the son of a lawyer of Alcántara in Estremadura, he studied law at Salamanca before joining the strict Observant Franciscan Order at Majar-etes in 1515. Noted as a preacher and for his austere and penitent lifestyle, Peter went on to found a friary at Badajoz in 1521 and was ordained in 1524. In the years that followed he served with missions throughout Spain and Portugal and was for a time chaplain to the court of King John III of Portugal. He was elected provincial for Saint Gabriel in Estremadura in 1538 but found himself unsuited to a political life and after two years resigned the post in order to assume the life of a hermit at Arabida, near Lisbon. Around 1556 he published a *Treatise on Prayer and Meditation*, a highly successful text that was translated into several other languages. At much the same time he organized the hermits who had gathered about him into the Reformed Friars Minor of Spain (the Alcantarines) at Pedrosa, where his friars observed the strictest austerity, living in tiny cells just seven feet in length and spending most of their time in prayer and contem-plation. The order was absorbed into the Conventuals and the Observants before the time of its founder's death. Peter also served as confessor to St TERESA OF AVILA, whom he first met in 1560, and it was with his encour-agement that she set up the first convent of reformed Carmelite nuns in 1562. He was canonized in 1669. He is honoured as the patron saint of Brazil, Estremadura and also of night watchmen (a reference to the tradition that for 40 years he slept for just an hour and a half each night, in a sitting position).

Feast Day: 19 October.

Peter of Tarentaise   (1102–1174) French bishop. Born into a religious family of Saint-Maurice near Vienne, Peter entered the Cistercian order and in due course rose to the position of abbot of Tamié in the Tarentaise

region of Savoy. In 1142 he was elected archbishop of Tarentaise and set about reforming the neglected diocese along Cistercian lines. His good works included the rebuilding of a hospice in the Little St Bernard pass for the benefit of travellers from Italy and Switzerland and the establishment of a charity to provide for impoverished rural communities. He yearned for a solitary life, however, and in 1155 abandoned his post and went into hiding as a laybrother in a Swiss abbey, where he was not located until a year later. As an elderly man he also paid visits to the Grande Chartreuse near Grenoble, where he became a friend of the young St HUGH OF LINCOLN. Having proved an effective supporter of Pope Alexander III against the antipope Victor, he was engaged in diplomatic efforts to restore peace between Louis VII of France and Henry II of England at the time of his death. He was canonized in 1191.
Feast Day: 8 May.

Peter Canisius (1521–1597) Dutch priest and theologian. Born Peter Kanis, the son of a burgomaster of Nijmegen in Holland, he studied law at Cologne University and at Louvain before entering the Jesuit order at Mainz under the influence of PETER FAVRE. He established a reputation as a powerful preacher and in 1547 attended the Council of Trent as procurator for the bishop of Augsburg. He went on to spend six months with St IGNATIUS OF LOYOLA in Rome, to teach at the Jesuit school at Messina and to reform the university at Ingolstadt in Bavaria. Subsequently he continued his reforming work at the University of Vienna, emerging as a prominent figure in the Counter-Reformation. In 1556 he became provincial superior of the Jesuits in southern Germany, Austria and Bohemia and went on to prove tireless in the founding of educational and religious establishments and in the conducting of missions throughout the area, effectively renewing the Catholic faith in a substantial swathe of western Europe. He was much admired both for the energy with which he dedicated himself to his work and for his theological writings, most notably his celebrated Catechism published as *Summa Doctrinae Christianae* in 1555. He died at Fribourg in Switzerland, where he had founded a school, and was canonized and named a doctor of the church in 1925.
Feast Day: 21 December.

Peter Celestine *See* CELESTINE V.

Peter Chanel (1803–1841) French missionary martyr. Born Peter Mary Chanel, the son of a peasant of Cuet near Belley, he was ordained a priest before enrolling as one of the founder-members of the missionary Society of Mary established at Lyons in 1822. In 1836 he was among a group of Marist missionaries sent to conduct evangelical work in the French territory of Wallis and Futuna in the Pacific. He and two companions were cordially received on their arrival in Futuna and Father Chanel determined to learn the local language in order to further his evangelical mission. Relations with the indigenous people gradually soured, as the gathering of new converts to Christianity (who included the son of the local chief) aroused suspicion and resentment. Three years after arriving in Futuna Father Chanel was attacked and beaten to death on the chief's orders, in the process becoming the first martyr in the South Seas. His work had not been in vain, however, and within two years the whole island of Futuna had converted to Christianity. Father Chanel was canonized in 1954 and is honoured today as the patron saint of Australia, New Zealand and the other countries of Oceania.

Feast Day: 28 April.

Peter Chrysologus   (*c*.400–*c*.450) Italian archbishop. Born at Imola, near Ravenna, Peter Chrysologus (meaning 'golden-worded') converted to Christianity as an adult and served as a deacon in Ravenna before being appointed bishop of the city either by SIXTUS III or by LEO THE GREAT in 433. Information about his life is sparse, though it seems he was a dedicated opponent of paganism, and he is usually remembered for his simply-worded sermons, the only examples of his many writings that have survived. As archbishop Peter Chrysologus presided over much new building and also involved himself in attempts to heal the rift threatened by the emergence of Monophysite heresy. He was declared a Doctor of the Church in 1729.

Feast Day: 30 July.

Peter Claver   (1580–1654) Spanish missionary. Born at Verdu in Catalonia, Peter Claver studied at the University of Barcelona before entering the Jesuit order at Tarragona in 1600. In 1610 he was sent to Cartagena (in what is now modern Colombia), the capital of the slave trade in South America, and there dedicated himself to the fight against the slavery of Black Africans. He spent the next 40 years working on their behalf, providing food, clothing and medical treatment for slaves in local plantations and mines, as well as conducting evangelical work among them and securing perhaps as many as 300,000 converts to the Christian faith. He also worked in local hospitals, offered pastoral care to prisoners of the

Inquisition and was reputed to hear as many as 5000 confessions a year. His work was hampered from 1650, when he contracted plague and never fully recovered. He died alone and neglected in his simple cell, was canonized in 1888 and is remembered today as the 'slave of the negroes' (a description he gave himself). In 1896 he was named patron saint of missionary activities among Black peoples.

Feast Day: 9 September.

Peter Damian (1007–1072) Italian cardinal. Born into a poor family of Ravenna, Peter Damian was orphaned at a young age and was brought up by a brother, who provided him with a good education, as a result of which he became a respected university teacher. In 1035 he joined a community of Benedictine hermits at Fonte Avellana, adopting an austere lifestyle of fasting, prayer and religious study. He was elected abbot of the community in 1043 and went on to found several other similar institutions. He earned a reputation as a leading reformer of the church, taking as his inspiration the lives of the early Desert Fathers and determining to counter clerical misconduct and corruption among his contemporaries. He was appointed bishop of Ostia and was raised to the rank of cardinal by Pope Stephen X in 1057. Subsequently he served under Popes Nicholas II and Alexander II, being entrusted with various important diplomatic missions and with responsibility for church renewal. At his own request he spent his final years living the life of a simple monk at the monastery at Fonte Avellana (although he still conducted diplomatic missions from time to time). His many writings included sermons, treatises, letters and hymns. He was declared a Doctor of the Church in 1828.

Feast Day: 21 February.

Peter Eymard (1811–1868) French founder. Peter Julian Eymard served in the parochial ministry and as a member of the Marist congregation at Lyons before establishing (1856) the Priests of the Blessed Sacrament in Paris, dedicated to the celebration of the Eucharist. A colleague of JOHN-BAPTIST VIANNEY, he went on to found the Servants of the Blessed Sacrament for women, and other similar organizations for priests and lay people, inviting their members to devote an hour each day to praying at the tabernacle. He was canonized in 1962.

Feast Day: 3 August.

Peter Favre (1506–1546) Italian Jesuit reformer. Born into a peasant family from Savoy, Peter Favre studied at the College of Saint Barbara in

Paris, where he became a friend and colleague of both FRANCIS XAVIER and
IGNATIUS LOYOLA. He was the first to join Ignatius Loyola's Society of
Jesus (the Jesuits) and, having been ordained in 1534, celebrated the mass
at which the first seven Jesuits took their vows. He went on to take part
in the diets of Worms and Regensburg in 1540, which attempted unsuccessfully to heal the rift between the Protestant and Catholic parties in
Germany, and to argue for spiritual renewal of the Catholic church.
Subsequently he preached throughout Germany and won widespread
support for his campaign for such renewal. In 1546 he was summoned
to Rome by Pope Paul III to act as his representative at the Council of
Trent, but, exhausted by the journey, he died in the arms of St Ignatius
shortly after his arrival.
Feast Day: 1 August.

Peter Fourier   (1565–1640) French founder. Born at Mirecourt in Lorraine,
Peter Fourier lived as an Augustinian canon regular at the abbey of Chau-
mozey until 1597 when, aged 32 and feeling the need to be of practical use
in the world, he chose the most impoverished and neglected parish he
could find, at Mattaincourt in Lorraine. There he volunteered to serve as
pastor. For the next 30 years or more he dedicated himself to the service
of his parishioners, doing much charitable work, promoting religious
education and inspiring a renewal of the Catholic faith in the area. His
foundation (in collaboration with Alix Le Clercq) of a free school for
young women in 1598 proved a particular success and stimulated the
establishment of similar institutions elsewhere in France, run by what
became the Cannonesses of Our Lady. In Peter Fourier's last years he also
successfully undertook the reform of various Augustinian establishments
in Lorraine, uniting them as one religious congregation. He was canonized
in 1897.
Feast Day: 9 December.

Peter Nolasco   (c.1182–1256) Spanish founder. Little is known for certain
about the life of Peter Nolasco. He was probably born into a merchant
family of Barcelona and in due course distinguished himself as a laybrother for his dedication to the cause of captives seized by the Moorish
occupiers of much of Spain. The order to which Peter Nolasco belonged
gradually evolved (1234) into the Mercedarian Order, of which he is
considered the founder. With Peter Nolasco as its master-general from
1249, the Mercedarians followed the rule of St AUGUSTINE and secured the

release of hundreds of Christian captives through the payment of ransoms. The order won papal approval from Gregory IX in 1235.
Feast Day: 28 January.

Peter Orseolo (928–987) Doge of Venice. Born into the powerful Orseoli family of Udine, Peter Orseolo served as a soldier before being elected doge of Venice in 976. He proved a capable statesman and successfully restored law and order to the city, but it appears that all the time he yearned secretly for a religious life. Accordingly, in 978, he abandoned his wife and son in Venice in order to enter the Benedictine abbey of Cuxa in the Pyrenees and there to pursue a life of asceticism and contemplation. Ultimately he left even this retreat and opted instead to live as a hermit nearby.
Feast Day: 10 January.

Petroc (6th century) Cornish founder. The life of St Petroc is largely a matter of legend. He may have been of Welsh origin, possibly a relative of St CADOC, and after arriving in Cornwall established a monastery at Wethinoc – now renamed Padstow (or 'Petroc's Stow'). This monastery became an important religious centre and the starting-point for numerous evangelical missions throughout Cornwall and beyond. Petroc himself is supposed to have travelled as far as Ireland (where he may have taught St KEVIN), Rome and Jerusalem. One legend claims he even set up a hermitage on an island in the Indian Ocean and lived there for seven years. He is reputed to have died back in Padstow and his relics were subsequently enshrined at Bodmin. His emblem is a stag (a reference to a legend that he prevented some hunters from killing a stag and then converted them).
Feast Day: 4 June.

Phileas (d.306) Martyr of Alexandria. Phileas is reputed to have converted to Christianity as an adult and in due course to have risen to the post of bishop of Thmuis in Lower Egypt. A scholarly and eloquent man, he was arrested not long after his consecration at Alexandria and imprisoned. While in prison he wrote a lengthy letter describing the tortures to which his fellow-Christians were subjected; fragments of his last interrogation by the prefect Culcianus are also extant. It appears that Phileas resisted all efforts to persuade him to apostatize, even for the sake of his wife and children, and ultimately he was taken out and beheaded.
Feast Day: 4 February.

Philibert (*c*.608–685) French founder. Born the son of a bishop in Gascony, he studied under his father and under St OUEN before himself serving as a monk in the monastery at Rebais. He was promoted to the position of abbot at the monastery but soon resigned in the face of opposition from the other monks and moved to Rouen, where in 654 he was granted land by Clovis II to found the influential abbey of Jumièges. Subsequently, in 674, he fell foul of Ebroin, the notorious West Frankish mayor of the palace, and was thrown into prison and then banished. He went on to found the monastery of Noirmoutier on the island of Heriou (Poitou) and, after the death of Ebroin in 681, established further houses for monks or nuns throughout Neustria, thus consolidating his standing as one of the most important founders of the early monastic tradition.
Feast Day: 20 August.

Philip (1st century) Apostle. According to the New Testament, Philip lived in Bethsaida in Galilee before being recruited as a disciple and himself persuading Nathanael (St BARTHOLOMEW) to join the group. He was present at several of the most important episodes of Christ's ministry, including the Feeding of the Five Thousand and the Last Supper. After the Crucifixion he is said to have preached the gospel in Phrygia and ultimately to have died at Hierapolis, possibly being martyred for his faith during the reign of Domitian. Today he is honoured as a patron saint of Uruguay. His emblem is loaves of bread.
Feast Day: 3 May.

Philip of Heraclea (d.304) Bishop and martyr of Heraclea. Philip of Heraclea in Thrace was an old man at the time of the persecution of Christians instituted during the reign of Diocletian. When the authorities closed his church down the aged bishop simply conducted services in the open, arguing that God dwelt in the heart of men rather than in buildings. When the authorities then demanded that he hand over the religious books of his church, he refused. On declining to worship the gods of the Romans, he was scourged and thrown into prison along with his deacon Hermes. Together with another priest, St **Severus**, he was taken to Adrianople where they were interrogated twice more before being beaten and then burned to death at the stake.
Feast Day: 22 October.

Philip Benizi (1233–1285) Italian friar. Born in Florence, Philip Benizi

studied medicine and philosophy at the universities of Paris and Padua
before enrolling as a laybrother in the Servite order at the monastery of
Monte Senario and working as a humble gardener until his talents as a
scholar were found out. He went on to become a priest and to win respect
as a preacher and in 1267 was elected head of the order. He is said to have
fled in terror when proposed as a successor to pope Clement IV in 1268
but attended the general council held at Lyons in 1274 and continued as
leader of the Servite friars, who prospered under his guidance. He also
helped to restore peace between warring factions in northern Italy and
when **Peregrine Laziosi**, a member of the Ghibelline faction, struck
Philip Benizi in the face the patience and calmness which the latter
displayed so impressed his attacker that he resolved immediately to
abandon his previous way of life and himself became a Servite friar
and a saint, being canonized in 1726. Philip Benizi himself was canonized
in 1671.

Feast Day: 22 August.

Philip Neri   (1515–1595) Italian founder. Born the son of a Florentine
notary, he studied under the Dominicans at the convent of San Marco in
Florence and worked in his uncle's business for a time before abandoning
his career in 1533 in favour of life as a hermit in Rome, studying philosophy and theology. When these studies palled, he dedicated himself to
charitable work, giving away most of his money to the poor and working
particularly on behalf of the young men of the city, trying to persuade
them to reject evil ways. In 1544 he underwent a profound revelatory
experience, which not only left him with permanent physical disabilities
but also spurred him on to pursue a deeply religious life. In 1548 he
founded a confraternity to organize care for the thousands of pilgrims
attracted to Rome and was himself ordained a priest in 1551. Living
among other priests at San Girolamo della Carita, he built a reputation
for his devotion to prayer, hearing confessions and preaching, earning the
nickname 'the Apostle of Rome'. He continued to combine his work on
behalf of the city's young men with charitable efforts to assist the sick and
needy and in time organized his assistants into what became in 1575 the
Congregation of the Oratory. Although Philip Neri had opponents, he won
widespread fame for his unswerving commitment to restoring the common
people to a Christian way of living and for his apparent ability to divine
the thoughts of others. The Oratory that he founded spread throughout the
world after the death of its founder, numbering among its many adherents

such notable names as JOHN HENRY NEWMAN. Philip Neri was canonized in 1622 and is honoured today as a patron saint of Rome.
Feast Day: 26 May.

Philomena   (dates unknown) Roman martyr. The wholly fictitious legend of the virgin martyr Philomena was inspired by the discovery of a set of human bones, evidently those of a young girl, in the catacomb of Priscilla in Rome in 1802. The bones were enshrined in a church at Mugnano near Naples and stimulated a substantial cult following, with various miracles being attributed to the so-called St Philomena, despite the complete lack of detail about her life and death. Mugnano became a place of pilgrimage and numerous churches were dedicated to the saint. In 1961 the total lack of historical evidence for the existence of a St Philomena, combined with doubts over the identification of the bones as those of a Christian martyr, persuaded the Roman Catholic church to order the feast of Philomena to be suppressed and the shrine at Mugnano to be destroyed – although to date no action has been taken and the shrine continues to flourish.
Feast Day: 10 August.

Phocas   (dates unknown) Martyr of Sinope. The story of Phocas is shrouded in mystery and little can be said for certain about him beyond the fact that a person of that name probably died the death of a martyr at Sinope on the southern shore of the Black Sea, possibly around the 4th century. Tradition claims that he was a hermit and gardener of Sinope who was sentenced to death for his Christian faith. When soldiers arrived at his house asking for the Christian called Phocas, he invited them in to stay the night in his home. While the soldiers slept Phocas quietly dug a grave for himself in his garden. In the morning he revealed his identity to his guests and was duly put to death. For unexplained reasons, Phocas was subsequently honoured as the patron saint of sailors on the Adriatic. Another St Phocas, supposedly bishop of Sinope, and a third St Phocas of Antioch are probably the same person as Phocas the gardener.
Feast Day: 22 September.

Pier Giorgio Frassati   (1901–1925) Italian philanthropist. Born the son of a wealthy newspaper editor in Turin, Pier Giorgio Frassati distinguished himself through his cheerful generosity to the poor and needy while still very young himself. Though born into a rich family, he preferred to give away his possessions and to dedicate himself to assisting the weak and vulnerable. A prayerful yet sociable character, he organized his friends into providing help for the poor of the city. Included among those he sought to assist were lepers, beggars and the homeless. Handsome and strong, he became famous throughout Turin for his many kindnesses and his premature death from poliomyelitis at the age of 24 was greatly lamented. He was beatified in 1990.

Feast Day: 4 July.

Pionius (d. *c*.250) Martyr of Smyrna. A priest of Smyrna well-known both for his eloquence and his learning, Pionius was arrested along with a woman named Sabina and a man called Asclepiades for celebrating the anniversary of another saint of Smyrna, St POLYCARP. A detailed record of the subsequent interrogation of Pionius has survived and describes how he stubbornly refused to sacrifice to the gods or in any other way to recant his faith. He protested vehemently when legal niceties were ignored and was forthright in his denunciation of those who persecuted Christians. When torture failed to produce any change in the belligerent prisoner's attitude the exasperated consul finally sentenced Pionius to death by burning and he was accordingly put to death in the stadium. The fate of his two companions is unknown.

Feast Day: 11 March.

Piran (d. *c*.480) Cornish abbot. Piran (or **Perran**) probably came from south Wales (or possibly Ireland) but is associated primarily with north Cornwall, specifically with the vicinity of Perranporth, where he established a monastic community. Little more is known of his life, although it is possible that he travelled to Brittany, where he was also venerated. He is thought to have died back in Cornwall and his shrine became a popular site of pilgrimage in medieval times. Piran became the patron saint of tin miners and is often identified as a patron saint of Cornwall itself. St Piran's flag, comprising a white cross on a black background, is also the traditional flag of Cornwall.

Feast Day: 5 March.

Pius V (1504–1572) Italian pope. Born Michael Ghislieri into a humble family of Bosco in Liguria, he joined the Dominican order and, having been ordained in 1528, soon distinguished himself as a preacher and teacher. Noted for his personal piety and concern for the spiritual welfare of others, he became bishop of Nepi and Sutri in 1556 and a year later was raised to the rank of cardinal and inquisitor-general. In 1559 he became bishop of Mondovi and ultimately, in 1556, was elected pope. Over the next six years Pius V proved a vigorous defender of Roman Catholicism and a prominent figure of the Counter-Reformation, encouraging the use of the inquisition and other strict measures to suppress the threat of Protestantism and to reassert the authority of the papacy in both spiritual and secular affairs. Specific targets of papal wrath during his reign included the Ottoman empire (against which he employed the Inquisition in both Italy and Spain and also oversaw the destruction of the Turkish fleet at Lepanto), corruption among the clergy, prostitution and bullfighting. Other notable reforms included an insistence upon bishops having to reside in their dioceses. More controversially, his decision to excommunicate England's Elizabeth I (thus releasing English Catholics from their allegiance to her) proved to be a damaging mistake based on a misunderstanding of the religious context in England and his inflexibility also provoked confrontation with the powerful Philip II of Spain. Pius V was canonized in 1712.

Feast Day: 30 April.

Pius X   (1835–1914) Italian pope. Born Giuseppe Sarto into a poor family of Riese in Venetia, he was ordained priest in 1858 and in due course was raised to the rank of canon of Treviso in 1875 and then to that of bishop of Mantua in 1884, effectively reviving a neglected diocese. In 1893 he was made patriarch of Venice and cardinal and finally, after some 45 years serving parish and diocese, was elected pope in 1903 in succession to Leo XIII. As pope he sought to revitalize the church, reorganizing the papal government, chartering a codification of canon law and promoting greater spiritual awareness among the laity. He also encouraged frequent taking of Holy Communion and reading of the Bible and argued in favour of allowing children as young as seven years old to participate in the Eucharist. He was an opponent, however, of Modernism (a movement aiming to reconcile Roman Catholicism with modern philosophy) and formally condemned it as heretical in 1907, thus unintentionally creating a rift between the church and the intellectual community that was to persist for half a century or more. His final years were darkened by the failure of his efforts to avert World War I, which broke out days before his own death. Much-loved for his simple goodness and for his embracing of poverty and virtue in his personal life, he was canonized in 1954. He is honoured as a patron saint of pilgrims.

Feast Day: 21 August.

Pius of Pietrelcina   *See* PADRE PIO.

Placid (6th century) Italian monk. Tradition has it that Placid trained as a monk under St BENEDICT at Subiaco and only narrowly escaped death by drowning in the lake there when rescued by St MAURUS. The events of Placid's later life are shrouded in mystery, although medieval legend (based on a forged document) claims he subsequently settled in Sicily and there died the death of a martyr along with several companions. Whatever the facts, he is remembered as a monk of unusual holiness. *Feast Day: 5 October.*

Pol de Léon *See* PAUL AURELIAN.

Polycarp (*c*.69–155) Bishop and martyr of Smyrna. Details of the life of Polycarp of Smyrna, one of the early leaders of the Christian church, are scant. He is said to have been converted to Christianity by JOHN THE BAPTIST at the age of 10 and to have gone on to become one of the saint's disciples, earning a reputation for wisdom and prudence. When he was aged about 26 he became bishop of Smyrna, in which post he served for many years. As an old man he was among those who travelled to Rome to confer with Pope Anicetus over the date of Easter (only for the two parties to agree to differ). He was subsequently betrayed by a servant during a wave of anti-Christian feeling in Smyrna and, aged 86, was arrested and condemned to death by burning. When his body miraculously failed to burn he was stabbed to death by the executioner. He is honoured as a Greek Father of the Church and as the patron saint of earache sufferers. *Feast Day: 23 February.*

Pontian (d. *c*.235) Roman pope and martyr. Born in Rome, he succeeded to the papacy in 230 but five years later was banished to the mines on the island of Sardinia on the orders of the emperor Maximinus the Thracian. Here he was reconciled with his rival, the antipope St HIPPOLYTUS, and thus brought about the end of his schism. Both Pontian and Hippolytus died in captivity in Sardinia. Pontian's relics were subsequently taken to Rome and placed in the papal crypt of the Catacomb of Callistus. *Feast Day: 13 August.*

Potamiaena and Basilides (d. *c*.208) Martyrs of Alexandria. According to Eusebius, Potamiaena was a maiden of Alexandria whose Christian devotion attracted much admiration in her native city. She was reputed to have fought off several attempts on her chastity and was ultimately sentenced to death by burning for her faith. Basilides, the officer who led her and her mother Marcella to execution, treated her with much consider-

ation and after Potamiaena's death similarly converted to Christianity, for which he too suffered the death of a martyr, in his case by beheading.
Feast Day: 28 June.

Pothinus   (d.177) French martyr. Bishop Pothinus was the leader of a group of martyrs who were executed as Christians in Lyons in 177 (*see* LYONS, MARTYRS OF). Aged around 90 years old, he showed no sign of fear when brought before the court at the demand of a hostile mob and his refusal to recant his faith led to him being viciously beaten. He died from his injuries two days later in prison.
Feast Day: 2 June.

Primus and Felician   (d. *c*.297) Roman martyrs. Legend has it that Primus and Felician were the sons of a Roman nobleman who in their old age were executed as Christians at Nomentum (Mentana) near Rome and buried on the Via Nomentana during the persecutions carried out under Diocletian and Maximian. Subsequently they became the first martyrs to have their remains exhumed and reburied within the walls of Rome (the church of San Stefano Rotundo being erected over their tombs).
Feast Day: 9 June.

Prisca   (*c*.3rd century) Roman martyr. Virtually nothing is known of the life and death of Prisca (otherwise called **Priscilla** and identified with a woman of that name in the Acts of the Apostles) beyond the plain fact that she was martyred for her faith in Rome some time in the 3rd century. The church on the Aventine hill is named after her and she appears to have been the object of an early Roman cult
Feast Day: 18 January.

Priscilla   *See* PRISCA.

Proclus   (*c*.390–446) Patriarch of Constantinople. Born in Constantinople, Proclus proved a promising scholar and, after studying under St JOHN CHRYSOSTOM, became secretary to Atticus, patriarch of Constantinople. He was ordained priest but it was not until around 434 that he himself succeeded to the post. Much respected as a preacher, he proved a dedicated opponent of the Nestorian heresy (which emphasized the dual nature of Christ), but nonetheless allowed heretics to be readmitted to the church. He was also the author of numerous treatises and homilies, including the *Tome of St Proclus*, which criticized the teachings of Theodore of Mopsuestia.
Feast Day: 24 October.

Prosper of Aquitaine (c.390–c.460) French theologian. Born Prosper Tiro in Aquitaine, he is thought to have spent his life as a monk and lay theologian, although little more is known about his career beyond suggestions that he lived among monks in Marseilles for a time and also served in the papal chancery in Rome, possibly as secretary to LEO THE GREAT. He is remembered as one of the most important theologians of his era, his views on such topics as grace and predestination reflecting the ideals of St AUGUSTINE. His influential writings included poems, prose and an informative chronicle discussing theological controversies of the day. *Feast Day: 25 June.*

Protase *See* GERVASE AND PROTASE.

Protus and Hyacinth (dates unknown) Roman martyrs. Little is known for certain about the martyrdom of Protus and Hyacinth, although legend identifies them as two brothers or fellow-teachers who were executed for their Christian faith in the 4th century or earlier. The story of their martyrdom enjoyed a boost in 1845 when the tomb of St Hyacinth was located and found to contain a set of charred bones (supporting the tradition that the saints were burned to death). The tomb of St Protus was empty (his relics having reportedly been transferred to Rome in the 9th century). Whatever the truth behind their martyrdom, the two saints were the subject of a considerable early cult, with churches dedicated to their honour as far distant as Cornwall. *Feast Day: 11 September.*

Quattro Coronati   *See* FOUR CROWNED MARTYRS.

Quentin   (dates unknown) Roman martyr. According to BEDE, Quentin (or **Quintin**) was martyred for his Christian faith at Augusta Veromanduorum (now renamed Saint-Quentin) in Gaul some time late in the 3rd century. He is thought to have been sent to Gaul as a missionary and is said to have earned a considerable reputation as a preacher before being imprisoned on the orders of the Roman prefect Rictiovarus, tortured and finally beheaded.
Feast Day: 31 October.

Queran   *See* CIARAN OF CLONMACNOISE.

Quintin   *See* QUENTIN.

Quiricus   *See* CYRICUS AND JULITTA.

R

Radegund (518–587) French queen. The daughter of the ruler of the German kingdom of Thuringia, she was kidnapped by Frankish raiders at the age of 12 but survived this experience and, after receiving religious instruction, converted to Christianity. Radegund became greatly admired both for her beauty and gentle nature and for her virtuous way of life. These qualities attracted the Frankish king Clotaire I, whose queen she became at the age of 18. Clotaire proved a challenging husband, however, continuing a violent and unchristian career that included among many other misdeeds the taking of many mistresses and the murder of Radegund's brother in around 550. On this final outrage, after six years of trying to serve her husband faithfully, Radegund persuaded Clotaire to allow her to withdraw from the Frankish court in order to become a nun at Noyon. Raised to the rank of deaconess, she went on to found the double monastery of the Holy Cross at Poitiers (the first such community for both men and women anywhere in Europe) and saw it become a centre of learning through the influence of St CAESARIUS OF ARLES and other notable figures. She also busied herself trying to reconcile various warring parties and took great joy in securing for her monastery a relic of Christ's cross, brought all the way from Constantinople.
Feast Day: 13 August.

Raphael the Archangel The biblical angel who is identified (at John 5:1–4) as the angel who moved the waters of the healing pool at Jerusalem and (at Tobit 2 and 6) as the bearer of healing (his name meaning 'God has healed'). Because of his identification as the travelling companion of Tobias he is particularly linked with the making of pilgrimages. His association with healing, and his reputation as the most approachable and sympathetic of the three archangels, is reflected by the veneration of his statue at Lourdes. He is honoured as the patron saint of travellers, the blind and of doctors and nurses.
Feast Day: 29 September.

Raymond of Capua (1330–1399) Italian priest. Raymond of Capua is remembered for his association with St CATHERINE OF SIENA, whom he served as confessor for six years until the latter's death. St Catherine

selected Raymond as her confessor after witnessing him celebrating Mass,
although he only gradually became convinced of the authenticity of her
mystical experiences. Such was the impact of St Catherine's revelations
that Raymond had to spend many hours each day hearing the confessions
of the many converts she had won for the church. He also worked alongside her in treating victims of the plague, contracting the disease himself
but allegedly being cured by Catherine's prayers. The two saints also
sought to restore peace between the cities of northern Italy and the papacy
and tried to heal the Great Western Schism between the rival popes at
Rome and Avignon when it broke out in 1378. After Catherine's death
in 1380 Raymond was made master-general of the Dominican order and
presided over a far-reaching programme of reform aimed at the restoration
of the rule of St DOMINIC (to the extent that he is sometimes identified as
the second founder of the order).
Feast Day: 5 October.

Raymund of Peñafort (c.1180–1275) Spanish friar. Born into a noble
   family of Peñafort in Catalonia, Raymund worked as a lawyer and scholar
   in Barcelona and Bologna until he was in his forties, when he opted
   instead for the life of a Dominican priest and preacher. His preaching did
   much to encourage Christian resistance to the Moorish occupiers of much
   of Spain and helped reclaim the country for Christianity. Having been
   summoned to Rome in 1230 as confessor to Pope Gregory IX, he composed
   a book entitled the *Decretals*, a collection of decrees issued by popes and
   councils since 1150. This volume proved profoundly influential and
   became a standard source of canon law over the next 700 years. Another
   important publication by his hand was the *Summa casuum* on the subject of
   penitential discipline. Illness allowed him the excuse to decline the post of
   archbishop of Tarragona at the age of 60 but three years later he was (reluctantly on his own part) elected as the third master-general of the Dominican Friars Preachers. After instituting various reforms of the order he
   resigned the post in 1240, although he was destined to spend another 35
   years working actively towards the conversion of Jews and Muslims before
   dying in Barcelona at around the age of 100. He was canonized in 1601
   and is honoured as a patron saint of canon lawyers and librarians.
   Feast Day: 7 January.

Raymund Nonnatus (1204–1240) Spanish cardinal. The life of Raymund
   Nonnatus is shrouded by legend. His name (meaning 'not born') is
   supposed to relate to the circumstances of his birth (at Portello in

Catalonia), during which he was removed from his mother's womb after her death in labour. Tradition claims that he was received as a member of the Mercedarian order at Barcelona by its founder St PETER NOLASCO and that subsequently he offered himself as a slave in Algiers in order to secure the release of others. Legend further claims that he was made a cardinal in Rome in 1239. He died at Cardona while on his way to Rome. Because of the manner in which Raymund was born he is honoured as a patron saint of midwives.

Feast Day: 31 August.

Remigius　(d.533) French bishop. Known as the Apostle of the Franks, Remigius (or **Remi**) was born at Laon, the son of a count, and rose quickly through the ranks to become bishop of Rheims while only 22 years old. Little is known of his subsequent career as bishop except for the fact that he devoted most of his energy towards securing converts among the Frankish peoples, making the most of his undoubted gifts as a preacher. His most significant achievement was the baptism of Clovis I, king of the Franks, at Rheims in 496.

Feast Day: 13 January.

Richard of Chichester　(1197–1253) English bishop. Born Richard Wych, the son of a yeoman farmer of Droitwich in Worcestershire, he studied canon law at Oxford, Paris and Bologna and after his return to England was appointed chancellor of Oxford University in 1235. He was then recruited as chancellor to St EDMUND OF ABINGDON at Canterbury and subsequently accompanied the archbishop into exile to France, where he was ordained priest. Having returned once more to England he was elected bishop of Chichester in 1244, although Henry III refused to accept the appointment for two years. Once in post, Richard was considered a model bishop, a humble man who was capable of both generosity and mercy as well as being stern and authoritative as the occasion demanded. He pushed forward a number of important reforms of his diocese in order to suppress corruption and abuses among the clergy and also preached in favour of the Crusades. He died after consecrating a new church in Dover and his shrine behind the high altar of Chichester cathedral became a popular site of pilgrimage. He was canonized in 1262.

Feast Day: 3 April.

Rita of Cascia　(1377–1447) Italian nun. Born at Roccaporena in Umbria, Rita obeyed her parents' wishes and married, but had to draw heavily on

her religious faith for support after her husband proved both violent and unfaithful. Having borne two sons, she was widowed after 18 years when her husband was murdered in the course of a vendetta. Her two sons fell ill and died before they could avenge their father's death (apparently in answer to their mother's prayer), upon which Rita entered an Augustinian convent at Cascia. Here she distinguished herself not only through her ceaseless praying and mortification but through the appearance of a wound on her forehead, as though pierced by a crown of thorns. The wound remained open until Rita's death from tuberculosis 15 years later, when her incorrupt body was reverently placed in an elaborate tomb. Venerated for her great holiness and for the miracles associated with her name, Rita of Cascia became the focus of a substantial worldwide cult, which continues to attract devotees in large numbers today. She was canonized in 1900 and is honoured as a patron saint of desperate cases, especially those of a matrimonial nature. Roses are her emblem (a reference to the tradition that a rose in her old garden bloomed out of season in order to provide a bloom for her deathbed).
Feast Day: 22 May.

Robert of Molesme   (1027–1110) French abbot. Born into a noble family of Troyes, he became a monk and progressed quickly to the rank of prior, serving first at Moûtier-la-Celle and later at Tonnerre before responding to a request to assume the post of abbot for the hermits of Collan. The community moved to Molesme around 1075 but Robert's ambition to see the house develop along strict Benedictine lines was only partially realised and instead, in 1090, he settled in the forest of Cîteaux near Dijon with several of the other monks and here founded a new community. After 18 months he returned to Molesme, which had gone into decline in his absence, and there he remained for the rest of his life. He is remembered chiefly as the first of the abbots of Cîteaux and consequently as one of the precursors of the Cistercian movement. He was canonized in 1222.
Feast Day: 29 April.

Robert of Newminster   (c.1100–1159) English abbot. Born at Gargrave in Yorkshire, he served as parish priest there before joining the Benedictines at Whitby. In 1132 he became one of the founders of Fountains Abbey and six years later he was made abbot of Newminster, near Morpeth in Northumberland. Although little is recorded of his subsequent life, he is remembered as an exceptionally able and holy abbot who was also credited with several visionary experiences and a number of miracles. He

is also known to have established further Cistercian houses at Sawley in West Riding, at Roche in south Yorkshire and at Pipewell in Northampton-shire and to have been a close friend of the hermit St GODRIC.
Feast Day: 7 June.

Robert Bellarmine   (1542–1621) Italian cardinal and theologian. Born Roberto Bellarmino into a noble family of Montepulciano in Tuscany, he joined the Jesuits in 1560 and worked as a teacher of classics before being ordained priest at Ghent in 1570. He went on to become the first Jesuit professor at the University of Louvain and to hold prominent posts at the College of Rome before being appointed provincial of Naples and, in 1597, theologian to Pope Clement VIII as well as examiner of bishops and consultor of the Holy Office. He was raised to the rank of cardinal in 1599, made archbishop of Capua in 1602 and in 1605 was appointed head of the Vatican Library. He was twice considered for the papacy, but failed to be elected. Considered a leading theologian in the debate between Roman Catholicism and emerging Protestantism, he played a leading role in a number of church disputes and also campaigned against various heresies (although his critics considered him too moderate in many of his views). It also fell to him to voice the church's accusations against Galileo concerning his heretical theories concerning the movement of the earth around the sun, although his own attitude towards the affair was fairly relaxed and he sought to calm the emotions of those involved. Of his many influential writings the most significant was his *Controversies of the Christian Faith Against the Heretics of This Time*. Others included two catechisms, treatises and commentaries upon the Bible. Robert Bellarmine was canonized in 1930 and a year later was named a Doctor of the Church.
Feast Day: 17 September.

Robert Southwell   (1561–1595) English martyr. Born in Horsham Saint Faith in Norfolk, Robert Southwell studied in Douay and Paris before being ordained a Jesuit priest in 1584. Two years later he was sent to England to serve in secret as a priest to the Catholics suffering under official persecution during the reign of Elizabeth I. He was employed as chaplain to Countess Anne of Arundel and worked diligently within the Catholic community until 1592, when he was betrayed to the authorities and imprisoned. While in prison he was subjected to cruel torture, includ-ing being placed on the rack on no less than nine occasions, and was then kept in solitary confinement in the Tower of London. After three years in the Tower he was condemned to death as a traitor and executed at

Tyburn. He is also remembered as a poet and was canonized in 1970 as one of the Forty Martyrs of England and Wales.

Feast Day: 21 February.

Roch (*c*.1350–1380) French hermit. Roch (otherwise referred to as **Rock** or, in Italy, as **Rocco**) was born into a wealthy merchant family of Montpellier in Languedoc and is remembered for the lengthy pilgrimages he undertook during his lifetime. During one of these, to Rome, he is alleged to have earned a reputation as a nurse and worker of miraculous cures among sufferers of the plague that he encountered in northern Italy. When he contracted plague himself, at Piacenza, he was said to have been tended by a dog until he recovered. Upon his eventual return home he was not recognized by his relatives and was thrown into prison as an imposter, where he died. Another version of his life story claims that he was imprisoned in Lombardy on charges of being a spy. He became the focus of a substantial cult following, and was venerated in France and Italy as a patron of sufferers of physical disease. He is also honoured as the patron saint of cattle (a reference to the tradition that he employed miraculous means to cure sick cattle).

Feast Day: 16 August.

Romanus and David *See* BORIS AND GLEB.

Romaric *See* ARNULF OF METZ.

Romuald of Ravenna (*c*.950–1027) Italian abbot. Born into a noble family of Ravenna, he decided to withdraw from the world when his father killed a relative in a duel. Accordingly, he enrolled as a monk at the Cluniac monastery of San Miniato and in due course became a great proponent of monasticism and in particular of the solitary life, effectively bringing the tradition of the hermit within the Benedictine rule. After leaving San Miniato he spent many years wandering northern Italy, founding a number of hermitages and monastic communities as he went. The most celebrated of these were the monasteries of Fonte Avellana in the Apennines and Camaldoli near Arezzo. The so-called Camaldolese order is still in existence today. Romuald was canonized in 1595.

Feast Day: 19 June.

Roque Gonzalez (1576–1628) Paraguayan martyr. Born into a noble Spanish family of Asunción, Paraguay, he was ordained priest in 1599 and joined the Jesuits ten years later. He spent the rest of his life working as a

missionary among the indigenous people of Paraguay, helping to establish independent villages (called 'reductions') for Christian converts from the jungle and seeking to protect them from the injustices of their Spanish rulers. He was widely respected for his evangelical work in the remotest regions, penetrating into the depths of Brazil and winning the love and gratitude of those he tried to assist. He died in Caaró in south Brazil when he and two other Jesuit missionaries were put to death on the orders of a medicine man who resented the influence of the Jesuits on the local population. In 1934 these three men became the first American martyrs to be beatified. Roque Gonzalez was canonized in 1988.
Feast Day: 19 November.

Rose of Lima (1586–1617) Peruvian recluse. Born Isabel de Flores y del Olivia in Lima, Peru, she was of impoverished Spanish parentage and spent her early years trying to earn money to augment the family income. Later, despite her personal beauty (which earned her the nickname 'Rose'), she decided against marrying and instead became a Dominican tertiary at the age of 20, taking up residence in a hut in her garden. She became well known for her dedication to her prayers and for the excessive nature of the penances she inflicted upon herself. She also became celebrated as a mystic and for her charitable work among the sick and the poor as well as among the indigenous American population, thus winning recognition as a fore-runner of the social services in Peru. When Lima largely survived power-ful earthquakes the presence of 'Rose of Lima' was widely assumed to be the reason that the damage had been limited. Rose died at the age of just 31 and was canonized in 1671, in the process becoming the first canonized saint of the Americas. She is honoured today as the patron saint of South America, Lima and Peru and of florists and gardeners.
Feast Day: 23 August.

Rose of Viterbo (1235–1252) Italian mystic. Born into a poor but pious family of Viterbo, Italy, Rose is supposed to have exhibited miraculous powers of healing from a very young age, allegedly restoring an aunt to life when just three years old. By the age of seven, Rose had taken up the life of a recluse and was earning a reputation for the penances she inflicted upon herself. She was also becoming known as a mystic, reporting visions of the Virgin Mary from the age of eight. When she was aged 12 she spoke out publicly against the excommunicated Holy Roman Emperor Frederick II of Germany, whose family had taken over the town of Viterbo, with the result that she and her whole family were temporarily banished.

Unabashed, while in exile in Sorbiano she campaigned against pagan heresy. Upon their return to the town Rose sought to gain admittance to the convent of St Mary of the Roses, but was turned down because she had no dowry and spent the rest of her life living at her father's house. Weakened by her early penances, she died prematurely at the age of 17. She is honoured as a patron of exiles and of people rejected by religious orders.

Feast Day: 4 September.

Rupert   (d. *c.*710) Bishop of Salzburg. Possibly of Frankish or Irish birth, Rupert (sometimes referred to as **Rupert of Salzburg**) served as bishop of Worms for several years before going as a missionary to Regensburg in Bavaria. He extended his evangelical activities over a wide area and established his base at Salzburg, where he founded the monastery of St Peter. He also founded a nunnery at Nonnberg. He is remembered as one of the most important of the early evangelizers of the German peoples. His emblem is a barrel of salt (a reference to the tradition that he instituted the first salt-mining activity in Salzburg).

Feast Day: 27 March.

Rusticus   *See* DENIS.

S

Sabas   *See* SAVA.

Sabas of Jerusalem   (439–532) Cappadocian abbot. Born near Caesarea in
Cappadocia, Sabas of Jerusalem became a follower of St EUTHYMIUS THE
GREAT and as a young man lived both as a solitary and as a monk in a
number of small communities in the vicinity of Jerusalem. After the death
of St Euthymius he established a community of hermits in a desolate area
in the desert around 478 and reluctantly agreed to be ordained priest in
491. Two years later he was entrusted with responsibility for all the hermit
monks in Palestine and in the years that followed he went on to found
several more early monastic houses in the region. The patriarch of
Jerusalem also sent him on two missions to Constantinople, where he
voiced his opposition to the Monophysite heresy, and he is reputed to
have travelled widely through the Middle East preaching on the topic.
When Sabas was aged 90 the emperor Justinian demonstrated his respect
and support for the saint and his monastery by agreeing, at the saint's
request, to reduce taxes in Palestine, to build a hostel for pilgrims to
Jerusalem and to erect a fortress to protect his monks from raiders. Sabas
died soon afterwards at his chief monastery, which exists to this day at
Mar Saba.
Feast Day: 5 December.

Samson   (*c*.490–*c*.565) Welsh bishop. Born in south Wales, Samson is said
to have been educated and ordained priest under St ILLTYD in Glamorgan
and then gone on to serve as abbot at a monastery on Caldey Island.
After a visit to Ireland and a period spent as a hermit on the banks of the
Severn, he was made a bishop by St DYFRIG. The epitome of a wandering
Celtic monk-bishop, he next moved to Cornwall as the result of a vision
and from there travelled to northern France, where he founded monasteries at Dol and Pental. He is also thought to have evangelized in the
Channel Islands and the Scilly Isles (where one of the islands bears his
name) and to have represented the Breton ruler Judual before the Frankish
king Childebert I. Recognized as the leader of the British colonizers of Brittany, he died at his monastery at Dol. Numerous miracles were attributed

to Samson and his memory is preserved in various placenames and churches in southwest Britain and Brittany.
Feast Day: 28 July.

Saturninus *See* SERNIN.

Sava (1173–1236) Serbian archbishop. Born in Tirnovo in modern Bulgaria, Sava (or **Sabas**) was the third son of Stephen Nemanya, ruler of the Serbs. In 1191 he became a monk on Mount Athos, where he was joined four years later by his father after he abdicated his throne in favour of another of his sons. Together Sava and his father (who adopted the name Simeon) founded the monastery of Khilandari on Mount Athos, making it an important centre of Serbian cultural and religious activity. Conflict between his brothers prompted Sava to return to Serbia in 1208 in order to undertake the reorganization of the church in Serbia and coordinate missionary work among the population from his base at Studenitsa. He went on to build several churches and to establish the independence of the Serbian church from Rome. In 1219 he was consecrated as Serbia's first archbishop. He also involved himself actively in secular affairs and helped to restore peace throughout the Serbian kingdom. His other achievements included the foundation of the monastery of St John in Jerusalem and the drawing up of a rule for the guidance of monks there as well as the translation of various religious books into the Serbian language. He is honoured today as the patron saint of Serbia.
Feast Day: 14 January.

Scholastica (d. c.543) Italian abbess. Born in Norcia, she was the sister (possibly the twin sister) of St BENEDICT and became the first of the Benedictine nuns. She established a nunnery at Plombariola, five miles away from Benedict's monastery at Monte Cassino, and for the rest of her life enjoyed yearly reunions with her brother at a house nearby. The story goes that on the occasion of their last meeting she sought to persuade Benedict to stay a little longer: when he declined she prayed for a violent storm to be whipped up and thus delay his departure – the storm duly blew up and Benedict stayed the night. Scholastica died three days later and in due course when Benedict died he was laid to rest in the same grave. Scholastica is honoured today as the patron saint of all Benedictine nunneries.
Feast Day: 10 February.

Scillitan martyrs (d.180) Group of African martyrs. The Scillitan martyrs were a group of seven men and five women from Scillium (an unidentified

location in north Africa) who were put to death for their faith in Carthage on the orders of the Roman proconsul Saturninus. Led by their spokesman St **Speratus** they refused stubbornly to recant their religious beliefs when arrested and interrogated and were immediately taken out and beheaded by the sword.
Feast Day: 17 July.

Sebastian (d. *c.*300) Roman martyr. Possibly born in Milan, or educated there, Sebastian ranks among the best known of the early martyrs through the many celebrated depictions by sculptors and painters during the Renaissance of his execution. Very little is known for certain about his life beyond the fact that he was put to death for his Christian faith by being shot to death with arrows and buried on the Appian Way in Rome during the reign of Diocletian. Legend has added the tradition that he was born at Narbonne in Gaul and served as an officer in the Roman Pretorian Guard before being revealed as a Christian, arrested and condemned to death. A further embellishment of his story has him being healed of his wounds by Irene, the widow of St **Castulus**, and then confronting the emperor directly about his cruelty, upon which he was beaten to death with clubs. He is honoured as the patron saint of archers and soldiers. His emblem is an arrow.
Feast Day: 20 January.

Sebastian Valfré (1629–1710) Italian priest. Born into a poor family of Verduno in Piedmont, he entered the Congregation of the Oratory in Turin in 1651 and was ordained priest a year later. He rose steadily through the ranks but turned down an offer of the archbishopric of Turin and opted instead to dedicate himself to working with the poor and conducting evangelical missions through northern Italy, holding religious meetings, helping the sick and hearing confessions, always with unfailing optimism. He died at the age of 80 after some 60 years of service to his flock. He was also well known as a prophet and visionary.
Feast Day: 30 January.

Sebbi (664–694) King of the East Saxons. As king, Sebbi (or **Sebbe**) supported the evangelization of his people by bishop Jaruman of Mercia but ultimately surrendered his throne in order to become a monk, becoming well known for his generosity and pious ways. He was buried in Old St Paul's in London and was listed among the saints on the strength of a biography written by the VENERABLE BEDE.
Feast Day: 29 August.

Senan of Scattery   (d. c.544) Irish abbot. Born near Kilrush in County Clare, Senan became a monk and studied at Cassidan in Irrus and at Kilnamanagh in Kilkenny before founding several monasteries at various locations throughout Ireland, including Slaney in Wexford and Scattery Island (Inis Cathaig) near Kilrush. Several legends accumulated about his name and he is also said to have visited St DAVID in Wales.
Feast Day: 8 March.

Seraphim of Sarov   (1759–1833) Russian monk. Born Prokhor Moshnin, the son of a builder of Kursk, near Moscow, he was admitted to the monastery of Sarov at the age of 20 and was ordained priest in 1793. Drawn to the life of a hermit, he spent 16 years living alone in a small wooden hut deep in a forest, dedicating his time to praying and studying the Bible. He retreated to a nearby monastery for a period in 1804 to recover after being assaulted by robbers and left for dead but then returned to his hut for another six years before ill-health obliged him to pursue the solitary life in a cell at the monastery, where he remained for the next 23 years. He became well-known for his visions of the Virgin Mary, the first of which he experienced in 1783, and was also renowned as a prophet and a miraculous healer. Having adopted the harshest penitential practices early in his life, he took a vow of silence in 1807 and did not speak again. He was canonized by the Russian Orthodox Church in 1903.
Feast Day: 2 January.

Serapion of Thmuis   (d. c.365) Egyptian martyr. Serapion of Thmuis (otherwise known as **Serapion the Scholastic**) is known to have served as bishop of Thmuis on the Nile delta. Little more is known of the details of his life and death beyond the facts that he was a disciple of St ANTONY in the desert early in his career, was a friend of St ATHANASIUS (supporting him against the heretic Arians) and was eventually martyred for his faith. He is remembered chiefly for a collection of prayers, apparently by his hand, that was discovered towards the end of the 19th century.
Feast Day: 21 March.

Sergius of Radonezh   (1313–1392) Russian monk. Born into a noble family of Rostov, he fled his home with his family because of civil war with the Tartars and was brought up in Radonezh, near Moscow, becoming a monk following the death of his parents. At the age of 20 he and his brother adopted the life of hermits in the forest nearby and in due course attracted a number of like-minded companions, who by 1354 formed the

basis of the monastery of the Holy Trinity, under the leadership of Sergius. Having thus fostered the re-establishment of the monastic tradition among the Tartars, Sergius founded around 40 more similar communities and became arguably Russia's most renowned religious figure, celebrated not only for his role as a monastic reformer but also for his personal qualities, which included humility, gentleness and willingness to serve others. He turned down an offer of the bishopric of Moscow in 1378 but continued to work actively to maintain peace between Russia's princes. Also credited with having had many visions of the Virgin Mary during his lifetime, his shrine in the Trinity monastery at Zagorsk became a popular site of pilgrimage. He was canonized in Russia before 1449 and is honoured as patron saint of Moscow and of all Russia.
Feast Day: 25 September.

Sernin (3rd century) French/Spanish martyr. Tradition claims that Sernin (or **Saturninus**) preached on both sides of the Pyrenees before becoming the first bishop of Toulouse. His success in converting thousands to Christianity enraged pagan priests of the city, who kidnapped him in the street and forced him into their temple, where they insisted that he make sacrifice to their gods. When Sernin refused, they tied him to one of the temple bulls and he was dragged through the city until he was dead. His body was laid to rest in the basilica of St Sernin in Toulouse.
Feast Day: 29 November.

Seven Brothers *See* FELICITY OF ROME.

Seven Founders (13th century) Italian founders of the Servants of Mary (Servites). The Seven Founders (also known as the **Seven Servite Founders** or **Seven Holy Helpers**) were seven prominent citizens of Florence who in 1233 decided to set themselves up as hermits on Monte Senario outside the city, building a church there and dedicating themselves to a life of austerity and prayer. From this beginning developed the order of mendicant friars called the Servants of Mary (or Servites). The seven included St **Buonfiglio Monaldo**, who served as the group's first leader, and St **Alexis Falconieri**, a laybrother who established a Servite community at Siena and was the last of the original group to die (in 1310 at the alleged age of 110). The order now has houses in many parts of the world. The Seven Founders were canonized in 1888.
Feast Day: 17 February.

Seven Holy Helpers *See* SEVEN FOUNDERS.

Seven Sleepers   (dates unknown) Group of seven young Christians
of Ephesus. According to 6th-century legend, the Seven Sleepers were
arrested at Ephesus during the persecution of Christians instituted during
the reign of Decius and walled up in a cave on Mount Anchilos. They then
fell into a miraculous sleep, awaking 200 years later during the reign of
Theodosius II, by which time Ephesus had become Christian. Their appearance created a sensation, even though all seven (named **Dionysius**,
Maximianus, Malchus, Martinianus, Joannes, Serapion and
Constantinus) died shortly afterwards. Their supposed tomb
subsequently became a site of pilgrimage. The legend probably represents
a Christian version of a much older folkloric tradition.
Feast Day: 27 July.

Severinus of Noricum   (d.482) Missionary to Austria. Apparently of
Middle Eastern birth, Severinus settled in Noricum (Austria) some time
after 453 and dedicated himself to the evangelization of the region's
barbarian conquerors, the Huns. He is known to have travelled to many
towns on the Danube, preaching and founding the country's first monasteries (at Passau and Favianae). He was also credited with prophetic
powers and with various miracles of healing. On his death his body was
laid to rest in Naples.
Feast Day: 8 January.

Severinus Boethius   (c.475–524) Roman scholar and martyr. Born Anicius
Manlius Severinus Boethius into one of the great noble families of Rome,
he was orphaned at an early age and was brought up by another noble
family, into which he eventually married. Boethius became a highly
respected scholar and the author of many profoundly influential works,
among them works on theology, mathematics and music. His translations
of Aristotle, Euclid, Plato, Ptolemy and Pythagoras were particularly influential, becoming standard works for scholars in the medieval period. He
was raised to the rank of consul by the Ostrogoth emperor Theodoric (to
which post his two sons were also subsequently appointed) but fell out
of imperial favour after defending in court a former consul accused of
conspiring against the throne. He was arrested and imprisoned in Pavia,
accused of treason, sacrilege and conducting impious studies, and after
nine months tortured and executed. While incarcerated he wrote the *Consolation of Philosophy*, his most celebrated work and one which was translated
by, among others, Alfred the Great, Geoffrey Chaucer and Elizabeth I.
Feast Day: 23 October.

Severus   *See* PHILIP OF HERACLEA.

Sexburga   (d. *c*.700) English abbess. Daughter of King Anna of the East Angles, she became the wife of King Erconbert of Kent and bore him four children before being widowed in 664. She then retired as abbess to the nunnery she had founded at Minster-in-Sheppey and, in 679, succeeded her sister St ETHELDREDA as abbess of Ely.
Feast Day: 6 July.

Sigebert   (d.635) English king and martyr. According to Bede, Sigebert became a Christian while in exile in Francia. After succeeding Redwald to the throne of East Anglia in 630 he promoted Christianity and, with the support of St HONORIUS OF CANTERBURY, had FELIX OF DUNWICH installed as bishop of East Anglia. He also provided the funds for Felix to establish a monastery at Burgh Castle and a number of schools. After a relatively short reign Sigebert resigned the throne and became a monk at Burgh Castle. When the kingdom was subsequently attacked by Penda, king of Mercia, however, Sigebert was forced to leave the monastery and go into battle with the East Anglian army (though he refused to carry anything more lethal than a staff). He was among those killed in the ensuing defeat.
Feast Day: 16 January and 27 September.

Sigfrid   (d. *c*.1045) Swedish bishop. Tradition claims that Sigfrid was of English birth, serving as a priest in York or Glastonbury before travelling to Scandinavia with two other bishops to conduct missionary work there. Based at Växjo in southern Sweden, where he built a church, he baptized the Swedish king Olaf and visited various remote areas in the course of his evangelical mission. His campaign, which took him as far as Denmark, aroused some opposition and while he was away his church at Växjo was attacked and his two nephews, who served as his assistants, were murdered. Sigfrid, however, persuaded Olaf to spare the lives of the murderers and set about rebuilding his church at Växjo, where ultimately he died.
Feast Day: 15 February.

Silas   (1st century) Companion of St PAUL. Silas (otherwise referred to as **Silvanus**) is identified in the Acts of the Apostles and elsewhere as a companion of St PAUL and may be the secretary called Silvanus mentioned in the epistles to the Thessalonians and at 1 Peter 5:12. Legend has it that he accompanied Paul on his travels through Syria, Cilicia and Macedonia, where he died.
Feast Day: 13 July.

Silvanus   *See* SILAS.

Silvester I   (d.335) Roman pope. Born in Rome, Silvester (or **Sylvester**) succeeded St MILTIADES as pope in 314. Few details are known of his life and papacy, although a number of legends became associated with his name. These included the probably erroneous tradition that it was under Silvester that the emperor Constantine granted the papacy supremacy over all other bishops and secular rulers in Italy. More reliable is the claim that Constantine granted Silvester the Lateran palace, which became St John Lateran, Rome's cathedral church. It was also during Silvester's reign that the first general council of the church was held at Nicaea in 325. His emblem is a chained dragon or bull and a tiara.
Feast Day: 31 December.

Silvester Gozzoli   (1177–1267) Italian abbot. Born at Osimo, Silvester Gozzoli studied law before defying parental opposition and being ordained priest and becoming a canon in the cathedral at Osimo. He remained there until the age of 50, when he found fault with the behaviour of his bishop and resigned from his post. He spent the next four years living as a hermit but in 1231 went on to found a monastery at Monte Fano, near Fabriano, and serve there as abbot. The monastery prospered under his direction, which obliged monks to observe a very strict version of the Benedictine rule, and several more similar so-called Silvestrine houses were established before the time of the founder's death.
Feast Day: 26 November.

Simeon the New Theologian   (949–1022) Abbot and mystic. Born in Galatine in Paphlagonia in Asia Minor, Simeon (or **Symeon**) was brought up in Constantinople and eventually (after two refusals) was admitted as a monk to the monastery of Studius in 984. He found the rule there too lenient, however, and moved to the monastery of St Mamas, where subsequently he served as abbot for 25 years. Eventually criticism of his radical reforms at St Mamas obliged him to go into exile, though ultimately he founded another small monastery at Chrysopolis, where he remained until his death. He is remembered chiefly for his influential writings, such as the *Catechetical Discourses* and *Hymns of Divine Love*, which developed the Byzantine mysticism of St JOHN CLIMACUS and St MAXIMUS THE CONFESSOR and contributed towards a renewal of the church in the East.
Feast Day: 12 March.

Simeon the Stylite   (390–459) Syrian ascetic and first of the pillar
hermits. Born the son of a shepherd in Cilicia, Simeon the Stylite (or
Simeon Stylites) adopted a lifestyle of extreme austerity and fasting as a
child and went on to spend some 20 years in hermitages and monasteries
in northern Syria. The severity of his austerities proved too much for the
other monks, however, and after only narrowly recovering from his
injuries after binding his arm with a tight noose of rope made from
palm leaves he was obliged to live in seclusion in a hut for three years.
Finding himself mobbed there by people attracted by his reputation for
meeting requests for prayers and advice, he made the decision in 423 to
remove himself literally from the world of ordinary men by taking up residence on top of a nine-foot pillar, at Telanissus (Dair Sem'an). He spent
the remaining 36 years of his life on a platform on top of a series of pillars,
the height of which was gradually raised to around 60 feet. Ironically, his
decision to live on a pillar only served to attract even larger crowds of the
faithful seeking his advice, from humble pilgrims to emperors. He
preached to these throngs of people twice daily, urging them to give up
their licentious and unjust ways. By the time of his death Simeon the
Stylite had become the most famous of all the ascetics to take up such a
mode of life and a monastery and sanctuary were later built over the
remains of his columns. Among those inspired to imitate his extraordinary
lifestyle were St DANIEL THE STYLITE and St **Simeon Stylite the
Younger** (d.592), who occupied a pillar near Antioch for many years.
Feast Day: 5 January.

Simeon Stylite the Younger   *See* SIMEON THE STYLITE.

Simon   *See* PETER.

Simon the Zealot   (1st century) Apostle. Few details of the life of
Simon are provided in the Bible, where he is variously called Simon the
Canaanite or Simon the Zealot (possibly a reference to his former association with a strict Jewish sect). He is listed among the 12 apostles by
Matthew and is said to have preached the gospel in Egypt and Persia
after the Crucifixion. Tradition maintains that he was martyred in Persia,
possibly alongside St JUDE. His emblem is a boat or a falchion (a sickle-
shaped sword or saw with which he is supposed to have been cut in two
by pagan priests).
Feast Day: 28 October.

Simon Stock   (d.1265) English friar. Born in England, possibly at Ayles-

ford in Kent, he may have made a pilgrimage to the Holy Land and been exposed to the influence of early Carmelite hermits there some time before emerging as prior general of the Carmelite order in London around 1247. He had a dynamic impact upon the order, founding new Carmelite houses in Cambridge, Oxford, Paris and Bologna and securing papal approval for the Carmelites changing from an order of hermits to an order of mendicant friars, thus strengthening the order's influence throughout the West. In 1251 he is said to have had a vision of the Virgin Mary while in Cambridge, a revelation that inspired the devotion of the brown scapular among Roman Catholics (Mary having allegedly promised Simon Stock that anyone who died wearing the brown habit of the Carmelites would be admitted to heaven). Simon Stock is also believed to have been the author of the Latin hymn *Flos Carmeli* ('Flower of Carmel'). He died in Bordeaux but was reburied in the old friary in Aylesford in 1951.
Feast Day: 16 May.

Simplicius, Faustinus and Beatrice   (d. *c*.304) Roman martyrs. The story of the martyrdom of Simplicius, Faustinus and Beatrice depends almost entirely upon legend. Popular tradition claims that Simplicius and Faustinus were brothers who were executed on the road to Porto after refusing to make sacrifices to the gods. Their sister Beatrice (or Viatrix) buried their bodies and was subsequently denounced to the authorities, strangled and buried alongside them.
Feast Day: (formerly) 29 July.

Sitha   *See* ZITA.

Sixtus II   (d.258) Roman pope and martyr. Sixtus (or **Xystus**) became pope in 257 but only remained in post for 12 months before being arrested while preaching in the catacombs on the Appian Way and summarily put to death, probably with a sword, after the emperor Valerian ordered the execution of all Christian clergy. According to some versions of the event four deacons were executed with him. He was buried in the cemetery of Callistus on the Appian Way and became one of the most popular martyrs of the early Roman church.
Feast Day: 6 August.

Sophronius   (*c*.560–638) Bishop of Jerusalem. Sophronius was born in Damascus and lived as a monk in Egypt and Palestine before being made patriarch of Jerusalem in 634. He emerged as a leading critic of the Monothelite heresy and defended the interests of the Christian community after the Arabs seized the city in 637. He had some success persuading the Arabic leader the Khalif Omar to act with tolerance towards the Christians before his death the following year. Sophronius was also admired as a writer, although few of his writings, which included lives of the martyrs John and Cyrus, have survived.

Feast Day: 11 March.

Speratus *See* SCILLITAN MARTYRS.

Stanislas of Cracow (1010–1079) Polish bishop and martyr. Born into a noble family of Szczepanow in Poland, he was elected bishop of Cracow in 1072 and proved a vigorous reformer, generous to the poor and an energetic preacher. Subsequently, however, he came into conflict with King Boleslav II after finding fault with the king's personal behaviour. When Stanislas had the temerity to excommunicate the king for abducting the wife of one of his nobles after she refused his advances (amid other misdeeds), Boleslav apparently responded by having his bishop assaulted and murdered while conducting Mass – although there is some confusion about what actually happened. One version of the story claims that Boleslav killed the bishop himself after his guards found themselves physically incapable of completing the deed. Whatever the case, Stanislas was canonized in 1253 and is venerated today in Poland, Lithuania, Belarus and Ukraine. He is also honoured as the patron saint of both Cracow and Poland.

Feast Day: 11 April.

Stanislas Kostka (1550–1568) Jesuit novice. Born into a noble family living in the castle of Rostkovo in Poland, Stanislas Kostka was educated at the Jesuit college in Vienna and in due course, after a life-threatening illness, resolved to become a Jesuit himself (in defiance of his father's wishes and the attempts of his brother Paul to dissuade him). Refused admittance to the order in Vienna, he travelled on foot all the way to Rome, where he was finally allowed in by St FRANCIS BORGIA. Despite his wealthy background, Stanislas Kostka proved an ideal recruit. He had a saintly demeanour and the ability to see visions, but died at the age of 17 after a final vision of the Virgin Mary just nine months into his novitiate. He was canonized in 1726, and is a patron saint of Lithuania.

Feast Day: 13 November.

Stephen (d. *c*.35) The first of the Christian martyrs. According to the Acts of the Apostles, Stephen (probably a Greek-speaking Jew) became the first of the seven deacons to whom the apostles entrusted the care of Greek-speaking Christian widows living in Jerusalem. He proved a powerful preacher and worker of miracles, but soon fell foul of the Jewish authorities, who accused him of blasphemy. When brought before the court he roundly condemned his accusers for having brought about the death of the Messiah and stirred up such indignation that he was dragged out of the city and stoned to death. Among the witnesses to Stephen's martyrdom was Saul, who was subsequently moved to embrace Christianity under the name PAUL. He is honoured as the patron saint of deacons, stonemasons and headache sufferers. His emblem is a book of the Gospels and a stone. *Feast Day: 26 December.*

Stephen I   (d.257) Roman pope. Born into a noble family of Rome, he served as a priest in the city before succeeding Lucius I as pope in 254. His brief reign of three years is usually remembered for the eruption of the Novatian controversy concerning the validity of baptism when carried out by heretics or apostates (which Stephen stubbornly considered valid). He also emphasized the authority of the papacy over the rest of the Christian church, involving himself in confronting heresy in Gaul and intervening in a religious dispute in Spain. One tradition claims that he died the death of a martyr, being seized on the orders of the emperor Valerian while celebrating Mass in the catacombs.
Feast Day: 2 August.

Stephen of Hungary   (c.975–1038) King of Hungary. The son of the duke of the Magyars in Hungary, Stephen (or **Istvan**) was baptized at an early age by St ADALBERT OF PRAGUE, married the sister of the Holy Roman Emperor St HENRY II and succeeded to his father's dukedom in 997. He proved a highly capable ruler, restoring law and order throughout the region and going on to be crowned the first king of Hungary in 1001. As king, Stephen actively encouraged the evangelization of his people, founding monasteries and supporting his bishops as well as doing many works of charity (often incognito). Where he met determined opposition from rival pagans, however, he suppressed it with a firm hand, forbidding, for instance, marriages between Christians and pagans and severely punishing anyone suspected of observing pagan superstitions. Pope Silvester II recognized Stephen's achievements by granting him the title king and bestowing upon him a papal crown, part of which is supposedly incorporated into the extant crown of St Stephen still preserved in Budapest. Unfortunately, much of the good work Stephen had carried out was

undone after his death due to the premature demise of his son Emeric (whom Stephen had carefully brought up to be a responsible Christian monarch) in a hunting accident. Stephen was canonized in 1083 and is honoured today as the patron saint of Hungary and kings.
Feast Day: 16 August.

Stephen Harding (d.1134) English abbot. Probably born in Dorset, Stephen Harding was educated at Sherborne abbey before going abroad and becoming a monk at Molesme in Burgundy. In 1098 he moved to Cîteaux and 10 years later succeeded St ALBERIC as abbot there. Together with Alberic and ROBERT OF MOLESME, Stephen Harding is considered one of the three founders of the Cistercian movement. Particularly influential was his formulation (by 1119) of the Charter of Charity (*Carta Caritatis*), which set in place the rules under which the movement was to develop through the generations. Monks joining the order were expected to renounce all luxury and to dedicate themselves to public and private prayer and manual labour. Heads of the all houses of the order were required to meet on a yearly basis and similarly to expect a visit from the abbot of the founding house every 12 months. Stephen Harding experienced some difficulty in his early years as abbot at Cîteaux through a lack of novices and disease among those who did actually join, but (with the assistance of St BERNARD and others) he survived these to witness the foundation of many more Cistercian houses before his death, with Cîteaux itself remaining the inspiration for the movement as a whole.
Feast Day: 28 March.

Sturm (d. *c.*779) Bavarian abbot. Born into a Christian family, he studied under BONIFACE OF CREDITON at Fritzlar before being ordained priest and undertaking missionary work in Hesse. After a period in retreat in the forest of Hersfeld, he sought to establish a Benedictine monastery at Fulda in co-operation with Boniface and became abbot there in 744, using it as a base to convert the Saxons. Subsequently, however, he became embroiled in a lengthy argument with the local bishop St LULL over which of them had the right to exercise jurisdiction over Fulda. Sturm was deposed temporarily as abbot on the orders of King Pepin and experienced further difficulty when the Saxons rose up in protest at the aggressive evangelization pursued by Charlemagne. He died after the Saxons drove the monks out of Fulda (although they returned later). Sturm was canonized in 1139.
Feast Day: 17 December.

Sulpice   (d.647) French bishop. Born into a wealthy family, Sulpice (or **Sulpicius**) served as bishop of Bourges in Aquitaine and became highly popular for his efforts to protect his flock from the tyranny of the Merovingian kings. He was also renowned for his generosity and concern for the welfare of the poor and needy. He is honoured as patron of the celebrated seminary of Saint-Sulpice in Paris.
Feast Day: 17 January.

Sulpicius   *See* SULPICE.

Swithun   (d.862) English bishop. Born in Wessex, Swithun (or **Swithin**) was educated in Winchester and in due course became chaplain to the Wessex kings Egbert and Ethelwulf. In 852 he was made bishop of Winchester, in which role he proved highly energetic, building several churches and promoting the welfare of the poor. He is usually remembered today for his association with the folkloric belief that if it rains on St Swithun's feast day then it will continue to rain for the next 40 days. This tradition has its origins in a story that describes how attempts made to move the saint's body 100 years after his death from a humble spot in the churchyard to a more prestigious location within Winchester cathedral were delayed by heavy rain (interpreted as a sign that Swithun preferred to remain where he was).
Feast Day: 2 July.

Sylvester   *See* SILVESTER I.

Symeon   *See* SIMEON THE NEW THEOLOGIAN.

Symphorian   (d. *c.*200) French martyr. According to legend, Symphorian was brought before the Roman governor after refusing to honour the pagan goddess Cybele at a festival in Autun. All attempts by verbal persuasion and flogging to make Symphorian demonstrate obeisance to Cybele proved futile and he was sentenced to death by beheading. As the sentence was carried out Symphorian's mother called out encouragement to him from the city wall. He was buried in a cave over which a church was later erected.
Feast Day: 22 August.

Syncletica   (4th century) Egyptian hermit. The daughter of wealthy Macedonian parents, Syncletica inherited a fortune but decided to distribute her riches among the poor and instead to retreat from the world in search of a life of solitude and simplicity. She and her blind sister accordingly took up residence in an unused burial chamber on a relative's estate and there pursued a life imitative of that of the desert fathers for the next 50 years. She became widely respected as a source of wise counsel to other aspiring Christian women.

Feast Day: 5 January.

Tarsicius   (*c*.3rd or 4th century) Roman martyr. The details of the martyrdom of Tarsicius are hazy, although it appears that he was unmasked as a Christian when stopped and searched in the street by a pagan mob and found to be carrying the consecrated host (possibly while taking it to imprisoned fellow-Christians). When he attempted to protect the host from interference he was beaten to death. One version of the story identifies Tarsicius as a young boy, while another suggests he was a deacon. He is honoured as the patron saint of altar boys and of the Blessed Sacrament. *Feast Day: 26 August.*

Tecla   *See* THECLA OF ICONIUM.

Teilo   (6th century) Welsh bishop. Information about the life and career of St Teilo is scant and unreliable. He is said to have been born in the vicinity of Penally, near Tenby, in south Wales and legend has it that he accompanied St DAVID on pilgrimage to Jerusalem. He is usually remembered, however, as the influential founder of a monastery at Llandeilo Fawr in Carmarthenshire. Another tradition claims he also served as the second bishop of Llandaff. When plague hit Wales he is thought to have visited St SAMSON at Dol and to have remained in Brittany for seven years before returning to Wales and dying at Llandeilo Fawr. He was buried in a tomb in Llandaff cathedral and his memory is preserved in a number of placenames in both south Wales and Brittany. *Feast Day: 9 February.*

Telesphorus   (d. *c*.136) Greek-born pope and martyr. Probably of Greek birth (possibly from Calabria), Telesphorus succeeded Sixtus I as pope around 125. His papacy lasted 11 years and ended with his martyrdom in obscure circumstances (making him probably the only one of the first 14 popes to follow St PETER whose reputation as a martyr is factually correct). He is said to have celebrated Easter on a Sunday, but to have been tolerant of others who celebrated the festival on other days. *Feast Day: 5 January.*

Telmo   *See* ERASMUS.

Teresa of Avila (1515–1582) Spanish foundress. Teresa (or **Theresa**) de Cepeday Ahumada was born into an aristocratic family near Avila in Castile and at the age of 15 was sent to be educated at the local Augustinian convent. Here she decided to become a nun and accordingly entered the Incarnation of the Carmelite nuns in Avila in 1536. As a young woman she suffered several bouts of serious illness, only narrowly surviving, and through this experience discovered the power of prayer. Once recovered, she had the first of many mystical revelations, going into ecstatic raptures and feeling herself projected out of her body. Henceforth she spent much of her time in prayer, often going into deep religious trances. In 1559 she underwent the rare experience of a transverberation, in which she felt her heart pierced by an arrow of divine love plunged into her by an angel. In 1562 she founded the reformed Discalced (meaning 'barefooted') Carmelite order to further her ambition of reforming Carmelite convents throughout Spain, returning to the strict rule under which the order was originally established. Over the years that followed she travelled extensively through the country, founding a total of 17 reformed Carmelite houses. She was joined in this work by St JOHN OF THE CROSS, whom she first met when she was aged 53. The two became close friends and corresponded regularly, St John undertaking similar reform among friars of the order. Greatly loved by her nuns, St Teresa was also celebrated for her written works on spiritual matters, which included her autobiography *Life* and the classic mystical treatises *The Interior Castle* and *The Way of Perfection*. She was canonized in 1622 and in 1970 became the first woman to be declared a Doctor of the Church. She is also honoured as the patron saint of lacemakers. Her emblems are a heart, an arrow and a book.
Feast Day: 15 October.

Teresa of the Andes (1900–1920) Chilean novice. Born Juanita Fernandez Solar into a wealthy family of mixed Chilean, Spanish and English descent at Santiago in Chile, Teresa showed a strong inclination for the religious life as a young child and was well educated at the local convent. After suffering great pain from appendicitis, at the age of 15 she took a vow of celibacy and set about living simply and doing good works, taking as her example the lifestyle of the Carmelites. In 1919 she began preparation for becoming a nun at the Carmel in Los Andes, but the following year was found to be suffering from typhus. She died shortly after making her vows as a Carmelite novice, aged 19. After her death Teresa's deep religious belief (evidenced by entries in her diary) combined with the poig-

nancy of her premature demise made her the focus of a substantial cult following and thousands of pilgrims continue to visit a shrine erected in her memory at La Riconda near Los Andes. She was canonized in 1993 and is widely considered a role model for young Catholics.
Feast Day: 12 April.

Teresa Benedicta of the Cross   *See* EDITH STEIN.

Thaddeus   *See* JUDE.

Thais   (dates unknown) Egyptian penitent. Legend identifies Thais as a beautiful Egyptian prostitute of the 4th century who made a fortune from her work but surrendered all her wealth willingly after a revelatory meeting with the desert monk St PAPHNUTIUS (or possibly one of his companions). She immediately burned her rich clothes and jewellery, joined a community of nuns and spent the rest of her life living as a penitent in her cell. She died three years later. Scholars doubt that there ever was a historical character called Thais and contend that she is more likely to have been the creation of early Christian moralists.
Feast Day: 8 October.

Thecla of Iconium   (1st century) Virgin martyr. Details of the life and death of St Thecla (or **Tecla**) of Iconium depend almost wholly on legend dating from the 2nd century. Tradition claims that she was born in Iconium (Konya) in Asia Minor and became a follower of St PAUL, breaking off her engagement in order to embrace a celibate Christian life. When her conversion was discovered, however, Paul was driven out of Iconium and Thecla herself was condemned to death by burning. When a storm put out the flames that threatened Thecla she was thrown into the arena to be killed by wild beasts, but the animals refused to go near her. She then managed to escape and was reunited with Paul at Myra. She spent the remaining 72 years of her life as a hermit in a cave at Seleucia, earning a reputation as a miracle worker. At the age of 90 Thecla was assaulted by pagan rivals but was protected from them when the rock of her cave opened up to surround her and she was never seen again. She became the focus of a considerable cult following (suppressed in 1969) and her cave at Seleucia became a site of pilgrimage. Scholars have suggested that St Thecla may never have existed in reality.
Feast Day: 23 September.

Theodore   (4th century) Martyr. Little is known about St Theodore beyond the fact that he was a Roman soldier who refused to pay homage to the

pagan gods at Amasea in Pontus and then burned down a temple dedicated to the Mother Goddess, upon which he was tortured and sentenced
to death as a Christian. While in prison awaiting execution he is said to
have been consoled by visions of heaven. He died after being thrown into
a furnace and was buried at Euchaita, where his tomb became a place of
pilgrimage. Along with St GEORGE and St DEMETRIUS, he is remembered as
one of the three celebrated soldier-saints of the East. Later additions to his
legend led to the invention in the 10th century of another St Theodore,
identified as a Roman general.
Feast Day: 9 November.

Theodore of Canterbury   (602–690) Greek-born archbishop. Born in
Tarsus in Cilicia, Theodore of Canterbury (otherwise known as **Theodore
of Tarsus**) was educated at Antioch and Constantinople and lived as a
monk first in Greece and then in Rome until he was in his sixties, when
he was unexpectedly appointed to the vacant see of Canterbury by Pope
Vitalian (667). Theodore accordingly came to England, accompanied by
St ADRIAN and St BENEDICT BISCOP, and in 672 presided over the first
synod of the whole English church, held at Hertford. He also appointed
bishops to fill vacant sees, set up a celebrated school in Canterbury, negotiated in the argument between St CHAD and St WILFRID over their jurisdiction of the see of York, created a number of new sees and assumed
responsibility for unifying the hitherto disorganized English church as one
body, effectively laying the foundations for the modern church in England
and becoming the first archbishop of Canterbury to enjoy universal authority. Evidently much respected in his own lifetime not only as an administrator but also as a teacher and scholar, Theodore remains one of the most
important figures in the early history of the English church. On his death
he was laid to rest close to St AUGUSTINE in the monastery of SS. Peter and
Paul in Canterbury.
Feast Day: 19 September.

Theodore of Sykeon   (d.613) Bishop of Galatia. Theodore was the illegitimate son of a prostitute who ran an inn-cum-brothel at Sykeon in Galatia.
As a young man he came under the influence of the family cook – a
Christian – and himself converted his mother, grandmother and aunt (who
also worked as prostitutes), persuading them to give up their immoral
ways. He went on to live as a hermit in a cave near Sykeon before being
ordained priest at the age of 18 and then conducting a pilgrimage to Jerusalem. On his return Theodore acquired a reputation for his extreme ascetical

practices (which included having himself suspended in a cage between Christmas and Palm Sunday each year) and attracted many disciples, in response to which he founded a substantial monastic community at Sykeon. Though reluctant to accept the position, he was elected bishop of Anastasiopolis, near Ankara, around 590 and remained in the post for some 10 years before resigning in order to resume the life of a humble monk at Sykeon. According to a biography written by one of his followers, Theodore was revered in his own lifetime for his apparently miraculous powers of healing and was generally much admired for his personal virtues.

Feast Day: 22 April.

Theodore the Studite   (759–826) Greek abbot and theologian. Born the son of a treasury official in Constantinople, he became a monk in the monastery of Sakkoudion in Bithynia, where his uncle was abbot, and was ordained priest in 787. He succeeded to his uncle's post of abbot at Sakkoudion in 794 but incurred imperial wrath shortly afterwards when he criticized the emperor Constantine's adulterous remarriage and was banished for a brief period. He then moved to Constantinople and took over the monastery founded by the Roman consul Studius in 463, going on to make it an influential centre of Byzantine monasticism. He proved a steadfast defender of the church's independence from secular interference and instituted important monastic reforms, although these were not achieved without difficulty. He was banished once more in the years 809–811 on the orders of Constantine and again in 814 after he opposed the adoption of Iconoclasm by Leo V the Armenian. He was then imprisoned for seven years and flogged but eventually released after Leo V's death in 820 (although prevented from ever returning to the Studite monastery in Constantinople and ultimately dying in a monastery on the Akrita Peninsula). Theodore the Studite was also the author of a number of significant writings, among them theological and liturgical works, sermons, letters and poems. He remains one of the most revered of all saints in the eastern church.

Feast Day: 11 November.

Theodosius of the Caves   (*c*.1002–1074) Ukrainian abbot. Born into a wealthy family of Vasilkov in the Ukraine, Theodosius of the Caves (otherwise referred to as **Theodosius of Kiev**) defied the wishes of his mother at a relatively young age by adopting an ascetic way of life and by selflessly dedicating himself to helping the poor and needy. Around 1032 he was admitted to a monastic community inhabiting the caves of Kiev and in due course (1063) was raised to the rank of abbot there. He reorganized the community along the lines of the monasticism recommended by St THEODORE THE STUDITE, encouraging the monks to live more active lives and extending the monastery physically beyond the original cave dwellings. Believing that monasteries should participate in wider society, he welcomed travellers as well as the sick and needy to the monastery and urged the monks to live by the ideals of love, peace and unity. The monastery attracted the support of the country's rulers, although Theodosius was careful to maintain independence from secular influence, even in the face of threatened banishment. He was canonized by the Russian church in 1108 and remains one of the most celebrated saints of early Russian Christianity.

Feast Day: 3 May.

Theodosius the Cenobiarch (*c.*423–529) Cappadocian abbot. Born in Cappadocia, he moved to Palestine aged around 30 and founded a small community of hermit monks near Bethlehem. The community prospered and became well known for its charitable work on behalf of the sick and needy. In recognition of his achievements Theodosius was placed in charge of all monks living in communities in Palestine (hence his title 'Cenobiarch', meaning 'head of those living in common'). His opposition to the Monophysite heresy concerning the nature of Christ provoked the emperor Anastasius, who responded by attempting to bribe him into taking his side. Theodosius accepted the money, distributed it among the poor but declined to change his views, upon which the emperor dismissed him from his post for a brief period. Theodosius is said to have died at the age of 105.

Feast Day: 11 January.

Théophane Vénard (1829–1861) French martyr. Born the son of a schoolmaster of Saint-Loup-sur-Thouet, Poitiers, he survived childhood illnesses to become a priest and, in 1850, to enter the College of the Foreign Missions of Paris. Ordained in 1852, he was sent to Tonkin (Vietnam) to assist the persecuted Christian community numbering thousands of converts there, though continuing to suffer ill health. He was expelled in 1856 and moved to Hanoi but was forced to go into hiding as the persecution continued and was eventually betrayed and arrested. His captors confined him in a bamboo cage for several months before beheading him for his Christian faith. He was canonized in 1988.

Feast Day: 2 February.

Theresa of Avila   *See* TERESA OF AVILA.

Theresa of Lisieux   (1873–1897) French mystic and nun. Theresa (or **Thérèse**) of Lisieux was born Marie Françoise Martin in Alençon in Normandy and dreamed initially of becoming a missionary and a martyr. Realising this was unrealistic, she became a Discalced Carmelite nun at Lisieux in 1888, having obtained special permission from the local bishop as she was aged only 15 and was thus technically too young to enter a convent. Calling herself Thérèse of the Child Jesus, over the next nine years she demonstrated great piety and inexhaustible love of God and impressed all with her simple faith, which she termed her 'little way of spiritual childhood'. In 1896, however, she was diagnosed with tuberculosis and was ordered by her superiors to commit an account of her life to writing before her illness could claim her. This she obediently did before dying at the premature age of 24. Her thoughts and recollections, together with details of her various mystical experiences, were subsequently published as *The Story of a Soul*, which became one of the most loved of all Catholic bestsellers. Theresa of Lisieux was canonized in 1925 and named a Doctor of the Church in 1998. Her shrine at Lisieux became an important site of pilgrimage, attracting admirers from all over the world. Popularly known as 'the Little Flower' or the 'Saint of the Little Way', Theresa of Lisieux is honoured as the patron saint of France, of foreign missions and of florists, air crews and AIDS sufferers.
Feast Day: 1 October.

Theresa Margaret of the Sacred Heart   (1747–1770) Italian mystic and nun. Born Anna Maria Redi in Arezzo, Italy, she entered the Carmelite convent of St TERESA OF AVILA in Florence in 1764 at the age of 17 and immediately made an impression upon the other nuns with her cheerful, purposeful demeanour. She proved a caring nurse of the other nuns when they were sick and was respected for her great piety and wisdom. Ultimately, in 1767, she became one of the few individuals in the history of the church credited with having experienced a transverberation, in which she felt her heart pierced and set aflame by a burning arrow of divine love. She died prematurely, at the age of 23, and was canonized in 1934.
Feast Day: 11 March.

Thomas   (1st century) Apostle. According to the Gospel of St JOHN, Thomas was termed 'Didymus' (meaning 'twin'). He was present at the Last Supper but famously was absent at the moment of Christ's

Resurrection. When he was subsequently told of it by the other apostles he declined to believe what he was hearing until Christ appeared to him and allowed him to touch his wounds, upon which Thomas expressed immediate conviction. He is often referred to as 'Doubting Thomas' on the strength of this episode (John 20:24-29). It is unclear what became of Thomas after these events. One tradition has it that he preached the gospel in India and may have died the death of a martyr when speared at Myla-pore near Madras. Another claims that he spent the rest of his life evan-gelizing in Parthia. He is honoured as the patron saint of builders and architects (a reference to the legend that he once built a heavenly palace for an Indian king) and of theologians.

Feast Day: 3 July.

Thomas of Canterbury   *See* THOMAS BECKET.

Thomas of Hereford   (1218–1282) English bishop. Born Thomas Cantel-upe into a family of aristocratic Norman descent at Hambledon in Bucking-hamshire, he was educated at Oxford, Paris and Orléans and was probably ordained priest while accompanying his father (Baron William de Cantel-upe) at the general council of Lyons in 1245. At the same time it appears he received papal permission to hold a plurality of benefices simul-taneously and throughout his life he paid great interest in these, often visiting the parishes in his care without warning in order to satisfy himself that the clergy beneath him were behaving correctly. He went on to teach canon law at Oxford and was appointed chancellor of the university in 1262. While in this post he sided with the barons against King Henry III and briefly served as chancellor of England under the barons' leader Simon de Montfort. He was obliged to go into temporary exile in France after de Montfort's defeat. He also served as adviser to King Edward I. In 1275 he was elected bishop of Hereford, in which role he frequently resorted to the courts to protect his authority throughout his see from encroachment by rivals. He became very popular with the common popu-lace and was much respected both for his generosity and for the austerity he embraced in his personal life. In 1282, however, a dispute with the Arch-bishop of Canterbury, John Peckham, resulted in Thomas of Hereford being excommunicated, obliging the bishop to make the long journey to Rome to petition the pope, only for him to die at Montefiascone near Orvieto. His remains were laid to rest in Hereford cathedral (the scene of many miracles attributed to his intervention) and he was canonized in 1320, thus becoming the only canonized saint to have been excommunicated at the time of his death.

Feast Day: 2 October.

Thomas of Villanueva   (1486–1555) Spanish archbishop. Thomas of Villanueva (or **Villanova**) was born near Villanueva in Castile and after attending university became an Augustinian friar at Salamanca. He was ordained priest in 1518 and quickly rose to the rank of prior, establishing a reputation as a capable administrator and preacher who was known for great personal piety and kindness. Having served as prior in various houses for over 25 years and as chaplain to the emperor Charles V, he was appointed to the post of Archbishop of Valencia in 1544. He went on to do much to restore a previously neglected diocese, giving generously to the needy (whatever their station in life) and trying to tackle the problem posed by the large numbers of Moors in the area who had been forcibly converted to Christianity in the years before he came to office. By the time of his death in Valencia he had effectively renewed the Catholic church throughout northeastern Spain. His other notable achievements included sending the first Augustinian missionaries to Mexico. Credited with miraculous healing powers, he was canonized in 1658.

Feast Day: 8 September.

Thomas Aquinas   (1225–1275) Italian priest, philosopher and theologian. Born the son of a nobleman of Roccasecca near Aquino in Italy, he was educated by the Benedictines at Monte Cassino but in 1245 chose instead to become a lowly Dominican mendicant friar (ignoring the opposition of his family). He went on to study philosophy and theology under St ALBERT THE GREAT in Cologne, taking particular inspiration from the writings of Aristotle, and then spent the next 20 years from 1256 teaching fellow Dominicans in Paris and Italy and writing. His *Summa Contra Gentes*, written between 1259 and 1264, attempted to give Christianity a rational basis for the benefit of Jews, Muslims and pagans. In 1266 he began writing his most important work, the treatise *Summa Theologica*, in which he summarized the whole philosophy of the Christian doctrine, discussing such issues as God, angels, human nature, grace and the sacraments. The book remained uncompleted at his death after its author had a profound religious experience in 1273, in response to which he devoted himself entirely to prayer. Though unfinished the book remains one of the most influential of Christian theological writings and a focus of intense debate and discussion (especially since the late 19th century). Other works by the hand of Thomas Aquinas included biblical treatises, commentaries on Aristotle and polemical tracts, among them *De Ente et Essentia, De Regimine Principium, Contra Impugnantes Religionem, De Perfectae Vitae Spiritualis, De Unitate Intellectus Contra Averroistas, Quaestiones Disputatae* and *Quaestiones Quodlibetales.* Considered the father of Christian philosophy and theology, the overweight and overworked Thomas Aquinas died at the abbey of Fossanuova near Terracina. Known as the 'Universal Teacher', he was canonized in 1323, declared a Doctor of the Church and Doctor Angelicus in 1567 and is honoured as the patron saint of philosophers, theologians, universities, schools, booksellers and students. His emblem is a star. *Feast Day: 28 January.*

Thomas Becket (1118–1170) English archbishop and martyr. Born of noble Norman descent in the Cheapside district of London, Thomas Becket (otherwise referred to as **Thomas à Becket** or **Thomas of Canterbury**) entered the service of Archbishop Theobald of Canterbury around 1142 and studied canon law abroad before being made a deacon and archdeacon of Canterbury in 1154. In 1155 he was appointed royal chancellor by his friend King Henry II and for the next seven years he enjoyed unquestioned royal support in his roles as statesman and diplomat, enjoying life at court and making the most of his royal patronage. In 1159 he even led the king's army into battle at Toulouse. In 1162, however, Thomas Becket was appointed Archbishop of Canterbury and everything changed. He immediately renounced his former extravagance, giving away much of his wealth, donning a hair shirt and living in conditions of austerity. He quickly fell out of favour with the king, obstinately refusing to acknowledge the authority of the state over clergy, disputing taxation issues and generally defending the church's independence from royal interference. Lacking the support of many of his bishops, Thomas Becket was forced to go into exile in France in 1164 and it was six years before the two sides were reconciled and the archbishop felt ready to return to England. Once back, however, the conflict between Becket and the king quickly flared up again, this time over the issue of disciplining rebellious bishops, and an enraged Henry hinted (probably unwittingly) that he wanted his turbulent archbishop dead. Four knights immediately set out for Canterbury and there murdered Thomas Becket as he prayed in his own cathedral. When Henry II heard the news of the murder he was horrified and in 1174 performed public penance in a bid to atone for the deed. The dead archbishop, meanwhile, was immediately declared a martyr and was canonized by Pope Alexander III in 1173, just three years after the murder. Thomas Becket's shrine at Canterbury (destroyed by Henry VIII in 1538) became the most celebrated site of pilgrimage in England and the archbishop's murder remains one of the most infamous episodes in the history of the English church.

Feast Day: 29 December.

Thomas Cantelupe   *See* THOMAS OF HEREFORD.

Thomas More   (1478–1535) English martyr. Born in London, lawyer's son Thomas More served as a youth in the household of Archbishop of Canterbury John Morton and studied for a time at Canterbury College, Oxford, before taking up a career as a barrister and (from 1504) as a member of parliament. He filled various posts in government, including those of Speaker of the House of Commons, High Steward of Cambridge University and Chancellor of the Duchy of Lancaster, and was knighted by King Henry VIII in recognition of his work. In his private life, he was a devoted family man, twice married and the father of four children. In 1529 he succeeded Cardinal Thomas Wolsey as Lord Chancellor of England after Wolsey failed to secure a divorce for Henry from his queen Catherine of Aragon. More incurred the king's wrath himself, however, when he too opposed the king's decision to divorce his wife and declare himself head of the church in England and he eventually resigned the chancellorship in 1532. When More then refused to sign the 1534 Act of Succession, acknowledging the children of Henry VIII and his second wife Anne Boleyn as rightful heirs to the throne, he was arrested, charged with treason and ultimately beheaded on London's Tower Hill. On the day of his execution he reiterated his loyalty to the king, but made it clear that he felt he owed a greater loyalty to God. Celebrated as a leading figure of the Renaissance period, More is also remembered as the author of *Utopia* (1515–16), a vision of an ideal, enlightened society that drew in part on the teachings of St AUGUSTINE. His other writings included *The Four Last Things* (1520) and *Dialogue of Comfort Against Tribulation* (1553). He was canonized in 1935 and is honoured as the patron saint of lawyers and adopted children.

Feast Day: 22 June.

Thorfinn   (d.1285) Norwegian bishop. Born in Trondheim, Thorfinn is thought to have lived as a Cistercian monk in the area prior to being appointed bishop of Hamar. Few details of his career have been recorded, but it appears that he and several other bishops came into conflict with

King Eric II over state interference in church affairs and had to go into exile abroad after being outlawed. He is said to have visited Rome and to have died at the Cistercian abbey of Ter Doest near Bruges. Contemporaries were evidently much impressed by Thorfinn's personal qualities and another Cistercian monk praised his goodness in a poem later placed over his tomb.
Feast Day: 8 January.

Thorlac of Skalholt (1133–1193) Icelandic bishop. Born into a noble family of Iceland, Thorlac became a priest in Iceland before travelling to Paris and Lincoln to continue his religious studies. He returned to Iceland in 1161 and dedicated himself to a celibate life of study, prayer and charitable work. In 1168 he founded a house of canons regular at Thykkviboer, with himself as abbot, to put into practice the monastic ideals to which he had been exposed abroad. He was consecrated bishop of Skalholt in 1178 and instituted various reforms, including the prohibition of marriage among the clergy and greater independence from secular interests. He also provided a code of laws to guide the daily lives of both clergy and lay persons. He was canonized by other Icelandic bishops in 1198.
Feast Day: 23 December.

Timothy (d.97) Bishop and martyr. Born the son of a Gentile father and a Jewish mother of Lystra in Laconia (in modern Turkey), Timothy was converted to Christianity by St PAUL and became his closest disciple (as described in the Acts of the Apostles). Paul sent him as his representative to the Thessalonians, the Corinthians and the Ephesians and he is sometimes identified as the first bishop of Ephesus, assuming responsibility for all the Christians living there. The New Testament includes two letters of encouragement and advice sent by Paul to Timothy. Tradition has it that Timothy was beaten to death with stones and clubs by an angry mob after he spoke out against their pagan rites in honour (probably) of Dionysus. His emblem is a club and a stone.
Feast Day: 26 January.

Titus (1st century) Bishop of Crete. Of Gentile birth, Titus was converted to Christianity by St PAUL, after which he became one of Paul's most trusted assistants and companions. He probably travelled with Paul on several of his journeys, was Paul's representative to Corinth and was then given charge of organizing the church in Crete as first bishop of the Cretan city of Gortyna. In a lettter sent to Titus in Crete Paul recommended a firm

hand in conducting his ministry among the Cretans, whom Paul considered lazy, greedy and dishonest.
Feast Day: 26 January.

Titus Brandsma (1881–1942) Dutch journalist and author. A Catholic priest, Father Titus Brandsma taught philosophy and theology at the Catholic University of Nijmegen for 19 years but with the German invasion of the Netherlands took on a new role, at the age of 60, as spiritual adviser to Dutch Catholic journalists. He immediately spoke out strongly against the printing of Nazi propaganda in Dutch Catholic publications, knowing very well that in doing so he was endangering his own life. The Germans quickly arrested him and imprisoned him first in Scheveningen and ultimately in Dachau concentration camp, where he was badly treated and subjected to medical experiments. When faced with death by lethal injection he behaved with great courage, as a consequence of which the nurse who administered the injection herself rediscovered her Catholic faith and returned to the Church after the war. Father Brandsma was beatified in 1985.
Feast Day: 26 July.

Tola   *See* OLAF.

Toribio of Lima (1538–1606) Spanish-born Peruvian archbishop. Toribio Alfonso de Mogroveio (otherwise referred to as **Turibius of Mogroveio**) was born in Mayorga in Spain and studied law, in due course becoming professor of law at the University of Salamanca. His prowess as a lawyer attracted the admiration of Philip I, who chose him to serve as chief judge of the Inquisition in Granada (despite the fact that he was a layman). Subsequently, even more remarkably for a layman (and in the face of Toribio's own reluctance), he was selected as the next archbishop of Lima in Peru and was accordingly ordained, consecrated and despatched to the New World. Arriving in Lima in 1581, Toribio proved both determined and tireless as he set about reforming the church in Peru, which was both disorganized and ill-disciplined. He also intervened to prevent abuses of the native Indian population by the Spanish authorities, took steps against those who broke the rules of the church and (in Lima in 1591) founded the first seminary in the Americas. He travelled widely despite the poor communications in that part of the world, led missionary campaigns (having learned several Indian languages), built churches and exhibited great generosity towards the poor and needy. He was canonized in 1726, becoming one of the first saints of the New World. He is honoured today as the patron saint of Peru and of the bishops of Latin America. *Feast Day: 23 March.*

Turibius of Mogroveio   *See* TORIBIO OF LIMA.

Ubaldo   (d. 1160) Italian bishop. Born Ubaldo Ballasini at Gubbio in Umbria, he was brought up in the household of his uncle, bishop of Gubbio. Ubaldo (or **Ubald**) went on to serve as dean at the cathedral in Gubbio and managed to muster support from several of the hitherto disorderly canons of the chapter to form a new monastic community under his rule. Though he yearned personally to assume the solitary life of a hermit (he turned down the bishopric of Perugia in 1126), he eventually allowed himself to be persuaded into accepting the bishopric of Gubbio and remained in the post for 32 years, earning the lasting love and praise of his flock through his gentleness and concern. He was canonized in 1192. *Feast Day: 16 May.*

Uganda, Martyrs of   *See* CHARLES LWANGA AND COMPANIONS.

Ulric of Augsburg   (*c*.890–973) Swiss bishop. Born near Zurich, Ulric (or **Ulrich**) was educated at the monastery of St GALL and spent time in the household of his uncle Adalbero, bishop of Augsburg. In due course, despite ill-health, he rose to the rank of bishop himself and served in the post for some 50 years, earning a reputation for his dedication to prayer and for his tireless work on behalf of the diocese, which was much traumatized by the effects of war. He founded many religious houses and made regular visits to all parts of his diocese to encourage his clerics and maintain standards. After Ulric's death many miracles supposedly took place at his tomb and just 20 years later, in 993, he became the first individual to be canonized by a pope when named a saint by Pope John XV. *Feast Day: 4 July.*

Ulric   *See* WULFRIC OF HASELBURY.

Ultan   (d.686) Irish monk. Brother to St FOILLAN and St FURSEY, he accompanied them as missionaries to East Anglia in 630 and there helped to found the Benedictine monastery of Cnobheresburg (Burgh Castle), near Yarmouth. Foillan succeeded Fursey as abbot of the monastery but subsequently both he and Ultan were obliged to follow Fursey into exile in Neustria in the face of Mercian attacks. After Foillan was murdered by robbers Ultan succeeded him as abbot of the monastery at Fosses near Nivelles.

Feast Day: 1 May.

Uncumber   *See* WILGEFORTIS.

Urban   (d.230) Roman pope and martyr. Born in Rome, Urban was elected pope in 222 in succession to the martyred St CALLISTUS I. Virtually nothing is known about his relatively peaceful papacy, which seems to have witnessed steady growth in the size of the Christian community in Rome, or of the circumstances of his death beyond the tradition that he died a martyr.

Feast Day: 25 May.

Ursula   (dates unknown) Virgin martyr. The story of St Ursula depends almost entirely upon legend and little is known of the historical basis for her tale. According to an inscription found on a stone at the church of St Ursula in Cologne and dated from around 400, Ursula was the name of a local virgin martyr put to death for her faith together with an unknown number of companions in otherwise obscure circumstances. By the 10th century, however, the legend had been much embellished and Ursula was becoming established as one of the most popular saints of the whole medieval period. She was now identified as the daughter of a Christian king in Britain, who asked for and got a postponement to her marriage to a pagan prince in order to make the lengthy journey to Rome, together with 10 ladies-in-waiting and 1000 maidens. The party reached Rome safely, but were all massacred for their faith by Huns on the return trip after Ursula refused to marry their chief. Another version of the legend identified Ursula as a Cornish princess who was sent together with 11,000 maidens and 60,000 servants to provide wives for British settlers in Armorica, only for their ships to be wrecked and all the women murdered or enslaved. A third variant describes Ursula and her companions as an army of women who died after fighting a battle. The figure of 11,000 companions is thought to have been arrived at through misinterpretation of the Latin for '11'. Due to the lack of any historical backing for the legend, the cult of St Ursula and her companions was officially suppressed in 1969. She is honoured as a patron saint of schoolgirls and young women.

Feast Day: (formerly) 21 October.

Vaast   *See* VEDAST.

Vaclav   *See* WENCESLAS.

Valentine   (3rd century) Roman martyr. Virtually nothing is known of the historical Valentine beyond the tradition that he was a priest who was martyred for his faith in Rome during the reign of Claudius II and was subsequently commemorated by a church of St Valentine on the Flaminian Way. Legend has it that when imprisoned Valentine converted his gaoler to Christianity by restoring his daughter's eyesight and that when taken out to execution he left a message for the girl signed "from your Valentine". Another tradition claims that he performed secret marriages on behalf of betrothed couples after Claudius II prohibited weddings because he needed more single men as recruits for his army. Some details of his legend appear to owe a deal to the lives of the saints **Marius** and **Martha**, who were also martyred in Rome and buried on the Via Cornelia. This Valentine may or may not be the same person as a bishop of Terni called Valentine who was martyred in Rome around 273. It is uncertain why either of these two historical Valentines (or a third, one Bishop Valentine of Genoa) became so uniquely associated with love and romance, specifically with the sending of 'valentines' in the form of anonymous cards to potential lovers on 11 February. The custom may be a relic of the Roman festival of Lupercalia, or it may owe more to the fact that the feast day of St Valentine falls on the date when birds were once believed to start seeking mates. St Valentine is honoured as the patron saint of beekeepers, betrothed couples, travellers and the young.
Feast Day: 14 February.

Vaubourg   *See* WALBURGA.

Vedast   (d.539) Bishop of Arras. Vedast (otherwise referred to as **Foster** or **Vaast**) is remembered primarily as the priest who coached Clovis, king of the Franks, before baptism by St REMIGIUS in 496. Clovis agreed to be converted after appealing to Christ to help him defeat his enemy, the Alamanni, in battle. His ensuing victory persuaded the king to come forward for baptism and accordingly he invited Vedast to prepare him for the sacrament. While on their way to Rheims to meet Remigius the king's resolve

to become a Christian was confirmed when Vedast apparently achieved the miraculous cure of a blind man they encountered on a bridge over the River Aisne. The king's baptism proved a crucial development as it encouraged many of his court to follow suit and abandon their pagan ways. Vedast was appointed bishop of Arras in 499 and over the next 40 years did much to promote the spread of Christianity in what is now Belgium. He also had some influence upon the fostering of the Christian faith in England, although he probably never visited the country.
Feast Day: 6 February.

Venantius Fortunatus (*c*.530–610) Bishop of Poitiers. Born near Treviso in Italy, he studied at Ravenna and first came to France at the age of 30 when he visited the shrine of St MARTIN OF TOURS to give thanks for the cure for an eye problem. Subsequently he settled in Poitiers, where he was ordained priest and became an intimate of St RADEGUND. He served as chaplain at the monastery of the Holy Cross before being made bishop of Poitiers around 600. He is usually remembered as a religious poet whose most celebrated works included such hymns as 'The royal banners forward go' and 'Sing, my tongue, the glorious battle' as well as poems and verse and prose biographies of the saints.
Feast Day: 14 December.

Vergil *See* VIRGIL.

Veronica (1st century) Woman of Jerusalem. Veronica is traditionally identified as the woman who was moved by pity to wipe the face of Christ when he fell under the weight of the cross while carrying it to Calvary. She is not mentioned in biblical descriptions of the event, however, and only makes her first appearance in accounts of the Crucifixion dating from around the 5th century. She is sometimes tentatively linked with other biblical characters, including MARTHA and the unnamed woman whom Christ cured of her bleeding. Another suggestion is that she was the wife of a Roman officer or of a tax collector called Zacchaeus. Though probably a wholly fictitious character, Veronica became a focus of great veneration in the medieval period and a cloth supposedly bearing the imprint of Christ's face and known as 'St Veronica's veil' has been preserved at St Peter's in Rome since the 8th century. Veronica (whose name is sometimes said to come from the Latin *vera icon*, meaning 'true image') is honoured as the patron saint of washerwomen.
Feast Day: 12 July.

Veronica Giuliani (1660–1727) Italian mystic and nun. Born into a wealthy family of Mercatello, she served as mistress of novices at a Capuchin convent at Città di Castello in Umbria for 34 years before being raised to the rank of abbess in 1716 and going on to prove herself a capable and determined, though humble, administrator and leader. She is usually remembered, however, for her many striking mystical experiences, which included powerful visions of Christ's Passion and the manifestation of the stigmata on her body (as detailed in her ten-volume diary, later published). These phenomena were closely studied by the local bishop, who placed Veronica under constant observation for some time before finally accepting the authenticity of her experiences. Veronica was canonized in 1839.
Feast Day: 9 July.

Viatrix *See* SIMPLICIUS, FAUSTINUS AND BEATRICE.

Vicelin (*c*.1086–1154) Bishop of Oldenburg. Born into a wealthy family of Hameln (Hanover), he studied at Paderborn (Detmold) and in due course became a canon at a school in Bremen. He was ordained priest at Magdeburg and subsequently, supported by the Danish nobleman CANUTE LAVARD, spent many years evangelizing among the Wends. He founded a number of religious houses and did much to promote the growth of Christianity throughout the region, ultimately serving as bishop of Oldenburg from 1149.
Feast Day: 12 December.

Victor of Marseilles (3rd century) French martyr. Little is known about the life of Victor of Marseilles beyond the fact that he was martyred for his faith late in the 3rd century. One tradition claims that he was a Roman soldier put to death during the reign of Maximian alongside three other guards he had converted to Christianity. His tomb in Marseilles became a popular early site of pilgrimage.
Feast Day: 21 July.

Vietnam, Martyrs of (d.1745–1862) Group of martyrs put to death in the former Vietnamese kingdoms of Tonkin, Annam and Cochin China. Of the 100,000 individuals who died in the cause of promoting the Christian gospel in what is now Vietnam 117 are recognized as saints. The group comprises eight bishops, 50 priests and 59 lay people, of which 96 were Vietnamese. Prominent among them are the French missionary THÉOPHANE VÉNARD, the Dominican Vincent Liem (who became the first Vietnamese

martyr), the Spanish bishop Dominic Henarez, the French bishop Stephen Cuénot and the Vietnamese priest **Andrew Dung-Lac**, a typical representative of numerous Vietnamese Christian clergy to die. Details of the deaths of many others are now lost. Many of their number were exposed to the most barbarous cruelty and died in agony as their limbs were hacked off or the flesh removed in strips. Many were also branded or made to take harmful drugs. The 117 Martyrs of Vietnam were canonized in 1988.
Feast Days: 2 February, 11 July, 26 November.

Vincent of Lérins (d. *c*.450) French monk and theologian. Little is known for certain about his life and career. Of noble birth and possibly the brother of St LUPUS OF TROYES, who became bishop of Troyes, Vincent is thought to have lived the life of a soldier before entering the church and, as far as can be ascertained, remaining a monk and priest in the island monastery of Lérins near Cannes. He is remembered chiefly as a scholar and teacher, his best-known work being a treatise upon the theme of scripture and orthodoxy entitled the *Commonitory*. In this short but classic piece he advises how to distinguish between Christian truth and falsehood. He is honoured as a Father of the Church.
Feast Day: 24 May.

Vincent of Saragossa (d.304) Spanish martyr. Vincent of Saragossa (or **Vincent of Zaragoza**) became a deacon and is known to have died for his faith at Valencia during the reign of Diocletian, although exact details of his life and death are not recorded. Tradition claims that he died after being viciously tortured, his sufferings including being beaten, flayed and roasted on a grid iron. Some say that Vincent of Saragossa was put to death alongside St **Valerius of Saragossa** (or **Valerius of Zaragoza**), bishop of Saragossa and Vincent's mentor, although another insists that the elderly Valerius was allowed to die peacefully in exile. Vincent of Saragossa is honoured as patron saint of Portugal.
Feast Day: 22 January.

Vincent de Paul (1581–1660) French founder of the Vincentian (or Lazarist) Congregation and of the Sisters of Charity. Born into a peasant family of Ranquine (now renamed Saint-Vincent-de-Paul) in Gascony, he studied at the universities of Toulouse and Saragossa before joining the Franciscans and being ordained at the young age of 19. An unreliable legend has it that in 1605, while travelling by sea, he was seized by pirates and sold into

slavery in Tunis. After two years, however, he managed to escape and by 1609 was back in Paris, where he became tutor and chaplain to the Count of Joigny. Subsequently, in 1617, he served as pastor of the parish church at Châtillon-les-Dombes in eastern France. Initially he seemed content to settle for a life of relative ease, but under the influence of Peter de Bérulle (who later became a cardinal), he became determined to devote the rest of his life to the service of the poor. He established a reputation for behaving with equal generosity and compassion towards both the rich and powerful and the poor and needy and in particular used his connections to better conditions for prisoners on galleys. Having come under the influence of St FRANCIS DE SALES, and with funds provided by a wealthy patron he went on, in 1625, to found the Congregation of the Mission (or Vincentians) to provide help for the vulnerable in rural areas and to establish seminaries to provide better training for the clergy. Priests who joined the order were encouraged to preach simply and directly and to renounce their ambitions of preferment within the church. They became known as Lazarists after 1633, when the order was installed in the Paris priory church of Saint-Lazare. Also in 1633 he collaborated with St LOUISE DE MARILLAC in founding the Sisters (or Daughters) of Charity, the first unenclosed order of women dedicated to caring for the poor and sick and now spread worldwide. Funds for the order were raised by an organization of wealthy women donors called the Ladies of Charity. He also promoted tolerance of Protestantism, sent relief to those affected by war in Lorraine, paid ransoms for the release of Christian slaves in Africa, despatched missionaries to Scotland and other foreign countries and served as adviser to Anne of Austria. One of the most celebrated religious figures of his era, St Vincent de Paul was confined to an armchair through illness in his last years, but continued to participate in charitable works and was also prominent in campaigns against heresy. His name is preserved in the Society of St Vincent de Paul, a lay confraternity founded in Paris in 1833 by Frederick Ozanam. He was canonized in 1737 and is honoured as patron saint of all charitable societies.
Feast Day: 27 September.

Vincent Ferrer   (1350–1419) Spanish friar and missionary. Born in Valencia of an English father and Spanish mother, he became a Dominican at the age of 17 and subsequently studied and taught in Barcelona, earning a reputation as a powerful preacher. He then moved to Toulouse to serve as papal legate for Cardinal Pedro de Luna and, when the cardinal became the antipope Benedict XIII, Vincent became his confessor and apostolic penitentiary. He went on to play a crucial role in ending the Great Western Schism that had resulted in the creation of rival popes in Avignon and Rome by withdrawing his support for Benedict after the pope at Rome promised to step down, thus opening the way for the election of a new pope. In 1398 Vincent fell seriously ill and as a result of a vision of the saints DOMINIC and FRANCIS DE SALES he resolved to spend the rest of his life preaching penance for sin and urging the faithful to prepare themselves for divine judgment. After 20 years as a travelling preacher throughout western Europe, attracting huge crowds wherever he went, he returned to Spain and spent another eight years preaching, working miracles and securing the conversion of thousands of Moors and Jews. He died at Vannes in Brittany while on a preaching tour of the region and was canonized in 1455. He is honoured as a patron saint of builders. *Feast Day: 5 April.*

Virgil   (d.784) Irish-born bishop of Salzburg. Virgil (otherwise referred to as **Fergal** or **Vergil**) is thought to have lived as a monk at Aghaboe in Ireland before going abroad around 740 and, after representing Peppin the Short to his defeated rival Duke Odilo of Bavaria, becoming abbot at the monastery of Salzburg. A controversial figure, he clashed with St BONIFACE OF CREDITON on at least two occasions, the second of which concerned Virgil's unorthodox notion that there existed another world beneath the familiar one, complete with its own sun, moon and peoples. Pope St ZACHARIAS was scandalized when these ideas were reported to him by Boniface and subsequently Virgil seems to have adopted a more orthodox philosophy. He was appointed bishop of Salzburg in 767 after the death of Boniface and is remembered as a scholar and leading figure in the evangelization of the province of Carinthia. He was canonized in 1233. *Feast Day: 27 November.*

Vitus, Modestus and Crescentia   (d. *c*.303) Italian martyrs. The exact details of the lives and martyrdom of **Vitus** (sometimes called **Guy**), **Crescentia** and **Modestus** are shrouded in obscurity. It seems that there may have been two saints called Vitus, the earlier Vitus being martyred in Lucania in southern Italy and the second being put to death after cruel torture with his nurse Crescentia and her husband Modestus in Sicily during the reign of Diocletian. One version of the legend has Vitus casting an evil spirit out of the son of Diocletian himself, an act that only served to convince the authorities to have the Christian executed. Whatever the truth of the matter, Vitus became particularly associated with various physical ailments, including epilepsy and chorea (otherwise known as 'St Vitus's dance') and he has long been considered the patron saint of people suffering from such nervous disorders as well as from snakebite or rabies. He is also the patron saint of dancers and actors. His emblem is a cock or a dog.

Feast Day: 15 June.

Vladimir   (955–1015) Prince of Kiev. Born in Scandinavia, the grandson of St OLGA, he had a pagan Viking upbringing but was baptized as a Christian around 989. He married Ann, sister of the Byzantine emperor, and renounced his former bloodthirsty and immoral ways. Vladimir established a reputation as a kindly ruler, who behaved with generosity towards the poor and with mercy towards convicted criminals. He also encouraged missionary work among his people (although he was criticized for imposing Christianity by force on occasion). He is honoured as a patron saint of Russia as well as of converts, kings, murderers and parents of large families.

Feast Day: 15 July.

Walburga   (d.779) English-born abbess of Heidenheim. The daughter of a West Saxon chief and sister of the saints WILLIBALD and WINEBALD, she spent her early adulthood as a nun at Wimborne in Dorset, Walburga (otherwise referred to as **Vaubourg**, **Waldburg** or **Walpurgis**) before being recruited to assist St BONIFACE OF CREDITON in his missionary campaign in Germany. In 761 she was made head of the double monastery of Heidenheim in succession to Winebald, where she remained for the rest of her life. Virtually nothing is known about her life as abbess, although there is a tradition that she was highly skilled in medicine. After her death her bones were said to exude a miraculous clear fluid that continues to be dispensed by Benedictine nuns to selected patients to this day. Walburga is perhaps most familiar today, however, through Walpurgisnacht, the night of 1 May (the date of the removal of her relics to Eichstätt) when witches were formerly reputed to gather on a peak in the Hartz mountains. *Feast Day: 25 February.*

Waldburg   *See* WALBURGA.

Waldetrudis   *See* WAUDRU.

Walpurgis   *See* WALBURGA.

Waudru   (d. *c*.688) Belgian patroness. Waudru (or **Waldetrudis**) was a wealthy married woman who, after her husband Madelgaire became a monk, dedicated herself to caring for the sick and needy of Mons in Belgium. She went on to found a convent in Mons and in due course to achieve sainthood, as did both her parents, her sister and her husband. *Feast Day: 9 April.*

Wenceslas   (907–929) Duke of Bohemia and martyr. Wenceslas (otherwise referred to as **Wenceslaus**, **Vaclav** or **Wenzel**) was the son of Duke Wratislaw of Bohemia and succeeded to the dukedom himself in 922. Having been brought up by his Christian grandmother **Ludmilla**, he did much to encourage his people to assume a Christian way of life. He also established peaceful relations with his German neighbours but met with opposition from pagan nobles within his own land. In 929 he fell out with his brother Boleslav after Wenceslas acknowledged the overlordship of the German king Henry the Fowler, upon which supporters of Boleslav set upon Wenceslas and killed him. The body of Wenceslas was laid to rest in the church of St Vitus in Prague and both Wenceslas and his grand-mother (who had been similarly murdered by pagan enemies in 921) were declared martyrs. The memory of Wenceslas is preserved in the enduringly popular carol 'Good King Wenceslas', although the events depicted are fictional. Wenceslas is honoured as the patron saint of Czech Republic. *Feast Day: 28 September.*

Wenefred   *See* WINIFRED.

Wenzel   *See* WENCESLAS.

Werburga   (d. *c.*700) English abbess. The daughter of King Wulfhere of Mercia and St Ermengild, Werburga became a nun at Ely under ETHELD-REDA and may have become abbess there herself. She seems to have had connections with a number of religious houses, including the nunneries at Weedon in Northamptonshire, Hanbury in Staffordshire and Threck-ingham in Lincolnshire, where she died. Her shrine at Chester became an important site of pilgrimage but was destroyed during the reign of Henry VIII. Her emblem is a goose (referring to the legend that she made a goose leave with just a single word).
Feast Day: 3 February.

Wilfrid   (*c.*633–709) English bishop. Born into a noble family of Northum-bria, Wilfrid (or **Wilfrith**) studied at the monastery of Lindisfarne and in Lyons and Rome before returning to England and, his abilities being quickly recognized, being appointed abbot at Ripon. Here he introduced the rule of St BENEDICT and, at the Synod of Whitby in 664, argued success-fully in favour of the Roman dating of Easter as opposed to the Celtic date. He went on to be appointed bishop of York, replacing St CHAD in the post in 669. In 678 he came into conflict with St THEODORE over the division of the diocese and had to go to Rome to secure papal support for his position (the first time an English bishop ever took a lawsuit to Rome). While on this mission he was diverted to Friesland and spent a year there preaching and evangelizing, in the process winning thousands of converts. On his return to England he was thrown into prison for nine months by King Egfrith of Northumbria (after having encouraged his queen ETHELD-REDA to enter a convent) and was subsequently sent into exile in Sussex. Here he organized evangelical missions among the South Saxons and estab-lished a monastery at Selsey. He was eventually invited back to the north

in 686 but three years later was forced to make another trip to Rome after further disagreements with Egfrith's successor Aldfrith. Forced to retreat to Mercia, he was made bishop of Lichfield and busied himself founding several more monasteries in the Midlands. In 705 he was made bishop of Hexham, a post he retained until his death while visiting a monastery he had founded at Oundle in Northamptonshire. He was buried at Ripon. Though his life was dogged by controversy and conflict with both ecclesiastical and secular powers (not least because of the opulence of his own lifestyle), Wilfrid is remembered as one of the most courageous and visionary leaders of the early English church and as a key figure in bringing the church in England more into line with the church in Rome.
Feast Day: 12 October.

Wilgefortis (dates unknown) Legendary Portuguese princess. Tradition has it that Wilgefortis (sometimes called **Uncumber** in English folklore) was one of the seven daughters of the king of Portugal, a pagan, who promised her in marriage to the king of Sicily. Wilgefortis objected to this match, however, having become a Christian and having made a vow of chastity, and she prayed that she might be made less attractive to her suitor. Accordingly, a beard miraculously sprouted on her face. The king of Sicily duly abandoned his plans to marry her and the enraged king of Portugal had Wilgefortis crucified. Ever since then she has been honoured as the patron saint of wives with troublesome husbands.
Feast Day: 20 July.

Willehad (d.789) English missionary. Born in Northumbria, Willehad was educated in York and subsequently dedicated his life to evangelizing on the continent of Europe. He arrived in Frisia around 766 and eventually settled in Utrecht, where he furthered the work already done by WILLIB-RORD. In 780 he embarked on a mission to foster the spread of Christianity among the Saxons after their conquest by Charlemagne, but this campaign ended within two years in the face of a rebellion and the massacre of many missionaries. Willehad personally reported progress back to the pope in Rome but returned to Germany after the restoration of peace. He became bishop of Bremen in 787 and built a cathedral there before his death.
Feast Day: 8 November.

William of Montevergine (1085–1142) Italian founder. Born into a noble family of Vercelli, William of Montevergine (otherwise called **William of**

Vercelli) was orphaned as a boy and as a young adult settled on life as a hermit. After conducting pilgrimages to Compostela and Jerusalem he spent a period as a hermit at Monte Solicoli (Basilicata) but later moved to Montevergine near Benevento, where he erected a cell and a church. Here he was joined by several other hermits, whom he organized into a small community around 1124. Under his guidance members of this monastic community observed an austere regime, against which they finally rebelled. William then abandoned his monastery and lived an itinerant life throughout southern Italy. He founded several other monasteries, but only the Benedictine abbey of Montevergine has survived. Various legends accrued around his name, including one in which a prostitute was sent to corrupt him: William simply lay himself down on the burning coals of his fire and, unharmed, invited her to join him, upon which the woman was immediately converted.
Feast Day: 25 June.

William of Norwich   (d.1144) English martyr. The legend of William of Norwich was apparently inspired by the discovery in 1144 of the unburied body of a 12-year-old boy in a wood near Norwich. The rumour spread that the boy (a skinner's apprentice from Norwich) had been crucified by local Jews in ritual mockery of Christ's Crucifixion and, despite the refusal of the authorities to accept this story, William of Norwich acquired the status of a martyr in the locality. His cult was relatively shortlived, however, and gradually dwindled after repeated papal refutations of the belief that Jews enacted ritual murders such as this.
Feast Day: (formerly) 26 March.

William of Rochester   (d.1201) Scottish martyr. William of Rochester (or **William of Perth**) was a fisherman of Perth who is said to have lived a devout Christian life as a young man, dedicating himself to charitable works on behalf of orphans and the poor. In 1201 he set out on a pilgrimage to the Holy Land with a young man as his single companion, only to be robbed and murdered by this unnamed individual while they reached Rochester. Various miracles were then reported in association with his corpse, which was laid to rest in Rochester cathedral.
Feast Day: 23 May.

William of Roskilde   (d.1070) English bishop. Details of the life of William of Roskilde are sparse, but it appears that he became a priest and in due course served as chaplain to King Canute, accompanying him on his trips to Scandinavia. Realising the need for renewal of the evangelical effort in Denmark, he eventually settled permanently in that country, accepting the post of bishop of Roskilde (Zeeland). He is said to have shown great courage in confronting the Danish king Sweyn Estridsen after the latter killed some suspected criminals who had sought sanctuary in a church. King Sweyn was duly impressed by the bishop's fortitude and from then collaborated closely with him in promoting the gospel throughout that part of the world. William and Sweyn were eventually buried together at Roskilde cathedral.

Feast Day: 2 September.

William of Vercelli   *See* WILLIAM OF MONTEVERGINE.

William of York   (d.1154) English archbishop. Born into a noble family, William Fitzherbert served as treasurer of York and chaplain to his uncle King Stephen before being appointed archbishop of York in 1140. Unfortunately, his election as archbishop provoked intense opposition from the Cistercians and others, who accused William of simony and immoral behaviour. Pope Innocent II confirmed William's appointment in 1143 but his election remained the cause of continuing resentment. A kindly, easy-going man who was very popular with the common populace, William did not prove a particularly good archbishop, neglecting some of his duties and failing to curb the violence of some of his supporters. After being deposed in 1147, he retired to Winchester and remained there for six years, living quietly as a monk, until restored to his archbishopric. Once back in his post he won respect for his forgiving attitude to his former rivals but died a few months later, possibly as the result of poisoning. Various miracles were subsequently reported at his tomb in York cathedral and he was canonized in 1227.

Feast Day: 8 June.

Willibald   (d.786) English-born bishop of Eichstätt. Born in Wessex, brother of the saints WALBURGA and WINEBALD, Willibald became a monk at Bishops Waltham in Hampshire. He is usually remembered as the first Englishman known to have made a pilgrimage to the Middle East, recording his travels as the *Hodoeporicon*, which he dictated to a nun at Heidenheim. After his experiences in the Middle East and time spent in Rome and Constantinople he assumed the life of a monk in the abbey of Monte Cassino, where he remained for 10 years (730–740). Subsequently he was sent by Pope St Gregory III to Germany to assist St BONIFACE OF CREDITON, who ordained him priest, and for the next 40 years he dedicated himself to pastoral and missionary work (from 742 as bishop of Eichstätt). He also founded monasteries for men and women at Heidenheim based upon the principles established by Boniface.

Feast Day: 7 July.

Willibrord   (658–739) English-born archbishop of Utrecht. Born in York- shire, Willibrord studied at Ripon under St WILFRID before moving to Ireland in 678 and being ordained priest there in 688. In 690 he was one of the first group of English missionaries to travel to Friesland (part of the modern Netherlands) to spread the gospel there. He was made archbishop of the Frisians by the pope in 695 and subsequently established Utrecht as a centre of missionary activity. He went on to found a substantial monas- tery at Echternach in Luxembourg and, despite extensive disruption in the years 715–719 due to war between the Frisians and the Franks, this too became an important religious centre. Encouraged by his success in Fries- land, Willibrord decided to extend his missionary work to Denmark but here experienced greater difficulties and only succeeded in baptizing 30 boys before returning to Friesland. He died at his monastery at Echternach. Willibrord and his contemporary BONIFACE OF CREDITON are remembered as two of the most important early missionary leaders in western Europe and their work laid the foundation for subsequent generations of evangel- ists. Willibrord's memory is celebrated annually by a procession through the streets of Echternach, and he is honoured as the patron saint of Luxembourg and the Netherlands.

Feast Day: 7 November.

Willigis   (d.1011) Archbishop of Mainz. Born into a poor family of Schönin- gen in Brunswick, Willigis became a priest and a canon of Hildesheim near Hanover. In due course he became chaplain to Otto II and, in 971, imperial chancellor. He was made archbishop of Mainz in 975 and did much to promote the Christianization of Schleswig, Holstein, Denmark and Sweden. He proved highly capable as an administrator in both the secular and ecclesiastical spheres, installing efficient bishops and building many churches. He went on to crown Otto III as emperor and then his successors Henry II and his queen Cunegund, serving each loyally. The only negative note was sounded by a prolonged dispute he had with St Bernward of Hildesheim over a question of jurisdiction, which eventually ended with Willigis conceding that he was in the wrong.

Feast Day: 23 February.

Winebald   (d.761) English-born abbot. The brother of the saints WILLIBALD and WALBURGA, Winebald (otherwise referred to as **Winnibald** or **Wynbald**) went on pilgrimage to Rome and remained there for seven years before returning to England. In 739 he and several companions travelled to Thuringia to assist St BONIFACE OF CREDITON in his missionary work there. Winebald was ordained priest and subsequently joined his brother Willibald in founding a Benedictine monastery for both men and women at Heidenheim. With Winebald as its first abbot, this monastery (then the only double monastery in Germany) became an important centre of evangelical activity in the region. After Winebald's death control of the monastery passed to his sister Walburga.
Feast Day: 18 December.

Winifred   (7th century) Welsh maiden. The story of Winifred (otherwise called **Gwenfrewi**, **Wenefred** or **Winefride**) depends almost entirely upon legend. Supposedly a niece of St BEUNO, she attracted the amorous attentions of a chieftain's son named Caradoc. When she spurned his advances the indignant young man struck her head off with his sword, upon which the ground opened beneath his feet and swallowed him up. Beuno replaced Winifred's head and restored her to life and she spent the rest of her days living as a nun at Gwytherin in Derbyshire. The location of these events is traditionally supposed to be Holywell (Treffynnon) in Flintshire and a spring that is said to have burst out at the spot where Winifred's head fell has long been considered a site of miraculous cures, attracting thousands of pilgrims.
Feast Day: 3 November.

Winnibald   *See* WINEBALD.

Winnoc   (d. *c*.717) Welsh abbot. Winnoc (otherwise called **Winnow** or **Wunnoc**) was probably of Welsh birth (although it is possible he was born in Brittany) and is thought to have founded the church of St Winnow in Cornwall before entering the monastery of Sithiu (Saint-Omer) under St BERTIN. Subsequently Bertin chose Winnoc, with three companions, to found a new monastery at Wormhoudt near Dunkirk. His memory is preserved in the placename Saint Winnow, near Lostwithiel.
Feast Day: 6 November.

Winnol   *See* WINWALOE.

Winnow   *See* WINNOC.

Winwaloe   (6th century) French abbot. Winwaloe (otherwise referred to as **Winnol** or **Guénolé**) is traditionally supposed to have been the child of British parents who fled to Brittany before he was born. He is said to have received a religious education from St BUDOC and, after a time spent as a hermit on an island off the Breton coast, in due course to have founded the monastery of Landévennec in Cornouaille, where he served as abbot and eventually died. His memory is preserved in various placenames in Brittany and Cornwall.
Feast Day: 3 March.

Wolfgang   (*c*.924–994) Bishop of Regensburg. Born in Swabia, Wolfgang studied at the abbey of Reichenau on Lake Constance and taught in cathedral schools in Würzburg and Trier before entering the Benedictine monastery at Einsiedeln. In 972, after a brief period as a missionary in Pannonia Superior (Hungary) he was made bishop of Regensburg, in which post he did much to promote standards among the clergy and to reform monastic life in the region. He was much loved for his generosity and widely respected for his great wisdom, even serving as tutor to the future Holy Roman Emperor HENRY II. He died at Puppingen near Linz and was canonized in 1052.
Feast Day: 31 October.

Wulfric of Haselbury   (*c*.1080–1154) English priest and hermit. Wulfric (or **Ulric**) was born at Compton Martin in Somerset and in due course lived as a priest at Deverill, near Warminster. He spent much of his time hunting with hawks and dogs but later gave up this passion in order to adopt a more austere lifestyle. After a time as parish priest back in Compton Martin he opted for the life of a recluse at Haselbury Plucknett, near Exeter. He became well known for his penitential practices, which included sitting for many hours at a time in a tub of cold water. He was also credited with the gifts of prophecy and clairvoyance. Many notable people consulted him in his cell, among them the kings Henry I and Stephen. After his death his cell became a popular site of pilgrimage.
Feast Day: 20 February.

Wulfstan   (*c*.1008–1095) English bishop. Born at Long Itchington in Warwickshire, Wulfstan (or **Wulstan**) studied at the abbeys of Evesham and Peterborough before becoming a Benedictine monk at Worcester. He was appointed prior around 1050 and proved an energetic leader, restoring the priory's finances and reforming the monastic life there. In 1062 his achievements were recognized when he was made bishop of Worcester. A popular and effective bishop, he instituted many reforms and among his many good works opposed the slave trade between Bristol and Viking Ireland, built many new churches and rebuilt Worcester cathedral itself. He managed to retain his post after the Norman Conquest and became a rare example of an Anglo-Saxon to remain in high office after the coronation of William I. After his death Wulfstan's tomb in Worcester cathedral was reportedly the scene of numerous miraculous cures. He was canonized in 1203.

Feast Day: 19 January.

Wunnoc *See* WINNOC.

Wynbald *See* WINEBALD.

Xystus *See* SIXTUS II.

Zachariah   *See* ZECHARIAH AND ELIZABETH.

Zacharias   (d.752) Greek-born pope. Born at San Severino in Calabria, Zacharias served as a deacon in Rome before being elected pope in 741. As pope he demonstrated skill as a diplomat, retrieving lands lost to the Lombard king Liutprand through negotiation and establishing friendly relations with the Franks. He also opposed the iconoclasm of the Emperor Constantine Copronymus, sought an end to the trade in Christian slaves and supported the missionary work of St BONIFACE OF CREDITON in Germany. Two of his letters to Boniface have survived and he was also the author of a translation into Greek of the Dialogues of St GREGORY THE GREAT.
Feast Day: 15 March.

Zechariah and Elizabeth   (1st century) The parents of JOHN THE BAPTIST. Nothing is known of the lives of Zechariah and Elizabeth beyond the details given in St LUKE's Gospel, which identifies Zechariah (alternative names, *Zachariah* or *Zachary*) as a priest in the temple of Jerusalem. Elizabeth is described as a close relative of Jesus' mother Mary and came from the priestly family of Aaron. The elderly couple seemed destined to remain childless until visited by the angel GABRIEL, who told them that Elizabeth would give birth to a son who would prove a new Elijah. When Zechariah refused to believe this he was immediately struck dumb and did not regain his voice until after the baby was born. Zechariah's heartfelt words of thanks upon the birth of John became enshrined as the canticle known as the Benedictus, which begins 'Blessed be the Lord God of Israel . . .' One tradition has it that Zechariah died a martyr in the Temple of Jerusalem on the orders of Herod.
Feast Day: 5 November.

Zeno   (d.371) Bishop of Verona. Born in Africa, he lived as a hermit before being made the first bishop of Verona in 361. As bishop he built several churches, founded a number of nunneries and opposed the heresy of Arianism. He is usually remembered, however, as a preacher whose 93 surviv-

ing sermons (comprising the earliest collection of Latin homilies) provide unique glimpses of Christian ritual and teaching in the 4th century.
Feast Day: 12 April.

Zephyrinus   (d.217) Roman pope. Born in Rome, Zephyrinus succeeded Victor I as pope in 198. Little is known in detail of his papacy, which was characterized by disputes with various heretical sects, notably with Theodotus (whom he excommunicated) and his group the Monarchians, who denied the Trinity. Legend has it that Zephyrinus died a martyr's death during the reign of the emperor Severus, although there is no evidence for this and this may be merely a reflection of the trials he underwent while in office.
Feast Day: (formerly) 26 August.

Zita   (1218–1272) Italian maidservant. Zita (otherwise referred to as **Citha** or **Sitha**) was born into a poor family of Monsagrati near Lucca and spent her life as a maidservant in the house of a wealthy weaver of Lucca. Hardworking and generous to those worse off than herself, she proved initially unpopular with the other servants but gradually won everyone over with her goodness. Many tales were told of Zita's charitable acts and she came to be credited with various miraculous powers. It was commonly said that when she stayed too long at her prayers in church (which she often did) her household chores were performed by angels. By the time of her death Zita was already being considered a saint and she was eventually canonized in 1696. She is honoured as the patron saint of maidservants. Her emblem is a bunch of keys.
Feast Day: 27 April

Zosimus of Syracuse   (d. *c.*660) Sicilian bishop. The son of Sicilian landowners, Zosimus was entrusted to the care of the monastery of Santa Lucia at the age of seven and remained there for the next 30 years, living quietly as a monk and serving as the monastery's doorkeeper. When the abbot of the monastery died the bishop of Syracuse chose the unassuming Zosimus as his successor and he was ordained priest. Zosimus proved a conscientious and able abbot who earned a reputation for his great wisdom and charity. Ultimately, when the bishop himself died in 649 Pope Theodore had Zosimus consecrated as bishop of Syracuse. He died at the age of 90.
Feast Day: 30 March.

INDEXES

Note that the lists below are confined to saints described in the main text.

FEAST DAYS

January
1 Odilo
2 Basil, Gregory of Nazianzus, Seraphim of Sarov
3 Geneviève
4 Elizabeth Seton
5 Edward the Confessor, John of Nepomuk, John Nepomucene Neumann, Simeon the Stylite, Syncletica, Telesphorus
6 Brother André
7 Canute Lavard, Charles of Sezze, Lucian of Antioch, Raymund of Peñafort
8 Gudule, Pega, Severinus of Noricum, Thorfinn
9 Adrian of Canterbury
10 Paul the Hermit, Peter Orseolo
11 Paulinus of Aquileia, Theodosius the Cenobiarch
12 Benedict Biscop, Marguerite Bourgeoys
13 Hilary of Poitiers, Kentigern, Remigius
14 Macrina the Elder, Sava
15 Ita, Macarius the Great
16 Berard and Companions, Fursey, Honoratus of Arles, Marcellus I, Sigebert
17 Antony, Sulpice
18 Margaret of Hungary, Prisca
19 Wulfstan
20 Euthymius the Great, Fabian, Henry of Finland, Sebastian
21 Agnes, Fructuosus of Tarragona, Meinrad
22 Anastasius the Persian, Vincent of Saragossa
23 Ildephonsus of Toledo
24 Francis de Sales
26 Eystein, Paula, Timothy, Titus
27 Angela Merici
28 Peter Nolasco, Thomas Aquinas
29 Gildas

30 Bathild, Sebastian Valfré
31 John Bosco, Maedoc of Ferns, Marcella

February
 1 Brigid
 2 Catherine dei Ricci, Joan de Lestonnac, Théophane Vénard, Martyrs of
   Vietnam
 3 Anskar, Blaise, Ia, Werburga
 4 Andrew Corsini, Gilbert of Sempringham, Isidore of Pelusium, Joan of
   France, John de Britto, Phileas
 5 Agatha
 6 Amand, Dorothy, Paul Miki and Lawrence Ruiz, Vedast
 8 Cuthman, Jerome Emiliani
 9 Apollonia, Teilo
10 Scholastica
11 Benedict of Aniane, Caedmon, Gregory II
12 Julian the Hospitaller
13 Lawrence of Canterbury
14 Cyril and Methodius, Valentine
15 Claude La Colombière, Jordan of Saxony, Sigfrid
16 Juliana
17 Finan, Fintan of Clonenagh, Seven Founders
18 Colman of Lindisfarne
20 Wulfric of Haselbury
21 Peter Damian, Robert Southwell
22 Margaret of Cortona
23 Milburga, Polycarp, Willigis
25 Ethelbert of Kent, Walburga
26 Alexander
27 Gabriel Francis Possenti, Leander
28 Angela of Foligno, Oswald of Worcester

March
 1 David
 2 Chad, Henry Suso
 3 Aelred, Cunegund, Katharine Drexel, Marinus, Winwaloe
 4 Casimir
 5 Ciaran of Saighir, John Joseph of the Cross, Piran
 6 Chrodegang, Colette

7 Perpetua and Felicity

8 Felix of Dunwich, John of God, Senan of Scattery

9 Catherine of Bologna, Dominic Savio, Four Crowned Martyrs, Frances of Rome, Gregory of Nyssa, Pacian of Barcelona

10 (suppressed 1969) Frances of Rome, John Ogilvie

11 Eulogius of Cordoba, Oengus the Culdee, Pionius Sophronius, Theresa Margaret of the Sacred Heart

12 Paul Aurelian, Simeon the New Theologian

13 Euphrasia

15 Clement-Mary Hofbauer, Louise de Marillac, Zacharias

17 Gertrude of Nivelles, Patrick

18 Cyril of Jerusalem, Edward the Martyr

19 Joseph

20 Cuthbert, Martin of Braga

21 Enda, Nicholas von Flue, Serapion of Thmuis

23 Gwinear, Toribio of Lima

24 Catherine of Sweden

25 Dismas

26 Braulio, Ludger, (formerly) William of Norwich

27 John the Egyptian, Rupert

28 Stephen Harding

30 John Climacus, Osburga, Zosimus of Syracuse

April

1 Hugh of Grenoble, Mary of Egypt

2 Francis of Paola

3 Agape, Chionia and Irene, Richard of Chichester

4 Benedict the Black, Isidore of Seville

5 Vincent Ferrer

6 Irenaeus of Sirmium

7 Aphraates of Persia, John-Baptist de La Salle

8 Julie Billiart

9 Waudru

10 Hedda of Peterborough

11 Gemma Galgani, Guthlac, Stanislas of Cracow

12 Julius I, Teresa of the Andes, Zeno

13 Carpus, Papylus and Agathonice, Margaret of Castello, Martin I

14 Bénézet

15 Damien de Veuster

16 Benedict Joseph Labre, Bernadette, Magnus
17 Donnan
19 Alphege, Leo IX
20 Agnes of Montepulciano
21 Anselm, Beuno
22 Conrad of Parzham, Theodore of Sykeon
23 Adalbert of Prague, George
24 Egbert, Euphrasia Pelletier, Fidelis of Sigmaringen, Mellitus
25 Mark
26 Cletus
27 Maughold, Zita
28 Louis Grignion de Montfort, Peter Chanel
29 Catherine of Siena, Hugh of Cluny, Robert of Molesme
30 Erconwald, Marie of the Incarnation, Pius V

May
 1 Asaph, Brieuc, Joseph, Ultan
 2 Athanasius, Mafalda of Portugal
 3 Elizabeth Leseur, James the Less, Philip, Theodosius of the Caves
 4 Gothard, Hallvard
 5 Hilary of Arles
 6 Marian and James
 7 John of Beverley
 8 Peter of Tarentaise
 9 Pachomius
10 Antoninus, Comgall, John of Avila
11 (Ireland) Comgall, Francis di Girolamo, Ignatius of Laconi, Mayeul
12 Epiphanius of Salamis, Germanus of Constantinople, Nereus and
   Achilleus, Pancras, Ubaldo
13 Andrew Fournet, Julian of Norwich
14 Matthias
15 Isidore the Farmer
16 Andrew Bobola, Brendan the Voyager, Simon Stock, Ubaldo
17 Paschal Baylon
18 Eric, John I
19 Celestine V, Dunstan, Ivo of Brittany
20 Bernardino of Siena
21 Godric
22 John Fisher, Rita of Cascia

23 Euphrosyne of Polotsk, John Baptist Rossi, Montanus and Lucius, William of Rochester
24 David of Scotland, Vincent of Lérins
25 Aldhelm, Venerable Bede, Gregory VII, Madeleine Sophie Barat, Mary MacKillop, Mary Magdalen dei Pazzi, Urban
26 (England) Augustine of Canterbury, Mariana, Philip Neri
27 Augustine of Canterbury, Julius of Durostorum
28 Germanus of Paris
30 Dympna, Ferdinand III of Castile, Hubert, Joan of Arc

June

1 Justin, Pamphilus
2 Blandina, Erasmus, Martyrs of Lyons, Marcellinus and Peter, Oda, Pothinus
3 Charles de Foucauld, Charles Lwanga and Companions, Clotilde, Genesius of Arles, John XXIII, Kevin
4 Francis Caracciolo, Petroc
5 Boniface of Crediton
6 Jarlath of Tuam, Norbert
7 Matt Talbot, Meriasek, Robert of Newminster
8 William of York
9 Columba of Iona, Diana D'Andalo, Ephraem, Pelagia of Antioch, Primus and Felician
11 Barnabas
12 Eskil, John of Sahagun, Leo III
13 Antony of Padua
14 Francis Solano
15 Edburga of Winchester, Germaine of Pibrac, Vitus, Modestus and Crescentia
16 Cyricus and Julitta, John Regis, Lutgard
18 Elizabeth of Schönau, Mark and Marcellian
19 Gervase and Protase, Juliana Falconieri, Romuald of Ravenna
20 Adalbert of Magdeburg, Osanna of Mantua
21 Aloysius, Méen
22 Alban, John Fisher, Nicetas of Remesiana, Paulinus of Nola, Thomas More
23 Etheldreda, Joseph Cafasso
24 John the Baptist
25 Maximus of Turin, Prosper of Aquitaine, William of Montevergine
26 Anthelm, John and Paul, Josemaría Escrivá

27 Cyril of Alexandria
28 Irenaeus of Lyons, Potamiaena and Basilides
29 Paul, Peter
30 Josemaría Escrivá

July

1 Junípero Serra, Oliver Plunket
2 Swithun
3 Thomas
4 Andrew of Crete, Elizabeth of Portugal, Pier Giorgio Frassati, Ulric of
  Augsburg
5 Antony Zaccaria, Athanasius the Athonite
6 Godelive, Maria Goretti, Modwenna, Moninne, Sexburga
7 Hedda of Winchester, Palladius, Willibald
9 Veronica Giuliani
10 Canute IV
11 Benedict, Olga, Martyrs of Vietnam
12 John Gualbert, Veronica
13 Eugenius of Carthage, Henry II, Mildred, Silas
14 Camillus, Humbert of Romans, Kateri Tekawitha, Nicodemus of the Holy
   Mountain
15 Bonaventure, Donald, Felix of Thibiuca, Vladimir
16 Eustathius, Helier
17 Alexis, Kenelm, Scillitan martyrs
18 Arnulf of Metz
19 Arsenius, Macrina the Younger
20 Margaret of Antioch, Wilgefortis
21 Lawrence of Brindisi, Victor of Marseilles
22 Mary Magdalen
23 Apollinaris of Ravenna, Bridget, John Cassian
24 Boris and Gleb
25 Christopher, James the Greater
26 Joachim and Ann, Titus Brandsma
27 Celestine I, Pantaleon, Seven Sleepers
28 Botvid, Samson
29 Lazarus, Lupus of Troyes, Martha, Olaf, (formerly) Simplicius, Faustinus
   and Beatrice
30 Peter Chrysologus
31 Germanus of Auxerre, Ignatius of Loyola, Neot

August

1 Alphonsus Liguori, Ethelwold, Peter Favre
2 Eusebius of Vercelli, Stephen I
3 Peter Eymard
4 John-Baptist Marie Vianney
5 Afra
6 Hormisdas, Sixtus II
7 Cajetan
8 Dominic
9 Oswald of Northumbria
10 Edith Stein, Lawrence, Philomena
11 Blane, Clare of Assisi, John Henry Newman
13 Hippolytus, John Berchmans, Maximus the Confessor, Pontian, Radegund
14 Maximilian Kolbe
15 Hyacinth of Cracow, Mary
16 Roch, Stephen of Hungary
17 Clare of Montefalco
18 Alipius, Helen
19 John Eudes
20 Bernard of Clairvaux, Oswin, Philibert
21 Pius X
22 Philip Benizi, Symphorian
23 Rose of Lima
24 Bartholomew, Emily de Vialar, Joan Thouret, Ouen
25 Genesius the Actor, Louis IX
26 Elizabeth Bichier des Âges, Fillan, Maximillian, Ninian, Tarsicius
   (formerly) Zephyrinus
27 Caesarius of Arles, Little Saint Hugh, Monica
28 Augustine of Hippo, Hermes, Joaquina, Moses the Black
29 Sebbi
30 Felix and Adauctus, Fiacre, Pammachius
31 Aidan, Cuthburga, Joseph of Arimathea, Raymund Nonnatus

September

1 Beatrice da Silva, (France and Ireland) Fiacre, Giles
2 William of Roskilde
3 Gregory the Great
4 Rose of Viterbo
5 Bertin, Lawrence Giustiniani

 7 Cloud
 8 Adrian and Natalia, Frederic Ozanam, Thomas of Villanueva
 9 Ciaran of Clonmacnoise, Omer, Peter Claver
10 Aubert of Avranches, Finnian of Moville, Nicholas of Tolentino
11 Deiniol, John Gabriel Perboyre, Paphnutius, Protus and Hyacinth
12 Guy of Anderlecht
13 Eulogius of Alexandria, John Chrysostom, Notburga
15 Catherine of Genoa, Nicomedes
16 Cornelius, Cyprian, Edith of Wilton
17 Hildegard of Bingen, Francis of Comporosso, Lambert, Robert Bellarmine
18 Joseph of Cupertino, Juan Macías, Methodius of Olympus
19 Alphonsus de Orozco, Emily de Rodat, Januarius, Theodore of Canterbury
20 (formerly) Eusebius of Vercelli, Martyrs of Korea
21 Matthew
22 Maurice, Phocas
23 Adamnan, Linus, Padre Pio, Thecla of Iconium
24 Gerard of Csanad
25 Cadoc, Euphrosyne, Finbar, Sergius of Radonezh
26 Cosmas and Damian, Cyprian and Justina, Isaac Jogues, John de Brébeuf,
   Nilus of Rossano, Martyrs of North America
27 Elzear, Sigebert, Vincent de Paul
28 Eustochium, Faustus of Riez, Lioba, Wenceslas
29 Gabriel the Archangel, Michael the Archangel, Raphael the Archangel
30 Gregory the Enlightener, Honorius, Jerome, Otto of Bamberg

October
 1 Bavo, Nicetius of Trier, Theresa of Lisieux
 2 Leger, Thomas of Hereford
 3 Hewald the Black, Hewald the White
 4 Ammonas the Hermit, Francis of Assisi
 5 Faustina Kowalska, Maurus, Placid, Raymond of Capua
 6 Bruno, Faith
 7 Osyth
 8 Demetrius, Keyne, Pelagia the Penitent, Thais
 9 Denis, John Leonardi, Louis Bertrand
10 Francis Borgia, Gereon, Paulinus of York
11 Canice, Ethelburga of Barking
12 Edwin, Wilfrid
13 Agostina Pietrantoni, Gerald of Aurillac

14 Callistus I
15 Euthymius the Younger, Teresa of Avila
16 Gall, Gerard Majella, Hedwig, Lull, Margaret Mary Alacoque, Marguerite d'Youville
17 Ignatius of Antioch
18 Justus of Beauvais, Luke
19 Frideswide, Paul of the Cross, Peter of Alcántara
20 Bertilla Boscardin
21 Hilarion, John of Bridlington, (formerly) Ursula
22 Donatus of Fiesole, Philip of Heraclea
23 Felicity of Rome, John of Capistrano, Severinus Boethius
24 Antony Mary Claret, Proclus
25 Crispin and Crispinian, Edmund Arrowsmith, Edmund Campion, Forty Martyrs of England and Wales, Gaudentius of Brescia, Margaret Clitherow
26 Cedd
27 Frumentius, Ia
28 Jude, Simon the Zealot
30 Alphonsus Rodriguez, Marcellus the Centurion
31 Foillan, Quentin, Wolfgang

November
 1 Benignus
 2 Eustace
 3 Malachy, Winifred
 4 Charles Borromeo
 5 Martin de Porres, Zechariah and Elizabeth
 6 Illtyd, Leonard, Martyrs of Vietnam, Winnoc
 7 Willibrord
 8 Cybi, Elizabeth of the Trinity, Forty Martyrs of Sebaste, Godfrey, Willehad
 9 Theodore
10 Andrew Avellino, Justus of Canterbury, Leo the Great
11 John the Almsgiver, Martin of Tours, Mennas, Theodore the Studite
12 Josaphat, Nilus of Ancyra
13 Brice, Frances Xavier Cabrini, Homobonus, Nicholas I, Stanislas Kostka
14 Dyfrig, Gregory Palamas, Lawrence O'Toole
15 Albert the Great, Felix of Nola, Leopold III, Malo
16 Edmund of Abingdon, Eucherius of Lyons, Gertrude, Margaret of Scotland

17 Dionysius of Alexandria, Elizabeth of Hungary, Gregory of Tours, Gregory the Wonderworker, Hilda, Hugh of Lincoln
18 Mawes, Odo of Cluny
19 Mechtilde of Helfta, Roque Gonzalez
20 Edmund
21 Columban, Gelasius I
22 Cecilia
23 Alexander Nevsky, Clement I, (Ireland) Columban, Felicity of Rome, Miguel Pro
24 Chrysogonus, Martyrs of Vietnam
25 Catherine of Alexandria
26 Leonard of Port Maurice, Silvester Gozzoli
27 Gregory of Sinai, Virgil
28 Catherine Labouré, Gregory III, James of the March
29 Sernin
30 Andrew

December
 1 Eloi
 2 John Ruysbroeck
 3 Birinus, Francis Xavier
 4 Barbara, John Damascene, Osmund
 5 Clement of Alexandria, Crispina, Sabas of Jerusalem
 6 Nicholas
 7 Ambrose
 8 Budoç
 9 Juan Diego, Peter Fourier
10 Eulalia of Merida, Miltiades
11 Damasus I, Daniel the Stylite
12 Edburga of Minster, Finnian of Clonard, Jane Frances de Chantal, Vicelin
13 Lucy
14 John of the Cross, Odilia, Venantius Fortunatus
15 Mary di Rosa
16 Adelaide, Charles de Foucauld, Mary of the Angels
17 Olympias, Sturm
18 Flannan, Winebald
21 Peter Canisius
23 John of Kanti, Thorlac of Skalholt
24 Charbel Makhlouf

25 Anastasia, Eugenia
26 Stephen
27 Fabiola, John
28 Holy Innocents
29 Thomas Becket
30 Egwin
31 Melania the Younger, Silvester I

EMBLEMS

Anchor	Clement I
Anvil	Eloi
Apparition of the Lord	Ignatius of Loyola
Arrow	Edmund, Giles, Sebastian, Teresa of Avila
Axe	Matthias
Ball of fire	Martin of Tours
Barrel of salt	Rupert
Basket of fruit and flowers	Dorothy
Bear	Columban
Beehive	Bernard of Clairvaux, John Chrysostom
Birds	Francis of Assisi
Boat	Simon the Zealot
Book	Ignatius of Loyola, Paul, Teresa of Avila
Book of the Gospels	Stephen
Breasts on dish	Agatha
Broken cup	Benedict
Broken heart	Augustine of Hippo
Broom	Martha
Bull	Silvester I
Bunch of keys	Martha, Zita
Butcher's knife	Bartholomew
Camel	Hormisdas
Candle	Geneviève
Cardinal's hat	Bonaventure
Chalice	Hugh of Lincoln
Chasuble	Ignatius of Loyola
Child in cradle	Hilary of Poitiers
Club	Jude, Timothy
Cobbler's last	Crispin and Crispinian
Cock	Vitus

Cow	Brigid
Cross	Helen
Cross saltire	Andrew
Crossed keys	Peter
Crown	Leopold III
Crowned skull	Francis Borgia
Dog	Dominic, Vitus
Dove	David
Dragon	George, Leo the Great, Margaret of Antioch, Martha, Silvester I
Eagle	John
Falchion	Simon the Zealot
Fire	Brice
Fish and key	Egwin
Fish and ring	Kentigern
Fishing net	Andrew
Fuller's club	James the Less
Goose	Martin of Tours, Werburga
Gridiron	Lawrence
Halberd	Matthias
Hammer	Eloi
Heart	Teresa of Avila
Holy Communion	Ignatius of Loyola
Horseshoe	Eloi
Jar of ointment	Mary Magdalen
Ladder to heaven	Bathild
Ladle	Martha
Lamb	Agnes, John the Baptist
Lily	Dominic
Lion	Jerome
Loaves of bread	Philip
Model of a church	Leopold III
Monstrance	Norbert
Pair of camels	Mennas
Pig	Antony
Pilgrim's hat	James the Greater
Plough	Isidore the Farmer
Raven	Benedict
Raven with ring	Oswald of Northumbria

Ray of light	Bruno
Ring	Edward the Confessor
Roses	Rita of Cascia
Scales	Antonino
Scallop-shell	James the Greater
Shamrock	Patrick
Shield	Gabriel
Ship	Anselm, Bertin
Shoe	Crispin and Crispinian
Sickle	Isidore the Farmer, Notburga
Snakes	Patrick
Spade	Fiacre, Isidore the Farmer
Spear	Gabriel
Staff with mouse	Gertrude of Nivelles
Stag	Aidan, Hubert, Petroc
Star	Dominic, Thomas Aquinas
Stone	Stephen, Timothy
Supernatural fire	Basil
Swan	Hugh of Lincoln
Sword	Paul
Three gold balls	Nicholas
Three loaves	Mary of Egypt
Tiara	Silvester I
Tooth in forceps	Apollonia
Tower	Barbara
Wheel	Catherine of Alexandria
Windlass	Erasmus
Winged lion	Mark
Winged man	Matthew
Winged ox	Luke
Wool-comb	Blaise

PATRON SAINTS

Abandoned children	Jerome Emiliani
Abused parents	Clotilde
Accountants	Matthew
Actors	Vitus
Adopted children	Clotilde, Thomas More
Aids sufferers	Aloysius, Theresa of Lisieux

Air crews	Theresa of Lisieux
Air travellers	Joseph of Cupertino
Alcoholics	Monica
Altar servers	John Berchmans, Tarsicius
Animals	Francis of Assisi
Apothecaries	James the Less
Apprentices	John Bosco
Archeology	Damasus I
Archers	Sebastian
Architects	Thomas
Artists	Catherine of Bologna, Luke
Astronomers	Dominic
Bakers	Elizabeth of Hungary
Barbers	Cosmas and Damian, Louis IX
Beekeepers	Ambrose, Valentine
Beggars	Elizabeth of Hungary, Giles, Martin of Tours
Bell-founders	Agatha
Benedictine nunneries	Scholastica
Bereaved parents	Clotilde, Holy Innocents
Betrothed couples	Agnes, Valentine
Biblical scholars	Jerome
Birds	Gall
Bishops of Latin America	Toribio of Lima
Blacksmiths	Brigid, Dunstan, Eloi, Giles, James the Greater
Blessed Sacrament	Tarsicius
Blind people	Clare of Assisi, Dunstan, Lucy, Odilia, Raphael the Archangel
Blood banks	Januarius
Bookbinders	Bartholomew, Columba of Iona
Bookkeepers	Matthew
Booksellers	John of God, Thomas Aquinas
Brewers	Amand, Boniface of Crediton
Brides	Clotilde, Dorothy, Elizabeth of Portugal, Nicholas
Bridge-builders	Peter
Builders	Louis IX, Thomas, Vincent Ferrer
Butchers	Luke
Cabinetmakers	Ann
Cambridge University	Etheldreda

Cancer victims	Bernard of Clairvaux
Candlemakers	Ambrose
Canon lawyers	Raymund of Peñafort
Carpenters	Joseph
Catholic press	Francis de Sales
Cattle	Cornelius, Roch
Cave explorers	Benedict
Charities	Elizabeth of Hungary, Vincent de Paul
Childbirth	Margaret of Antioch
Children	Bathild, Nicholas, Pancras
Choirboys	Dominic Savio
Christian youth	Aloysius
Circus performers	Julian the Hospitaller
Clerics	Gabriel Francis Possenti
Clockmakers	Peter
Clothworkers	Homobonus
Cobblers	Bartholomew, Crispin and Crispinian
Computer users	Isidore of Seville
Confessors	Alphonsus Liguori
Converts	Alban, Vladimir
Cooks	Lawrence
Cripples	Giles
Customs officers	Matthew
Cutlers	Lawrence
Dancers	Vitus
Deacons	Stephen
Dead children	Holy Innocents, Isidore the Farmer
Dentists	Apollonia
Desert caravans	Mennas
Desperate situations	Gregory the Wonderworker, Rita of Cascia
Difficult marriages	Monica, Rita of Cascia, Wilgefortis
Disaster victims	Geneviève
Distillers	Louis IX
Doctors	Raphael the Archangel
Domestic livestock	Cornelius
Drought victims	Geneviève
Drug addicts	Maximilian Kolbe
Dying people	James the Less
Earache sufferers	Polycarp

Ecologists	Francis of Assisi
Ecology and environment	Kateri Tekawitha
Embroiderers	Louis IX
Eucharist	Paschal Baylon
Exiles	Clotilde, Joaquina, Rose of Viterbo
Falsely accused	Dominic Savio, Margaret of Cortona
Farmers	Isidore the Farmer
Farriers	John the Baptist
Fathers	Joseph
Ferrymen	Julian the Hospitaller
Firefighters	Barbara
Fishermen	Andrew, Peter
Florists	Dorothy, Rose of Lima, Theresa of Lisieux
Foreign missions	Francis Xavier, Theresa of Lisieux
French monarchy	Louis IX
Fullers	James the Less
Funeral directors	Dismas
Furriers	Bartholomew
Gardeners	Agnes, Fiacre, Gertrude of Nivelles, Rose of Lima
Glaziers	Lawrence, Lucy, Mark
Goldsmiths	Dunstan
Grooms	Hormisdas, Louis IX
Gunners	Barbara
Haberdashers	Louis IX
Hairdressers	Louis IX
Hatters	James the Less
Headache sufferers	Stephen
Healers	Brigid
Hired hands	Notburga
Homeless	Benedict Joseph Labre, Margaret of Cortona
Hospitals	Catherine of Alexandria, Jude
Housewives	Ann, Martha
Human race	Mary
Hunters	Eustace, Hubert
Immigrants	Frances Xavier Cabrini
Innkeepers	Julian the Hospitaller, Martin of Tours
Insane people	Dympna
Irish women	Brigid

Italian hospitals	Catherine of Genoa
Jesuit order	Ignatius of Loyola
Jewellers	Dunstan
Kings	Louis IX, Stephen of Hungary, Vladimir
Knights Hospitallers	John the Baptist
Labourers	James the Greater, John Bosco
Lacemakers	Elizabeth of Hungary, Teresa of Avila
Lawyers	Thomas More
Lay sisters	Martha
Lead-founders	Fabian
Learning	Ambrose
Leatherworkers	Crispin and Crispinian
Librarians	Catherine of Alexandria, Jerome, Raymund of Peñafort
Lighthouses	Clement of Alexandria
Livestock	Isidore the Farmer
Local rulers	Ferdinand III of Castile
Locksmiths	Dunstan
Lost articles	Antony of Padua
Lost causes	Jude
Maidservants	Zita
Manual workers	Joseph
Martyrs	Agostina Pietrantoni
Masons	Louis IX, Peter, Stephen
Medical social workers	John Regis
Medical workers	Pantaleon
Mentally ill	Benedict Joseph Labre
Merchants	Mennas, Nicholas
Metalworkers	Eloi
Midwives	Dorothy, Margaret of Cortona, Raymund Nonnatus
Milliners	James the Less
Miners	Barbara
Missionaries	Leonard of Port Maurice, Peter Claver
Moral theologians	Alphonsus Liguori
Mothers	Monica
Motorists	Christopher
Murderers	Vladimir
Music	Cecilia

Musicians	Benedict Biscop, Cecilia, Dunstan, Gregory the Great
Needleworkers	Louis IX
Nervous disorders	Vitus
Nightwatchmen	Peter of Alcántara
Notaries	Mark
Nurses	Camillus, John of God, Raphael the Archangel
Nursing services	Catherine of Siena
Old maids	Andrew
Orphans	Jerome Emiliani
Oxford University	Frideswide
Painters	Benedict Biscop
Papacy	Peter
Parents of large families	Clotilde, Margaret of Scotland, Vladimir
Parish priests	John-Baptist Marie Vianney
Pawnbrokers	Nicholas
Penitent women	Afra
Pharmacists	Gemma Galgani, James the Less
Philosophers	Catherine of Alexandria, Justin, Thomas Aquinas
Physicians	Cosmas and Damian, Luke
Pilgrims	James the Greater, Pius X
Poetry	Cecilia
Poets	Brigid, Columba of Iona, David
Poor	Ferdinand III of Castile
Post office	Gabriel the Archangel
Potters	Catherine of Alexandria, Fabian
Preachers	Catherine of Alexandria, John Chrysostom
Pregnant women	Leonard
Prisoners	Beatrice da Silva, Dismas, Ferdinand III of Castile, Joan of Arc, Joseph Cafasso, Leonard, Louis IX, Mark
Purse-makers	Brieuc
Queens	Clotilde, Elizabeth of Portugal, Margaret of Scotland
Rabies sufferers	Hubert, Vitus
Race relations	Martin de Porres
Recently deceased	Gertrude of Nivelles
Rejects of religious orders	Marguerite Bourgeoys, Rose of Viterbo

Retarded children	Hilary of Poitiers
Retreats	Ignatius of Loyola
Runaways	Dympna
Saddlers	Paul
Sailors	Brendan the Voyager, Cuthbert, Erasmus, Francis of Paola, Nicholas, Phocas
Salesmen	Lucy
Scholars	Bede
Schoolgirls	Ursula
Schools	Thomas Aquinas
Sculptors	Louis IX
Security guards	Matthew
Servants	Martha
Shipbuilders	Peter
Sick children	Hugh of Lincoln
Sick people	Camillus, John of God, Louis IX, Michael the Archangel, Roch
Singers	Gregory the Great
Single laywomen	Margaret of Cortona
Sinners	Mary Magdalen
Sisters of Mercy	Elizabeth of Hungary
Snakebite cures	Hilary of Poitiers
Snakebite sufferers	Vitus
Social justice	Martin de Porres
Social workers	Louise de Marillac
Soldiers	Ignatius of Loyola, Joan of Arc, Louis IX, Martin of Tours, Michael the Archangel, Sebastian
Spinners	Catherine of Alexandria
Spiritual exercises	Ignatius of Loyola
Stable-boys	Hormisdas
Stomach ailments	Erasmus
Stroke victims	Andrew Avellino
Students	Aloysius, Isidore of Seville, Joseph of Cupertino, Thomas Aquinas
Students of natural science	Albert the Great
Surgeons	Cosmas and Damian, Luke
Tailors	Boniface of Crediton, Homobonus, John the Baptist

Tanners	Bartholomew
Tax collectors	Matthew
Teachers	Gregory the Great, John Baptist de La Salle
Teenaged girls	Maria Goretti
Telecommunication workers	Gabriel the Archangel
Television	Clare of Assisi
Tent-makers	Paul
Tertiaries	Margaret of Cortona
Theologians	Augustine of Hippo, John, Thomas, Thomas Aquinas
Therapists	Dismas
Tin miners	Piran
Trappers	Hubert
Travellers	Christopher, Gertrude of Nivelles, Joseph, Nicholas, Raphael the Archangel, Valentine
Tuberculosis sufferers	Gemma Galgani
Undertakers	Dismas
Universities	Thomas Aquinas
Veneral disease sufferers	Fiacre
Victims of abuse	Agostina Pietrantoni, Joaquina
Victims of torture	Alban
Victims of unfaithful marriages	Elizabeth of Portugal, Marguerite d'Youville, Monica
Virgins	Agnes, Joan of Arc
Wanderers	Julian the Hospitaller
Washerwomen	Veronica
Wet-nurses	Agatha
Widows	Elizabeth of Portugal, Elizabeth Seton, Joaquina, Margaret of Scotland, Marguerite d'Youville, Monica
Winemakers	Amand
Women in labour	Ann
Writers	Francis de Sales, John, Lucy
Young girls	Catherine of Alexandria
Young people	Valentine
Young women	Ursula
Youth	Dominic Savio, Gabriel Francis Possenti, John Berchmans

PATRON SAINTS OF PLACES

Africa (central)	Mary
Africa (northern)	Cyprian
Africa (eastern)	Mary
Albania	Mary
Alexandria	Cyril of Alexandria
Algeria	Cyprian
Alsace	Odilia
Antwerp	Mary
Aragon	Braulio
Argentina	Francis Solano, Mary
Armenia	Gregory the Enlightener
Assisi	Francis of Assisi
Australia	Mary, Peter Chanel
Austria	Leopold III
Avignon	Bénézet
Belarus	Euphrosyne of Polotsk
Belgrade	Demetrius
Bohemia	John of Nepomuk, Norbert
Bolivia	Francis Solano
Brazil	Mary, Peter of Alcántara
Brittany	Ann
Brussels	Gudule, Michael the Archangel
Bulgaria	Cyril and Methodius
Canada	Ann
Catania	Agatha
Chile	Francis Solano, James the Greater
China	Joseph
Colombia	Louis Bertrand, Mary
Cornwall	Piran
Cracow	Stanislas of Cracow
Cremona	Homobonus
Cuba	Mary
Cyprus	Barnabas
Czech Republic	Wenceslas
Denmark	Anskar, Canute IV
Dublin	Kevin
Ecuador	Mary

England	(formerly) Edmund, (formerly) Edward the Confessor, George
Estremadura	Peter of Alcántara
Europe	Benedict, Cyril and Methodius
Finland	Henry of Finland
France	Denis, Joan of Arc, Martin of Tours, Mary, Theresa of Lisieux
Genoa	Catherine of Genoa, George
Germany	Boniface of Crediton
Gibraltar	Bernard of Clairvaux
Glasgow	Kentigern
Greece	Andrew, Nicholas, Paul
Guatemala	James the Greater
Hungary	Stephen of Hungary
Iceland	Anskar
India	Francis Xavier
Indonesia	Mary
Ireland	Columba of Iona, Patrick
Italy	Catherine of Siena, Francis of Assisi
Lima	Rose of Lima
Lithuania	Casimir, Cunegund, Stanislas Kostka
London	Erconwald
Luxembourg	Cunegund, Mary, Willibrord
Madrid	Isidore the Farmer
Magdeburg	Norbert
Majorca	Alphonsus Rodriguez
Malta	Paul
Montepulciano	Agnes of Montepulciano
Moscow	Nicholas, Sergius of Radonezh
Naples	Andrew Avellino, Januarius, John Joseph of the Cross
Netherlands	Willibrord
New Zealand	Mary, Peter Chanel
Nicaragua	James the Greater
Norway	Magnus of Norway, Olaf
Oceania	Peter Chanel
Oslo	Hallvard
Pakistan	Francis Xavier
Palermo	Benedict the Black

Palestine	Mary
Paraguay	Francis Solano, Mary
Paris	Geneviève, Germanus of Paris
Peru	Francis Solano, Joseph, Rose of Lima, Toribio of Lima
Poland	Adalbert of Prague, Casimir, Mary, Stanislas of Cracow
Portugal	Antony of Padua, Francis Borgia, George, Mary, Vincent of Saragossa
Prussia	Adalbert of Prague
Romania	Cyril and Methodius
Rome	Catherine of Siena, Lawrence, Peter and Paul, Philip Neri
Russia	Andrew, Basil, Nicholas, Sergius of Radonezh, Vladimir
St Petersburg	Alexander Nevsky
Scotland	Andrew, Margaret of Scotland
Serbia	Sava
South America	Rose of Lima
Spain	George, James the Greater, Mary
Sri Lanka	Lawrence, Mary
Sweden	Bridget, Eric, Gall
Switzerland	Gall, Nicholas von Flue
Turkey	John the Baptist, John Chrysostom
United States of America	Mary
Uruguay	James the Less, Mary, Philip
Venezuela	Mary
Venice	George, Mark
Vienna	Clement-Mary Hofbauer
Wales	David
West Indies	Gertrude
Westphalia	Hewald the Black, Hewald the White

PLACES IN BRITAIN AND IRELAND ASSOCIATED WITH SAINTS

Abernethy	Donald
Abingdon	Edmund of Abingdon, Ethelwold
Aghaboe	Canice
Amesbury	Edith of Wilton

Andressey Island	Modwenna
Anglesey	Cybi
Annadown	Brendan the Voyager
Armagh	Brigid, Moninne
Aranmore	Cybi
Ardfert	Brendan the Voyager
Armagh	Malachy, Oliver Plunket, Patrick
Aylesford	Simon Stock
Bamburgh	Aidan
Bangor	Columban, Comgall, Deiniol, Gall
Bangor Fawr	Deiniol
Bangor Iscoed	Deiniol
Bardsey Island	Deiniol, Dyfrig
Barking	Edith of Wilton, Erconwald, Ethelburga of Barking
Barra	Finbar
Bath	Alphege
Berkshire	Edmund Campion
Beverley	John of Beverley, John Fisher
Bishops Waltham	Willibald
Bodmin Moor	Neot, Petroc
Boyne valley	Enda
Bradwell-on-Sea	Cedd
Bridlington	John of Bridlington
Burgh Castle	Foillan, Fursey, Sigebert, Ultan
Burton-on-Trent	Modwenna
Bury St Edmunds	Edmund
Bute	Blane
Caerleon	Dyfrig
Caldey Island	Samson
Camborne	Meriasek
Cambridge	Etheldreda, John Fisher, Simon Stock, Thomas More
Canterbury	Adrian of Canterbury, Aldhelm, Alphege, Anselm, Augustine of Canterbury, Benedict Biscop, Dunstan, Edmund of Abingdon, Honorius, John of Beverley, Justus of Canterbury, Lawrence of Canterbury, Mellitus, Oda, Oswald of Worcester, Paulinus of York, Richard of Chichester, Theodore of Canterbury, Thomas Becket, Thomas More
Cape Clear	Ciaran of Saighir

Cardiganshire	Brieuc
Cassidan	Senan of Scattery
Castledermot	Lawrence O'Toole
Channel Islands	Helier, Samson
Chertsey	Erconwald
Chester	Werburga
Chich	Osyth
Chichester	Richard of Chichester
Clonard	Finnian of Clonard
Clonenagh	Fintan of Clonenagh, Oengus the Culdee
Clonfert	Brendan the Voyager
Clonmacnoise	Ciaran of Clonmacnoise
Cluain Fois	Jarlath of Tuam
Clydeside	Gildas
Clynnog Fawr	Beuno
Compton Martin	Wulfric of Haselbury
Connacht	Ciaran of Clonmacnoise, Colman of Lindisfarne, Maedoc of Ferns
Connor and Down	Malachy
Cooldrevne	Columba of Iona
Corfe	Edward the Martyr
Cork	Finbar
Cornwall	Brieuc, Budoc, Cadoc, Cybi, Gwinear, Ia, Keyne, Mawes, Meriasek, Neot, Petroc, Piran, Samson, Ursula, Winnoc, Winwaloe
Coventry	Osburga
Crediton	Boniface of Crediton
Crowland	Guthlac
Deerhurst	Alphege
Derry	Canice, Columba of Iona
Deverill	Wulfric of Haselbury
Disertbeagh	Oengus the Culdee
Donegal	Adamnan, Columba of Iona
Dorchester	Birinus
Dorset	Stephen Harding
Dover	Richard of Chichester
Downpatrick	Brigid
Droitwich	Richard of Chichester
Dromore	Finnian of Moville

Drumlane	Maedoc of Ferns
Drum-na-Keith	John Ogilvie
Dublin	Edmund Campion, Kevin, Lawrence O'Toole, Matt Talbot
Dumfries	Finnian of Moville
Dunblane	Blane
Dundalk	Brigid
Dunfermline	David of Scotland, Margaret of Scotland
Dunwich	Felix of Dunwich
Durham	Cuthbert, Godric
Durrow	Columba of Iona
Dysert Enos	Oengus the Culdee
East Anglia	Edmund, Edwin, Etheldreda, Felix of Dunwich, Foillan, Fursey, Oda, Sexburga, Sigebert, Ultan
Edinburgh	John Ogilvie
Eigg Island	Donnan
Ely	Edward the Confessor, Etheldreda, Sexburga, Werburga
Essex	Cedd
Etargabail	Finbar
Evesham	Egwin, Oswald of Worcester, Wulfstan
Exeter	Boniface of Crediton
Exning	Etheldreda
Eynesbury	Neot
Falmouth	Mawroc
Farne Islands	Cuthbert
Faversham	Crispin and Crispinian
Felixstowe	Felix of Dunwich
Ferns	Maedoc of Ferns
Finchale	Godric
Flannan Islands	Flannan
Flat Holm Island	Cadoc, Gildas
Fountains Abbey	Robert of Newminster
Galway	Brendan the Voyager, Jarlath of Tuam
Gargrave	Robert of Newminster
Gilling	Oswin
Glamorgan	Samson
Glasgow	John Ogilvie, Kentigern

Glastonbury	Dunstan, Ethelwold, Joseph of Arimathea, Neot, Sigfrid
Glendalough	Kevin, Lawrence O'Toole
Gougane Barra	Finbar
Greenwich	Alphege
Gwynedd	Deiniol
Gwytherin	Winifred
Hambledon	Thomas of Hereford
Hanbury	Werburga
Harpham	John of Beverley
Hartlepool	Hilda
Haselbury Plucknett	Wulfric of Haselbury
Henfynw	David
Hereford	Thomas of Hereford
Hertford	Theodore of Canterbury
Hexham	Aelred, Cuthbert, John of Beverley, Oswald of Northumbria, Wilfrid
Holy Loch	Fillan
Holyhead	Cybi
Holywell	Winifred
Holywood	Finnian of Moville
Horsham Saint Faith	Robert Southwell
Inishbofin	Colman of Lindisfarne, Flannan
Inishdroum	Brendan the Voyager
Inishmore	Ciaran of Clonmacnoise, Enda
Iona	Adamnan, Aidan, Canice, Colman of Lindisfarne, Columba of Iona, Donnan, Egbert, Finan, Oswald of Northumbria
Isle of Man	Maughold
Jarrow	Bede, Benedict Biscop
Jersey	Helier
Kells	Columba of Iona
Kemsing	Edith of Wilton
Kent	Crispin and Crispinian, Ethelbert of Kent, Sexburga
Kerry	Brendan the Voyager
Kildare	Brigid
Kilkenny	Canice
Killaloe	Flannan
Killeedy	Brendan the Voyager, Ita

Killeevy	Moninne
Kilmanach	Kevin
Kilnamanagh	Senan of Scattery
Kilrush	Senan of Scattery
Kirkwall	Magnus
Lancaster	Edmund Arrowsmith, Thomas More
Lastingham	Cedd, Chad
Leinster	Columban, Finnian of Clonard, Fintan of Clonenagh, Gall, Kevin
Lichfield	Chad, Wilfrid
Lincoln	Little Saint Hugh, Hugh of Lincoln
Lincolnshire	Aelred, Chad, Guthlac
Lindisfarne	Aidan, Cedd, Chad, Colman of Lindisfarne, Cuthbert, Egbert, Finan, Wilfrid
Llancarfan	Cadoc
Llandaff	Dyfrig, Teilo
Llanddeusant	Paul Aurelian
Llandeilo Fawr	Teilo
Llandovery	Paul Aurelian
Llanelwy	Asaph, Kentigern
Llaniltud	Gildas
Llantwit Major	Illtyd
London	Claude la Colonbière, Edmund Campion, Edward the Confessor, Erconwald, Giles, Hugh of Lincoln, John Henry Newman, Mellitus, Oliver Plunket, Pancras, Robert Southwell, Uebbi, Simon Stock, Thomas Becket, Thomas More
Long Itchingdon	Wulfstan
Lothian	Kentigern
Lough Corrib	Flannan
Lough Erne	Comgall
Loughcrew	Oliver Plunket
Lyford Grange	Edmund Campion
Madley	Dyfrig
Malmesbury	Aldhelm, Lull
Mayo	Colman of Lindisfarne
Meath	Ciaran of Clonmacnoise, Enda, Finnian of Clonard, Oliver Plunkett
Mellifont	Malachy

Melrose	Cuthbert
Minster-in-Sheppey	Sexburga
Minster-in-Thanet	Edburga of Minster, Mildred
Moville	Finnian of Moville
Mynyw	David
Newminster	Robert of Newminster
Northumbria	Adamnan, Aidan, Bede, Benedict Biscop, Chad, Cuthbert, Cuthburga, Edwin, Egbert, Ethelreda, Hewald the Black and Hewald the White, Hilda, Oswald of Northumbria, Oswin, Paulinus of York, Wilfrid, Willehad
Norwich	Julian of Norwich, William of Norwich
Nursling	Boniface of Crediton
Ogilvy	Donald
Orkney Islands	Magnus, Maughold
Ossory	Canice, Ciaran of Saighir
Oundle	Wilfrid
Oxford	Edmund of Abingdon, Edmund Campion, Frideswide,, Giles, John of Bridlington, John Henry Newman, Richard of Chichester, Simon Stock, Thomas of Hereford, Thomas More
Padstow	Petroc
Peakirk	Pega
Penally	Teilo
Perranporth	Piran
Pershore	Edburga of Winchester, Oswald of Worcester
Perth	William of Rochester
Peterborough	Hedda of Peterborough, Wulfstan
Pipewell	Robert of Newminster
Pittenweem	Fillan
Ramsbury	Oda
Ramsey	Oswald of Worcester
Raphoe	Adamnan
Renfrew	John Ogilvie
Repton	Guthlac
Revesby	Aelred
Rievaulx	Aelred
Ripon	Wilfrid, Willibrord
Roche	Robert of Newminster

Rochester	Augustine of Canterbury, Ethelbert of Kent, John Fisher, Justus of Canterbury, Paulinus of York, William of Rochester
Rossinver	Maedoc of Ferns
St Albans	Alban
St David's	David, Enda
St Helier	Helier
St Ives	Ia
St Michael's Mount	Michael the Archangel
St Neot	Neot
St Neots	Neot
St Ninian's	Enda
St Osyth	Osyth
St Winnow	Winnoc
Saighir	Ciaran of Saighir
Salisbury	Edmund of Abingdon, Osmund
Saul	Patrick
Sawley	Robert of Newminster
Scattery Island	Senan of Scattery
Scilly Isles	Samson
Selsey	Wilfrid
Sempringham	Gilbert of Sempringham
Severn	Samson
Shaftesbury	Edward the Martyr
Sherborne	Aldhelm, Stephen Harding
Slaney	Senan of Scattery
Soham	Felix of Dunwich
Somerset	Aldhelm, Alphege
Steyning	Cuthman
Strangford Lough	Patrick
Strathclyde	Deiniol
Strathfillan	Fillan
Tallacht	Oengus the Culdee
Threckingham	Werburga
Tilbury	Cedd
Tiree	Comgall
Tuam	Jarlath of Tuam
Tyburn	Edmund Campion, Oliver Plunkett, Robert Southwell
Ulster	Comgall, Onegus the Culdee

Walpole	Godric
Wareham	Edward the Martyr
Waterford	Ita
Wearmouth	Bede, Benedict Biscop
Weedon	Werburga
Wenlock	Milburga
West Cork	Ciaran of Saighir
Westbury-on-Trym	Oswald of Worcester
Whitby	Caedmon, Cedd, Colman of Lindisfarne, Edwin, Hedda of Winchester, Hilda, John of Beverley, Robert of Newminster, Wilfrid
Whithorn	Finnian of Moville, Ninian
Wicklow	Kevin, Palladius
Wilton	Edith of Wilton
Wimborne	Cuthburga, Lioba, Walburga
Winchcombe	Kenelm
Winchester	Alphege, Edburga of Winchester, Edith of Wilton, Ethelwold, Hedda of Winchester, Oswald of Worcester, Swithun, William of York
Witham	Hugh of Lincoln
Worcester	Egwin, Oswald of Worcester, Wulfstan
York	Chad, Edwin, John of Beverley, Margaret Clitherow, Oswald of Worcester, Paulinus of York, Sigfrid, Wilfrid, Willehad, William of York
Yorkshire	Willibrord